PRINCIPLES
AND
PRACTICES
OF
HEAVY
CONSTRUCTION

RONALD C. SMITH

Structural Technology Department
Southern Alberta Institute of Technology

PRENTICE-HALL, INC.

Englewood Cliffs, N.J.

PRENTICE-HALL INTERNATIONAL, INC., London
PRENTICE-HALL OF AUSTRALIA, PTY. LTD., Sydney
PRENTICE-HALL OF CANADA, LTD., Toronto
PRENTICE-HALL OF INDIA (PRIVATE) LTD., New Delhi
PRENTICE-HALL OF JAPAN, INC., Tokyo

Current printing (last digit):

10 9 8 7 6 5 4

Library of Congress Catalog Card Number 67-10752
Printed in the United States of America

C-70189

PREFACE

The term *heavy construction,* as used in this title, is intended to encompass those buildings constructed with heavy timber, steel, concrete, or a combination of these materials. Such buildings would include office buildings, hotels, factories, apartment houses, churches, hospitals, schools, etc. It is hoped that this book may provide the reader with some insight into the problems involved in the construction of a large building. It is further hoped that some knowledge and understanding of the methods used to solve these problems will be gained at the same time.

Our great public buildings—office buildings, churches, universities—stand today as tribute to their builders' ingenuity and skills. They are the realization of the architect's plans. Any man who has participated in a large construction project can be justifiably proud of his contribution to community and nation.

CONTENTS

SITE INVESTIGATION

1

One of the basic steps in the planning and construction of a large building is a thorough investigation of the building site. This must first be done early in the planning stage, and it must be done again when construction is about to begin.

PRELIMINARY INVESTIGATION

Soil Bearing Capacity

Investigation of the site early in the planning stage is essential for a number of reasons. One reason is the necessity of determining the load-bearing capacity of the soil. Heavy buildings require soils of high bearing capacity, rock in some cases, to carry their loads. The depth at which this bearing is available will determine the feasibility of locating the building on the proposed site. If the project is feasible from this standpoint, this investigation will help to estimate the cost and influence the design of the foundations.

The proposed building plans will indicate the distribution of building loads and the proposed size of footings under various parts of the building. A site investigation will show whether the load-bearing capacity of the soil is constant over the entire area or whether special footing plans must be made to overcome an unequal bearing problem.

Topography

The topography of the area will also be studied during this investigation. Is the site relatively level? Will it be necessary to remove large quantities of earth or, alternatively, to do considerable filling? Is there rock to be removed and, if so, how much?

Kinds of Soil

It is important to know the kinds of soil that will be encountered during excavation. Are they loose—requiring shoring—or are they relatively firm? What type of machinery will be best for excavating this soil? Must the excavated earth be removed from the site or is there room for storage on the property?

Ground Water Level

Another reason for preliminary site investigation is the necessity of determining the level of the water table and the possible presence of underground streams. If ground water is close to the surface, what are the possibilities of lowering the water table in order to excavate? The presence of an underground stream could present a serious problem if uncovered during excavating operations. If water is there, a decision must be made as to the best method of removing and disposing of it. One means of assessing the possibility of an underground stream is to study available data on investigations of the surrounding area.

Proximity of Other Buildings

How close are other buildings to the construction site? If the excavation is close to an existing building, some means must be found of protecting it from being undermined. If blasting is required, surrounding buildings must be protected from flying debris and from the shock of blasting.

Area of Site

The area of the site must be known. How much of the total area will actually be occupied by the building? Is there room left for adequate storage of building materials? If space is at a premium, a careful schedule will have to be worked out for the ordering and delivery of materials, so that the right ones will be on hand at the right time. Too many materials stored in a limited area can only result in confusion and work delays.

Subsurface Exploration

Subsurface exploration for the purpose of determining the type or types of soil to be encountered is a matter

Fig. 1-1. Sounding rod

of prime importance in preparing for the construction of a heavy building. Neglecting to investigate the subsurface properly can result in foundation faults that may be very expensive to remedy.

There are a number of methods available for examining subsurface conditions, and the one adopted in any particular case will depend on circumstances. It may be that more than one method will have to be used to make the investigation complete. These methods include the use of: (1) sounding rods; (2) augers; (3) test pits; (4) wash borings; (5) dry sample borings; (6) rock drillings; (7) geophysical instruments.

(1) A sounding rod is not used to bring up soil for examination but rather to determine the depth below the surface at which rock appears and whether the soil resistance is increasing or decreasing as the test proceeds. This method cannot be used in soil containing rocks of any significant size since the rod would be deflected from its vertical course.

The rod is of solid steel, from $\frac{5}{8}$ in. to $1\frac{1}{2}$ in. diameter, about 5 ft. long. It has a pointed and enlarged head (see Fig. 1-1) for easy penetration and reduced friction. The length is increased by adding sections by means of threaded couplings. The top end is fitted with a flat driving cap. The rod may be driven either by hand or by a mechanical driver.

Fig. 1-2. Hand operated auger (Courtesy Erie Iron Works)

(2)   An auger is useful for bringing up samples from relatively shallow depths in soils which are cohesive enough to be retained in the tool while it is being raised to the surface. It consists of a cylinder, usually 2 in. in diameter, with cutting lips on the lower end (see Fig. 1-2). It is connected by ordinary couplings to a series of pipe sections. As the auger is turned, layers of earth are peeled off and forced up into the auger cylinder. When the cylinder is full, the auger is brought to the surface, emptied, cleaned, and returned. Power augers, like the one shown in Fig. 1-3, bring up what are known as *disturbed auger borings*.

(3)   The use of test pits is probably the best method of examining subsurface soil because it is possible, by this method, to examine the layers of earth exactly as they exist. In addition, soil moisture conditions are evident and load tests can be made at any desired depth. This method is relatively expensive and the depth to which examination can be carried out is limited. Excavating is usually done by hand, but if a required depth cannot readily be reached by hand, mechanical digging equipment may be used.

(4)   The wash boring method requires the use of water and, as a result, the borings are in the form of mud. Any given sample may be a mixture of two or more layers of soil. A particular stratum may thus not be detected at all.

The equipment for wash boring consists of an outer casing, inside of which is a hollow drill rod with a cross-chopping bit, like the one shown in Fig. 1-4. Boring is done by raising, lowering, and turning the rod while water is forced down the rod and out through ports in the sides of the bit. Loose material is forced up between the drill rod and the outer casing by water pressure and collected through an opening near the top of the casing. This is known as a *wet* sample.

(5)   A *dry* sample may be taken by removing the drill rod and inserting a rod which has a sampling spoon on the end. The spoon, which is similar to a short length of pipe split vertically, is driven into the cuttings at the bottom of the casing and lifted for inspection (see Fig. 1-5).

(6)   A number of systems are employed for drilling rock, among them *diamond drilling, shot drilling,* and *churn drilling*.

A diamond drill consists of a diamond-studded bit, like the one shown in Fig. 1-6, attached to a core barrel. The barrel is in turn attached to a drill rod mounted in a rig similar to the one shown in Fig. 1-7. The drill rod is rotated and water is forced down through the hollow rod to cool the bit and carry the drill cuttings to the surface. The bit cuts a circular groove, and the core is forced up into the core barrel. When it is of the desired length, the core is broken off by a

Fig. 1-3.   Power auger (Courtesy Mobile Drilling Inc.)

special device and brought to the surface for inspection. Diamond drilling may be done either vertically or at an angle.

Shot drilling is similar to diamond drilling except for the bit. It consists of a circular, hollow, hard steel bit with a slot around the bottom edge to allow circulation of shot. A flow of chilled steel shot is fed through the drill rod to the bit, and as the bit turns, the shot cuts the rock and forms a core, which is forced up into the core barrel. Cores as large as 72 in. in diameter can be taken with a shot bit.

Churn drilling consists of operating a hard steel chopping bit attached to a drill stem inside a casing. A cable,

Fig. 1-4.   Cross-chopping bit (Courtesy Soiltest Inc.)

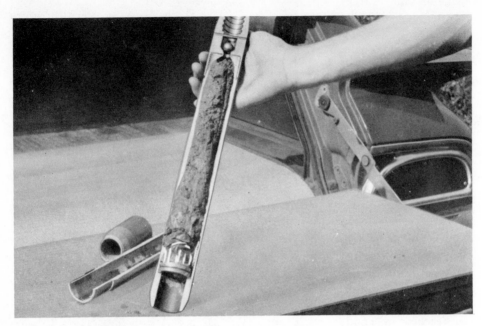

Fig. 1-5. Split spoon sampler (Courtesy Soiltest Inc.)

to which is fastened a set of weights, raises and drops the bit so that it strikes the bottom, chipping the rock. Water is forced down the side of the casing and the resulting slurry is removed from the hole with a bucket.

(7) There are two basic types of geophysical instruments used for shallow (100 ft or less) subsurface investigation and exploration. They are refraction seismographs and earth electrical resistivity units. The techniques involved in the use of these instruments have been known and used successfully for many years for deep exploration common to the oil and mineral industries.

Through advances in electronic technology, the heavy, bulky equipment once required for this deep exploration has been reduced to small, compact units which can be carried quite readily by a two-man crew.

The seismic refraction theory is based on the fact that shock waves travel at particular and well-defined velocities through materials of various densities. The denser the material, the greater the speed. The velocities may range from as low as 600 ft/sec in light, dry

Fig. 1-6. Diamond drill bit (Courtesy Soiltest Inc.)

Fig. 1-7. Drilling rig (Courtesy Canadian Industries Ltd.)

top soil to 20,000 ft/sec in unseasoned granite. If the speed of the shock wave is known, the type, hardness, and depth of the stratum responsible for the refracted wave can be accurately determined.

A portable refraction seismograph consists of a hand-operated tamper to initiate the shock waves (see Fig. 1-8), a geophone to detect the refracted shock wave, and an instrument (see Fig. 1-9) to measure the time (in milliseconds) required for the shock wave to travel from the point of initiation to the geophone. It contains an oscilloscope on which the wave is displayed.

The operation of the unit consists of selecting a line along which to work and setting up the receiving instrument at one end of it. A shock wave is then initiated 10 ft from the receiver. A series of blows are struck at 10 ft intervals for a distance of 100 ft or so, depending on the depth to be investigated. Figure 1-10 illustrates the positions at which shock waves are initiated and the manner in which the waves will travel through layers of materials. At 10 and 20 ft the wave near the ground surface reaches the receiver first. From 30, 40, and 50 ft the waves traveling through the fractured rock arrive first. All waves beyond 50 ft will travel through the bedrock and reach the receiver first. The interval between the initiation of the shock and its arrival at the geophone is plotted (see Fig. 1-11) and the depth, hardness, and types of material are calculated from this data. Figure 1-12 plots the hammering point distances against the seismic wave travel

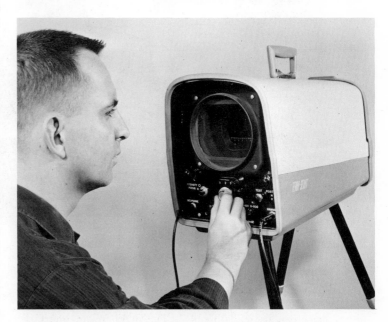

Fig. 1-8. Refraction seismograph unit in operation (Courtesy Soiltest Inc.)

Fig. 1-9. Refraction seismograph instrument (Courtesy Soiltest Inc.)

Fig. 1-10. Schematic diagram of seismic wave refraction principle

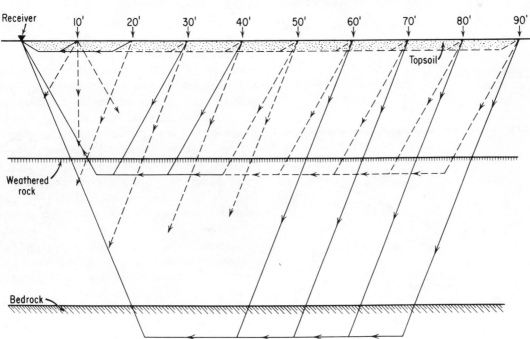

Fig. 1-11. Plotting refraction seismograph readings (Courtesy Soiltest Inc.)

times for each distance. The points are joined by a series of sloping lines, the slope of each line representing seismic velocity. Velocity charts are available which may be laid over the graph so that the velocity at each layer can be read directly. The depth to an interface is calculated by using the formula:

$$\frac{\text{Distance from point to point} \times \text{velocity of that line}}{2000} = \text{depth in feet}$$

For example, the depth to the first interface at A, Fig. 1-12, is

$$\frac{0 \text{ to } A \times \text{Vel. 1}}{2000} = \frac{10 \times 1000}{2000} = 5 \text{ ft}$$

Fig. 1-12. Time-distance plot of instrument readings

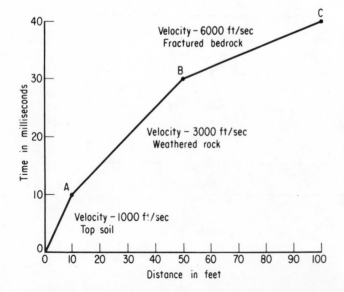

The earth electrical resistivity measurement method depends on the ability of earth materials and formations to conduct electrical current, which follows relatively good conductors and avoids poor ones. Conductivity of the material depends upon its electrolytic properties. Conductivity and resistivity vary according to the presence and quantity of fluids, mineral salt content of the fluids, volume of pore spaces, pore size and distribution, degree of saturation, and a number of other factors.

In operating a resistivity unit, four electrodes are placed into the ground at equal distances from one another. A current is passed between the two outside electrodes and a measurement of electrical potential is made between the two inner electrodes. The measured potential is proportionate to the resistance present in the subsurface material. In the latest equipment, the measurements may be read directly in ohms.

Loose materials such as loam, peat, etc., offer low electrical resistivity. Granular soils, nonpermeable rocks, and materials lacking pore space, such as ice and frozen soils, show a high resistivity. By plotting the resistance readings obtained at regular intervals along a straight line, the character of the subsurface may be plotted with reference to depth, thickness, and makeup in much the same way that data gained from using the refraction seismograph was plotted and interpreted.

Because the seismic and resistivity methods measure different physical characteristics of the subsoil, a technique combining both methods has recently been developed. It is called *complementary usage,* and by its use correlation values have been established for various materials. At the same time, the limitations of each individual system have been overcome. Some typical correlation values are as follows:

Bedrock—high velocity, high resistance
Ground water—high velocity, low resistance
Soil—low to medium velocity, low to medium resistance
Sand and gravel—low to medium velocity, high resistance

Of course, the use of this type of equipment does not eliminate the need for test boring. Drilling and sampling are necessary for foundation investigations where accurate information on the bearing capacity of a soil is required and where samples are needed for laboratory analysis. But the use of electronic equipment may materially reduce the amount of drilling necessary and may help in the intelligent selection of drilling sites.

Nature of Soil

In order to make use of the samples taken during subsurface exploration, it is necessary to understand something of the nature of soil, types of soil, and how they react under various circumstances. This topic, in all its facets, is a complete study in itself and it is intended here to deal with the subject only insofar as it pertains to construction.

What is meant by *soil?* It is the word used by engineers and architects to denote all the fragmented material found in the earth's crust. Included within the meaning of the word is material ranging all the way from individual rocks of various sizes, through sand and gravel, to fine-grained clays. It should be noted that while particles of sand and gravel are visible to the naked eye, particles of some fine-grained clays cannot even be distinguished when viewed through low-powered microscopes.

All soils are thus made up of large or small particles derived from solid rock. They consist of one or more of the minerals which make up solid rock. These particles have been transported from their original location by various means. For example, there are notable deposits of *eolian soil* in western North America which were deposited by wind. There are also numerous deposits of *glacial till*, a mixture of sand, gravel, silt, and clay, moved and deposited by glaciers. Other soils have been deposited by the action of water, while others—known as *residual soils*—consist of rock particles which have not been moved from their original location but are products of the deterioration of solid rock.

Soils are generally described and defined by the size of the particles of which they are composed. Soil types, as determined by particle size, are as follows:

Cobbles and boulders:	larger than 3 in. in diameter.
Gravel:	smaller than 3 in. and larger than #4 sieve (approximately $\frac{1}{4}$ in.).
Sand:	particles smaller than #4 sieve and larger than #200 sieve (40,000 openings per sq in.).
Silts:	particles smaller than 0.02 mm and larger than 0.002 mm in diameter.
Clays:	particles smaller than 0.002 mm in diameter.

For purposes of establishing the abilities of these soils to safely carry a load, they are classified as *cohesionless soils, cohesive soils, miscellaneous soils,* and *rock.* Table 1-1 lists the allowable bearing values, in pounds per square foot, for the various types of soil indicated.

Table 1-1

Bearing Strengths of Soils

Type of Soil	Allowable bearing strength, psf
Cohesionless soils	
Dense sand, dense sand & gravel	6,000
Cohesive soils	
Dense silt	3,000
Medium dense silt	2,000
Hard clay	6,000
Stiff clay	4,000
Firm clay	2,000
Soft clay	1,000
Miscellaneous soils	
Dense till	10,000
Cemented sand & gravel	20,000
Rock	
Massive	100,000
Foliated	80,000
Sedimentary	40,000
Soft or shattered	20,000

Cohesionless soils include sand and gravel, soils in which the particles have little or no tendency to stick together under pressure. Cohesive soils include dense silt, medium dense silt, hard clay, stiff clay, firm clay, and soft clay. The particles of these soils tend to stick together, particularly with the addition of water. Miscellaneous soils include glacial till and conglomerate. The latter is a mixture of sand, gravel, and clay, with the clay acting as a cement to hold the particles together. Rock is subdivided into *massive, foliated, sedimentary,* and *soft* or *shattered.* Massive rocks are very hard, have no visible bedding planes or laminations, and have widely spaced, nearly vertical or horizontal joints. They are comparable to the best concrete. Foliated rocks are also hard, but have sloping joints which preclude equal compressive strength in all directions. They are comparable to sound structural concrete. Sedimentary rocks include hard shales, sandstones, limestones, and silt-stones, with softer components. Rocks in this category may be likened to good brick masonry. Soft or shattered rocks include those that are soft or broken but not displaced from their natural beds. They do not become plastic when wet and are comparable to poor brick masonry.

One of the problems caused by soil in building operations is related to backfilling around foundation walls and in service trenches. Once soil has been removed from its original location it tends to increase in bulk, because pressure is no longer keeping the particles closely packed. When this soil is returned to the excavation it is still in this bulked state, and, unless some special measures are taken during backfilling, time and weather will bring about a return to the original volume, causing shrinkage in the hole. This can be overcome by compacting the soil while it is being replaced.

Tests have shown that mixing a certain amount of water with the soil enable the particles to be packed more closely together so that all the voids that existed between the particles during the bulked state have been filled. The addition of too much water will simply tend to separate the particles and so increase the overall volume.

The practical implications are important. If soil can be replaced and packed with this optimum amount of water, no shrinkage will take place later. The optimum moisture condition is usually close to the condition of the soil as it was removed. Thus, it is clear that soil removed from an excavation should be protected against drying out as much as possible, if it is to be used again as backfill. However, if the moisture content is changed, it should be allowed to dry or water should be added, as the case may be, before it is returned. Soil should be replaced in thin layers, not more than 6 in. thick, in order to get it into place at its maximum density. Each layer must be treated by some type of compaction machinery. If this process is followed carefully, it is possible to backfill trenches, even very large ones, so that the soil approximates its original condition, and no appreciable settling of the surface occurs.

Frost Penetration

Another problem relating to soils that is of great importance to the building industry in colder areas is that of frost penetration, and the resulting heaving of the soil that may sometimes take place.

In many cases where ground freezes no outward change is visible, but the strength of soil is increased, partly because of the binding of the soil particles by ice. In other cases the ground heaves and the resultant displacement of the soil may cause considerable damage.

As the mean air temperature drops, the surface of the ground will freeze. With the lower temperature of approaching winter, the freezing plane slowly penetrates the soil. In a fine-grained and moist soil, a peculiar phenomenon occurs. At the freezing plane, the water in the soil turns to ice. This is in effect a drying action, and water in the unfrozen soil beneath moves toward the freezing plane in the same way as water will move from moist to dry soil. This water, upon reaching the freezing plane, is able to flow through and around the soil particles and to join the ice crystals above, thus adding to the growth of a layer of pure ice. Pressure develops so that the ice and soil above it are lifted.

Heaving pressures range over wide limits and depend mainly on the type of soil and its moisture content. A saturated soil will develop the maximum heaving pressure; as the moisture content drops, heaving pressure drops also, and is reduced to zero in a soil with low moisture content. The type of soil is influential, with finer-grained soils developing more pressure than coarser-grained ones. Thus, clay soils develop higher pressure than silts, and silts higher pressure than fine sands. In general, it can be said that coarse sands and gravels do not heave.

The three basic requirements for frost heaving are: (1) a freezing plane in the soil; (2) a fine-grained soil through which moisture can move; and (3) a supply of water. If any of these factors can be controlled, frost heaving can be prevented. In a site investigation for a building project, it may be necessary to determine whether ice lenses will form in the soil. Since it is seldom economically possible to control soil temperature, frost heaving is usually prevented by replacing the fine-grained soil with coarse, granular material. Soil moisture can also be controlled by careful attention to drainage, thus greatly reducing the extent of frost heaving.

SECONDARY INVESTIGATION

Secondary does not necessarily refer to importance, but to chronological sequence. The primary investigations discussed in the first part of this chapter are carried out before plans and specifications are drawn—that is, they are made by the planners. But once the building has been decided upon and the tenders let, then the prospective contractor must carry out some investigations of his own.

Access to the Site

The contractor will want to know what roads or streets give access to the site and if it is feasible to move the necessary equipment over them. It may be necessary to build a private road.

If a navigable waterway is accessible, is it practical and economical to use it for the delivery of equipment and material to the site? Is air transportation available? It may be that fast transportation of urgently needed men and supplies will be economical in the long run.

In any case, it is most often advantageous to give some thought and study to the most practical and economical routes by which equipment and materials are to be moved to the job site.

Availability of Services

One of the most important considerations is the availability of electrical power at the job site. Practically no modern construction job can be carried out without it. Is power close at hand or must it be brought in over long distances? Will the power line be supplied by the power company or will this be the responsibility of the construction company?

Gas is another very important commodity at a construction site, for both heating and cooking. If there is gas in the area, the location and size of the main must be known in order to bring gas to the site.

Water must be available when a construction job begins. The builder must therefore ascertain whether or not there is a water main in the vicinity. If not, some other method of supplying water must be found. This may be accomplished by means of a well, pipeline, or tank trucks.

Local Building Bylaws

Local and national building codes and bylaws are formulated to set safety standards, to stipulate proper methods of construction, and to designate proper use and occupancy of buildings coming under their jurisdiction. Restrictions stipulate the type of construction required in various fire zones. Other rules govern the distance which a building must be set back from the street, the maximum height of buildings in various

localities, the number of stories allowed before there must be a setback in the building, location of fire escapes, etc. Other regulations provide safe working standards for workmen, specify types of scaffolds, ladders, etc., which must be used, and limit the loads allowed on streets and roads. All of these rules and bylaws must be known to the builder in order that he may govern his operations accordingly.

Local Labor Supply

An important consideration when planning a construction job is the availability of labor, both skilled and unskilled. The contractor will usually provide his own staff of technical men (engineers, estimators, and superintendents) but may wish to rely on local supply for the remainder. In some areas unskilled labor will be in adequate supply, while skilled workmen, such as carpenters, bricklayers, electricians, and plumbers, will have to be brought in. In other instances, the entire labor force may have to be imported, while in still other situations an adequate supply of labor of all kinds will be locally available. Importing help may mean that the contractor will have to feed and house these men during construction at his own expense.

Site Conditions

The prospective builder will of course want to know what sort of soil will be encountered during excavation and what problems he may have with underground water. He should be able to obtain this information from the planner, but if it is not available, subsurface exploration will have to be carried out as previously described.

Local Weather Conditions

Climate plays an important part when planning a construction job. Is the area subject to a great deal of rain, is it unusually dry, or just average? The answer to these questions will have an effect on how equipment and materials are to be stored, what types of equipment will work best under those conditions, and whether special construction schedules will have to be developed.

Is the job in an area where a long winter season is likely to be encountered? If so, this will affect the types of equipment to be used, the heating and lighting requirements, and the proper protection that must be provided in order to carry on winter work.

Unforeseen inclement weather may disrupt construction schedules to the extent that completion dates cannot be met. This could result in penalties which may significantly increase the overall cost of the project.

In short, the more a builder learns about the conditions to be met during the operation, the more likely

he is to complete the job with a minimum of trouble. He will be able to arrive at a realistic cost figure, to plan a reasonably smooth working schedule, and to complete the building in a manner satisfactory to both himself and the owner.

REVIEW QUESTIONS

1. Outline two basic differences between *preliminary* and *secondary* investigation.

2. (a) List four basic questions to be answered by a preliminary investigation; (b) explain why each is important.

3. What are three problems that may result from having an existing building in close proximity to a building site?

4. Describe briefly how to solve the problems in 3 above.

5. (a) How does the site area affect the planning of a new building; (b) how does it affect a building's cost?

6. What is meant by the *complementary* usage of soil testing methods?

7. Define the following soils: (a) eolian; (b) glacial till; (c) residual.

8. List five soil types according to particle size, beginning with the finest.

9. (a) Distinguish between *cohesive* and *cohesionless* soils; (b) give two types belonging to each classification.

10. (a) What is meant by the *bulking* of soil; (b) how does it affect backfilling operations; (c) what are two steps one might take to overcome this problem?

11. (a) Briefly describe the cause of frost heaving in soil; (b) how can it be prevented?

12. What six factors must be considered by a contractor making a secondary investigation of a building site?

SITE LAYOUT 2

Once the building site has been established, it is then necessary to locate the building precisely within the boundaries of the site. It is also necessary to indicate to what depth excavation must be carried out. When the site is not level, excavation depths will vary, and these variations must be shown.

Included among the drawings for a building is the site plan (see Fig. 2-1), which shows the property lines, available utilities, location of trees, etc., and the location of the building. Approaches and slopes of finished grades are usually shown. In addition, a *bench mark* is very often indicated on the plan. This is an established point—a manhole cover, some permanent point at or near ground level on an adjacent building, or a known elevation point in the vicinity. The bench mark is a datum point, to which all elevations in the building will refer. It is usually given an arbitrary elevation, e.g., +100′.

LEVELING INSTRUMENTS

Leveling instruments are used to run the lines, lay out the angles, and ascertain the various differences in elevation required during the construction of a building and its foundations. These are precision instruments incorporating a telescope, leveling devices, horizontal and vertical cross hairs, and finely calibrated scales for measuring horizontal and vertical angles.

Two basic types of leveling instruments are used in the building industry — the *builders'* (or *dumpy*) *level*, and the *transit level*. The builders' level, shown in Fig. 2-2, turns only in a horizontal circle, while a transit level—Fig. 2-3—can turn in a vertical arc as well as a horizontal circle. An automatic, or self-leveling, level is now also in common use. That instrument is illustrated in Fig. 2-4.

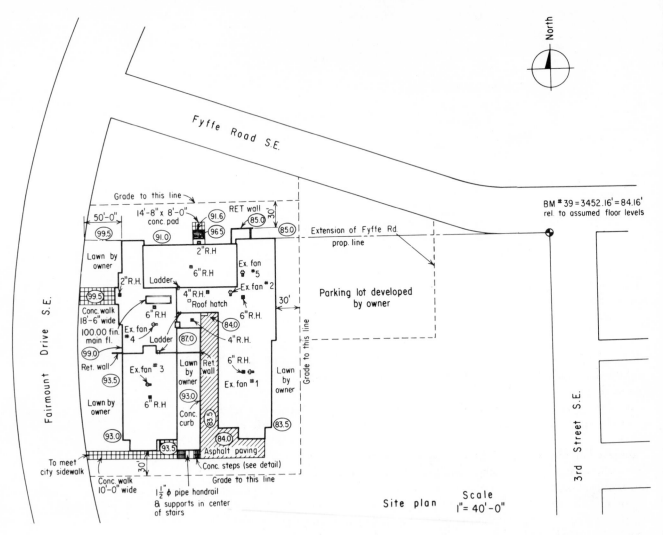

Fig. 2-1. Site plan

Figure 2-5(a) illustrates a transit level and indicates the main parts. The instrument consists of a telescope (1) with magnification powers ranging from 8 to 30 times, mounted on a frame (13). To the telescope is attached a level tube (14), similar to a small spirit level. The level tube and telescope are leveled by adjusting the leveling screws (12) in pairs until the bubble is centered, regardless of the direction in which the instrument is turned.

At the front end of the telescope is an objective lens (2) and at the rear is an eyepiece cap (4) which is turned to bring the cross hairs into focus. A focusing knob (3) allows the object being sighted to be brought into clear view.

At the bottom of the frame is a horizontal circle hous-

ing (15), cut away on one side to expose a graduated horizontal circle and a horizontal vernier scale (Fig. 2-5(b)). The telescope, frame, and housing revolve upon the horizontal circle, thus making possible the measurement of horizontal arcs of circles.

The telescope may be locked at any position in its horizontal travel by a horizontal clamp screw (8) and brought into fine adjustment by a horizontal tangent screw (9). The telescope is held in a horizontal position by locking levers (5) which, when unlocked, allow the telescope to tilt vertically. It can be locked in any tilted position by the vertical clamp screw (6) and fine adjustments are made by a vertical tangent screw (7).

The vertical arc (10) is divided into degrees and

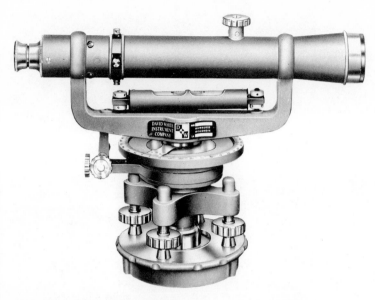

Fig. 2-2. Builder's level
(Courtesy David White Instruments).

Fig. 2-3. Transit level
(Courtesy David White Instruments).

Fig. 2-4. Automatic level
(Courtesy Hickerson Instrument Co.)

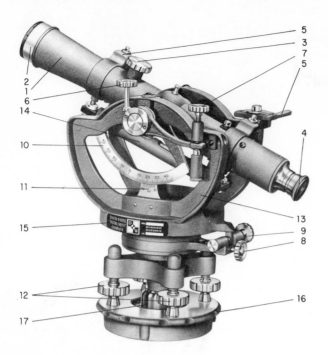

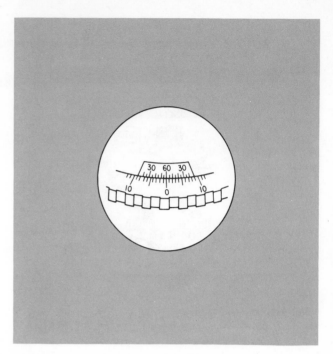

Fig. 2-5. Transit level parts

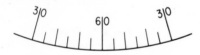

Fig. 2-6. Horizontal circle scale

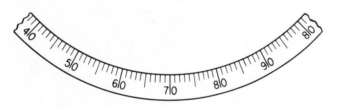

Fig. 2-7. Vernier scale

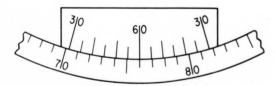

Fig. 2-8. Reading of 76° 0′

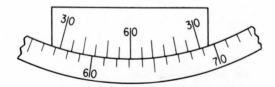

Fig. 2-9. Reading of 63° 5′

ranges to 45° on both sides of zero, the horizontal position. The vertical vernier (11) is graduated, as is the horizontal one, to give readings accurate to within 5′ ($\frac{1}{12}$ of a degree). The whole instrument rests on a leveling head (16), a flattened ring by means of which the instrument is fastened to the tripod. Projecting into the hollow center of the leveling head is a centering head (17), a part of the telescope frame. When the leveling screws are loose, the centering head —and the whole instrument—will move within the confines of the opening.

The horizontal circle and the vertical arc are marked off in degrees and numbered every 10° (see Fig. 2-6). The vernier is marked into twelve divisions of 5′ each, the twelve representing one degree (60′). Those 12 spaces are equal to 11 spaces (11°) on the circle or arc. The vernier has zero (marked 60) in the center and reads both right and left to 30′ (see Fig. 2-7).

The vernier makes it possible to take a reading to within 5′ ($\frac{1}{12}$ of a degree). If the zero (60) on the vernier coincides *exactly* with a degree mark on the circle, then the reading will be $x°$ 0′. Figure 2-8 shows a reading of 76° 0′. But if the zero on the vernier comes *between* two degree marks on the circle, we rely on the vernier to read the fraction of a degree involved.

Remember, each space on the vernier is $\frac{1}{12}$ smaller than a space on the circle. When zero on the vernier is just enough past a degree mark to allow the first line on the vernier to the right or left of zero to coincide with a line on the circle, the vernier zero must be $\frac{1}{12}$

of a degree (5') past the degree mark. Therefore, the reading would be $x°$ 5'. Figure 2-9 illustrates a reading of 63° 5'. If the second line on the vernier coincides with a degree mark, it means that the vernier zero is $\frac{2}{12}$ of a degree (10') past the degree reading. In other words, in order to read the number of minutes by which the vernier zero is past a degree mark, find a line on the vernier which coincides with a line on the circle. If none is found between zero and 30, in the direction being read, go back to the 30 at the opposite end of the vernier and read towards 60 again. Remember that each space on the vernier, to the right or left, equals 5'. Figure 2-10 shows a reading of 45° 50'.

The horizontal circle is marked off in quadrants, with the degrees reading from 0 to 90, then down to 0 again, repeated in the two other quadrants (see Fig. 2-11).

A leveling instrument is mounted upon a tripod and properly adjusted before use (Fig. 2-12). Proceed as follows:

1. Set the tripod in the desired location and spread the legs so that the eyepiece of the telescope will be in a comfortable position for sighting. A spacing of about three feet for the legs is generally satisfactory. The spacing of the legs should be adjusted so that the tripod head is as level as can be accomplished by eye.

2. Push the legs firmly into the ground. On a paved surface, be sure the points will hold securely.

3. Tighten the wing nuts at the top of the tripod legs into a reasonably firm position.

4. Remove the cap from the tripod head and place it in the instrument box. Lift the instrument from the box by the frame, *not by the telescope,* and set it on the tripod head. Make sure the horizontal clamp screw is loose.

5. Holding the level by the upper structure, screw the leveling head firmly into place.

Leveling is the most important operation in preparing to use the instrument. It is good practice to adopt the following procedure:

1. Make sure that the locking levers holding the telescope in a horizontal position are locked.

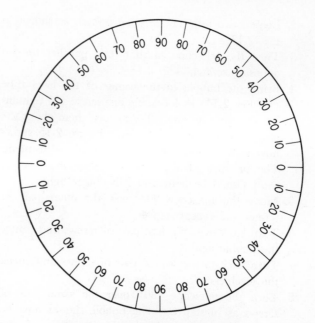

Fig. 2-11. Horizontal circle quadrants

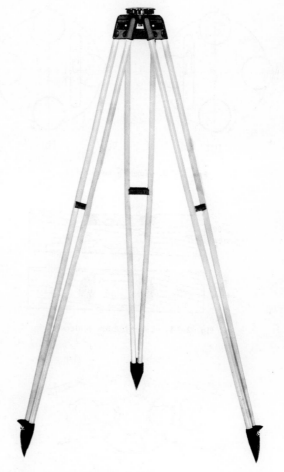

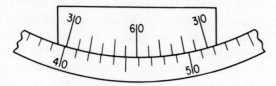

Fig. 2-10. Reading of 45° 50'

Fig. 2-12. Instrument tripod (Courtesy David White Instruments)

2. Loosen two adjacent leveling screws, as shown in Fig. 2-13(a).

3. Turn the telescope so that it is parallel to two opposing screws—Fig. 2-13(b).

4. Bring the bubble to the center of the level tube (see Fig. 2-14) by loosening one screw and tightening the opposite one. Try to turn them about the same amount simultaneously. Figure 2-15 shows how to hold and turn the screws for adjustment. The pressure of the screws against the leveling head should be light and only finger tight.

5. Move the telescope 90° over the other pair of screws and repeat step 4.

6. Turn back over the first pair of screws and center the bubble again.

7. Turn back to the second pair of screws and check the levelness.

8. Turn the telescope 180° over the same pair of screws as in step 6. The bubble should now be centered in this or any other position of the telescope.

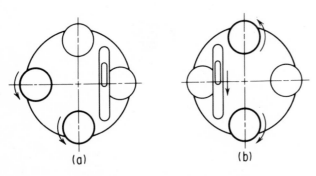

Fig. 2-13. Turning level screws

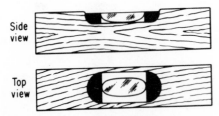

Fig. 2-14. Level bubble centered

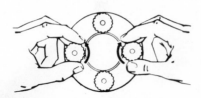

Fig. 2-15. Adjusting level screws

The instrument is now ready for sighting adjustments. These may vary slightly for different individuals.

1. Aim the telescope at the object and sight it first along the top of the tube.

2. Then look through the eyepiece and adjust the focus by turning the focusing knob until the object is clear.

3. Now turn the eyepiece cap or focusing ring until the cross hairs appear sharp and black.

4. Adjust the telescope until the object is centered as closely as possible. *Do not put your hands on the tripod.* Tighten the horizontal clamp screw.

5. Center the object exactly by bringing the vertical cross hair into final position with the horizontal motion tangent screw.

The point of intersection of the cross hairs is on the *line of sight*, which is horizontal in any direction of the telescope. The vertical distance from the ground on which the tripod stands to that line of sight is called the *height of instrument* (H.I.).

One of the important uses of a leveling instrument is to find the difference in *grade* or *elevation* between two points. To do this, it is necessary to use a *leveling rod*. A section of a leveling rod is shown in Fig. 2-16. Some rods are equipped with a *target* (see Fig. 2-16) which can be moved up or down the rod until the horizontal target line corresponds to the instrument's line of sight (horizontal cross hair).

The difference between the rod readings at two locations will be the difference in elevation or grade. This is illustrated in Fig. 2-17. To read this difference, set the instrument in a convenient location from which both points can be seen, preferably about midway between them. Level the instrument as explained previously. Have someone hold a rod straight up at one of the two points, or *stations*, and sight on it. Record the reading at which the horizontal cross hair cuts the graduations on the rod. Have the rod held over the second station and swing the instrument around without otherwise disturbing it and take another reading on the rod. The difference between the two readings is the amount that one station is above or below the other. For example, in Fig. 2-17, the reading at Station X is 4 ft 2 in. and at station Y, 2 ft 8 in. The difference between these two, 1 ft 6 in., is the amount by which station Y is higher than Station X. In other words, there is a difference in grade between the two points of 18 in. The elevation of a whole series of stations can be compared to a given point by the same method.

Another use of a leveling instrument is to find the elevation at a particular point or points, knowing the

Fig. 2-16. Leveling rod with target

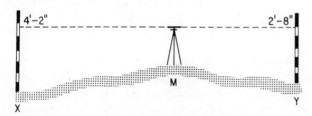

Fig. 2-17. Difference in grade

elevation of some designated point, called a *bench mark*. Proceed as follows:

1. Set up the instrument at a convenient point between the bench mark and the unknown elevation, where the rod (held on the bench mark) will be in sight. Level the instrument.

2. Take a sight on the rod and record the reading. This is called a *backsight*. That reading, *added* to the bench mark elevation, is the H.I., the height of instrument.

3. Have the rod moved to a convenient location between the instrument and the unknown elevation. Loosen the clamp screw and swivel the instrument around so that a reading can be taken on the rod at its new location. This is a *foresight*. Record that reading and *subtract* it from the H.I. The result is the elevation of the point on which the rod rests—Station 1.

4. Now move the instrument to a new position between Station 1 and the unknown elevation and take a backsight. Add that backsight reading to the elevation of Station 1 and you have a new H.I.

5. Have the rod moved to a new station and take a foresight. From it establish the elevation of Station 2.

6. This procedure is repeated until the final station reaches the unknown elevation.

Notice that a backsight was added to a known elevation to obtain the H.I. It is thought of as a *plus* quantity. A foresight is subtracted from the H.I. to obtain a station elevation. It is thought of as a *minus* quantity. In reality, this continuous process of adding and subtracting is not necessary. The backsights are merely all recorded as being *plus* and their sum is a *plus* quantity. The foresights are all recorded as *minus* and their sum is a *minus* quantity. The difference between these two totals is a net *plus* or *minus* quantity, depending on which is larger. The difference, added to or subtracted from the original bench mark, will give the elevation of the point in question.

For example, the elevation of a point *A* is required, from a bench mark recorded as 2642.62 ft, far enough away that three stations are required between the bench mark and the point *A*. The recorded readings were as follows:

	Backsights	Foresights
1	4.26 ft	3.19 ft
2	6.19 ft	8.27 ft
3	5.35 ft	6.92 ft
4	3.68 ft	7.75 ft
Totals	+ 19.48 ft	− 26.13 ft

Net difference = 26.13 − 19.48 = −6.65 ft.
Elevation of point A = 2642.62 − 6.65 = 2635.97 ft.

One particular use of a transit level is for running straight lines. A straight line must be run from a point in a given direction or to another point.

1. Set the instrument up over the starting point. To

do this, use the plumb bob in the instrument box. Attach its cord to the eyelet in the middle of the centering head. Adjust the position of the tripod legs until the plumb bob is as nearly centered as possible over the starting point.

2. Loosen two adjacent screws and move the centering head within its limits until the plumb bob is aligned exactly over the center of the starting point.

3. Level the instrument and unlock the locking levers.

4. Sight on the second point given or point the telescope in the given direction and lock it in that position with the horizontal clamp screw.

5. By tilting the telescope up or down, a number of positions can be sighted and marked on the ground, all of which will be in a straight line from the starting point (see Fig. 2-18).

The level or transit level is readily used for laying out angles or for measuring a given angle. To lay out an angle, the *intersection* of the two legs must be known, the *direction* of one leg, and the *size* of the angle.

1. Set up the instrument over the point of the angle, using the plumb bob, as previously described and level the instrument.

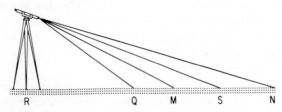

Fig. 2-18. Running a straight line

2. Unlock the locking levers and sight on a point (a stake) on the given leg of the angle. Record the reading on the horizontal circle or turn the horizontal circle to a zero reading. The bottom edge of the horizontal circle is knurled and the circle can be turned by applying light pressure with a finger.

3. Loosen the horizontal clamp screw and turn the instrument through the required angle. It can be brought to the required angle by using the horizontal tangent screw. Tighten the clamp screw again.

4. Run a line in this direction for the required distance.

For measuring angles already laid out, the procedure is much the same. Figure 2-19 shows a plot outline for which the angles may have to be measured.

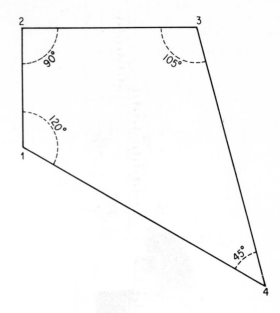

Fig. 2-19. Measuring angles

1. Set up the instrument at Station 1 and center it over the station pin.

2. Level the instrument and release the locking levers.

3. Sight on Station 2, centering the vertical cross hair on the station pin. Set the horizontal circle to zero or record the reading.

4. Turn the instrument and sight accurately on Station 4. Record the new reading on the circle. In this case it is 120°.

5. Now set up over Station 2, sight back to Station 1, and around to Station 3. Read the angle—90°.

6. Repeat the procedure at Station 3 and Station 4.

A transit level is required for taking vertical sights, such as plumbing building walls, piers, columns, doorways, and windows. First level the instrument, then release the locking levers that hold the telescope in the level position. Swing the telescope vertically and horizontally until the line to be established is directly on the vertical cross hair. Tighten the horizontal clamp screw. If the telescope is now rotated up or down, each point cut by the vertical cross hair is in a vertical plane with the starting point (see Fig. 2-20).

LAYOUT BEFORE EXCAVATION

The boundaries of the lot on which a building is to be constructed should be established by markers, called *monuments*, set by a registered surveyor. The site plan shows the positions of the boundary lines, relative to streets, roads, etc. (see Fig. 2-21). The contractor locates the boundary markers and, by running lines between them, can establish the boundaries. Now, from the distances given on the site plan and using a tape, the building can be laid out by driving stakes at the corners and on the column center lines (see Fig. 2-22). The accuracy of the staking may be checked by measuring the diagonals of the rectangles concerned. Each pair will be exactly equal if the stakes are set in their correct position.

These corner stakes will be lost during excavating operations, and it is therefore necessary to record their position beforehand. This is done by means of *batter boards*, on which are marked points that are on the various building and column lines. These batter boards are horizontal bars fastened to posts, which are set up singly or in pairs around the important points in the building (see Fig. 2-23). The basic purpose of the staking outlined above is to enable the workmen to locate batter boards correctly. They must be set far

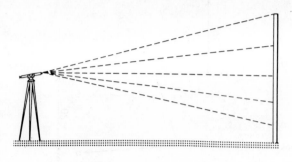

Fig. 2-20. Establishing a vertical line

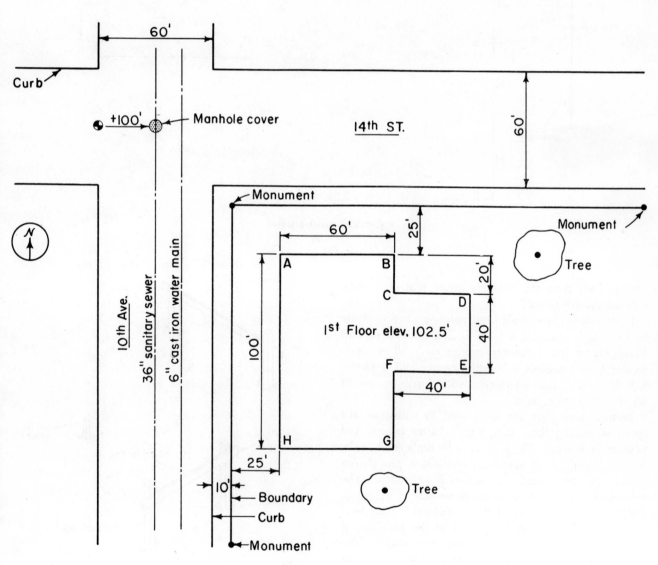

Fig. 2-21 Plot plan

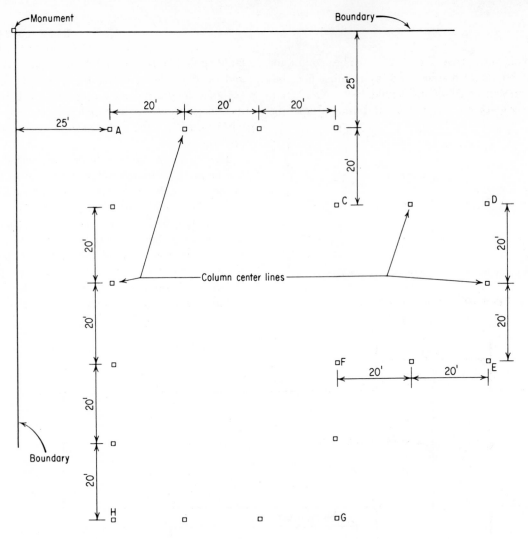

Fig. 2-22. Building stakes

enough back from the stakes to insure that excavating will not disturb them.

Lines run between designated points on two opposite batter boards represent a building line (outside of wall frame, center line of column footings, etc.). Two intersecting lines represent a building corner and a plumb bob dropped at that intersection will pinpoint a corner on the excavation floor.

Because wire lines are often used to withstand the strain of pulling them taut, strong batter boards and posts are required. The posts may be timbers (4 in. by 4 in. or larger), small steel beam sections, or pipe driven firmly into the ground and braced if necessary. The horizontal bars are then bolted or welded to the posts, making sure that all are at the same level. That level should coincide with a floor level of the building, if possible, or at least bear some definite relation to it. The elevation should be plainly marked on one or more of the batter boards. It is good practice to check these

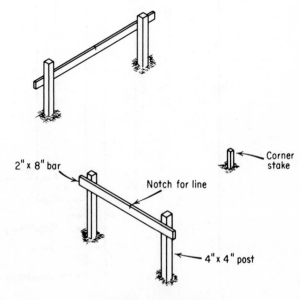

Fig. 2-23. Batter boards

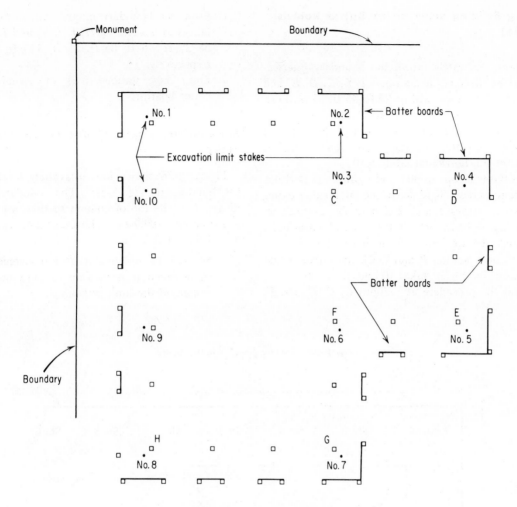

Fig. 2-24. Batter boards in place

elevations during excavation and foundation work to make sure that there has been no shift or displacement.

The limits of the excavation now have to be staked out. The excavation will usually extend 2 ft or more beyond the boundaries of the building itself—to the payline—in order to allow room to work outside the forms. Excavation limit stakes are accordingly driven at the required distance from the corner stakes, as shown in Fig. 2-24.

PRELIMINARY LAYOUT PROBLEMS

Setting Batter Boards to a Definite Level

For the building indicated in Fig. 2-21, it has been decided to set the batter boards to the first floor elevation, shown on the plan as 102.5 ft. Proceed as follows:

1. Set up the leveling instrument so that sights can be taken on the bench mark and the batter boards and level it.
2. Take a backsight on the bench mark. Suppose that the rod reading is 4.86 ft. The H.I. is then 104.86 ft.
3. The difference between the H.I. and the batter board elevation is $104.86 - 102.5 = 2.36$ ft. Set the target on the rod at 2.36 ft.
4. Now place the rod alongside a post of the batter board at A, Fig. 2-24, and move it up or down until the cross hair coincides with the target. Mark the height of the bottom of the rod on the post.
5. Fasten one end of a batter board to the post with its top edge at that mark. Level the batter board and fasten to the second post.
6. Set the remainder of the batter boards at exactly the same level, using the instrument to check their height and levelness.

Projecting Building Lines on to Batter Boards (Fig. 2-25)

1. Measure accurately (from the boundary intersection) the distances to Stations A, B, C, D, E, and F. These distances will be 25 ft, 45 ft, 65 ft, 85 ft, 115 ft, and 125 ft, respectively.
2. Set up the instrument over Station A, level it, and backsight on the boundary intersection marker. Now set the horizontal circle to 0.
3. Turn the telescope to 90° and tighten the horizontal clamp screw. Sight across the intervening batter boards at stakes 1 and 2 and mark carefully on each batter board where the vertical cross hairs intersect the top edge of the batter board.
4. Set up over Station B and mark the building line on batter boards at stakes 10 and 4.
5. Repeat the procedure at Stations C, D, E, and F.

6. From the boundary intersection, measure the distances to Stations G, H, I, J, K, and L. They will be 25 ft, 45 ft, 65 ft, 85 ft, 115 ft, and 125 ft, respectively.
7. From these stations mark the remainder of the batter boards.

Marking the Depth of Cut on Excavation Limit Stakes

Figure 2-26 shows the excavation limit stakes for the building in Fig. 2-21. The foundation plan indicates that the top of column footings are to have an elevation of +89.5 ft. The excavation is to be taken 6 in. below that level.

1. Set up the instrument at a convenient location from which it is possible to sight on the bench mark and the limit stakes.

Fig. 2-25. Running lines on batter boards

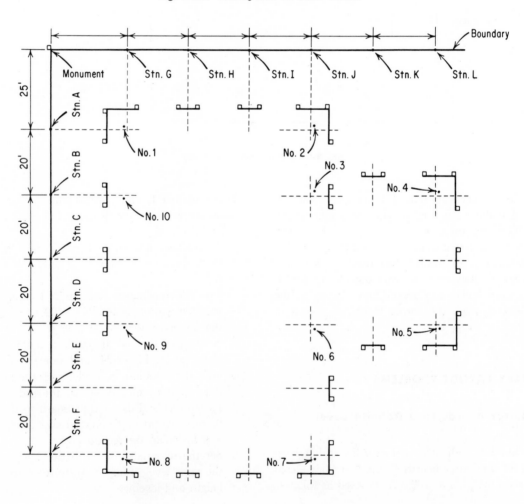

2. Find the differences in elevation between the bench mark and each of the limit stakes and record these differences. Suppose that they are:

Stake No.	Elevation	Difference
1	101.5 ft	+ 1.5 ft
2	99.2 ft	− 0.8 ft
3	99.0 ft	− 1.0 ft
4	98.0 ft	− 2.0 ft
5	96.5 ft	− 3.5 ft
6	97.5 ft	− 2.5 ft
7	95.0 ft	− 5.0 ft
8	99.0 ft	− 1.0 ft
9	100.0 ft	0.0 ft
10	100.8 ft	+ 0.8 ft

3. Calculate the difference in elevation between the bottom of the excavation and the bench mark. In this case the difference will be $100 - 89 = 11$ ft.
4. Calculate the cut at each stake and indicate it on the stake (see Fig. 2-27). These will be:

No. 1	Cut $11 + 1.5 = 12.5$ ft
No. 2	Cut $11 - 0.8 = 10.2$ ft
No. 3	Cut $11 - 1.0 = 10.0$ ft
No. 4	Cut $11 - 2.0 = 9.0$ ft
No. 5	Cut $11 - 3.5 = 7.5$ ft
No. 6	Cut $11 - 2.5 = 8.5$ ft
No. 7	Cut $11 - 5.0 = 6.0$ ft
No. 8	Cut $11 - 1.0 = 10.0$ ft
No. 9	Cut $11 - 0.0 = 11.0$ ft
No. 10	Cut $11 + 0.8 = 11.8$ ft

Running Grades

It is sometimes necessary to run *grade lines* at a construction site—lines which have a uniform drop throughout their length. This is usually expressed as a given number of feet of drop per 100 ft of length. For example, a 1% grade means that there is 1 ft of uniform drop per 100 ft of length.

One method of obtaining a uniform drop in any given distance is as follows:

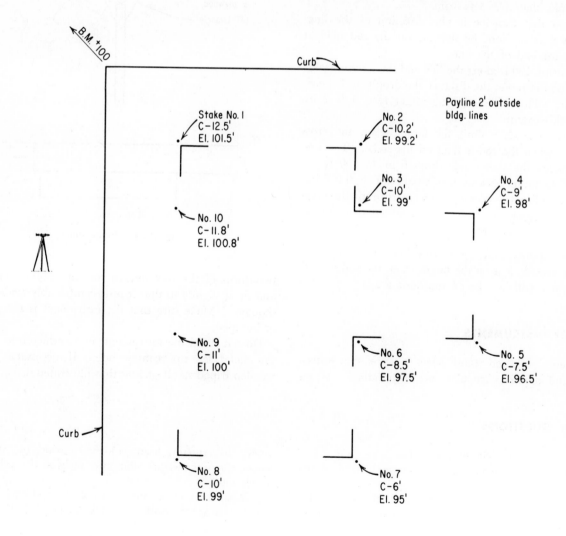

Fig. 2-27. Excavation stake marked for cut

1. Drive a stake to the required height at the start of the proposed line, set up the instrument over this stake, and level it.
2. Measure (with the rod or a tape) the height of the telescope above the stake; suppose, in this example, that it is 3 ft 8 in.
3. Align the telescope in the direction of the line; this may be done by sighting on the rod held at the far end of the line.
4. Measure 100 ft along the line and set another stake.
5. Raise the target the distance the drop is to be, e.g., 6 in. This will make the target read 4 ft 2 in. in this example.
6. Drive the stake until the target is on the cross hair when the rod is held on the stake. The line between the stakes now drops 6 in. in 100 ft.
7. Set the target back to its original reading, 3 ft 8 in., and incline the telescope downward until the cross hair is again on the target. Tighten the vertical motion clamp screw.

Stakes set anywhere along this line and driven in until the cross hair is on the target when the rod is held on the stake will now be on the same grade.

CARE OF INSTRUMENTS

Builders' levels and transit levels are precision instruments and require particular care in handling. When

the instrument is not attached to the tripod, see that it is properly placed in its carrying case. One end of the case is marked **eyepiece end,** so that the instrument can always be fitted in properly. Be sure that it is not subjected to shocks during packing, unpacking, or transportation.

If the instrument gets wet, let it dry—preferably in a relatively dust-free environment. If it has become dusty, clean the dust from the lens with the brush provided. Never rub the optical surfaces. Have the instrument checked and cleaned periodically by a reliable instrument man.

When the instrument is attached to its tripod, carry both as an incorporated unit. Grasp the tripod about

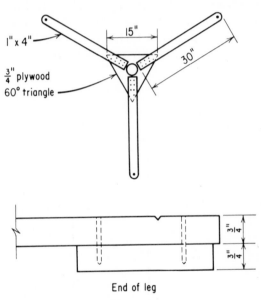

Fig. 2-28. Tripod stand

two-thirds of the way toward the top, closing the legs, and tip it slightly so that it rests comfortably against the shoulder. Make sure that the instrument is not jarred or bumped.

Do not stand the instrument on a surface into which the metal leg tips cannot bite. If necessary, use a wooden tripod stand such as that illustrated in Fig. 2-28.

REVIEW QUESTIONS

1. What is the purpose of a site plan?
2. Describe the leveling procedures for both standard and automatic levels.
3. Briefly describe the purpose of each of the following parts to be found in a level: (a) horizontal motion tangent screw; (b) centering head; (c) vernier scale; (d) vertical motion clamp screw; (e) adjustment screw at the end of the bubble tube.
4. What is meant by the *elevation* of an object?
5. Define the following: (a) backsight; (b) H.I.; (c)

turning point; (d) station.

6. A bench mark is recorded as 1656.121. What is the elevation of point (A), measured from this bench mark, if the recorded readings were as follows:

	T.P.1	T.P.2	T.P.3	T.P.4	T.P.5	T.P.6
Backsights	2.56′	6.63′	5.16′	4.20′	3.92′	6.08′
Foresights	3.12′	2.18′	6.31′	7.65′	1.58′	2.35′

7. We wish to determine the height of a chimney. The instrument is set up 100′ from the base and a level sight is found to be 4.6′ above ground level. When sighting on the top of the chimney from the same point, the angle of inclination is found to be 31°23′. What is the height of the chimney?

8. The elevations of the corner stakes at the site of an excavation are found to be (a) 102.6′ (b) 99.7′ (c) 94.8′ (d) 95.5′ relative to a datum point of +100.0′; calculate the amount of *cut* to be shown on each stake if the bottom of the excavation is to be 11′ below datum.

3

EXCAVATIONS AND
EXCAVATING EQUIPMENT

The type of foundation to be used for any particular building will have
been determined at the planning stage. The type chosen will depend to a
large extent on the soil or subsoil encountered at the site. Soil or subsoil
in its natural state is often sufficiently stable to support the foundations of
light buildings. Foundations for heavy buildings, on the other hand, will be
brought to a level with sufficient bearing strength, or to bedrock (unless
tests show that bedrock occurs at too great a depth to be reached by
conventional foundation walls). In that event, deep foundations will be
required, and these will be discussed in a subsequent chapter.

In order to build a normal foundation, an excavation is required, and
this operation will usually be carried out by some type of power excavating
equipment.

EFFECTS OF SOIL TYPES ON EXCAVATING EQUIPMENT

The type of soil at the site will be the major factor in determining the
type of excavating equipment needed for the job. If the soil is loose or
noncohesive—dry sand or gravel, for instance—excavating can usually be
started with a clamshell bucket and completed with a payloader—a shovel
mounted on a tractor—or it may be done completely by payloader or bulldozer. The use of these two machines requires access into and out of the
excavation. In restricted locations where such access is not possible, other
methods must be used.

More cohesive soils require more power, and in such cases a power shovel or pull shovel (backhoe) will be required. Again, a power shovel requires access to and from the excavation while a pull shovel can dig below its own level—within limits. A bulldozer may also be used for excavating cohesive soils. For very large excavations in soils of either of the above types, a scraper may be employed.

Soils that are too soft or wet to support machinery traveling over them may be excavated by means of a dragline. This machine will operate from one or two stable spots at the side of the excavation.

When narrow trenches or individual holes are required —for footings, or piers—a pull shovel or a trencher is the proper equipment to use.

Boulders and broken rock will probably be handled best by a power shovel, though a clamshell bucket could be used if the pieces are small enough. All these machines will be described in some detail in subsequent paragraphs.

Fig. 3-1. Pump draining excavation (Courtesy Homelite Pumps.)

REMOVING GROUND WATER

One of the serious problems sometimes encountered during operations is the presence of water in the excavation. This may be caused by rain, melting snow, an underground stream, or the fact that the *water table* in the area is high. The water table is the normal level of ground water, and if that level is close to the surface, excavating will allow the ground water to seep and collect in the excavation.

There are two principal methods of getting rid of water. One is to use a pump (or pumps) to empty the excavation or to keep it dry. This method is particularly useful in getting rid of collected rain water and runoff or to remove the water from an uncovered underground stream. Figure 3-1 illustrates the removal of collected rain water from a pier excavation by pump. Pumps are also used to get rid of seepage water. A sump, into which the water collects and from which the pump can then remove it, is required. Figure 3-2 shows a pump removing seepage water from behind a cofferdam.

The other method is to lower the water table in the area in which the excavating will take place. This is done by a *dewatering system*—a system which involves sinking a series of *well-points* around the area and extracting the water by suction pump. Figure 3-3 shows an excavation surrounded by a dewatering system to keep the working area dry. Figure 3-4 illustrates how a typical well-point system would be laid out, while Fig. 3-5 shows a section through such a system.

A system consists of a series of well-points (see Fig. 3-6), each with a riser pipe and a swing joint connecting

Fig. 3-2. Pump removing seepage water (Courtesy Homelite Pumps.)

to a common header or manifold. In Fig. 3-7, a profile of a well-point system shows the setup. Notice the normal water level and the predrained water level, brought about by the water extraction.

The header pipe is exhausted by a combination

Fig. 3-3. Excavation surrounded by well-point system. (Courtesy Moretrench Corp.)

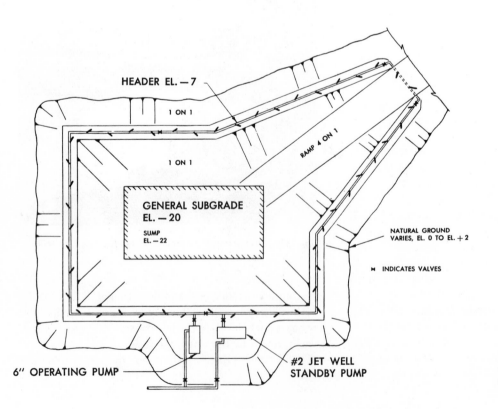

HEADER EL. — 7

1 ON 1

1 ON 1

RAMP 4 ON 1

GENERAL SUBGRADE
EL. — 20

SUMP
EL. — 22

NATURAL GROUND
VARIES, EL. 0 TO EL. + 2

⋈ INDICATES VALVES

6" OPERATING PUMP

#2 JET WELL
STANDBY PUMP

Fig. 3-4. Typical well-point layout plan. (Courtesy Moretrench Corp.)

Fig. 3-5. Typical well-point layout section. (Courtesy Moretrench Corp.)

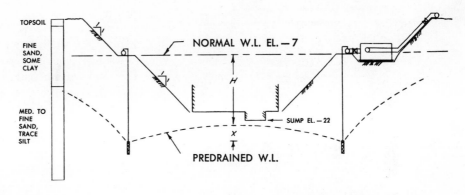

Fig. 3-6. Two inch self-jetting well-point. (Courtesy Moretrench Corp.)

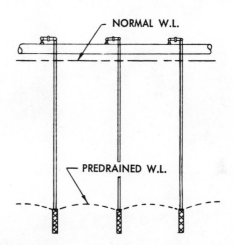

Fig. 3-7. Profile of well-point system. (Courtesy Moretrench Corp.)

riser and swings, and through the header to the pump. Any air entering the system is separated in the float chamber and passed to the vacuum pump. The water passes to the centrifugal pump which discharges it to a drainage system (see Fig. 3-8).

In coarse soils, easily drained, well-points are driven directly into the soil. In fine, dense soils, they are generally set in a column of sand, as shown in Fig. 3-9, which helps to prevent the well-point screen from becoming clogged with silt.

The well-point is a hollow, perforated tube, covered with a stainless steel filter screen which allows water to enter the well-point but keeps out sand and silt (see Fig. 3-6). The bottom end is serrated to enable it to penetrate the soil more easily. In the bottom end is a chamber containing a ball valve with a wooden center, so that it will float. When water is being drawn from the well-point, the ball floats up against a ring valve at the top of the chamber and prevents sand from being drawn into the system.

When placing the well-point in the ground, a jet of water can be forced down through the pipe, loosening the soil around the tip and making penetration easier.

pumping unit, which is a centrifugal pump continuously primed by a positive displacement vacuum pump. Atmospheric pressure forces water through the ground to the well-point screens, into the well-points, up the

Fig. 3-8. Dewatering pump. (Courtesy Moretrench Corp.)

Fig. 3-9. A properly sanded well-point. (Courtesy Moretrench Corp.)

During this operation, the ball valve is forced down into the retainer basket at the bottom of the chamber. Figure 3-10 shows a well-point being jetted into place.

Another type of dewatering operation is illustrated in Fig. 3-11. Here perforated drains are being installed into the bottom of a bank to facilitate slide control.

GENERAL AND SPECIAL EXCAVATIONS

Excavating operations are of two types, *general* and *special*. General excavations include all the work, other than rock excavation, which can be carried out by mechanical equipment. For example, excavating done with draglines, shovels, or scrapers, loading with pay-loader or clamshell, and hauling by truck all come under the heading of general excavation.

Special excavation includes the work that must be done by blasting, by special machines, by hand, or by a combination of hand and machine.

The contractor should be fully aware of the types of excavation with which he must deal, in order to estimate the cost properly and to insure that he has the right kind of equipment on hand to do the best job.

ESTIMATING AMOUNT OF MATERIAL TO BE REMOVED

Before an excavation is begun, its cost must be estimated. This estimate should be based on the cubic yards of material to be dug and hauled away. Plans show the area occupied by the building and the depth to which the excavation must be carried. Since there must usually be room to work around the outside forms in an excavation, a line is drawn at a reasonable distance (usually 2 ft) outside the building line and the excavating contractor is paid for the material excavated to this line—the *payline*.

When soil is taken from its compacted position and broken up, as in excavating, it increases in bulk. This is called the *soil swell*. Therefore, the volume of material to be removed from the site must be increased by a percentage, depending on the type of soil. Most soils will swell between 20 and 50%. Table 3-1 shows the percentages of bulking encountered with some common soil types.

If the soil is cohesive enough, or if some means of supporting the sides of the excavation are to be used, the compact volume to be removed is simply a matter of length × width × depth. But for loose, sliding soils, the excavation must have sloping sides, usually with a 1-1 slope. This fact must be taken into account when

TABLE 3-1

Soil Swell Percentage

Soil type	Percentage of swell from compact state
Silt	20%
Clay	25%
Sand & Gravel	50%
Loam	25%
Stone	50%

estimating the volume of material to be removed. A formula that may be used in calculating the volume in such cases is

$$\frac{(A + B + 6C)H}{8}$$

where $A =$ top area
$B =$ bottom area
$C =$ midsection area (average of top and bottom areas)
$H =$ vertical height

CHOOSING EXCAVATION EQUIPMENT

A number of factors must be taken into consideration when deciding what type or types of excavating ma-

Fig. 3-10. Jetting a well-point. (Courtesy Moretrench Corp.)

Fig. 3-11. Drill installing 1300 ft perforated drains to facilitate slide control. (Courtesy Mobile Drilling Co.)

Fig. 3-12. Crane lifting wall panels. (Courtesy American Hoist and Derrick Co.)

chinery will do the job most efficiently. The first point to consider is the volume of material to be removed. This will influence the size of the machines to be used. The depth of the excavation will determine the height to which material must be lifted to get it into trucks.

The disposal of the excavated material may influence the type of machinery used. If it can be deposited on a spoil bank at the site, one machine may do both digging and depositing. The distance from excavation to spoil bank is also a factor. On the other hand, if the material must be removed from the site, hauling units and special loading equipment may be required.

The type of soil to be excavated will influence the kind of equipment selected. Some machines work well in loose, dry soils, but not in wet or highly compacted earth.

The time allowed for excavation will also affect the type, size, and amount of equipment to be used.

Before discussing machines used specifically for excavating, it would perhaps be well to look at a machine that has many uses on a building site, including adaptations for digging. This is the crane, a machine designed primarily for lifting, but adapted to many other uses. Few building jobs are without a crane, and Figs. 3-12, 3-13, and 3-14 illustrate some typical uses of these machines.

A crane consists basically of a power unit mounted on crawler tracks or wheels, with a boom, and control cables for raising and lowering the load and the boom (see Fig. 3-15). A *gantry* is sometimes added (see Fig. 3-16) to provide better boom support. For greater reach, an extension may be added to the boom. This may be in the form of a *boom insert*, a section added between the upper and lower ends, or a *jib*, an extension

Fig. 3-13. Crane lifting bridge girders

Fig. 3-14. Crane with concrete bucket

with boom length and any extension of the boom reduces the rating. Lowering the boom also increases the radius and thus reduces the rated capacity.

3. The counterweight. This is added to the after-end of the machine and manufacturers' specifications provide standard and maximum counterweights, and give crane ratings for both. Counterweights may be increased to a specified maximum, but the operating radius *must* not exceed that given by the manufacturer.

The working range of a crane is limited horizontally for maximum lift only by the boom length. The reach below footing level is limited only by the length of the hoist cable. Figure 3-18 points out the various crane clearances involved in crane operation. A wide variety of tools which may be used with a crane boom are illustrated in Fig. 3-19. Three of these are excavating tools and will be discussed later.

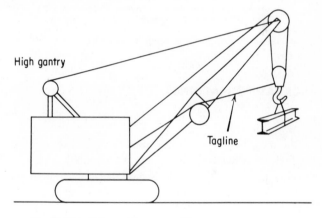

Fig. 3-16. Crane with gantry. (Courtesy Power Crane & Shovel Ass'n.)

to the end of the boom. Figure 3-17 illustrates these boom extensions. Notice that in Fig. 3-12, the crane boom has both an insert and a gooseneck jib.

The load capacity of a crane depends on:

1. The stability of the footing. The size of the crawlers is a factor because a longer or wider mounting increases the stability of any footing.
2. The strength of the boom. This is one of the major governing factors in establishing *load ratings*, and these should never be exceeded. Ratings vary

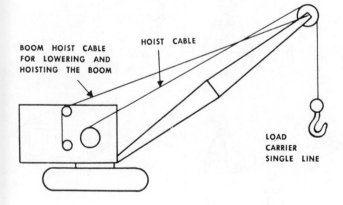

Fig. 3-15. Diagram of crane. (Courtesy Power Crane & Shovel Ass'n.)

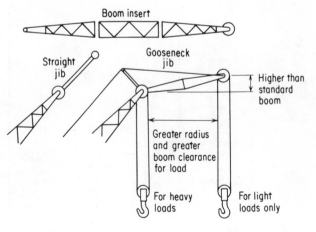

Fig. 3-17. Boom extensions. (Courtesy Power Crane & Shovel Ass'n.)

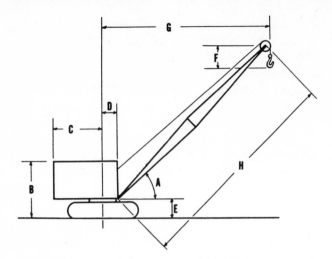

A Boom Angle
B Maximum Clearance Height of Cab
C Maximum Radius of Tail Swing
D Center of Rotation to Boom Foot Pin
E Height from Ground to Boom Foot Pin
F Distance from Center of Boom Point Sheave to Bottom of Hook
G Clearance Radius of Boom
H Length of Boom

Working radius, not shown in above diagram, is of course, of primary importance in crane selection.

Fig. 3-18. Crane clearance diagram. (Courtesy Power Crane & Shovel Ass'n.)

EXCAVATING MACHINES

Bulldozer

The term *bulldozer* is often used to mean any tractor, tracked or wheeled, on which is mounted a blade. Specifically, when the blade is mounted perpendicularly to the line of travel, the machine is a *bulldozer*, while if the blade is at an angle to the direction of travel, it is an *angledozer* (see Fig. 3-20).

Bulldozers and angledozers have limited use for excavating by themselves. They are able to loosen and remove soil from its original position, but can only dispose of this soil by pushing it beyond the limits of the excavation. For this reason, a bulldozer is useful for starting an excavation, for stripping valuable topsoil from the excavation site, or for use where earth must be excavated from one part of the site and deposited as fill in another. As an excavation deepens, a bulldozer's usefulness is reduced to loosening soil and readying it for removal by other means.

Loader

A *loader* is one machine in common use to pick up excavated material. It consists of a crawler or wheeled tractor with a shovel or bucket mounted in front. A loader can excavate loose soils, but its chief use is loading excavated material into trucks for removal. Figure 3-21 shows a wheeled tractor being used as both a loader and a dozer, while Fig. 3-22 shows a crawler tractor with bucket being used only as a loader.

Scraper

Scrapers have established an important position in the earth-moving field, particularly where large volumes must be excavated and hauled away. A scraper is a combination machine, in that it loads, hauls, and dis-

Fig. 3-19 Crane tools. (Courtesy Power Crane & Shovel Ass'n.)

Digging tools

Dragline buckets

Clamshell buckets

Orange peel buckets

Backfill blades

Hooks

Plain hook

Hook blocks

Slings

Hairpin hooks

Special hooks

Grabs

Tongs

Grabs

Clamps

Magnets

Grapples

Bulk material tools

Concrete buckets

Skips

Load platform

Bottom-dump platform

Weights

Skull crackers

Pile driver

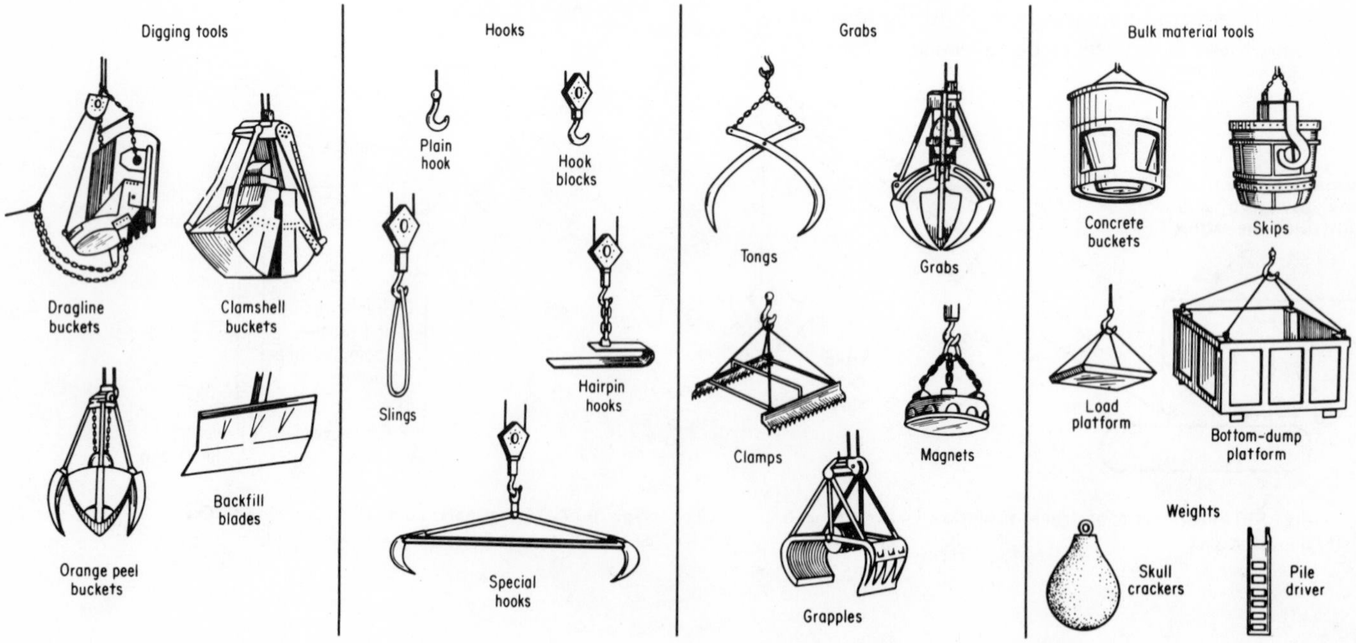

Fig. 3-20. Crawler bulldozer. (Courtesy J. I. Case Co.)

(a)

(b)

Fig. 3-21. (a) Wheeled tractor as a dozer; (b) wheeled tractor as a loader. (Courtesy Allis-Chalmers Co.)

Fig. 3-22. Crawler loader. (Courtesy J. I. Case Co.)

Fig. 3-23. Wheeled scraper. (Courtesy Euclid Division, General Motors Corp.)

Fig. 3-24. Power shovel. (Courtesy Insley Equipment Co.)

charges material. It may be powered by a crawler tractor or by one or two rubber-tired wheeled tractors. Some very large machines have an individual power unit driving each wheel. The crawler tractor scraper has good traction and does not usually require assistance in loading, but is a slow traveler. The rubber-tired scraper, on the other hand, often needs assistance in loading if the earth is very compact, but can travel at speeds in excess of 40 mph (see Fig. 3-23).

Power shovel

A *power shovel* is used primarily to excavate earth and load it into trucks, or deposit it on a spoil bank at the site. It may be mounted on crawler tracks or at the rear of a truck. A crawler-mounted unit has slow travel speeds, but wide tracks permit it to operate on soft soil. Figure 3-24 shows a crawler-mounted power shovel in operation.

A power shovel is designed to operate against a face or bank which it displaces as it moves forward. Its design permits power to be applied so as to force the dipper into the bank, and it is capable of digging into the hardest types of materials. Figure 3-25 illustrates its action and the basic parts of the digging apparatus.

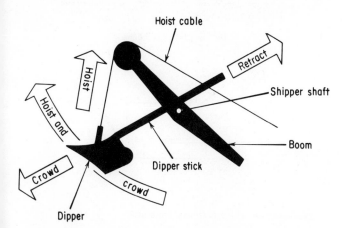

Fig. 3-25. Shovel digging action. (Courtesy Power Crane & Shovel Ass'n.)

This type of machine can be used in a number of ways, some of which are depicted in Fig. 3-26.

Since the shipper shaft acts as a fulcrum, both dipper and dipper stick can be raised or lowered by the hoist line as well as pushed out or retracted by the crowd mechanism. These motions can be performed simultaneously and permit a flexibility of operation. The

limits of this flexibility are commonly referred to as the *working ranges*. These are indicated in Fig. 3-27.

The size of power shovel to use for any particular job depends on a number of factors. These are:
1. The capacity of the dipper
2. The type of soil being extracted
3. The radius required to reach the digging area
4. The radius required to reach the hauling units
5. Distance required to reach a spoil bank or stock pile
6. The height of the face to be excavated
7. Clearance height required to reach hauling units located on top of the bank
8. Physical clearances of the machine when working in confined areas

TABLE 3-2

Hourly Shovel Handling Capacities in Cubic Yards

Shovel dipper sizes in cu yd	⅜	½	¾	1	1¼	1½	1¾	2	2½
Class of material									
Moist loam or sandy clay	85	115	165	205	250	285	320	355	405
Sand and gravel	80	110	155	200	230	270	300	330	390
Good common earth	70	95	135	175	210	240	270	300	350
Clay, hard, tough	50	75	110	145	180	210	235	265	310
Rock, well-blasted	40	60	95	125	155	180	205	230	275
Common, with rock & roots	30	50	80	105	130	155	180	200	245
Clay, wet & sticky	25	40	70	95	120	145	165	185	230
Rock, poorly-blasted	15	25	50	75	95	115	140	160	195

Conditions : 1) Cu yd bank measurement per hour
2) Suitable depth of cut for maximum effect
3) Continuous loading with full dipper
4) 90° swing, grade level loading
5) All materials loaded into hauling units
Reproduced by permission of Power Crane and Shovel Association.

Pull shovel

A *pull shovel* is often referred to as a *hoe* or *backhoe* and is quite similar to a power shovel as far as basic parts are concerned. The main difference is that the position of the bucket is the reverse to that of the power shovel. It digs by pulling the load toward the power unit rather than pushing it away as a power shovel does. Figure 3-28 shows a small pull shovel mounted on a wheeled tractor, and Fig. 3-29, a large, crawler-mounted shovel discharging into a truck.

Basic pull shovel parts consist of an auxiliary gantry, boom, dipper stick, braces and dipper, as illustrated in Fig. 3-30. The dipper stick, hinged at the boom point to provide lever action, acts as an arm for the dipper. The dipper is pulled inward as the digging cable is taken in, while the boom can be raised and lowered at the same time. All the motions of the

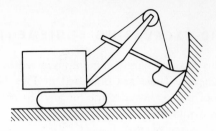

Embankment digging (above grade)

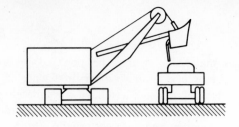

Loading into hauling units at ground level

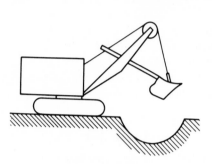

Digging below grade

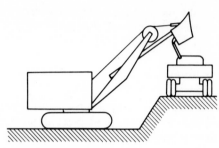

Loading into hauling units on top of bank

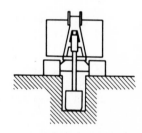

Handling shallow trenches

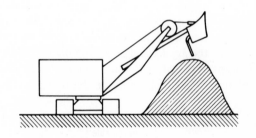

Dumping onto spoil bank

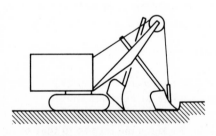

Digging along horizontal plane

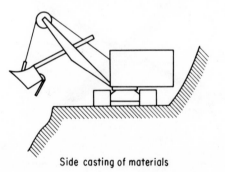

Side casting of materials

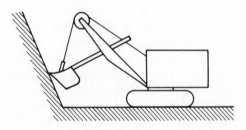

Digging slopes

Dumping onto belt, conveyor, hopper or grizzly

Fig. 3-26. Typical power shovel operations. (Courtesy Power Crane & Shovel Ass'n.)

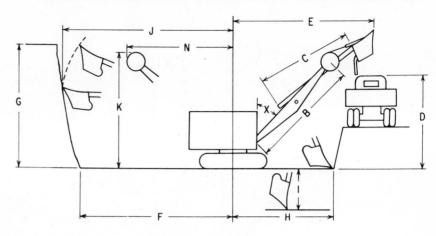

X Boom angle
B Boom length
C Dipper stick length
E Dumping radius at max. height
F Dumping radius (max.)
D Dumping height (max.)
G Height of cut (max.)

J Digging radius (max.)
H Floor level radius
I Max. digging depth below ground level
K Clearance ht. of boom point sheave
N Clearance radius of boom point sheave

Fig. 3-27. Power shovel working ranges. (Courtesy Power Crane & Shovel Ass'n.)

Fig. 3-28. Pull shovel on wheeled tractor

Fig. 3-29. Crawler mounted pull shovel. (Courtesy Miron Co., Ltd.)

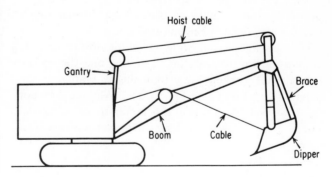

Fig. 3-30. Basic parts of pull shovel. (Courtesy Power Crane & Shovel Ass'n.)

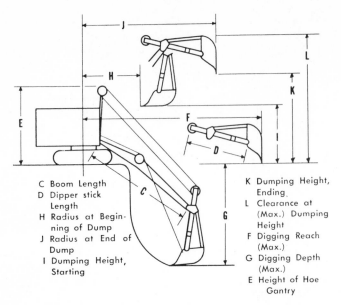

C Boom Length
D Dipper stick Length
H Radius at Beginning of Dump
J Radius at End of Dump
I Dumping Height, Starting

K Dumping Height, Ending
L Clearance at (Max.) Dumping Height
F Digging Reach (Max.)
G Digging Depth (Max.)
E Height of Hoe Gantry

Fig. 3-31. Pull shovel working ranges. (Courtesy Power Crane & Shovel Ass'n.)

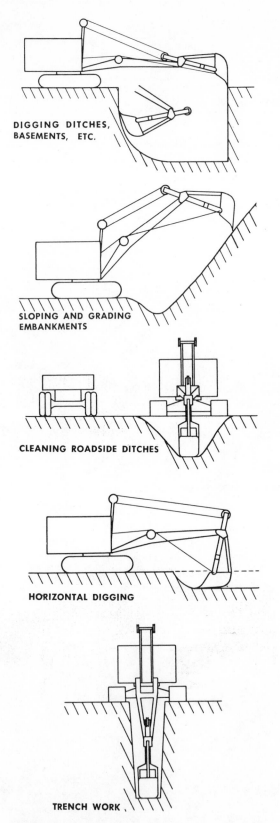

DIGGING DITCHES, BASEMENTS, ETC.

SLOPING AND GRADING EMBANKMENTS

CLEANING ROADSIDE DITCHES

HORIZONTAL DIGGING

TRENCH WORK

Fig. 3-32. Typical uses of pull shovel. (Courtesy Power Crane & Shovel Ass'n.)

machine combine to provide working ranges shown in Fig. 3-31.

The pull shovel is designed to dig below the level on which the machine rests, and to deposit the material on a spoil bank or in trucks. Because of its positive action, it is also capable of digging in the hardest materials. The most common uses of the pull shovel are illustrated in Fig. 3-32.

Dragline

One of the attachments used on a crane boom is a *dragline*, shown in Fig. 3-33. As illustrated in Fig. 3-34, the dragline attachment consists of a dragline bucket, hoist cable, dragcable, and fairlead—used with a crane boom. The machine is operated by pulling the bucket toward the power unit, regulating the digging depth by adjusting the tension on the hoist cable.

The dragline has a wide range of operations. It remains on firm or undisturbed ground and digs below its own level, backing away from the excavation as the material is removed (see Fig. 3-35). While it does not dig to as accurate a grade as a power shovel or a pull shovel, it has a larger working range—an advantage in many situations. Figure 3-36 outlines the dragline working range.

In addition to its large working range, the dragline has the further advantage of being suited to digging

Fig. 3-33. (Top) Dragline discharging bucket. (Courtesy Insley Mfg. Corp.)

Fig. 3-34. (Center) Basic parts of dragline. (Courtesy Power Crane & Shovel Ass'n.)

Fig. 3-35. (Bottom) Dragline working deep excavation. (Courtesy Miron Co., Ltd.)

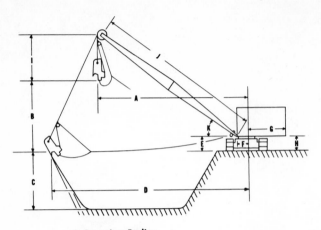

A Dumping Radius
B Dumping Height
C Maximum Digging Depth
D Digging Reach (Depends on Conditions and Operator's Skill)
E Distance from Ground to Boom Foot Pin
F Distance from Center of Rotation to Boom Foot Pin
G Rear End Radius of Counterweight
H Ground Clearance
I Length of Bucket (Depends on Size and Make)
J Boom Length
K Boom Angle

Fig. 3-36. Dragline working range. (Courtesy Power Crane & Shovel Ass'n.)

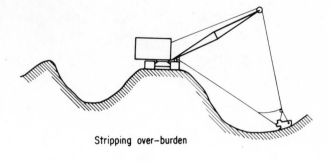

Stripping over–burden

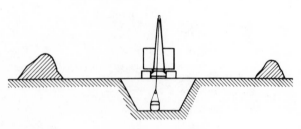

Excavating narrow ditches

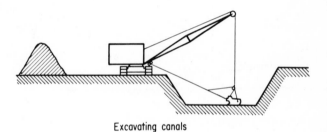

Excavating canals

in excavations below water level and in mud or quicksand. Figure 3-37 illustrates a few typical uses.

Clamshell

The crane boom is often used with a hinged bucket, called a clamshell (see Fig. 3-38), for vertical excavating below ground level and for handling bulk materials such as sand and gravel.

The clamshell bucket consists of two scoops hinged in the center, with holding arms connecting the headblock to the outer ends of the scoops. A closing line is reeved through blocks on the hinge and the head, so that the bucket closes when it is taken in. The bucket is opened by releasing the closing and hoisting line while holding the bucket with the holding and lowering line. Clamshells are usually equipped with a tagline to control the swing of the bucket (see Fig. 3-39).

Buckets are available in a wide variety of sizes and types. A heavy-duty type is available for digging, and lighter weight ones for general purpose work or handling light materials. Some buckets have removable teeth, used when digging in hard material, while others have special cutting lips.

Overcasting from borrow pit

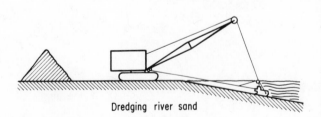

Dredging river sand

Fig. 3-37. Typical dragline operation. (Courtesy Power Crane & Shovel Ass'n.)

Fig. 3-38. Clamshell unloading sand

Trencher

Excavating trenches (for sewer lines, pipe lines, etc.) is a type of operation which usually requires specialized machines. A pull shovel may be employed, as shown in Fig. 3-40, but for speed and economy of operation, a *trencher* is used. It is a machine that digs and deposits the soil in one continuous operation. Figure 3-41 shows one type of trencher ready for operation. As earth is dug up by the wheel, it is dropped on a side delivery belt and deposited in a continuous pile alongside the trench. Backfilling the trench can be done in many ways, one of which is shown in Fig. 3-42. Bulldozers, angledozers, and loaders are also used for backfilling trenches and around foundations.

Trucks

No discussion of excavating machinery would be complete without mentioning the hauling units—usually *trucks*, with bodies made for that specific purpose. Figure 3-43 shows such a body, with a protective canopy over the cab and a tapered back for easy dumping. In Fig. 3-44, a pull shovel discharges into a truck with a square-end body.

Most trucks may be operated over sufficiently firm and smooth haul roads. Some units now in use are

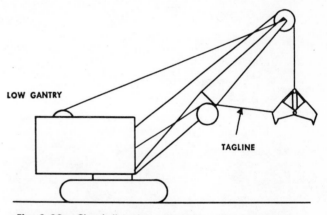

Fig. 3-39. Clamshell bucket with tagline. (Courtesy Power Crane & Shovel Ass'n.)

designated as *off-highway* trucks, because of their size and power.

Trucks may be classified in a great many ways, including the following:

1. According to size and type of engine
2. By the number of gears
3. As two-, four-, or six-wheel drive
4. By the number of wheels and axles
5. By the method of dumping
6. By the capacity

Fig. 3-40. Pull shovel used for trenching. (Courtesy Insley Mfg. Corp.)

Fig. 3-41. Trencher

Fig. 3-42. Backfilling trench

Fig. 3-43. Truck with special dump body

The truck in Fig. 3-44 is a 30-ton rear-dump, six-wheel hauler.

PROTECTION OF EXCAVATIONS

The protection of an excavation involves making certain that the side walls do not cave in and bring about extra digging, damage to forms, or injury to workmen. The amount of protection required will depend on the type of soil being excavated. The sides of an excavation dug in compact, stable soil may need no protection at all. In Fig. 3-45, the sides of the excavation are standing unprotected. Notice that near the top, where the soil is looser, the sides have been sloped to prevent cave-in. One of the reasons for the stability of the soil in this case is that the area has been kept dry by a dewatering system.

Fig. 3-44. Loading heavy dump truck. (Courtesy Miron Co., Ltd.)

Fig. 3-45. Free-standing excavation walls. (Courtesy Moretrench Corp.)

Fig. 3-46. Excavation with braced walls. (Courtesy Moretrench Corp.)

In less stable soils the excavation must be protected against cave-ins, and this may be done in one of two ways. One is to slope the sides of the excavation until the angle of repose of that particular soil is reached. In some cases, this will mean a slope of 1 and 1, or 45°. This method may not be possible where space is limited or where the extra cost of excavation is prohibitive. In such situations, it is necessary to provide temporary support around the excavation to hold back the earth.

Such supports may be placed after completing the excavation, and must be held in place while they are performing their job. If the excavation is narrow, braces may reach across it and hold the earth in place, as is the case in Fig. 3-46. Notice that only spaced pads are used here, because the earth is stable and is merely being reinforced.

In noncohesive soils, or in situations where workers must be protected against sudden cave-ins, solid walls of wood, concrete, or steel are used to hold back the earth. These protective walls are known as *sheeting*, or *sheet piling*, depending on how and when they are placed. When timbers, flat steel sections, or concrete sheet piles are driven beyond the final depth of excavation before any earth has been removed, they are

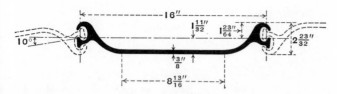

Fig. 3-47. Interlocking sheet piling. (Courtesy Bethlehem Steel Co.)

known as sheet piling. In Fig. 3-33, the dragline is excavating behind a line of interlocking steel sheet piling.

The steel sheet piling used in Fig. 3-33 is of a common type. The piles interlock as illustrated in Fig. 3-47 and are made in lengths of up to 70 ft.

Concrete sheet piles are precast, square or rectangular, reinforced, and with tongue-and-groove edges. The bottom end of the pile is beveled on one edge to facilitate driving.

Timber sheet piling is usually 3- or 4 in.-thick material in 10 or 12 in. widths. Length is more limited than that of steel sheet piling. Two layers of piling may be driven, one behind the other, with overlapping joints.

When material being used to hold back the earth is set in place as the excavation proceeds or after its completion, it is known as sheeting. Wood, concrete, or a combination of wood and steel are commonly used for this purpose.

One method consists of driving wooden or steel posts along the face of the excavation and placing wood, reinforced concrete, or steel sheeting behind them, as has been done in Fig. 3-48. The posts must be braced or shored at their ends, unless they have been driven a considerable distance below the excavation.

Another method involves the use of sections of sheeting set against the excavation face and braced in place.

PROTECTION OF ADJACENT BUILDINGS

In many instances, it is necessary to carry the excavation for a new building right up to the foundations of an existing one. This presents a problem if the new excavation is to be deeper than the footings of the existing building. Part of the support for those footings will be removed, and it is the responsibility of the builder to protect the building against movement caused by settlement during and after construction of the new building. Temporary support may be provided by *shoring* or *needling*, while permanent support is provided by *underpinning*—extending the old foundation to the level of the new one.

Shoring is the simplest method of providing temporary support, and involves only the use of shoring timbers and jacks (see Fig. 3-49). Screw jacks are most suitable if the pressure is to remain for an extended period of time.

There must be solid bearing for the end of the shoring

Fig. 3-48. Excavation protected with sheeting. (Courtesy Moretrench Corp.)

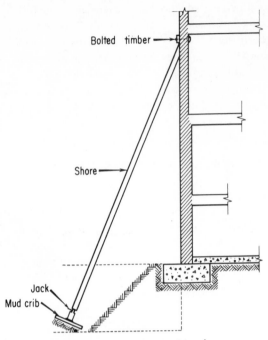

Fig. 3-49. Wall supported by shore

of the footings for the new building. If necessary, the projecting lip of the old footing is cut off, and a new foundation—*underpinning*—is poured, extending under the old footing down to the new level.

Where soil of high bearing strength and good stability is involved and old foundations are strong, underpinning may be carried out without shores or needles. In such instances, the underpinning is placed in spaced sections, a procedure known as *leg-and-leg* underpinning. Relatively small sections of earth are removed from under the old footings at spaced intervals, leaving the remainder intact to support the building for the time being. Forms are set and underpinnings are poured under each section. When the concrete has gained sufficient strength, a new section is excavated along each leg, thus transferring those portions of the building load to the newly poured legs. The adjoining sections are then formed and poured as before. Ad-

timber near the top of the wall being supported. Pockets may be formed in brick walls by removing a few of the face bricks. A timber may be fastened to the face of the wall by bolting through timber and wall, as is the case in Fig. 3-49. Shores may also bear against window lintels high up the wall.

The lower end of each shore rests on a jack head. Each jack rests on a *crib* large enough to spread the load safely over the earth below. Be sure to set the crib at the proper angle to insure that jacking pressure is in direct line with the shore.

There are disadvantages to the shoring method which should be kept in mind. First, it is only practical for relatively light buildings. Second, the height to which shores will reach is limited and therefore not practical for very tall buildings. Third, the lower ends of shores will extend into the new working area, and may inconvenience workmen and machines.

Needling involves the use of a *needle beam* which is thrust through the wall of the building being supported. The inner end stands on solid blocking while the outer end is supported by a post resting on a jack. Figure 3-50 illustrates how a needle beam is used. The post jacks must be set in pits dug in the working area to the depth of the new excavation. Work is then carried out around them until permanent support can be provided for the old building.

Once the wall is supported, the earth is excavated from below the existing footings to at least the depth

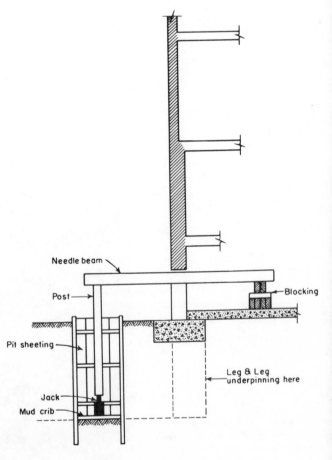

Fig. 3-50. Wall supported by a needle beam

joining sections should be tied together by keys or steel dowels. This process is repeated until the entire length of the wall has been underpinned.

Forms for underpinnings need special consideration. Where the soil is stable, no form may be necessary on the inside. The earth wall should be cut as straight as possible and lined with material such as polyethylene film, heavy wax paper, or thin plywood to keep concrete from coming in contact with the earth. The outer

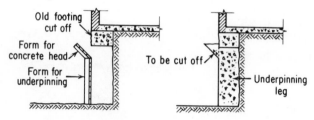

Fig. 3-51. Underpinning

form is simple except that it must have a *head* at the top to allow concrete to be poured above the level of the base of the old footing, as seen in Fig. 3-51. Concrete can then be poured and vibrated into place to make sure that it comes in contact with the under surface of the old footing. The projecting lip of concrete is cut off when the forms are removed.

ROCK EXCAVATION

Excavating sometimes includes the removal of solid rock, and this will involve blasting, a job that is normally carried out by specialists. It is important, however, that the basic principles of rock removal by blasting be understood by those involved with the construction job.

In the building construction industry, blasting is used for such purposes as rock excavation, demolition work on buildings and foundations, stump clearing, and the breaking-up of boulders too large to handle. The techniques of blasting have been made possible through the development of gunpowder and the refinement of explosives such as dynamite.

TYPES OF EXPLOSIVES

Explosives commonly used in commercial blasting are practically all solid-solid or solid-liquid mixtures capable of rapid and violent decomposition, with resultant conversion into large volumes of gas. Decomposition of a

Fig. 3-52. Demolition blasting. (Courtesy Canadian Industries Ltd.)

high explosive, such as dynamite, takes place with extreme rapidity, while a *low* explosive, such as black blasting powder, decomposes more slowly, simulating rapid burning. As a result, high explosives are called *detonating* explosives and low explosives are referred to as *deflagrating* explosives.

The most widely used high explosive in the construction field is dynamite. It is basically composed of liquid nitroglycerin as a *sensitizer*, sawdust or wood pulp as a *liquid absorber*, an *oxygen supplier* such as sodium nitrate, and a small amount of *antiacid* material such as zinc oxide or calcium carbonate. Several types of dynamite exist, the common ones being: (1) *straight*; (2) *extra* or *ammonia*; (3) *gelatin*; and (4) *permissive* dynamite.

Dynamite is produced in various grades, depending on the percentage (by weight) of nitroglycerin the material contains. Thus, a 30% grade contains 30% nitroglycerin, while a 60% grade contains 60% nitroglycerin, etc. This does not mean that 60% dynamite is twice as strong as 30% dynamite—in fact, it is only about 1⅓ times as strong.

For practical use, dynamite is rolled into cartridges covered with wax-impregnated, 70 lb manila paper. Cartridges range from ⅞ to 8 in. in diameter and from 8 to 24 in. in length.

In order to produce an explosion, dynamite may be ignited in any one of three ways, depending on the type of dynamite used and the general conditions at the time of blasting. One method is to use a safety fuse connected directly to the cartridge. Another is to use a blasting cap at the end of a fuse, and the third is the use of electric blasting caps.

A safety fuse consists of black powder protected by a flexible fabric tube. Safety fuses are available in two burning rates: 1 yd in 120 sec or 1 yd in 90 sec. Fuses are generally lit with matches and their burning time provides an opportunity to clear the blast area.

Many dynamites cannot be ignited by the burning action of a fuse, and must be set off by a primary blast wave. This is done by placing a blasting cap on the end of a safety fuse and inserting the cap into a cartridge. The burning fuse ignites the cap, which detonates, and in turn sets off the dynamite.

In many cases, safety fuses and detonators are replaced by electric blasting caps. These are small copper cylinders about $1\frac{1}{8}$ in. long and $\frac{3}{8}$ in. in diameter containing a small explosive charge. Two conducting wires lead into one end and are connected by a resistance bridge. When an electric current passes across this bridge, the heat generated ignites the charge, which in turn detonates the main charge. Two kinds of blasting caps known as *delay* caps are also made. They are the ordinary delay cap, that allows approximately $\frac{1}{2}$ sec between groups or firing periods, and the millisecond delay cap. In the latter, various delays are available, ranging from .025 sec to .1 sec.

Electric blasting circuits may be wired in series, in parallel, or in series-parallel (employed when a large number of caps are to be set off). Circuits are energized either by batteries or by a blasting machine. Batteries are used only when a blasting machine is not available. The latter produces the desired current, and produces it every time the machine is used. Three types of blasting machines are the twist handle, rack bar, and condenser-discharge.

Excavating with explosives is carried out primarily by drilling holes in the rock, loading the holes with explosives, and firing the charge. Holes are drilled

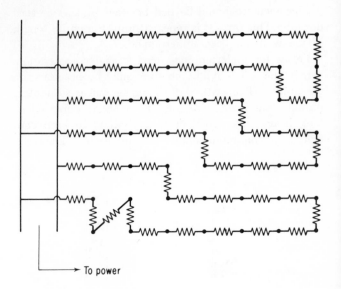

Fig. 3-54. Series-in-parallel electric blasting circuit

horizontally (Fig. 3-55), vertically (Fig. 3-56), or at an angle, depending on circumstances. Holes of all diameters and for different explosives are all loaded basically in the same manner.

When drilling is completed, holes should be cleaned with a jet of compressed air and tamped with a wooden pole. If they are to remain unused for some time after drilling, they should be sealed with paper plugs to keep them clean. Loading a hole consists of placing a primer charge and a number of cartridges in the hole and tamping them into place. A cap is placed in the primer charge by piercing a cartridge with a wooden poker and embedding the cap in the hole, allowing the leg wires to project. The primer charge is lowered into the hole, and additional charges are then placed and tamped. The cartridges are connected by slitting the end of each as it is placed. The pressure caused by tamping causes the slits to open and dynamite to bleed from one cartridge to another. The primer cartridge is not slit. Figure 3-57 illustrates one method of loading a hole.

After the hole has been loaded to the desired depth, it is *stemmed* with an inert material, such as sand or clay. The stemming confines the blast and prevents blowouts through the hole. During the placing, tamping, and stemming operations, the leg wires from the blasting cap must be held against one side of the hole to prevent their being damaged. Figure 3-58 shows a vertical section through a loaded and stemmed hole.

In order to achieve the best results, an organized and calculated pattern of holes must be set up, loaded with either *instantaneous* or *delay* caps. Instantaneous loading and shooting does not permit control of the direction

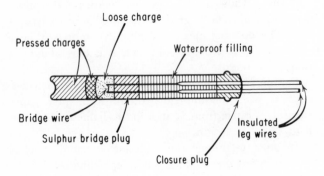

Fig. 3-53. Diagram of electric blasting cap

Fig. 3-55. Horizontal drilling. (Courtesy Canadian Industries Ltd.)

Fig. 3-56 Vertical drilling. (Courtesy Schramm Inc.)

Fig. 3-57. Loading a hole with cartridges. (Courtesy Canadian Industries Ltd.)

of rock throw, and tends to produce *muck* which is often too large to handle. With the use of delay time caps, the direction of rock throw is controlled, and fragmentation is generally improved. Figure 3-59 shows how the use of delay pattern has controlled the breakage of rock at the excavation face. Figure 3-60 illustrates good rock throw control and good fragmentation achieved with a delay pattern. Figure 3-61(a) and (b) shows two steps in a blasting operation, one at the height of the explosion and the other at its conclusion.

In Fig. 3-62, a typical delay pattern is illustrated.

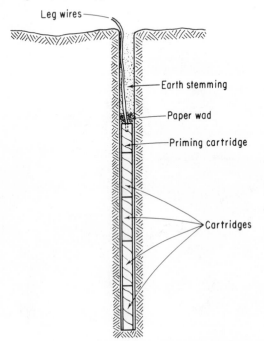

Fig. 3-58. Section through loaded and stemmed hole

Notice that the longer delays are used in the back rows of the holes and along the sides, and the short delay caps are used in the bore holes close to the working face. The short delay charges move the rock near the face and thus provide space for the material moved by the charges primed with long delay caps.

In some cases, large boulders or rock masses left after the *primary* blast may require *secondary* blasting for

Fig. 3-59. Clean rock face made possible with delay pattern blasting. (Courtesy Canadian Industries Ltd.)

complete breakage. Secondary blasting may be done in three ways: (1) by *mudcapping;* (2) by *blockholing;* or (3) by *snakeholing.*

In mudcapping, the required number of cartridges are tied together in a bundle and placed on top of the boulder or rock pile. They are covered with a piece of waterproof paper and a layer of mud about 6 in. thick. The mud contains the blast and directs the shock wave into the rock. Figure 3-63 shows a mudcapping operation before and after the blast.

If extremely hard rock such as granite or traprock does not respond to mudcapping, blockholing must be used. This consists of drilling one or more holes, depending on the size, and loading, stemming, and firing them as in primary blasting.

Snakeholing consists of tunneling under a boulder and placing a charge there in order to lift it and break it up. The excavated earth is replaced in the hole as stemming (see Fig. 3-64).

In primary blasting, the *burden* and the *spacing* of the holes are extremely important. The spacing is the distance between holes in a line, and the burden is the distance of a hole from the free face.

Hole sizes for general blasting range from 1 to 1½ in. and are drilled to a maximum of 20 ft. To illustrate how to plan a drilling pattern and how to determine

Fig. 3-60. Delay pattern blasting. (Courtesy Canadian Industries Ltd.)

(a)

(b)

Fig. 3-61. Controlled blasting: (a) explosion at maximum; (b) blast completed

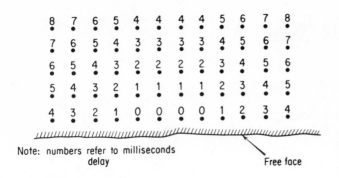

8	7	6	5	4	4	4	4	5	6	7	8
7	6	5	4	3	3	3	3	4	5	6	7
6	5	4	3	2	2	2	3	4	5	6	
5	4	3	2	1	1	1	1	2	3	4	5
4	3	2	1	0	0	0	0	1	2	3	4

Note: numbers refer to milliseconds delay

Free face

Fig. 3-62. Typical delay pattern

the amount of explosive required for a given situation, 1⅛ in. drill holes will be considered.

The maximum amount of explosive that can be placed in a hole 1⅛ in. in diameter and 1 ft deep is .69 lb. Under free breaking conditions, rock normally requires a load of 1 lb of explosive per cu yd. At that rate, the volume of rock that can be broken up with .69 lb of explosive is .69 cu yd, or 18.6 cu ft. A slab of rock 1 ft thick that produces 18.6 cu ft will have a square surface dimension of 4.3 ft × 4.3 ft. So if a number of holes 1 ft deep were drilled in a square pattern, the maximum spacing would be 4.3 ft in any direction. The general spacing and burden limit in instantaneous blasting is 4.3 ft, although this space may vary to some degree with the use of delay caps.

A variety of patterns may be developed by the use of delay caps. One basic pattern is illustrated in Fig. 3-65, where a shot is to be fired into a bank with both ends closed, leaving a vertical face.

The three top center holes, loaded with #0 delay caps, open the shot and release the burden on the #1 delay holes below and on each side. The burden of each successive hole is free-faced by the firing of the charge in front of it. This free-facing of the burden of every charge is the basic principle behind delay pattern blasting. The general load factor will be 1 lb of explosive per cu yd of rock, but the #0 delay charges probably have a load factor of 1.25 lb per cu yd, in order to produce a good, clean start for the pattern. Figure 3-61 shows a bank shot such as that described above being fired.

When there is danger of damage occurring because of rock throw, blasting mats should be used. Two most often used types are woven rope and wire mats. Wire mats must be weighted down to contain rock during a blast, whereas rope mats are heavy enough by themselves. Figure 3-66 shows an area covered with woven rope mats, about to be blasted in a residential section. In Fig. 3-67, rock is being contained by wire mats.

Safety is a prime factor in blasting operations, and following are fifteen general safety rules to practice when handling explosives:

1. Smoking must not be tolerated in the blasting area.
2. Only hardwood or nonspark pokers must be used to pierce cartridges.
3. Circuits should always be checked before firing.

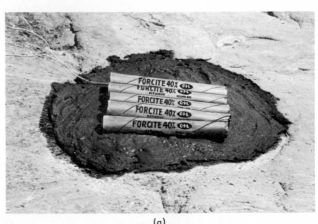

(a)

(b)

(c)

Fig. 3-63. Mudcapping: (a) setting a charge; (b) charge capped; (c) after the explosion. (Courtesy Canadian Industries Ltd.)

4. It must be made certain that the area has been cleared before firing a shot.
5. Shunts should always be used when setting up an electric circuit.
6. When there are electrical storms in the area, all electric blasting should be stopped.
7. Only nonsparking tape should be used for measuring hole depths during loading.
8. The *shucking* of dynamite—removal from the car-

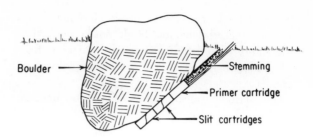

Fig. 3-64. Snakeholing

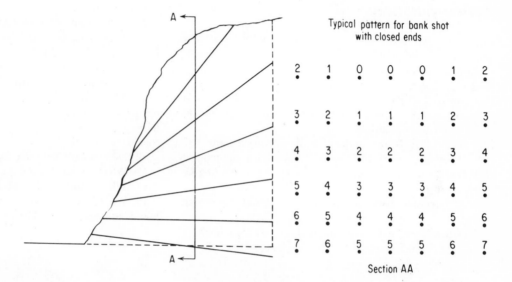

Fig. 3-65. Typical pattern for bank shot with closed ends

Typical pattern for bank shot with closed ends

Section AA

Fig. 3-66. Woven rope mats in place. (Courtesy Canadian Industries Ltd.)

Fig. 3-67. Blasting using wire blasting mats. (Courtesy Canadian Industries Ltd.)

tridge—should be avoided unless absolutely necessary. Shucked dynamite should not be tamped.

9. Inventory should be taken before and after firing of a shot to guard against mislaid explosives and caps.

10. Only blasting galvanometers should be used for testing the circuit.

11. Loaded hole areas should be clearly marked with appropriate signs.

12. Piles of cartridges should never be left beside a large-diameter hole.

13. Holes must be cool prior to loading. This should be checked.

14. The primer cartridge should never be forced into a hole and should never be tamped.

15. Storage or dry-cell batteries should never be used to activate electric blasting circuits.

REVIEW QUESTIONS

1. How may soil types influence the kind of excavating equipment to be used?

2. What is the basic difference between a *power shovel* and a *pull shovel*?

3. Briefly outline the operational difference between a *dragline bucket* and a *clamshell* bucket. What operational feature is common to both?

4. (a) What is the purpose of dewatering equipment? (b) What are the five basic parts of dewatering equipment? (c) What is a possible alternative to the use of dewatering equipment?

5. Differentiate between *general* and *special* excavating work.

6. What is meant by (a) soil swell, and (b) payline?

7. Differentiate between *shoring or needling* and *underpinning* as means of protecting adjacent buildings.

8. Differentiate between *sheeting* and *sheet piling* as used in an excavation.

9. What is a 500 millisecond delay blasting cap?

10. What is a *delay pattern* of blasting?

11. The working face of an open pit consists of soft shale overlaid by hard rock. If the entire face is to be moved in a single blasting operation, describe briefly how the holes should be loaded.

12. Differentiate between *high* and *low* explosives.

13. What is the *powder factor*?

14. What is the *burden* of a hole drilled for blasting?

15. What are eight safety precautions that must be followed throughout blasting operations?

FOUNDATION LAYOUT

4

The layout of the foundation structure must be carried out with great accuracy to insure that its various elements are placed exactly as called for in the building plans. A set of building plans will include a foundation plan, on which is shown the position of piles, footings, column bases, slab stiffeners, etc., with all elevations and necessary details.

Figure 4-2 is the foundation plan for the building shown in Fig. 4-1. This is a typical footing, wall and slab foundation, with the building loads transferred to the earth by the footings.

Figure 4-4 is a pile foundation plan for the office building shown in the site plan, Fig. 4-3. Here the building loads are transferred to solid bearing by perimeter and interior piles.

LOCATING POINTS FROM BATTER BOARD LINES

The first step in laying out the foundation, after completing the excavation, is to rig the batter board lines. They may be either cord or wire, depending on their length, but they must always be strung very tightly.

A plumb bob dropped from the intersection of two corner batter board lines (see Fig. 4-5) to the excavation floor establishes a corner position. A stake is driven at that point and a nail placed in the top of the stake so that it coincides exactly with the point of the plumb bob. All the outside corners are established in the same way. The perimeter of the building is thus outlined, as shown in Fig. 4-6. The accuracy of the staking should now be checked by measuring the diagonals of the rectangles involved. If there is no error, the diagonals will be exactly equal.

A further check may be made by measuring the angles with the leveling instrument. For example, for the layout shown in Fig. 4-6, proceed as follows:

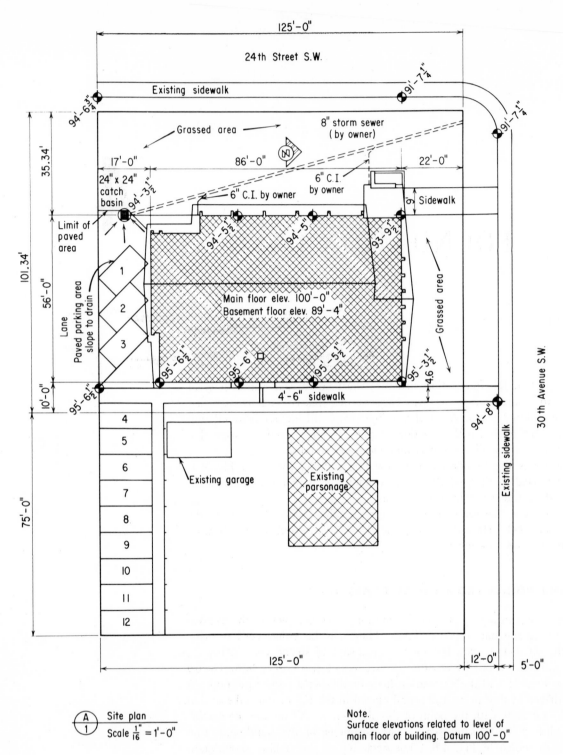

Fig. 4-1. Site plan for church

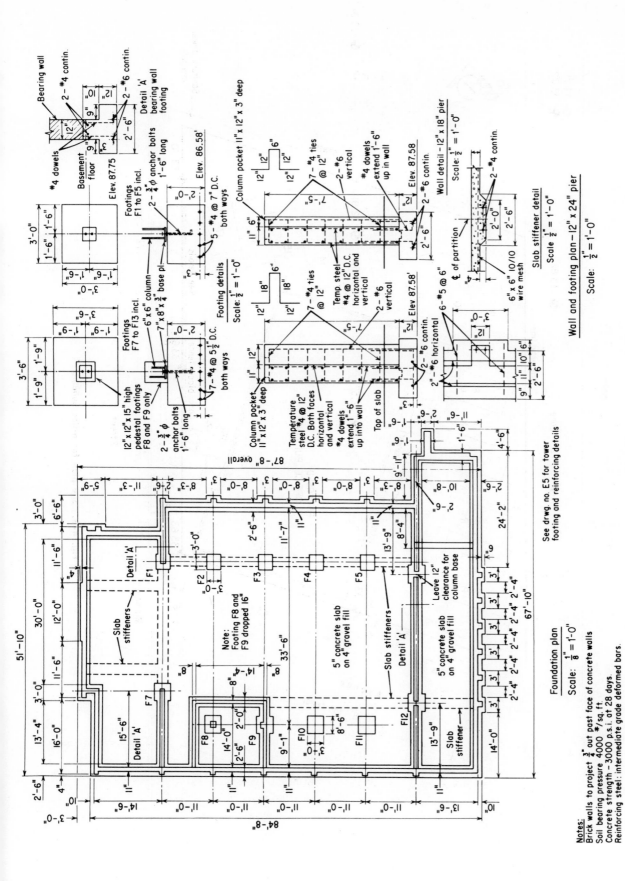

Fig. 4-2. Typical foundation plan

Foundation plan

Scale: $\frac{1}{8}$" = 1'-0"

See drwg. no. E5 for tower footing and reinforcing details

Notes:
Brick walls to project $\frac{3}{4}$" out past face of concrete walls
Soil bearing pressure 4000 #/sq. ft.
Concrete strength – 3000 p.s.i. at 28 days.
Reinforcing steel: intermediate grade deformed bars.

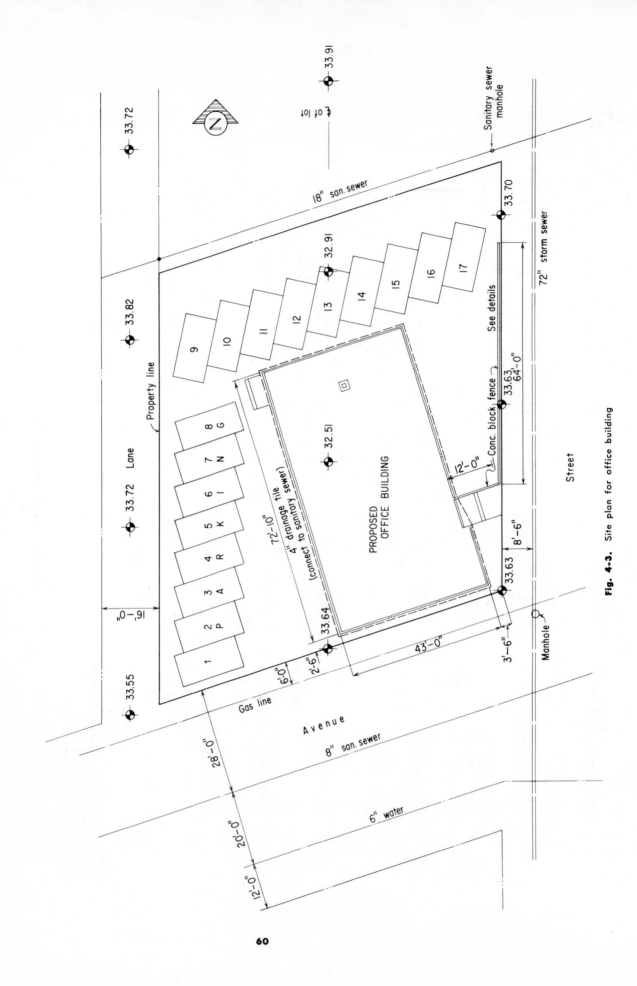

Fig. 4-3. Site plan for office building

60

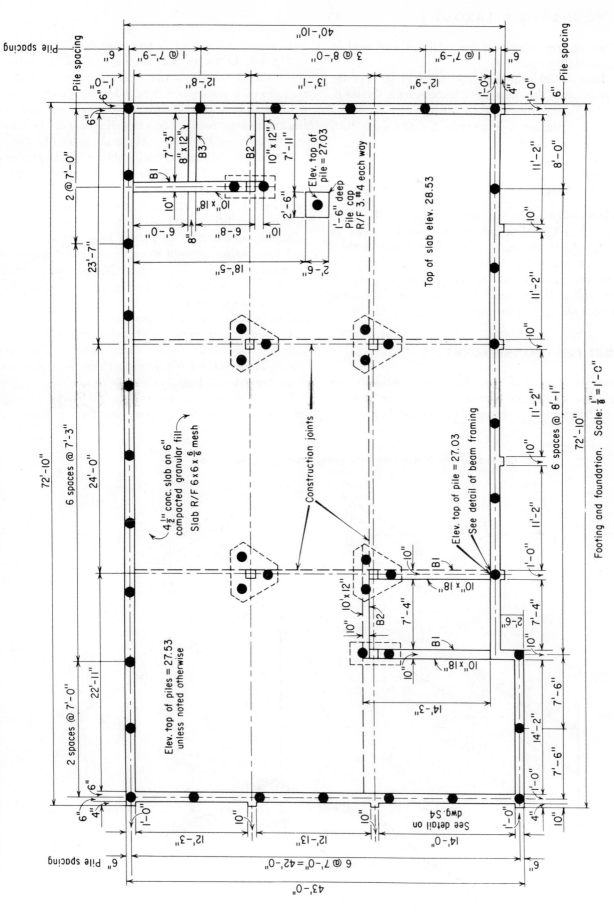

Fig. 4-4. Pile foundation plan

Footing and foundation. Scale: $\frac{1}{8}'' = 1'-0''$

61

1. Set up the instrument over stake *A* and level it. Backsight on stake *B*.
2. Turn the telescope and sight on stake *D*. For the dimensions shown on this plan, the angle should be 11°19′.
3. Turn again and sight on stake *C*. The angle *BAC* should be 18°26′.
4. Sight on stakes *E*, *F*, *G*, and *H* in order. The angles should be 30°58′; 45°0′; 59°2′; and 90°0′ respectively.

Column center lines can now be established. Drop a plumb bob from line intersections (see Fig. 4-7) on opposite sides of the building and drive stakes at those points. A line strung between these stakes represents the column center line, and the positions of column footing centers can be measured along this line and indicated by driving stakes at each point.

LAYOUT FOR FOOTING FORMS

There are a number of methods for establishing the outside line of exterior footing forms. If the footings are not large, the projection of the footing beyond the outside wall line can easily be measured. For example, in Fig. 4-2, the bearing wall footing extends 9 in. beyond the wall. From the corner stake already established, measure off a square with 9 in. sides (see Fig. 4-8), and drive a stake with one face on the line and one the thickness of the footing form material beyond the intersecting line (see Fig. 4-9). This stake should be driven or cut off exactly at the elevation shown for the footings. For example, in Fig. 4-2, the elevation of the bottom of footings *F1* to *F5* is shown as 86.58 ft and the footings are 2 ft thick. Therefore, the elevation of the top of the stakes here would be 88.58 ft.

Stakes are similarly placed at each outside corner, and lines strung between them to guide the driving of intermediate stakes. Figure 4-10 illustrates this. Stakes for the inside form are located by measuring from this line. The inside corner stake must be set away from the line in both directions, as shown in Fig. 4-11.

If footings are wide, their inside and outside extremities may be located on batter boards. The position of inside and outside forms can then be determined from batter board lines (see Fig. 4-12).

If column footings are not large, they can be positioned as in Fig. 4-13. Here the footing form has

Fig. 4-5. Establishing a foundation corner position from batter board lines

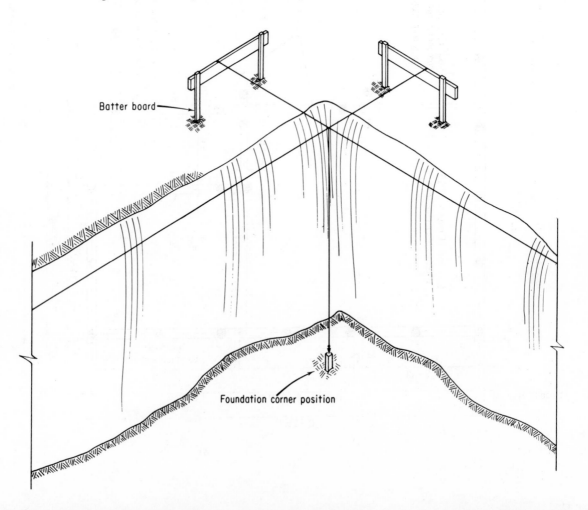

Batter board

Foundation corner position

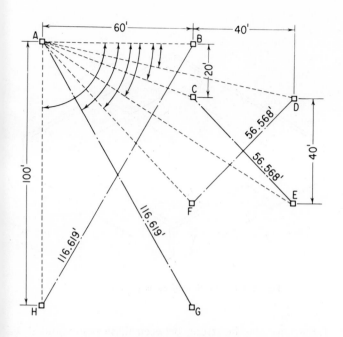

Fig. 4-6. Checking layout

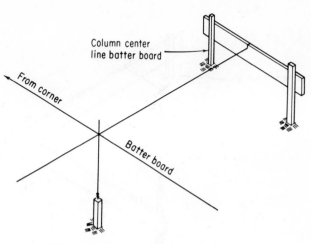

Fig. 4-7. Locating column center line stake

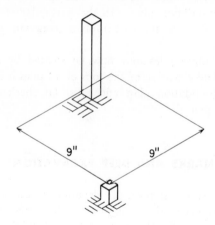

Fig. 4-8. Locating outside footing stake

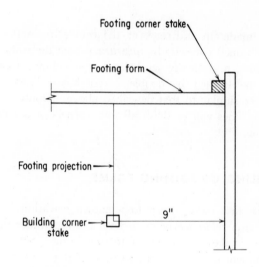

Fig. 4-9. Footing corner stake position

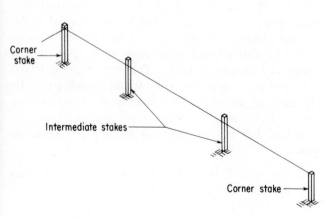

Fig. 4-10. Line for outside of footing

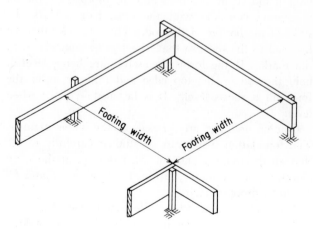

Fig. 4-11. Inside footing stake position

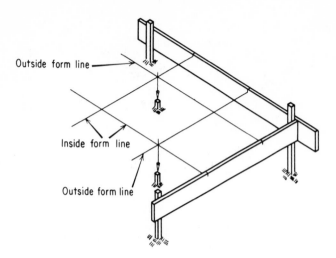

Fig. 4-12. Double batter board lines

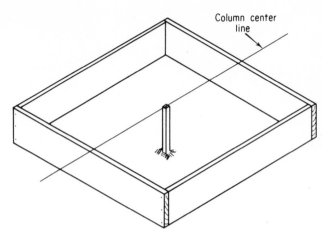

Fig. 4-13. Positioning column footing

been made up and set over the center line stake. It is positioned correctly by measuring from the stake and the line, and finally leveled. Large column footings may be located by double batter board lines, in a manner similar to that described above. Double intersecting lines will establish all four corners of a column footing.

LEVELING OF FOOTING FORMS

The first stake driven to a known elevation is now used as a reference point to level the remainder of the footing stakes or the top of footing forms. Set up the instrument in a convenient location within the perimeter of the building. Take a backsight on a rod held on the first stake and tighten the target in position. Now have the rod held alongside the next stake to be leveled and have it moved up or down until the horizontal line on the target coincides with the cross hair. Mark the stake at the bottom of the rod. The form can then be fastened to the stake so that its top edge coincides with the mark. If the forms themselves are being leveled, hold the rod on the top edge and raise or lower the form till it shows level. It is fastened in place when level.

Column footings are leveled in the same manner. The foundation plan must be studied carefully to see that all the footings and column bases are at the same elevation. For example, in Fig. 4-2, footings *F8* and *F9* are to be dropped 16 in.

The layout for perimeter pile centers (see Fig. 4-4) may be carried out by first establishing and staking the centers of the corner piles from batter board lines.

Lines may now be strung between these points and the location of the remainder of the perimeter piles found by measuring along the lines. Pile spacings are shown on the foundation plan. In the particular case shown in Fig. 4-4, 14 in. cast-in-place concrete piles are specified.

The column piles may now be located by measurement. The elevation of the tops of all piles is indicated on the foundation plan and must be checked as the piles are placed.

BENCH MARKS AND DEEP EXCAVATIONS

It is easy to establish an elevation at the bottom of a shallow excavation (no deeper than the rod being used) from a bench mark at ground level. But for deeper excavations, other methods must be used. One method is outlined in the following example. Remember that the *angles of depression* must be read very accurately. Let us suppose that for a particular building the elevation of the top of wall footings is to be $+76.5$ ft with relation to a bench mark of $+100.0$ ft established at ground level. The excavation is 105 ft wide and 25 ft deep (for a 100-ft wide building). The elevation of the excavation floor must be established. Figure 4-14 shows a vertical cross section of the excavation, 105 ft wide and 25 ft deep. Proceed as follows:

1. Set up and level the instrument at a convenient location near the edge of the excavation (see Fig. 4-14).
2. Take a backsight on the bench mark. Suppose

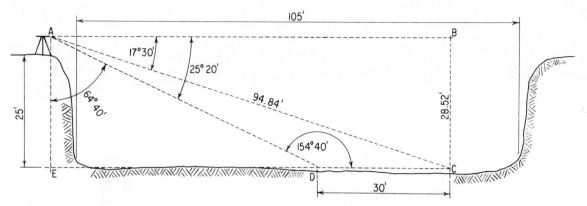

Fig. 4-14. Elevations in deep excavations

that the reading is 4.76 ft. Then the H.I. is 104.76 ft.

3. Pick a convenient spot on the floor of the excavation and drive a stake at that point (point C in Fig. 4-14). Lower the telescope and sight on the top of the stake. The angle of depression is found to be 17°30′.

4. Measure a definite distance (30 ft in this case) in the same line of sight and drive a second stake at D, level with the first. Let the angle of depression to the top of stake D be 25°20′. Both of these readings must be very accurate.

5. Calculate the size of angles DAC (7°50′) and ADC (154°40′).

6. Apply the sine rule to triangle ADC to find the length of side AC.

$$\frac{30}{\text{sine } 7°\ 50'} = \frac{AC}{\text{sine } 154°\ 40'}$$

$$30 \times .42788 = AC \times .13629$$

$$AC = \frac{30 \times .42788}{.13629} = 94.84 \text{ ft}$$

7. With respect to triangle ABC, $\dfrac{BC}{AC} = \text{sine } 17°\ 30'$.

Therefore $\dfrac{BC}{94.84} = .30071$

$$BC = .30071 \times 94.84 = 28.52 \text{ ft.}$$

8. The elevation of the top of stake C, relative to the bench mark, will be $104.76 - 28.52 = 76.24$ ft.

Stake C may now be used as a bench mark from which to establish the elevation of footing forms, etc., for the foundation.

REVIEW QUESTIONS

1. Give three reasons why it is usually better to establish column center lines rather than outside lines of footing when laying out column footing locations.

2. Explain why it may be preferable to have both inside and outside of wide footings established on batter boards.

3. Why should footing form stakes be cut-off to elevation?

4. Why is it good practice to check the elevation of the first piles in a group while the subsequent piles are being driven?

5. Suggest an alternative method of establishing the elevation at the bottom of an excavation from a datum point at ground level.

5

PILES, CAISSONS, AND SPREAD FOUNDATIONS

NEED FOR DEEP FOUNDATIONS

The foundations of a building are generally regarded as that part of the structure which transmits the load of the building to the earth on which it rests. They must be carried to a depth at which the earth has sufficient bearing strength to carry the load safely.

For lightweight buildings and for heavier buildings on good load-bearing soil, the foundations normally consist of footings and piers, or foundation walls. The footings are spread over a wide enough area to carry safely the load of the piers or walls that must rest on them.

When massive structures are involved, or where soils with low load-bearing capacity are encountered, the amount of concrete and steel necessary to construct adequate footings soon becomes uneconomical. One answer to this problem is the use of *bearing piles* or *caissons*. They provide a practical means of transmitting loads from structures to the supporting natural rock or earth below.

TYPES OF PILES

Piles are made from any of several materials, including wood, steel, and concrete. They may also be composite in structure—that is, made up of more than one material. A pile with a wood lower section and concrete upper section is the most common composite type.

There are three main classifications of piles used in the construction industry. The most common is the *bearing pile*. It transfers the heavy loads through the unstable surface soils to the denser, more stable soils below.

It should be noted that loads are carried vertically downward to bedrock, or other material of high-bearing strength.

The next is the *friction pile*. This type does not necessarily reach high-bearing materials, but does reach soil resistance to a point where the load is carried by the underlying soil and the soil pressure surrounding the pile. Friction piles thus depend on soil density and side pressure for a great percentage of their load-bearing ability.

The third type of pile is the *sheet pile*. It is not intended to carry vertical loads, but rather to resist horizontal pressure. The principal use for sheet piling is to hold back earth around the perimeter of an excavation.

PARTS OF A TYPICAL PILE

All piles, regardless of the type of material from which they are made, have certain basic parts. Figure 5-1 illustrates a typical pile and its parts. The following definitions apply to any such pile:

Head: The head of a pile is its upper part in final position.

Foot: The foot of a pile is its lower part in final position.

Tip: The tip of a pile is its small end before or after it is placed in position.

Butt: The butt of a pile is its large end before or after it is placed in position.

Pile ring: A pile ring is a wrought-iron or steel hoop that is placed on the head of the pile to prevent cracking, brooming, or splitting.

Driving head: A driving head is a device placed on the head of a pile to receive hammer blows and to protect it from injury while it is being driven. A driving head may be used instead of a pile ring.

Pile cut-off: The portion of the pile that is removed after completion of driving.

Pile shoe: A pile shoe is a metal cone placed on the tip of a pile to protect it from cracking or splitting. It also helps the pile to penetrate such materials as riprap, coarse gravel, shale, or hardpan.

BEARING CAPACITY OF PILE FOUNDATIONS

The design of pile foundations consists of two general steps: (1) the selection and design of the piles and the driving equipment to be used; and (2) the study of the soils to which the loads are transmitted. The allowable load limits for bearing soils range from 1 ton per sq ft for soft clay up to approximately 30 tons per

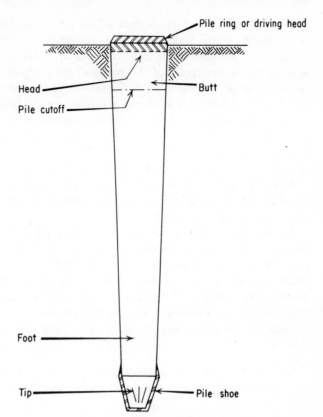

Fig. 5-1. Parts of a typical pile

sq ft for granite bedrock. The average gravel soil will support a compressive load of 5 or 6 tons per sq ft. The supporting strength of a pile is therefore proportional to its size and to the strength of the soil in which it is driven.

The following example will demonstrate the computation of the upward bearing strength of a pile of prescribed dimensions driven into a particular soil.

Given: Soil bearing = 4 tons per sq ft; skin friction = 700 lb per sq ft. A timber pile 35 ft long with an average diameter of 12 in. is to be driven. The pile tip diameter is 8 in.

End area = $22/7 \times 1/3$ ft $\times 1/3$ ft = .35 sq ft
End bearing = .35 $\times$ 8000 = 2800 lb
Pile area = $22/7 \times 1$ ft $\times 35$ ft = 110 sq ft
Bearing due to skin friction = 110 $\times$ 700 = 77,000 lb
Total bearing capacity of this pile = 2,800 + 77,000
   = 39.9 tons.

WOOD PILES

Considerable selection is necessary in order to obtain good wooden piles. They should be free from *large* or *loose knots, decay, splits,* and *shakes. Crooks* and *bends* should be not more than one-half of the pile diameter at the middle of the bend. Pile *sweep* should be limited so that: (1) for piles less than 70 ft in length, a straight line joining the midpoint of the butt and the midpoint of the tip does not pass through the surface of the pile; (2) for piles 70 to 80 ft in length, a similar straight line does not lie more than 1 in. outside the surface of the pile; (3) for piles 80 ft in length a similar straight line does not lie more than 2 in. outside the surface of the pile. The *taper* should be uniform from tip to butt.

Pile lengths are in increments of 1 ft. The minimum tip diameter is normally 6 in. and the maximum butt diameter for any length is 20 in.

Various species of trees are used for making piles, the most common being southern pine, red pine, lodgepole pine, Douglas fir, western hemlock, and larch. All of these can be pressure treated, a process designed to protect piles against deterioration. Creosote is the preservative most commonly used for this purpose.

Some of the advantages of using wood piles are as follows:

1. Wood piles have an indefinite life expectancy when placed under water or driven below groundwater level.
2. Wood piles are light.
3. In many areas, wood piles are readily available, relatively cheap, and easy to transport.
4. Wood piles produce greater *skin friction* than piles of most other materials.

However, wood piles are subject to attack by insects, marine borers, and fungi unless treated. They have a lower resistance to driving forces than other types of piles, and have a tendency to split or splinter while being driven. Wood piles support a smaller load than other types of comparable size, which means using more piles and larger footings.

CONCRETE PILES

There are two principal types of concrete piles, *cast-in-place* and *precast*. The cast-in-place pile is formed in the ground, in the position in which it is to be used. The precast pile is usually cast in a factory, where prestressing techniques can be employed, and after curing is driven or jetted like a wood pile.

Cast-in-place piles are divided into two general groups, the *shell* type and the *shell-less* type. Shell-type piles are made by first driving a steel shell or casing into the ground, filling it with concrete, and leaving the shell in place. The shell acts as a form and pre-

vents mud and water from mixing with the concrete. Such piles may or may not be reinforced, depending on circumstances.

Shell-type piles are useful where the soil is too soft to form a hole for an uncased pile, or where the soil is hard to compress and would deform an uncased pile.

Shells may be cylindrical or tapered, with smooth or corrugated outside surfaces. One type of tapered shell produced in sections is known as a *step-taper* pile (see Fig. 5-2).

A number of variations of shell-type piles are made. One is a cased pile with a compressed base section, as

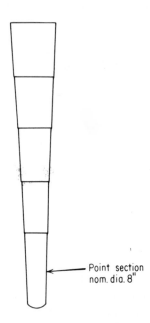

Point section nom. dia. 8"

Fig. 5-2. Typical step-taper pile

illustrated in Fig. 5-3. It is used where the side support of the soil is so slight that the pile must be used as a column or when the pile is designed to meet lateral forces arising from eccentric loading.

Another variation is the button-bottom pile shown in Fig. 5-4. It is used where an increase in end-bearing area is required. The enlarged bottom eliminates side friction support unless the soil is highly compacted around the pile.

Swage piles, shown in Fig. 5-5, are used where driving is very hard or where it is desired to leave watertight shells for some time before the concrete is placed. This type of pile consists of a steel shell driven over a conical precast concrete end plug.

Shell-less piles are made by driving a steel pipe, fitted with a special end or tapered shoe, into the ground for the full depth of the pile. The pipe is

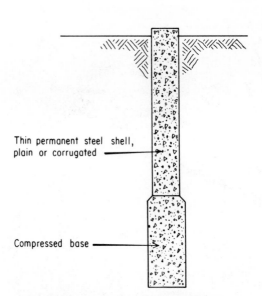

Thin permanent steel shell, plain or corrugated

Compressed base

Fig. 5-3. Cased pile with compressed base

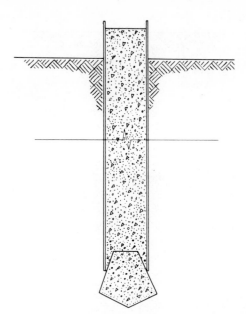

Fig. 5-5. Swage pile

then pulled up, leaving the shoe at the bottom, and the hole is filled with concrete. This type of pile is satisfactory where soil is cohesive enough so that a reasonably smooth inside surface is maintained when the shell is removed. Figure 5-7 illustrates the simplest type of shell-less pile. Sometimes concrete is poured as the shell is being lifted. This eliminates some of the possibility of earth becoming mixed with the concrete.

Variations of the shell-less pile are also made. One involves the use of a bored hole rather than a punched one. In some cases the bottom end of the hole is *belled* out to provide a pedestal for increased end bearing. Figure 5-8 shows a boring rig in place on a job site while Fig. 5-9 illustrates the belling attachment and Fig. 5-10, shows an auger discharging earth. Figure 5-11 illustrates a vertical section through a completed belled pile.

Fig. 5-4. Button-bottom cased concrete pile

Fig. 5-6. Cased, pedestalled concrete pile

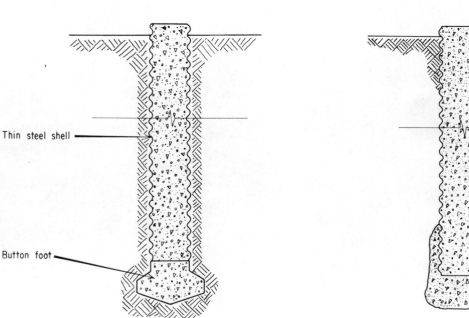

Thin steel shell

Button foot

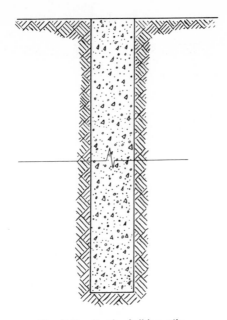

Fig. 5-7. Simple shell-less pile

Fig. 5-8. Pile boring rig. (Courtesy Calweld Inc.)

Fig. 5-9. Belling attachment. (Courtesy Calweld Inc.)

Fig. 5-10. Auger discharging earth. (Courtesy Calweld Inc.)

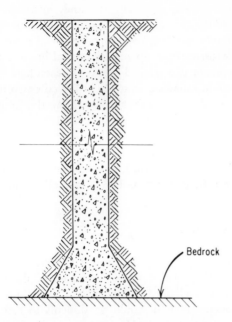

Fig. 5-11. Section through completed belled pile

Fig. 5-13. Bottom end of shell-less pile. (Courtesy Franki of Canada)

Another variation of the shell-less pile involves the use of a very dry concrete mix. The shell is driven by dropping a heavy hammer onto a plug made from this dry mix (see Fig. 5-12). When the shell has reached its full depth, the plug is driven out to form an enlarged base and extra concrete is added as required to make the base as large as necessary. A reinforcing cage is then dropped into place in the shell. As the shell is slowly withdrawn, dry mix is fed into the top and driven out the bottom by the drop hammer, forming a highly compacted pile with corrugated sides. Figure 5-13 shows

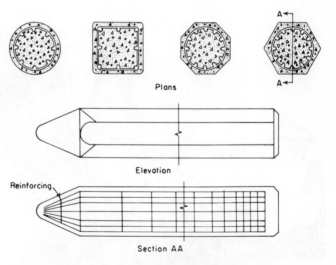

Fig. 5-14. Precast pile shapes

Fig. 5-12. Driving a shell with drop hammer and concrete plug

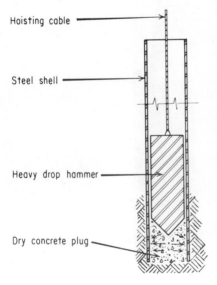

the bottom end of a pile such as this after removal from the earth.

Precast concrete piles are normally made in a casting yard under controlled conditions. This allows not only the development of high strength concrete, but also flexibility in design, reinforcing, length, etc.

Precast reinforced piles are made in round, square, hexagonal, and octagonal shapes, as illustrated in Fig. 5-14. Very long piles are made by casting hollow reinforced sections, usually 16 ft in length, and joining the sections together by stressed steel cables.

Precast concrete piles usually need assistance when

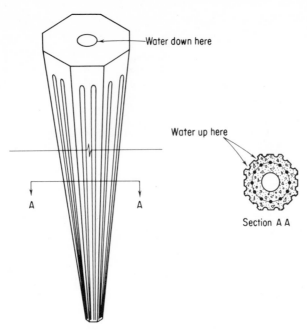

Fig. 5-15. Precast jetting pile

being driven, especially in sand, and one method of providing this is to use a water jet. One type of precast pile has been developed especially for installation by jetting. It is tapered, octagonal in cross section, and has one or two vertical grooves in each face. The center is hollow, allowing water to be forced down to loosen the soil at the tip. The grooves allow the jetted water to return to the surface (see Fig. 5-15).

Precast piles may be impregnated with asphalt to help prevent damage by seawater, spray, etc. Piles are pressure-treated with hot asphalt at 450 to 500° F., and penetrations of up to 1½ in. are obtained.

STEEL PILES

A steel pile may be a rolled H section or a steel pipe known as a tubular pile. Because of their small cross section, steel piles can often be driven into dense soils, through which it would be difficult to drive a pile of solid cross section. However, one point should be con-

Fig. 5-16. Driving H piles. (Courtesy Bethlehem Steel Co.)

sidered when driving long structural shapes. This is the possibility of the pile tip striking a large boulder below the surface. There have been many instances in which long steel pilings have been deflected by massive boulders below the surface, and as a result of continued driving, the pile tip has worked itself to the surface of the ground again. This, of course, makes it necessary to extract the pile and to determine the limits of the boulder before proceeding. This operation can become rather expensive, and points out the advisability of having a clause in the contract to protect the builder from such contingencies. Steel piles may be driven so that the top end, which extends above the ground, serves as a column. The upper ends of H piles may be encased in concrete to prevent corrosion.

Tubular piles vary in diameter from 8 in. to 72 in. They may be driven from the top—using a drop or mechanical hammer—or from the bottom, using a drop-hammer falling on a concrete plug. The pipe is usually filled with concrete, which means that if the pipe is driven open-ended, the earth must be removed from the inside by a water jet.

COMPOSITE PILES

Two materials may sometimes be combined to make up a single pile. The most common combination is wood and concrete, and the result is known as a composite pile.

This type of pile may be used to advantage under several conditions. One is if the permanent water head is not more than 70 ft below ground level. This is about the length limit for the upper concrete section of the pile. Another is where the use of wood piles alone would necessitate 10 ft or more of dry excavation, or as little as 4 ft of very wet excavation. This can be eliminated by the use of a composite pile. A third situation is when the overall length of the pile is so great that it would be economically impractical to obtain or handle either straight wood or concrete piles. Cast-in-place concrete piles of up to about 70 ft in length can rest on top of wood piles of any obtainable length. Wood piles are difficult to handle and expensive when longer than 80 ft. Precast concrete piles are very expensive in lengths beyond 55 ft.

The wooden pile is driven to ground level, and the head of the pile is fitted with a steel casing. Driving continues by means of a mandrel or core until the required depth is reached. The mandrel is then withdrawn and the shell filled with concrete.

The shell is fitted to the wooden pile head in several different ways. One is to simply set the end of the shell over the slightly tapered end of the pile head. Another method is to make a tenon with a square shoulder at the end of the pile, set a sealing ring over the tenon, and rest the shell on the ring. Another method involves the use of a wedge ring which is forced into the flat top of the pile head. Figure 5-17 illustrates these three methods of connection.

A number of piles are sometimes driven close together in a group, to be later capped with a common concrete cap. Several points pertaining to this particular operation warrant special consideration.

First of all, it is generally recognized that when a number of piles are driven close together, the load bearing value of each is reduced. As a result, a number of building codes have established a minimum center-to-center spacing for grouped piles. These vary from 2 ft 6 in. to 5 ft, with the latter considered less desirable.

When piles are driven close together, particularly in the case of friction piles, those driven later may cause the first ones to heave. This may necessitate some redriving but, in any case, a check should be made on the elevation of the tops of the piles driven first.

When piles are driven in a group, those driven later are generally more difficult to drive and pull up before the earlier piles. This is due to the increased compaction of the soil as it is displaced. In some cases, soil in the surrounding area is heaved, instead of the piles.

Driving piles in the proper order will help to avoid the heaving problem. The piles at the center of the group should be driven first, followed in succession by those closer to the outside.

When shell-type piles are being used, the increased compaction due to group driving may result in damage (distortion or crushing) to shells already in place. As a result, it may be difficult to pour concrete or the passage may be completely blocked.

Fig. 5-17. Composite pile connections

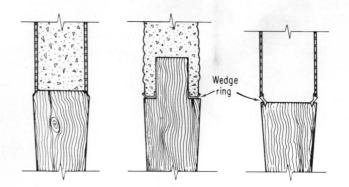

Wedge ring

PILE DRIVERS

Wood, precast concrete, steel H piles, and large tubular piles are driven into the ground by a pile driver striking the pile head. Small tubular piles and shells for cast-in-place concrete piles are more often pulled into the ground by a core. The core is forced into the earth by a tapered drop hammer and pulls the shell or tube with it.

Pile drivers may consist of a drop, mechanical, or vibratory hammer. A drop hammer is the simplest type of machine, consisting of a heavy weight, lifted by a cable and guided by *leads,* which is allowed to drop freely on the pile head.

The hammer of a mechanical driver operates like a piston, actuated by steam, compressed air, or the internal combustion of diesel fuel.

A vibratory hammer is secured to the head of a pile and operates by delivering vibrations to the pile head in up-and-down cycles at the rate of 100 cps. These vibrations set up waves of compression in the pile which in turn produce minute amounts of expansion and contraction. As the pile expands longitudinally it displaces soil at the pile tip, and the weight of the pile, hammer, and equipment forces the pile into the tiny void. At the same time as the pile expands in length, it contracts slightly in diameter and thus relieves the friction between the earth and the pile surface. This relief of friction helps the pile to move downward.

These movements are very small but occur 100 times every second and as a result, penetration may actually be quite rapid. For example, a pile which might require an hour to be set with a steam hammer can be driven in two or three minutes by a vibratory hammer. This type of equipment performs best in sandy soil, but may be used in silt, clay, or soil containing layers of gravel.

Assistance may have to be provided when piles are being driven. This is particularly true when driving precast piles in granular soils. The high friction rate makes driving very difficult. The assistance is usually in the form of a water jet which softens the soil at the pile tip. Water is jetted down the hollow center and returns to the surface around the outside of the pile.

Figure 5-12 illustrates the principle involved in *pulling* a tubular pile or pile shell into the ground. A tapered drop hammer is dropped on a core made up of very dry concrete mix, driving it into the ground. At the same time, the hammer's tapered point forces the concrete against the inside wall of the shell, creating tremendous friction. As a result, the friction between the core and the tube pulls the tube down as the core is driven into the ground.

CAISSONS

A *caisson* is similar to a cast-in-place pile, the distinction being in their size. Caissons are usually large structures, intended to carry the loads of massive buildings down to bedrock. They may be round or rectangular, 6 to 20 ft or more in diameter for round ones and 10 to 30 ft across for rectangular ones. They are merely shells, forced into the ground, excavated, and filled with concrete. In some cases, if the soil will withstand it, the hole may be dug first and the shell is then placed in it in one or more sections.

Caissons are classified according to make and usage. An *open* caisson is open at both top and bottom. A *box* caisson is open at the top but closed at the bottom. If it is open at the bottom and closed at the top, it will require compressed air to carry on the excavation work inside, and is then known as a *pneumatic* caisson.

If the hole is to be drilled first, machines capable of drilling holes from 2 to about 12 ft in diameter may be used. The machine shown in Fig. 5-18, for example, has a 6 ft drilling bucket and can be equipped with reamers which will enlarge the diameter to 10 or 12 ft. In Fig. 5-19, a 10 ft 6 in. diameter telescoping casing is being lowered into a hole made with a drilling bucket and reamers.

Where the soil will not permit the hole to be drilled first, excavating must be carried out inside the casing as it is being jacked into the ground. As the earth is removed at the bottom, the casing is forced further down until it has reached its full depth. Excavating may be done by hand or by machine. There are machines capable of digging holes from 2 to 8 ft in diameter and 100 ft deep. One such machine has an orange peel-type bucket operated at the end of a drill stem. Digging is done inside a casing which is forced downward as work progresses and to which sections are added until the desired depth is reached. Another machine operates an auger bit at the end of a drill stem.

One type of caisson is made in sections, each of which fits inside the one above. A pit is dug and the first section of steel casing placed in it. It is forced into the ground to its full depth by driving and excavating inside the cylinder. A cylinder 2 in. smaller in diameter is then placed inside the first and driven to its full depth. This continues until suitable bearing is reached. The excavation is then belled out at the bottom to provide a greater bearing area (see Fig.

Fig. 5-18. Six-foot drilling bucket with reamers. (Courtesy Calweld Inc.)

5-20). Box and pneumatic caissons are used in or under water and in very wet soils.

COFFERDAMS

Although *caissons* and *cofferdam*s fulfill the same general function, a caisson is a permanent structure used for protection while excavating and as a form for concrete whereas a cofferdam is a temporary box-like structure used to hold back water or earth while work is being done inside it, and is later removed.

A cofferdam consists of sections of sheeting driven side-by-side to form a watertight unit. The sheeting forms a box large enough to work inside it. The sections are usually driven in water or mud which is to be removed from the inside once the cofferdam is complete. If the bottom is too soft, a layer of concrete may be poured over it to provide a firm base. Whatever permanent structure is required can then be built inside the cofferdam, which is removed when the work has been completed.

SPREAD FOUNDATIONS

If building loads are not large enough to warrant being carried to bedrock by piles or caissons, but the

Fig. 5-19. Casing (10 ft 6 in.) lowered into drilled hole. (Courtesy Calweld Inc.)

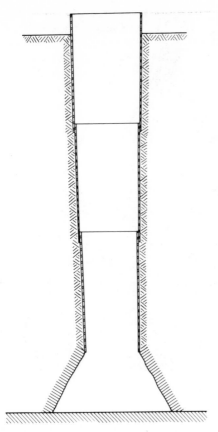

Fig. 5-20. Telescoping shell caisson

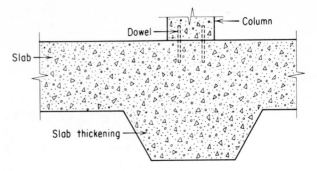

Fig. 5-21. Grillage footing

unit load. There are a number of different types, and the one to use in any particular case depends on soil strength, load concentration, depth of the foundation below grade level, etc.

One type of spread foundation is known as a *grillage* footing. It is made up of two or more tiers of steel beam sections, laid at right angles to one another. Each tier has a smaller number of units than the one below it, but the section modulus remains fairly constant.

When a grillage footing rests on compressible soil, a slab of concrete is cast first, 6 to 12 in. deep. The first tier of steel, bolted together, is set on the slab and leveled. The next tier is set on the first at a right angle and fastened down. Succeeding tiers (if any) follow, and a steel slab or billet is finally set on the top tier and fixed in place. A building column will rest on this billet. Finally, the whole grillage is encased in concrete (see Fig. 5-21).

Another type of spread foundation consists of a solid slab of heavily reinforced concrete covering the entire

soil bearing strength is low, a solution may be the use of *spread* foundations. These, as their name implies, are foundations which are extended over large areas in order to distribute the weight and thus reduce the

Fig. 5-22 Raft foundation deepened under columns

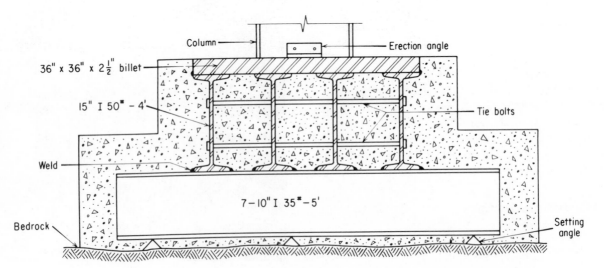

site. It may be from 3 to 8 ft thick, depending on the area to be covered and the loads to be carried. This is known as a *raft* foundation.

Still another type consists of two series of heavy, continuous ground beams, running at right angles to one another and intersecting under columns. A slab is usually cast monolithically with the beams, but sometimes the slab is placed at the bottom of the beams, making them and the slab inverted T beams. In other cases, the slab is placed at the top of the beams.

In the former case, the space between the slab and the top of the beams is filled with cinders or gravel, while in the latter case, the beams are set into the earth so that the slab is poured on grade.

A fourth type of spread foundation also features a continuous slab, but a much thinner one than the raft foundation described above. The slab thickness is increased under each column, as shown in Fig. 5-22. The whole structure thus resembles a flat slab with drop-panel type concrete floor (see Chapter 11).

REVIEW QUESTIONS

1. Name the two major types of piles and explain their difference in purpose.

2. What is the purpose of: (a) a pile ring; (b) a pile shoe; (c) piledriver leads?

3. Outline three methods of setting cast-in-place piles.

4. What two main problems are involved in driving precast piles?

5. Name the two principal disadvantages of using wood piles.

6. Give two advantages of composite piles.

7. What are two advantages of steel H-piles?

8. What is meant by *jetting* a pile?

9. Differentiate between *sheet piling* and *sheeting*.

10. What is the difference between a *cofferdam* and a *caisson*?

11. What is the distinctive feature of a Gow caisson?

12. What is meant by *pile rebound*?

13. Where would a *raft foundation* be used?

14. What is the purpose of a *grillage foundation*?

FORMWORK

## 6

Concrete structures require the use of *forms* into which the freshly mixed, plastic concrete can be placed. Forms must generally be built so that they may be easily removed after the concrete has gained sufficient strength. This form-building may be done in a plant that is producing precast concrete units, but for poured-in-place members, the forms are often built at the site.

FORM MATERIALS

Wood is the most widely used material for building forms, and no matter what material is used some wood is nearly always required. It may be either lumber or plywood.

Lumber is usually of the softwood variety, because of its availability, relative lightness, and ease of handling. Pine, fir, and western hemlock are the species generally considered most suitable. Partly seasoned lumber is best for formwork because dry lumber swells considerably when wet, while green lumber shrinks and warps in hot weather. When lumber is to be used for concrete surfaces the material should be planed, although rough lumber may be used for frames, bracing, and shoring.

Plywood has recently replaced boards to a large extent in making forms for concrete surfaces. The large, smooth surface of plywood sheets, its resistance to changes in shape when wet, and its ability to withstand rough usage without splitting has made it a popular form material.

Overlaid plywood is frequently used where very smooth, grainless surfaces are required. This is plywood surfaced with plastic resin which has been fused to the wood under heat and pressure. In addition to producing smoother surfaces, overlaid plywood is generally more resistant to abrasion and moisture penetration.

An additional advantage in the use of plywood for forms is its ability to bend, thus making it possible to produce curved surfaces. The degree of bending depends on the thickness of the sheet and on whether it is curved across the face grain or parallel to it. Table 6-1 gives the minimum bending radii for plywood.

Table 6-1

Minimum Bending Radii for Plywood Panels

Plywood thickness	Minimum bend radius	
	Perpendicular to face grain	Parallel to face grain
1/4 in.	16 in.	48 in.
5/16 in.	24 in.	60 in.
3/8 in.	36 in.	72 in.
1/2 in.	72 in.	96 in.
5/8 in.	96 in.	120 in.
3/4 in.	120 in.	144 in.

Average values; no regard for knots, patches, shot grain, etc.
Reprinted by permission of B.C. Plywood Manufacturing Association.

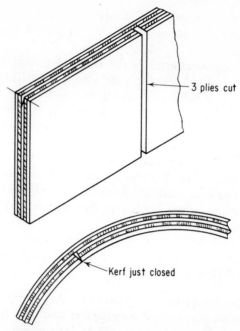

Fig. 6-1. Saw kerfing plywood for bending

Panels with clear, straight grain will permit greater bending than those shown in the table.

Thicker plywood may be bent by cutting saw kerfs across the inner face at right angles to the curve. The kerf should cut 3 plies of a 5-ply sheet or 5 plies of a 7-ply sheet. They should be spaced so as to just close up when the plywood is bent to the correct radius (see Fig. 6-1).

Another method of curving thick face material is to use two or more thicknesses of 1/4 in. plywood, bent one at a time.

A specially treated, tempered, 1/4 in. hardboard is also available for form facing material. In addition to being tempered, the surface is coated with plastic, which helps to prevent water from penetrating into the board. Hardboard is essentially a form liner material and should be applied to a supporting backing of lumber. Figure 6-2 illustrates how it may be applied to backing boards.

Steel is widely used in the construction of forms, for both frames and form facing. Steel angles and other structural shapes are finding increasing use in frames for formwork. They perform the same function as wood framing but often permit greater spans or heavier loads than would otherwise be possible.

A steel form frame may be faced with either ply-

Fig. 6-2. Hardboard form liners

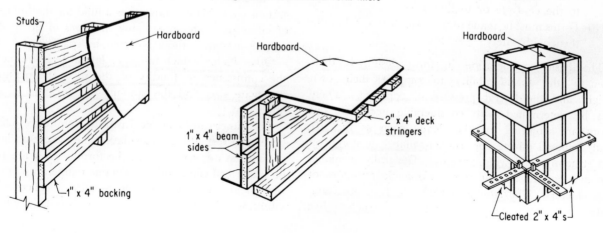

wood or sheet steel. The latter is widely used for form facing in plants specializing in precast concrete products.

Glass-fiber-reinforced plastic is another form facing material which is gaining wide acceptance. This type of form is prefabricated directly in the size and shape desired. Precast concrete plants use this type of form quite extensively and pan forms for ribbed concrete floors are often made from this material.

Various types of insulating board are often used as form liners. The material is fastened to one or both form faces and, when the form is removed, the insulation remains, either bonded to the concrete or held in place by clips.

FORM DESIGN

Forms should be so designed that they are practical and economical in both manufacture and use. A number of important factors should be kept in mind when forms are being built. They are:

(1) Forms must be strong enough to withstand the pressure of plastic concrete and to maintain their shape during the concrete pouring operation.

(2) They must be tight enough to prevent wet concrete from leaking through joints and causing unsightly fins and ridges.

(3) They must be as simple to build as circumstances will allow.

(4) They must be easy to handle on the job.

(5) Form sections must be of a size that can be lifted into place without too much difficulty and transported from one job to another if necessary.

(6) They must be made to fit and fasten together with reasonable ease.

(7) The design must be such that the forms, or sections of them, may be removed without damage to the concrete or to themselves.

(8) Forms must be made so that workmen can handle them with safety.

The basic consideration in form design is their strength—the forms' ability to support their own weight and the lateral pressure of concrete. These can be determined with considerable accuracy, but forms are subjected to other loads, such as the live loads imposed during construction, materials stored on the structure, and wind pressure. Generally speaking, the designer must make some reasonable estimates of these factors. The American Concrete Institute Committee 622 recommends a minimum construction live load of 50 psf of horizontal projection to provide for the weight of workmen, equipment runways, and impact.

Two types of strength problems are involved, based on the concrete itself. One deals with the weight of the concrete producing a vertical load and the other with the lateral pressure exerted on forms by fresh concrete in its *liquid* form.

Concrete may vary in weight from 40 to 600 lb per cu ft, depending on the aggregates from which it is made. Concrete made with natural sand and gravel aggregates weighs between 145 and 150 lb per cu ft. The formwork itself will vary from about 3 to 15 psf. With these weights and the addition of a definite imposed live load, it is possible to calculate the size of joists, stringers, and shores required to carry vertical loads.

The lateral pressure exerted by fresh concrete presents a different problem. Freshly poured concrete acts temporarily like a liquid, producing fluid or hydrostatic pressure which acts against vertical forms. This pressure varies, depending on a number of factors. One of them is the weight of the concrete being used. Hydrostatic pressure at any point in a liquid is the result of the weight of fluid above. But because fresh concrete is a composite material, rather than a true liquid, the laws of hydrostatic pressure apply only approximately and for limited periods.

The rate of placement also affects lateral pressure. The greater the height to which concrete is poured while the whole mass remains in the liquid stage, the greater the lateral pressure at the bottom of the form.

The temperatures of concrete and atmosphere affect the pressure because they affect the setting time. When these temperatures are low, greater heights can be placed before the concrete at the bottom begins to stiffen, and greater lateral pressures are therefore built up.

Vibration increases lateral pressures because the concrete is consolidated and acts as a fluid for the full depth of vibration. This may cause increases of up to 20% in pressures over those incurred by spading.

Other factors which influence lateral pressure include the consistency or fluidity of the mix, the maximum aggregate size, and the amount and location of reinforcement.

The American Concrete Institute Committee 622 has developed formulas for calculating the maximum lateral pressure at any elevation in the form. They are based on prescribed conditions of concrete temperature, rate of placement, slump of concrete, weight of concrete, and vibration. They may be used for internally vibrated concrete of normal density, placed at not more than 10 ft per hr, with no more than 4 in. of slump. Vibration depth is limited to 4 ft below the concrete surface. The two formulas for wall form design are as follows:

(1) For walls, with rate of pour not exceeding 7 ft per hr:

$$p = 150 + \frac{9000\,R}{T}$$

maximum $= 2000$ psf or $150\,h$, whichever is less.

(2) For walls, with rate of pour from 7 to 10 per ft hr:

$$p = 150 + \frac{43400}{T} + \frac{2800\,R}{T}$$

maximum $= 2000$ psf or $150\,h$, whichever is less.

$p =$ maximum lateral pressure, psf
$R =$ rate of placement, ft per hr
$T =$ temperature of concrete in the forms, degrees F
$h =$ maximum height of fresh concrete in the form, in ft

Table 6-2 gives the maximum lateral pressure to be used in designing wall forms, based on the above formulas.

Table 6-2

Maximum Lateral Pressure for Design of Wall Forms

Rate of placement (R), ft per hr	Maximum lateral pressure (p) psf for indicated temperature					
	90°F	80°F	70°F	60°F	50°F	40°F
1	250	262	278	300	330	375
2	350	375	488	450	510	600
3	450	488	536	600	690	825
4	550	600	664	750	870	1050
5	650	712	793	900	1050	1275
6	750	825	921	1050	1230	1500
7	850	938	1050	1200	1410	1725
8	881	973	1090	1246	1466	1795
9	912	1008	1130	1293	1522	1865
10	943	1043	1170	1340	1578	1935

Note: Do not use design pressures in excess of 2000 psf or 150 × height (in ft) of fresh concrete in forms, whichever is less.
Reprinted by permission of American Concrete Institute.

Column forms are frequently poured to their full height within the time it takes for concrete to set. In addition, vibration often extends to the full depth of the form. This means that greater lateral pressures are developed than in the case of walls. The A.C.I. Committee 622 has developed a formula for calculating the maximum pressure to be used in column form design, taking the aforementioned factors into consideration. It is:

$$p = 150 + \frac{9000\,R}{T}$$

maximum $= 3000$ psf or $150\,h$, whichever is less.

Table 6-3 gives the maximum lateral pressure to be used in designing column forms, based on the above formula.

Table 6-3

Maximum Lateral Pressure for Design of Column Forms

Rate of placement (R), ft per hr	Maximum lateral pressure (p) psf for indicated temperature					
	90°F	80°F	70°F	60°F	50°F	40°F
1	250	262	278	300	330	375
2	350	375	407	450	510	600
3	450	488	536	600	690	825
4	550	600	664	750	870	1050
5	650	712	793	900	1050	1275
6	750	825	921	1050	1230	1500
7	850	938	1050	1200	1410	1725
8	950	1050	1178	1350	1590	1950
9	1050	1163	1307	1500	1770	2175
10	1150	1275	1435	1650	1950	2400
11	1250	1388	1564	1800	2130	2625
12	1350	1500	1693	1950	2310	2850
13	1450	1613	1822	2100	2490	3000
14	1550	1725	1950	2250	2670	
16	1750	1950	2207	2550	3000	
18	1950	2175	2464	2850		
20	2150	2400	2721	3000		
22	2350	2625	2979			
24	2550	2850	3000			
26	2750	3000				
28	2950		(3000 psf maximum)			
30	3000					

Note: Do not use design pressures in excess of 3000 psf or 150 × height of fresh concrete in forms, whichever is less.
Reprinted by permission of American Concrete Institute.

The material to be used for forms (sheathing, studs, and wales) can be selected from Tables 6-4 to 6-15, based on the maximum pressures developed as indicated in Tables 6-2 and 6-3. In some cases tables have two sections, in others separate tables are shown, one for formwork with one or two uses and one for formwork subject to repeated usage. In the first instance, the working stresses used for lumber are as follows:

$f = 1875$ psi; $H = 180$ psi; $E = 1,600,000$ psi

for boards, and 1,760,000 psi for dimension lumber

These stresses are based on construction grade Douglas fir or its equivalent. For formwork subject to reuse, the working stresses are:

$$f = 1500 \text{ psi}; \quad H = 145 \text{ psi}; \quad E = 1,600,000 \text{ psi}$$

For plywood sheathing the working stresses are:

$$f = 2000 \text{ psi}; \quad E = 1,600,000 \text{ psi}$$

The size and spacing of ties should be based on the manufacturer's recommendations or on calculations of the load carried per lineal foot of wale. For example, if the load per lineal foot of wale is found to be 3000 lb and ties are spaced 2 ft o.c., the load per tie will be 6000 lb. Based on an allowable tensile stress of 20,000 lb per sq in., the cross-sectional area of this tie should be $\frac{6000}{20,000} = .30$ sq in. This will require a ⅝ in. diameter tie with an area of .31 sq in.

FOOTING FORMS

There are usually two factors of prime importance to consider in the construction of footings. One is that the concrete must be up to specified strength and the other that the footings be positioned according to plan. The appearance is seldom of importance since footings are usually below grade.

Old or used material may be employed for footing forms, provided it is sound. A certain amount of tolerance is allowed in footing size and thickness, but reinforcing bars and dowels must be placed as specified. Concrete is sometimes cast against the excavation, but care must be taken that this does not give inferior results, caused by the earth absorbing water from the concrete or by pieces of earth falling into it. Trenches may be lined with wax paper or polyethylene film to prevent this. It is sometimes desirable to form the top 4 in. of a footing cast in earth, as shown in Fig. 6-3.

In cases where wall footings are shallow, lateral pressure is small and the forms are simple structures as illustrated in Fig. 6-4. When the soil is firm, the form can be held in place by stakes and braces. If the soil

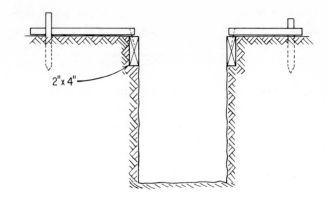

Fig. 6-3. Forming top of trench

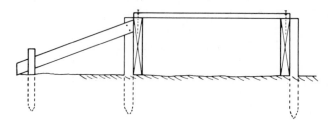

Fig. 6-4. Simple footing form

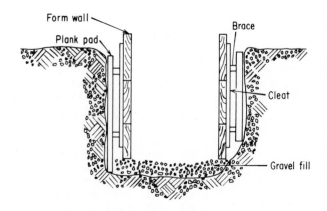

Fig. 6-5. Form braced against excavation

will not hold stakes, the forms may be secured by bracing them against the excavation sides, as shown in Fig. 6-5.

Table 6-4

Safe Spacing in Inches of Supports for Board Sheathing Continuous Over Four* or More Supports

Maximum deflection is $1/360$ of support spacing, but not more than $1/16$ in.

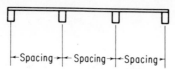

←Spacing→ ←Spacing→ ←Spacing→

Pressure or load from concrete, pounds per square foot	f = 1875 psi; H = 180 psi; E = 1,600,000 psi				f = 1500 psi; H = 145 psi; E = 1,600,000 psi			
	Nominal thickness of S4S boards, in.				Nominal thickness of S4S boards, in.			
	1	1¼	1½	2	1	1¼	1½	2
75	32	40	46	54	32	40	46	54
100	29	37	43	50	29	37	43	50
125	28	35	41	48	28	35	41	48
150	26	33	39	46	26	33	39	46
175	25	32	38	44	25	32	38	44
200	24	31	36	42	24	31	36	42
300	22	28	33	38	22	28	33	38
400	20	26	30	35	20	26	30	35
500	18	24	28	33	18	24	28	33
600	17	23	27	32	17	23	27	32
700	16	22	26	31	16	22	26	31
800	16	21	25	30	16	21	25	30
900	15	21	24	29	15	21	24	29
1000	14	20	24	28	14	20	24	28
1100	14	19	23	27	14	19	23	27
1200	14	19	23	27	13	18	22	27
1300	13	18	22	26	13	17	21	26
1400	13	18	22	26	12	17	20	26
1500	13	17	21	25	12	16	20	25
1600	12	17	21	25	11	16	19	24
1700	12	16	21	25	11	15	19	23
1800	12	16	20	24	11	15	18	23
1900	12	16	20	24	10	14	18	22
2000	11	16	19	24	10	14	17	21
2100	11	15	19	23	10	13	17	21
2200	11	15	18	23	10	13	16	20
2300	11	15	18	22	9	12	15	19
2400	10	14	18	22	9	12	15	18
2500	10	14	17	21	9	12	14	18
2600	10	13	17	21	9	11	14	17
2700	10	13	16	20	8	11	13	17
2800	9	12	16	20	8	11	13	16
2900	9	12	15	19	8	10	13	16
3000	9	12	15	19	8	10	12	15

Note : Calculations are based on span distances center to center of supports where supports are relatively narrow. Where supports may be wide in relation to the distance between them, such as 2" by 4"s used flat where the spacing is 8 in., use the tabulated spacing as the clear distance between supports.
* For sheathing with only three points of support (continuous over two spans) support spacing for simple span in Table 6-5 may be safely used.
Reproduced by permission of American Concrete Institute.

Table 6-5

Safe Spacing in Inches of Supports for Board Sheathing on Simple Span Supported at Two Points*

Maximum deflection is $1/360$ of support
spacing, but not more than $1/16$ in.

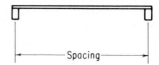

Spacing

Pressure or load from concrete, pounds per square foot	f = 1875 psi; H = 180 psi; E = 1,600,000 psi				f = 1500 psi; H = 145 psi; E = 1,600,000 psi			
	Nominal thickness of S4S boards, in.				Nominal thickness of S4S boards, in.			
	1	1¼	1½	2	1	1¼	1½	2
75	28	35	41	48	28	35	41	48
100	25	32	38	44	25	32	38	44
125	24	31	36	42	24	31	36	42
150	23	29	34	40	23	29	34	40
175	22	28	33	39	22	28	33	39
200	21	27	32	37	21	27	32	37
300	18	24	29	33	18	24	29	33
400	17	22	26	31	17	22	26	31
500	15	21	25	29	15	21	25	29
600	14	20	24	28	14	20	24	28
700	14	19	23	27	14	19	23	27
800	13	18	22	26	13	18	22	26
900	13	17	21	25	13	17	21	25
1000	12	17	21	25	12	17	21	25
1100	12	16	20	24	12	16	20	24
1200	11	16	20	24	11	16	20	24
1300	11	15	19	23	11	15	19	23
1400	11	15	19	23	11	15	18	23
1500	11	15	18	22	10	14	18	22
1600	10	14	18	22	10	14	17	21
1700	10	14	17	21	10	13	17	21
1800	10	14	17	21	9	13	16	20
1900	10	13	17	21	9	13	16	20
2000	10	13	16	20	9	12	15	19
2100	9	13	16	20	9	12	15	19
2200	9	13	16	20	8	12	15	18
2300	9	13	16	19	8	11	14	18
2400	9	12	15	19	8	11	14	17
2500	9	12	15	19	8	11	14	17
2600	9	12	15	19	8	11	13	17
2700	9	12	15	18	8	11	13	16
2800	8	12	15	18	7	10	13	16
2900	8	12	14	18	7	10	13	16
3000	8	11	14	17	7	10	12	15

Note : Calculations based on span distances center to center of supports, where supports are relatively narrow. Where supports are wide in relation to the distance between them, as a 3 in. wide support where the spacing is 8 or 9 in., use the tabulated spacing as the clear distance between supports.
* These values may also be used for sheathing that has three support points (continuous over two spans).
Reproduced by permission of American Concrete Institute.

Table 6-6

Safe Spacing in Inches of Supports for Plywood Sheathing, Continuous Over Four* or More Supports

Maximum deflection is $^1/_{360}$ of support spacing, but not more than $^1/_{16}$ in.

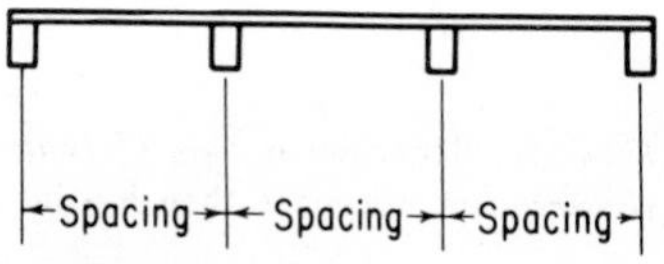

Pressure or load of concrete, pounds per square foot	f=2000 psi; E = 1,600,000 psi — 5-ply sanded, face grain parallel to span				f=2000 psi; E = 1,600,000 psi — 5-ply sanded, face grain perpendicular to span				f=1,500 psi; E=1,600,000 psi — 5-ply sanded, face grain parallel to span				f=1,500 psi; E=1,600,000 psi — 5-ply sanded, face grain perpendicular to span			
	½ in.	⅝ in.	¾ in.	1 in. (7-ply)	½ in.	⅝ in.	¾ in.	1 in. (7-ply)	½ in.	⅝ in.	¾ in.	1 in. (7-ply)	½ in.	⅝ in.	¾ in.	1 in. (7-ply)
75	20	24	27	32	14	19	24	31	20	24	27	32	14	19	24	31
100	18	22	25	30	13	17	22	29	18	22	25	30	13	17	22	29
125	17	21	23	29	12	16	21	27	17	21	23	29	12	16	21	27
150	16	19	22	27	11	15	20	26	16	19	22	27	11	15	20	26
175	15	18	21	26	10	14	19	25	15	18	21	25	10	14	19	25
200	14	17	20	25	10	14	18	24	14	17	20	25	10	14	18	24
300	12	15	17	23	9	12	15	22	12	15	17	23	9	12	15	22
400	11	14	16	21	8	11	14	20	11	14	16	21	8	11	14	20
500	10	13	15	19	7	10	13	18	10	13	15	19	7	10	13	18
600	10	12	14	18	7	9	12	17	10	12	14	18	7	9	11	17
700	9	11	13	17	7	9	12	16	9	11	13	16	6	8	10	15
800	9	11	13	16	6	8	11	15	9	9	12	15	5	7	8	13
900	9	10	12	16	6	8	10	15	8	8	11	13	4	6	7	12
1000	8	10	12	15	5	8	9	14	7	7	11	12	—	5	7	11
1100	8	10	11	15	5	8	8	14	6	7	10	11	—	5	6	10
1200	8	9	11	14	5	7	8	12	6	6	10	10	—	5	6	9
1300	7	9	11	13	4	7	7	11	5	6	9	9	—	4	5	8
1400	7	9	10	12	4	7	7	11	5	5	8	8	—	4	5	8
1500	6	9	10	11	4	6	6	10	5	5	8	8	—	4	5	7
1600	6	9	10	10	—	6	6	9	4	5	7	7	—	—	4	7
1700	6	8	9	10	—	5	5	9	4	4	7	7	—	—	4	6
1800	5	7	9	9	—	5	5	8	4	4	6	7	—	—	4	6
1900	5	7	8	9	—	5	5	8	4	4	6	6	—	—	4	6
2000	5	6	8	8	—	5	5	7	—	4	6	6	—	—	—	5
2200	4	6	7	7	—	4	4	7	—	—	5	5	—	—	—	5
2400	4	5	6	7	—	4	4	6	—	—	5	5	—	—	—	5
2600	4	5	6	6	—	4	4	6	—	—	4	5	—	—	—	4
2800	4	5	6	6	—	—	—	5	—	—	4	4	—	—	—	4
3000	—	4	5	5	—	—	—	5	—	—	4	4	—	—	—	4

Note: Rolling shear has been considered in determination of safe support spacing. Spans shorter than 4 in. are not shown. Calculations give distances center to center of supports where supports are relatively narrow. In the case of column or other forms where supports may be wide in relation to the distance between them, such as 2″ by 4″s used flat 7 or 8 in. apart, take the tabulated spacing as the clear distance between supports.

* For plywood continuous over three supports (two spans) support spacing for simple span shown in Table 6-7 may be safely used.

Reproduced by permission of American Concrete Institute.

Table 6-7

Safe Spacing in Inches of Supports for Plywood Sheathing With Only Two Points of Support*

Maximum deflection is $^1/_{360}$ of support
spacing, but not more than $^1/_{16}$ in.

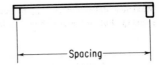

Spacing

Pressure or load of concrete, pounds per square foot	f = 2000 psi;				E = 1,600,000 psi				f = 1500 psi;				E = 1,600,000 psi			
	5-ply sanded, face grain parallel to span				5-ply sanded, face grain perpendicular to span				5-ply sanded, face grain parallel to span				5-ply sanded, face grain perpendicular to span			
	½ in.	⅝ in.	¾ in.	1 in. (7-ply)	½ in.	⅝ in.	¾ in.	1 in. (7-ply)	½ in.	⅝ in.	¾ in.	1 in. (7-ply)	½ in.	⅝ in.	¾ in.	1 in. (7-ply)
75	19	21	24	29	12	16	21	27	19	21	24	29	12	16	21	27
100	15	19	22	27	11	15	19	26	15	19	22	27	11	15	19	26
125	14	18	20	25	10	14	18	24	14	18	20	25	10	14	18	24
150	14	17	19	24	10	13	17	23	14	17	19	24	10	13	17	23
175	13	16	18	23	9	12	16	22	13	16	18	23	9	12	16	22
200	12	15	17	22	9	11	15	21	12	15	17	22	9	11	15	21
300	10	13	15	19	7	10	13	18	10	13	15	19	7	10	13	18
400	9	12	13	17	7	9	12	16	9	12	13	17	7	8	11	15
500	9	11	12	16	6	8	11	15	9	11	12	16	6	8	10	14
600	8	10	12	15	6	8	10	14	8	10	12	15	6	8	10	14
700	8	10	11	14	6	7	10	14	8	10	11	14	6	7	10	14
800	7	9	11	14	5	7	9	13	7	9	11	13	5	7	9	13
900	7	9	10	13	5	7	9	13	7	9	10	13	5	7	9	13
1000	7	8	10	13	5	7	9	12	7	8	10	12	5	7	9	12
1100	7	8	10	12	5	6	8	12	7	8	9	12	5	6	8	12
1200	6	8	9	12	5	6	8	11	6	8	9	11	5	6	7	11
1300	6	8	9	12	5	6	8	11	6	7	8	11	4	5	7	10
1400	6	8	9	11	5	6	8	11	6	7	8	10	4	5	6	9
1500	6	7	9	11	4	6	7	11	6	7	8	9	4	4	5	9
1600	6	7	8	11	4	6	7	10	5	7	7	9	—	4	5	8
1700	6	7	8	11	4	5	6	10	5	6	7	8	—	4	5	8
1800	6	7	8	10	4	5	6	10	5	6	7	8	—	4	4	7
1900	5	7	8	10	—	5	6	9	5	6	7	8	—	—	4	7
2000	5	7	8	10	—	5	6	9	4	6	7	7	—	—	4	6
2200	5	6	7	9	—	4	5	8	4	5	6	6	—	—	4	6
2400	5	6	7	8	—	4	5	7	—	5	6	6	—	—	—	5
2600	4	6	7	8	—	—	4	7	—	4	5	6	—	—	—	5
2800	4	5	6	7	—	—	4	6	—	4	5	5	—	—	—	5
3000	4	5	6	7	—	—	4	6	—	4	4	5	—	—	—	4

Note: Rolling shear has been considered in determination of allowable support spacing. Spans shorter than 4 in. are not shown. Calculations give distances center to center of supports where supports are relatively narrow. In the case of column or other forms where supports may be wide in relation to distance between them, such as 2" by 4"s used flat 6 or 7 in. apart, take the tabulated spacing as the clear distance between supports.
* May also be used for sheathing continuous over three points of support.
Reproduced by permission of American Concrete Institute.

Table 6-8

Safe Spacing in Inches of Supports for Joists, Studs (or Other Beam Components of Formwork), Continuous Over Four* or More Supports

$f = 1875$ psi; $E = 1,760,000$ psi; $H = 180$ psi

Maximum deflection is $\frac{1}{360}$ of spacing, but not more than $\frac{1}{4}$ in.

Nominal size of S4S lumber

Uniform load, lb per lineal ft (equals uniform load on forms times spacing between joists or studs, ft)	2×4	2×6	2×8	2×10	2×12	3×4	3×6	3×8	3×10	4×2	4×4	4×6	4×8	6×2	6×3	6×4	6×6	6×8	8×2	8×8	10×2
200	62	93	—	—	—	73	105	—	—	36	81	114	—	42	68	93	—	—	46	—	49
300	52	79	107	—	—	65	95	120	—	32	71	103	—	37	60	82	114	—	41	—	44
400	42	65	88	112	—	57	87	112	—	29	64	96	—	34	54	75	107	—	37	—	40
500	35	54	73	93	113	51	78	105	—	27	60	91	115	31	50	69	101	—	34	—	37
600	31	47	64	81	98	45	69	94	119	24	54	83	109	29	47	65	96	121	32	—	35
700	27	42	57	72	87	40	60	82	104	23	50	77	104	28	45	62	93	117	31	—	33
800	25	38	51	65	79	36	54	74	94	21	47	70	97	26	43	59	88	113	29	—	32
900	23	35	47	60	73	32	50	67	85	19	42	64	87	25	40	55	83	110	28	119	31
1000	21	32	44	56	68	30	46	62	79	17	39	59	80	24	38	53	79	107	27	116	29
1100	20	31	42	53	64	28	43	58	73	16	36	54	74	23	36	50	75	103	26	113	29
1200	19	29	39	50	60	26	40	54	69	15	33	51	69	22	35	48	72	98	25	110	28
1300	18	28	38	48	58	25	38	51	65	14	31	48	65	20	33	45	67	91	24	108	27
1400	17	26	36	46	55	23	36	49	62	13	30	45	62	19	31	42	63	86	23	106	26
1500	17	25	35	44	53	22	34	46	59	13	28	43	58	18	29	40	59	81	22	103	25
1600	16	24	33	42	51	21	33	45	56	12	27	41	56	17	28	38	56	77	22	99	24
1700	15	24	32	41	49	21	31	43	54	11	26	39	53	16	26	36	54	74	21	96	24
1800	15	23	31	40	48	20	30	41	52	11	25	38	51	16	25	35	51	70	20	94	23
1900	15	22	30	39	47	19	29	40	51	10	24	36	49	15	24	33	49	67	19	87	22
2000	14	22	30	38	45	19	28	39	49	10	23	35	48	14	23	32	47	65	18	83	22
2100	14	21	29	37	44	18	28	38	48	10	22	34	46	14	22	31	46	62	17	80	21
2200	14	21	28	36	43	18	27	37	46	10	21	33	45	13	21	30	44	60	17	77	20
2300	13	20	27	35	43	17	26	36	45	—	21	32	43	13	21	29	43	58	16	74	19
2400	13	20	27	34	42	17	25	35	44	—	20	31	42	12	20	28	41	56	16	72	19
2500	13	20	26	34	41	16	25	34	43	—	20	30	41	12	20	27	40	55	15	70	18
2600	13	19	26	33	40	16	24	33	42	—	19	29	40	12	19	26	39	53	15	67	18
2700	12	19	26	33	40	16	24	33	41	—	19	29	39	11	18	25	38	52	14	66	17
2800	12	19	25	32	39	15	23	32	40	—	18	29	38	11	18	25	37	51	14	64	17
2900	12	18	25	32	38	15	23	31	40	—	18	28	37	11	17	24	36	49	13	62	16
3000	12	18	25	31	38	15	23	31	39	—	18	27	37	11	17	23	35	48	13	60	16
3200	12	18	24	31	37	14	22	30	38	—	17	26	35	10	16	22	34	46	12	58	15
3400	11	17	24	30	36	14	22	29	37	—	16	26	34	10	16	22	32	44	12	55	14
3600	11	17	23	29	35	14	21	28	36	—	16	25	33	—	15	21	31	43	11	53	14
3800	11	17	23	29	35	13	21	27	35	—	15	24	32	—	15	20	30	41	11	51	13
4000	11	17	22	28	34	13	20	27	34	—	15	23	31	—	14	20	29	40	11	49	13
4500	10	16	22	27	33	12	19	25	32	—	14	22	29	—	13	18	27	37	10	45	12
5000	10	16	21	26	32	12	18	24	31	—	14	21	28	—	12	17	26	35	10	42	11

Note: Both light gage and standard structural steel sections may be used for framing forms; however, the available cross sections are too numerous to provide a comprehensive tabulation of permissible spans. Refer to manufacturers' handbooks and data sheets.

* For members continuous over three supports (two spans), spacing for simple span shown in Table 6-10 may be safely used.

Reproduced by permission of American Concrete Institute.

Table 6-9

Safe Spacing in Inches of Supports for Joists, Studs (or Other Beam Components of Formwork), Continuous Over Four* or More Supports

f = 1500 psi; E = 1,600,000 psi; H = 145 psi

Maximum deflection is 1/360 of spacing, but not more than 1/4 in.

Uniform load, lb per lineal ft (equals uniform load on forms times spacing between joists or studs, ft)	Nominal size of S4S lumber																				
	2×4	2×6	2×8	2×10	2×12	3×4	3×6	3×8	3×10	4×2	4×4	4×6	4×8	6×2	6×3	6×4	6×6	6×8	8×2	8×8	10×2
200	60	86	115	—	—	71	103	—	—	35	79	112	—	41	66	91	—	—	45	—	48
300	45	68	94	118	—	59	93	118	—	31	69	101	—	36	58	80	112	—	39	—	43
400	37	54	74	93	113	51	78	105	115	27	60	91	110	33	53	72	104	—	36	—	38
500	30	45	62	79	95	44	67	91	99	24	53	81	101	30	48	67	98	119	33	—	36
600	26	40	54	69	83	38	58	78	88	22	49	75	90	27	44	61	91	114	31	—	34
700	23	36	48	62	75	33	51	69	79	19	43	66	81	25	41	56	81	106	29	119	32
800	21	32	44	56	68	30	46	63	72	17	39	59	73	24	38	53	79	101	27	116	31
900	20	30	41	52	63	28	42	57	67	16	35	54	68	22	36	50	74	97	26	112	29
1000	19	28	39	49	59	26	39	53	63	15	33	50	63	21	34	47	69	88	24	107	27
1100	18	27	36	46	56	24	36	50	59	14	30	46	59	19	31	43	64	82	23	103	26
1200	17	25	35	44	53	22	34	47	56	13	28	43	55	18	30	40	60	77	22	99	25
1300	16	24	33	42	51	21	33	44	53	12	27	41	52	17	27	38	56	72	21	93	24
1400	15	23	32	40	49	20	31	42	51	11	25	38	50	16	26	35	53	68	20	87	23
1500	15	22	31	39	47	20	30	40	49	11	24	37	48	15	24	34	50	65	19	83	22
1600	14	22	30	38	46	19	29	39	47	10	23	35	46	14	23	32	48	62	18	79	22
1700	14	21	29	37	44	18	27	37	46	10	22	34	44	14	22	31	45	59	17	75	21
1800	14	21	28	36	43	18	27	36	44	10	21	32	43	13	21	29	43	57	16	72	20
1900	13	20	27	35	42	17	26	35	43	—	21	31	41	13	20	28	42	55	16	69	19
2000	13	20	27	34	41	17	25	34	42	—	20	30	40	12	20	27	40	53	15	67	18
2100	13	19	26	33	40	16	24	33	41	—	19	29	39	12	19	26	39	51	15	64	18
2200	13	19	26	33	39	16	24	32	40	—	19	29	38	11	18	25	38	50	14	62	17
2300	12	18	25	32	39	15	23	32	39	—	18	28	37	11	18	24	36	48	14	60	16
2400	12	18	25	31	38	15	23	31	38	—	18	27	36	11	17	24	35	47	13	59	16
2500	12	18	24	31	37	14	22	30	38	—	17	26	35	10	17	23	34	46	13	57	15
2600	12	18	24	31	37	14	22	30	37	—	17	26	34	10	16	23	34	45	12	55	15
2700	12	17	23	30	36	14	22	29	36	—	17	25	34	10	16	22	33	44	12	53	14
2800	11	17	23	30	36	14	21	29	36	—	16	25	33	10	16	21	32	43	12	51	14
2900	11	17	23	29	35	13	21	28	35	—	16	24	32	—	15	21	31	42	11	50	13
3000	11	17	23	29	35	13	20	28	34	—	16	24	31	—	15	20	30	40	11	48	13
3200	11	17	22	28	34	13	20	27	33	—	15	23	30	—	14	20	29	39	11	46	13
3400	11	17	22	28	34	13	20	26	32	—	15	22	30	—	14	19	28	39	10	44	12
3600	10	16	22	27	33	12	19	25	32	—	14	22	29	—	13	18	27	37	10	43	12
3800	10	16	21	27	33	12	19	25	31	—	14	22	28	—	13	18	26	36	10	41	11
4000	10	16	21	27	32	12	18	24	31	—	14	21	27	—	12	17	25	35	—	38	11
4500	10	15	20	26	31	11	18	23	30	—	13	20	26	—	12	16	24	33	—	36	10
5000	10	15	20	25	30	11	17	22	29	—	12	19	25	—	11	15	23	31	—	—	—

Note: Both light gage and standard structural steel sections may be used for framing forms; however, the available cross sections are too numerous to provide a comprehensive tabulation of permissible spans. Refer to manufacturers' handbooks and data sheets.

* For members continuous over three supports (two spans), spacing for simple span in Table 6-11 may be safely used.

Reproduced by permission of American Concrete Institute.

Table 6-10

Safe Spacing in Inches of Supports for Joists, Studs (or Other Beam Components of Formwork), on Two* Supports (Simply Supported)

Maximum deflection is $1/360$ of spacing, but not more than $1/4$ in.

$f = 1875$ psi; $E = 1,760,000$ psi; $H = 180$ psi

Uniform load, lb per lineal ft (equals uniform load on forms times spacing between joists or studs, ft)	2×4	2×6	2×8	2×10	2×12	3×4	3×6	3×8	3×10	4×2	4×4	4×6	4×8	6×2	6×3	6×4	6×6	6×8	8×2	8×8	10×2
													Nominal size of S4S lumber								
200	53	80	104	124	142	62	93	117	143	31	69	100	127	36	58	79	111	140	39	152	43
300	46	70	94	112	129	55	82	106	129	27	60	91	114	31	50	70	100	127	34	138	37
400	40	60	83	100	120	49	74	98	120	24	55	83	106	28	46	63	94	118	31	128	34
500	36	54	74	94	113	45	69	93	114	23	51	77	101	26	43	59	88	112	29	121	31
600	33	50	67	86	104	42	63	86	109	21	48	72	96	25	40	55	84	107	27	115	30
700	30	46	63	79	96	38	59	80	101	20	45	69	93	24	38	52	79	103	26	111	28
800	28	43	58	74	90	36	55	75	94	19	42	64	87	22	36	50	75	99	25	107	27
900	26	40	54	68	83	34	52	70	89	18	40	61	82	22	35	48	73	97	24	104	26
1000	24	37	50	63	77	32	49	67	84	17	38	57	78	21	34	47	70	94	23	102	25
1100	23	35	47	59	72	31	47	63	80	16	36	55	74	20	33	45	67	92	22	99	24
1200	21	33	44	56	68	29	44	61	77	15	34	52	71	19	31	43	64	88	22	97	23
1300	20	32	42	53	64	28	43	58	74	15	33	50	69	19	30	41	62	84	21	95	23
1400	19	30	40	51	61	27	41	55	70	14	32	49	66	18	29	40	60	81	21	93	22
1500	18	29	38	49	59	25	39	53	67	14	31	47	64	17	28	39	58	79	20	92	22
1600	18	28	37	47	57	24	37	50	64	13	30	45	62	17	27	37	56	76	19	88	21
1700	17	27	36	45	55	23	35	48	61	13	29	44	60	16	26	36	54	74	19	86	21
1800	17	26	35	44	53	23	34	47	59	13	28	43	58	16	26	35	53	72	18	84	20
1900	16	25	34	42	51	22	33	45	57	12	27	41	56	15	25	34	52	70	18	82	20
2000	16	25	33	41	50	21	32	43	55	12	26	40	54	15	24	33	50	68	17	80	19
2100	15	24	32	40	49	20	31	42	53	11	25	38	52	15	24	33	49	66	17	78	19
2200	15	23	31	39	48	20	30	41	52	11	24	37	51	14	23	32	48	65	17	76	19
2300	15	23	30	38	46	19	29	40	50	11	24	36	49	14	23	31	47	64	16	74	18
2400	14	22	30	38	45	19	28	39	49	10	23	35	48	14	22	30	46	62	16	73	18
2500	14	22	29	37	45	18	28	38	48	10	22	34	46	13	22	30	45	61	15	71	17
2600	14	21	29	36	44	18	27	37	47	10	22	33	45	13	21	29	44	60	15	70	17
2700	13	21	28	36	43	17	26	36	46	10	21	32	44	13	21	29	43	59	15	69	17
2800	13	21	28	35	42	17	26	35	45	—	21	31	43	13	20	28	42	57	15	68	16
2900	13	20	27	34	42	17	25	35	44	—	20	31	42	12	20	28	41	56	14	66	16
3000	13	20	27	34	41	16	25	34	43	—	20	30	41	12	20	27	40	55	14	65	16
3200	12	20	26	33	40	16	24	33	41	—	19	29	39	12	19	26	38	52	14	63	15
3400	12	19	25	32	39	15	23	32	40	—	18	28	38	11	18	25	37	50	13	61	15
3600	12	19	25	31	38	15	23	31	39	—	18	27	37	11	17	24	35	48	13	59	15
3800	12	18	24	31	37	14	23	30	38	—	17	27	36	10	17	23	34	46	13	58	14
4000	11	18	24	30	37	14	22	29	37	—	17	26	35	10	16	22	33	45	12	56	14
4500	11	17	23	29	35	13	21	27	35	—	16	24	32	—	15	20	30	41	11	51	13
5000	11	16	22	28	34	13	20	26	33	—	15	23	31	—	14	19	28	39	10	48	12

Note: Both light gage and standard structural steel sections may be used for framing forms; however, the available cross sections are too numerous to provide a comprehensive tabulation of permissible spans. Refer to manufacturers' handbooks and data sheets.

* Also applicable to members continuous over three supports (two spans).

Reproduced by permission of American Concrete Institute.

Table 6-11

Safe Spacing in Inches of Supports for Joists, Studs (or Other Beam Components of Formwork), on Two* Supports (Simply Supported)

Maximum deflection is $1/360$ of spacing, but not more than $1/4$ in.

$f = 1500$ psi; $E = 1,600,000$ psi; $H = 145$ psi

Nominal size of S4S lumber

Uniform load, lb per lineal ft (equals uniform load on forms times spacing between joists or studs, ft)	2×4	2×6	2×8	2×10	2×12	3×4	3×6	3×8	3×10	4×2	4×4	4×6	4×8	6×2	6×3	6×4	6×6	6×8	8×2	8×8	10×2
200	51	77	101	121	139	60	90	114	136	30	67	99	123	35	56	77	109	137	38	148	41
300	41	63	85	108	126	53	79	104	123	26	58	88	112	30	49	67	98	124	33	130	36
400	36	54	74	94	114	46	69	94	115	24	53	80	104	28	44	61	92	115	30	125	33
500	32	48	66	84	101	41	62	84	107	21	48	72	99	26	41	57	86	109	28	118	30
600	29	44	60	77	93	37	57	77	97	20	44	67	90	24	39	53	80	104	26	112	29
700	27	41	55	70	85	34	52	71	90	18	40	62	84	23	37	50	76	100	25	108	27
800	24	37	50	64	77	32	49	66	84	17	38	58	78	21	34	47	71	96	24	104	26
900	23	34	46	59	71	30	46	63	79	16	36	54	74	20	32	44	67	91	23	102	25
1000	21	32	43	55	66	29	44	59	75	15	34	51	70	19	31	42	63	86	22	99	24
1100	20	30	41	51	62	27	41	56	72	14	32	49	67	18	29	40	60	82	21	96	23
1200	19	28	39	49	59	26	39	53	67	14	31	47	64	17	28	39	58	79	20	92	22
1300	18	27	37	47	56	24	37	50	64	13	30	45	61	17	27	37	56	76	19	88	22
1400	17	26	35	45	54	23	35	48	60	13	29	43	59	16	26	36	53	73	18	85	21
1500	16	25	34	43	52	22	33	46	58	12	27	42	57	15	25	34	52	70	18	82	20
1600	16	24	33	41	50	21	32	44	55	12	26	40	54	15	24	33	50	68	17	80	19
1700	15	23	32	40	49	20	31	42	53	11	25	38	52	15	23	32	49	66	17	77	19
1800	15	22	31	39	47	20	30	40	51	11	24	37	50	14	23	32	47	64	16	75	18
1900	15	22	30	38	46	19	29	39	49	10	23	35	48	14	22	31	46	63	16	73	18
2000	14	21	29	37	45	18	28	38	48	10	22	34	47	13	22	30	45	61	15	71	17
2100	14	21	28	36	44	18	28	37	47	10	22	33	45	13	21	29	44	60	15	69	17
2200	14	20	28	35	43	17	27	36	45	—	21	32	44	13	21	28	43	58	15	68	17
2300	13	20	27	35	42	17	26	35	44	—	20	31	42	12	20	28	41	56	14	66	16
2400	13	20	27	34	41	17	26	34	43	—	20	30	41	12	20	27	40	55	14	65	16
2500	13	19	26	33	40	16	25	33	42	—	19	30	40	12	19	26	39	53	14	64	16
2600	13	19	26	33	40	16	25	33	41	—	19	29	39	11	19	26	38	52	14	62	15
2700	12	19	25	32	39	15	24	32	40	—	18	28	38	11	18	25	37	50	13	61	15
2800	12	18	25	32	39	15	24	31	40	—	18	28	37	11	18	24	36	49	13	60	15
2900	12	18	24	31	38	15	23	31	39	—	18	27	37	11	17	23	35	48	13	59	14
3000	12	18	24	31	38	15	23	30	38	—	17	26	36	10	17	23	34	47	13	58	14
3200	12	18	24	30	37	14	22	29	37	—	17	25	35	10	16	22	33	45	12	56	14
3400	11	18	23	30	36	14	21	28	36	—	16	25	34	—	15	21	32	43	12	53	13
3600	11	17	23	29	35	14	21	28	35	—	16	24	32	—	15	20	30	41	11	51	13
3800	11	17	23	28	34	13	20	27	34	—	15	24	32	—	14	20	29	40	11	49	13
4000	11	16	22	28	34	13	20	26	34	—	15	23	31	—	14	19	28	39	10	48	12
4500	10	16	21	27	33	12	19	25	32	—	14	22	29	—	13	18	26	36	10	44	12
5000	10	16	21	26	32	12	18	24	31	—	13	21	28	—	12	17	25	34	—	41	11

Note: Both light gage and standard structural steel sections may be used for framing forms; however, the available cross sections are too numerous to provide a comprehensive tabulation of permissible spans. Refer to manufacturers' handbooks and data sheets.

* Also applicable to members continuous over three supports (two spans).

Reproduced by permission of American Concrete Institute.

Table 6-12

Safe Spacing in Inches of Supports for Double Wales Continuous Over Four* or More Supports

Maximum deflection is $1/360$ of spacing, but not more than $1/4$ in.

Equivalent uniform load, lb per lineal ft (equals uniform load, psf, on forms times spacing of wales in ft)	f=1875 psi ;	E=1,760,000 psi ;	H=180 psi						
	Nominal size of S4S lumber used double								
	2 × 4	2 × 6	2 × 8	3 × 4	3 × 6	3 × 8	4 × 4	4 × 6	4 × 8
1000	36	54	74	51	77	105	60	90	115
1100	33	50	68	49	74	100	57	86	112
1200	31	47	64	46	69	94	54	82	109
1300	29	44	60	43	64	88	52	79	107
1400	28	42	57	40	61	83	51	76	104
1500	26	40	54	38	57	78	49	74	101
1600	25	38	52	36	54	74	47	71	97
1700	24	36	50	34	52	71	44	67	92
1800	23	35	48	33	49	68	42	64	88
1900	22	33	46	31	47	65	41	61	84
2000	22	32	44	30	46	62	39	59	80
2100	21	31	43	29	44	60	37	56	77
2200	20	31	42	28	42	58	36	54	74
2300	20	30	41	27	41	56	35	53	72
2400	19	29	39	26	40	55	34	51	69
2500	19	28	38	26	39	53	33	49	67
2600	18	27	38	25	38	52	32	48	65
2700	18	26	37	24	37	50	31	46	63
2800	17	26	36	24	36	49	30	45	62
2900	17	25	35	23	35	48	29	44	60
3000	17	25	35	23	34	47	28	43	59
3200	16	24	33	22	33	45	27	41	56
3400	16	24	32	21	31	43	26	39	53
3600	15	23	31	20	30	41	25	37	51
3800	15	23	30	19	29	40	24	36	49
4000	14	22	30	19	28	39	23	35	48
4200	14	22	29	18	28	38	22	34	46
4400	14	21	28	18	27	37	22	33	45
4600	13	21	28	17	26	36	21	32	43
4800	13	20	27	17	25	35	21	31	42
5000	13	20	27	17	25	34	20	30	41

* For members continuous over three supports (two spans), spacing shown in Table 6-14 may be safely used.
Reproduced by permission of American Concrete Institute.

Table 6-13

Safe Spacing in Inches of Supports for Double Wales Continuous Over Four* or More Supports

Maximum deflection is $1/360$ of spacing, but not more than $1/4$ in.

Equivalent uniform load, lb per lineal ft (equals uniform load, psf, on forms times spacing of wales in ft)	f = 1500 psi ;	E = 1,600,000 psi ;	H = 145 psi						
	Nominal size of S4S lumber used double								
	2 × 4	2 × 6	2 × 8	3 × 4	3 × 6	3 × 8	4 × 4	4 × 6	4 × 8
1000	30	46	62	44	67	91	53	81	111
1100	28	42	58	41	62	84	51	77	106
1200	26	40	54	38	58	79	49	74	101
1300	25	38	51	36	54	74	47	70	96
1400	24	36	49	34	51	70	44	66	90
1500	23	34	47	32	48	66	41	62	85
1600	22	33	45	30	46	63	39	59	81
1700	21	31	43	29	44	60	37	56	77
1800	20	30	41	28	42	57	36	54	73
1900	19	29	40	27	40	55	34	52	70
2000	19	28	39	26	39	53	33	50	68
2100	18	27	38	25	38	51	32	48	65
2200	18	27	37	24	37	50	31	46	63
2300	17	26	36	23	35	48	30	45	61
2400	17	25	35	23	34	47	29	43	59
2500	16	25	34	22	33	46	28	42	57
2600	16	24	33	22	32	44	27	41	56
2700	16	24	33	21	32	43	26	40	54
2800	15	23	32	21	31	42	26	39	53
2900	15	23	31	20	30	41	25	38	51
3000	15	23	31	20	30	41	24	37	50
3200	15	22	30	19	28	39	23	35	48
3400	14	21	29	18	27	38	22	34	46
3600	14	21	28	18	27	36	22	32	44
3800	13	20	27	17	26	35	21	31	43
4000	13	20	27	17	25	34	20	30	41
4200	13	19	26	16	24	33	19	29	40
4400	13	19	26	16	24	32	19	29	39
4600	12	19	25	15	23	32	18	28	38
4800	12	19	25	15	23	31	18	27	37
5000	12	18	24	15	22	30	18	26	36

Note: Steel members may also be used as wales; however, available cross sections are too numerous to provide a comprehensive tabulation of permissible spans. Refer to manufacturers' handbooks and data sheets.
* For members continuous over three supports (two spans), spacing shown in Table 6-15 may be safely used.
Reproduced by permission of American Concrete Institute.

Table 6-14

Safe Spacing in Inches of Supports for Double Wales, Simply Supported* at Two Points

Maximum deflection is $1/360$ of spacing, but not more than $1/4$ in.

Equivalent uniform load, lb per lineal ft (equals uniform load, psf, on forms times spacing of wales, ft)	$f = 1875$ psi; $E = 1,760,000$ psi; $H = 180$ psi								
	Nominal size of S4S lumber used double								
	2 × 4	2 × 6	2 × 8	3 × 4	3 × 6	3 × 8	4 × 4	4 × 6	4 × 8
1000	36	54	74	45	69	93	51	77	101
1100	34	52	71	43	66	90	49	74	98
1200	33	50	68	42	63	86	48	72	96
1300	31	48	65	40	60	83	46	70	93
1400	30	46	63	39	58	80	45	69	93
1500	29	44	61	37	56	77	44	66	90
1600	28	43	59	36	55	74	42	64	87
1700	27	42	56	35	53	72	41	62	85
1800	26	40	54	34	52	70	40	60	82
1900	25	39	52	33	50	68	39	59	80
2000	24	37	50	32	49	66	38	58	78
2100	23	35	49	32	48	65	37	56	76
2200	23	34	47	31	47	64	36	55	75
2300	22	33	46	30	46	62	35	54	73
2400	21	32	44	29	45	61	35	53	68
2500	21	31	43	29	44	60	34	51	67
2600	20	31	42	28	43	58	33	50	67
2700	20	30	41	28	42	57	33	49	66
2800	19	29	40	27	41	56	32	49	65
2900	19	29	39	26	40	54	32	48	65
3000	19	28	39	26	39	53	31	47	64
3200	18	27	37	25	37	51	30	45	62
3400	17	26	36	24	35	49	29	44	60
3600	17	25	35	23	34	47	28	43	58
3800	16	25	34	22	33	45	27	41	56
4000	16	24	33	21	32	44	26	40	54
4200	15	23	32	20	31	42	25	38	52
4400	15	23	31	20	30	41	25	37	51
4600	15	22	30	19	29	40	24	36	49
4800	14	22	30	19	28	39	23	35	48
5000	14	21	29	18	28	38	23	34	46

* May be used also for members supported at three points (continuous over two spans only).
Reproduced by permission of American Concrete Institute.

Table 6-15

Safe Spacing in Inches of Supports for Double Wales, Simply Supported* at Two Points

Maximum deflection is $1/360$ of spacing, but not more than $1/4$ in.

Equivalent uniform load, lb per lineal ft (equals uniform load, psf, on forms times spacing of wales, ft)	$f = 1500$ psi; $E = 1,600,000$ psi; $H = 145$ psi								
	Nominal size of S4S lumber used double								
	2 × 4	2 × 6	2 × 8	3 × 4	3 × 6	3 × 8	4 × 4	4 × 6	4 × 8
1000	32	48	66	41	63	84	48	73	99
1100	31	46	63	39	59	80	46	69	94
1200	29	44	61	37	56	77	44	66	90
1300	28	43	58	36	54	74	42	64	87
1400	27	41	55	34	52	71	40	61	83
1500	26	39	53	33	50	69	39	59	81
1600	24	37	50	32	49	67	38	57	79
1700	23	35	48	31	47	65	37	56	76
1800	23	34	46	30	46	63	36	54	74
1900	22	33	45	30	45	61	35	52	72
2000	21	32	43	29	44	60	34	51	70
2100	20	31	42	28	43	58	33	50	68
2200	20	30	41	27	42	57	32	49	67
2300	19	29	40	27	40	55	32	48	65
2400	19	28	39	26	39	53	31	47	64
2500	18	27	38	25	38	52	30	46	63
2600	18	27	37	24	37	50	30	45	61
2700	17	26	36	24	36	49	29	44	60
2800	17	26	35	23	35	48	29	43	59
2900	17	25	35	23	34	47	28	43	58
3000	16	25	34	22	33	46	28	42	57
3200	15	24	33	21	32	44	26	40	54
3400	14	23	32	20	31	42	25	38	52
3600	14	23	31	20	30	40	24	37	50
3800	13	22	30	19	29	39	23	35	48
4000	13	21	29	18	28	38	23	34	47
4200	13	21	28	18	27	37	22	33	45
4400	13	20	28	17	26	36	21	32	44
4600	12	20	27	17	26	35	21	31	42
4800	12	20	27	17	25	34	20	30	41
5000	12	19	26	16	24	33	20	29	40

Note: Steel members may also be used as wales; however, available cross sections are too numerous to provide a comprehensive tabulation of permissible spans. Refer to manufacturers' handbooks and data sheets.
* May also be used for members supported at three points (continuous over two spans only).
Reproduced by permission of American Concrete Institute.

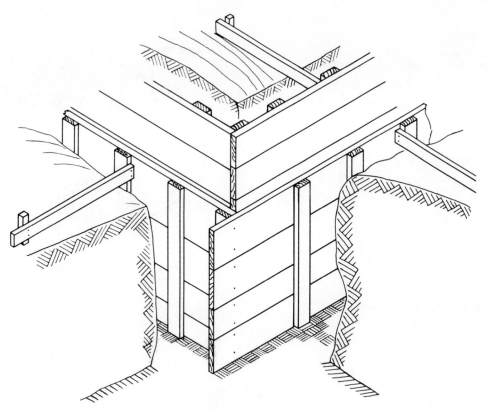

Fig 6-6. Heavy grade beam form

For deeper wall footings and grade beams, the formwork must be more elaborate and is constructed in much the same manner as wall forms (see *Wall Forms* on page 95).

When a wall footing is supported by sloping ground, the footing may be stepped longitudinally at intervals, the frequency of the steps depending on the slope. Figure 6-7 illustrates a method of forming such steps.

Simple rectangular column footing forms may be made as bottomless boxes, constructed in four pieces—two sides and two end sections. Two sections are made the exact dimensions of the footing and the two opposite ones long enough to take care of the thickness of the material and the vertical cleats used for holding the sections together (see Fig. 6-8). Ties are used to prevent the sides from bulging under pressure. A template for positioning dowels in the footing can be attached to the form box, as shown in Fig. 6-9. Figure 6-9 also illustrates an alternative method of tying the form.

Stepped column footings are shown in Fig. 6-10. The forms are made as a series of boxes stacked one on top of the other. The upper ones can be supported as shown in Fig. 6-10 and if the difference in size between the upper and lower forms is considerable, the

bottom one may require a cover. The whole assembly must be weighed or tied down to prevent uplift by freshly placed concrete.

Fig. 6-7. Stepped wall footing

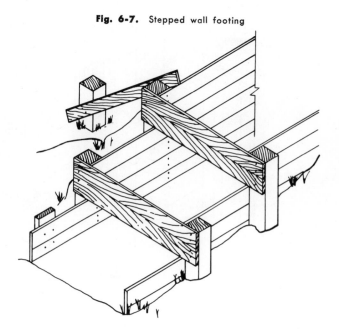

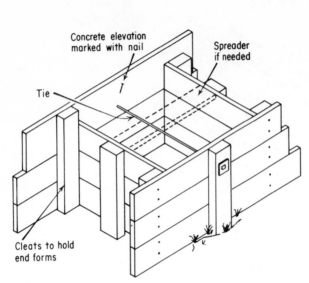

Concrete elevation
marked with nail

Spreader
if needed

Tie

Cleats to hold
end forms

Fig. 6-8. Simple column footing form

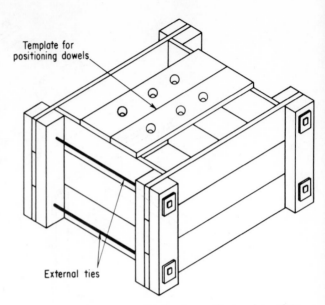

Template for
positioning dowels

External ties

Fig. 6-9. Column footing form with dowel template

Fig. 6-10. Stepped column footing form

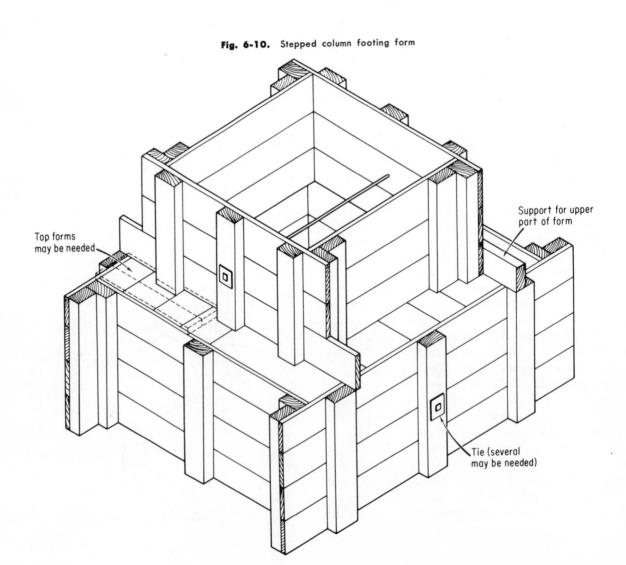

Support for upper
part of form

Top forms
may be needed

Tie (several
may be needed)

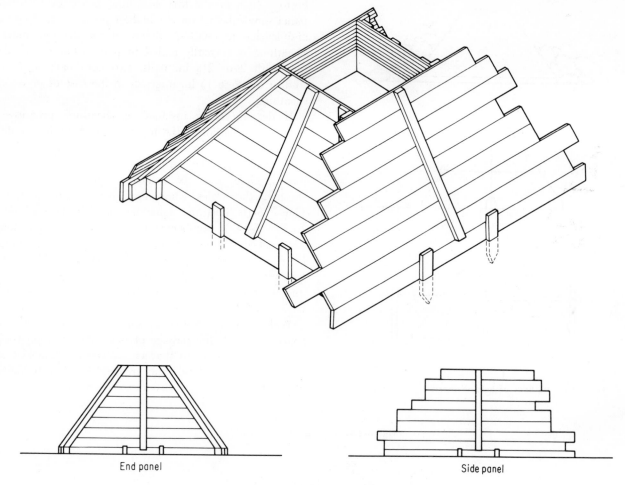

End panel

Side panel

Fig. 6-11. Tapered footing form

Tapered footing forms are made like a hopper. Two opposite panels are made to the exact dimension of the footing face. The other two are longer and do not have to be tapered (see Fig. 6-11). Cleats hold the side and end sections together and some method must again be used to hold the form in place. Figure 6-12 illustrates three alternate ways of holding down a tapered form.

It is sometimes necessary to transfer part of the load of one footing to another or to support two columns on a single footing. The footing is then known as a *combined*, or *strap* footing.

When two columns are supported on a single footing, the form is built the same way as a flat or stepped footing, except that it is longer. When part of the footing load is to be transferred to another pad, a strap or beam must be constructed between the two. When the footing and strap are cast monolithically, the form may be built as shown in Fig. 6-13. Depending on the available height, it may not be necessary to set the strap or beam into the footing, as in Fig. 6-13.

WALL FORMS

Wall forms are made up of five basic parts. They are: (1) *sheathing*, to shape and retain the concrete until it sets; (2) *studs*, to form a framework and support the sheathing; (3) *wales*, to keep the form aligned and support the studs; (4) *braces*, to hold the forms erect under lateral pressure; and (5), *ties and spreaders* or *tie-spreader units*, to hold the sides of the forms at the correct spacing (see Fig. 6-14).

Wall forms may be built-in-place or prefabricated, depending on shape and desirability of reuse.

The first step in building forms in-place is to attach a sole plate to the footing as a base for the studs. It must be set out from the proposed wall line the thickness of the sheathing and carefully aligned. It is fastened to the footing by concrete nails, powder-driven studs, or simply held in place by stakes, as illustrated in Fig. 6-15. Studs are then set and toe-nailed on the desired centers and are held vertical by temporary bracing. Sheathing is attached next. The

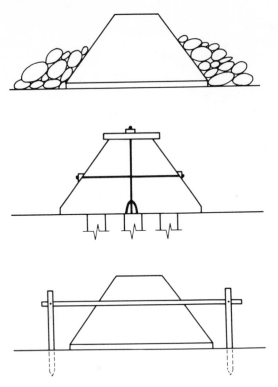

Fig. 6-12. Methods of holding tapered forms in place

bottom edge of the first sheathing board or plywood panel should be set on the highest point of the footing and leveled to establish alignment for the remainder. Sheathing is normally nailed in place from the inside face with 2 or 2½ in. nails, two per board at each stud or at 12 to 16 in. intervals in the case of plywood sheathing.

If ties are being installed as sheathing progresses, notches can be cut in the top edge of sheathing at the required locations to allow ties to pass through. Otherwise, holes must be drilled after the sheathing is in place. Holes must be located so that ties will pass through the wales when they have been installed. Figure 6-16 illustrates some inexpensive types of ties. In Fig. 6-17, a number of ties are shown in position. Some of these require separate spreaders which must be recovered as concrete is being poured. This may be done by running a wire through the upper spreaders and wrapping it around the bottom one, as illustrated in Fig. 6-18.

Wales may be double or single. Double wales are spaced to allow the passage of ties. Pieces of plywood may be used to act as spacers. Wales are attached to the outside of the studs and are held in place by nails, clips, or some other device (see Fig. 6-19).

Fig. 6-13. Form for strap footing

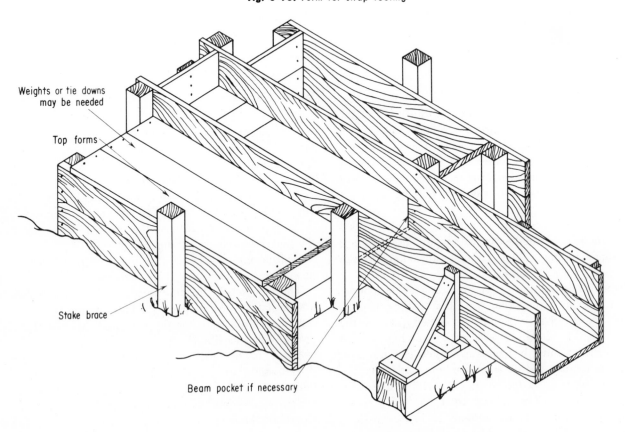

Weights or tie downs may be needed

Top forms

Stake brace

Beam pocket if necessary

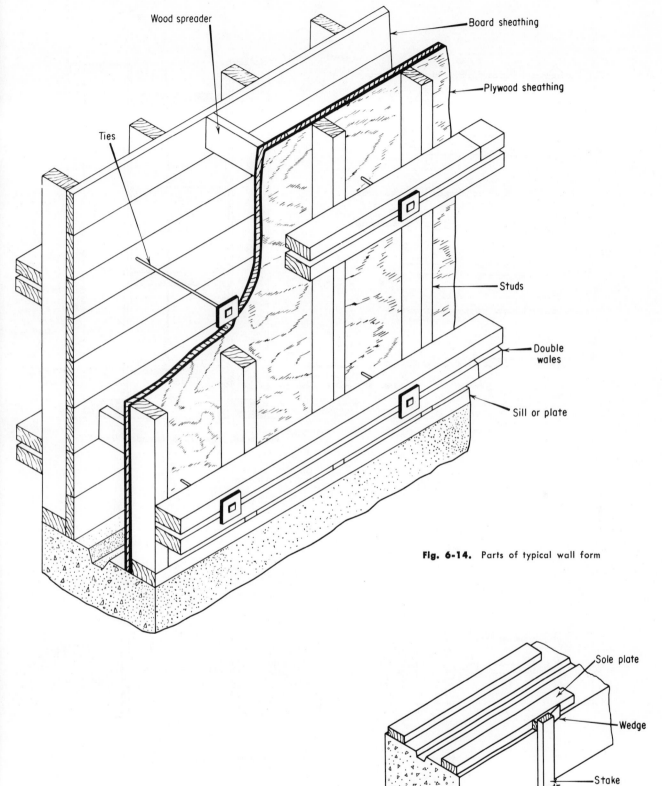

Fig. 6-14. Parts of typical wall form

Fig. 6-15. Wall form sole plate in place

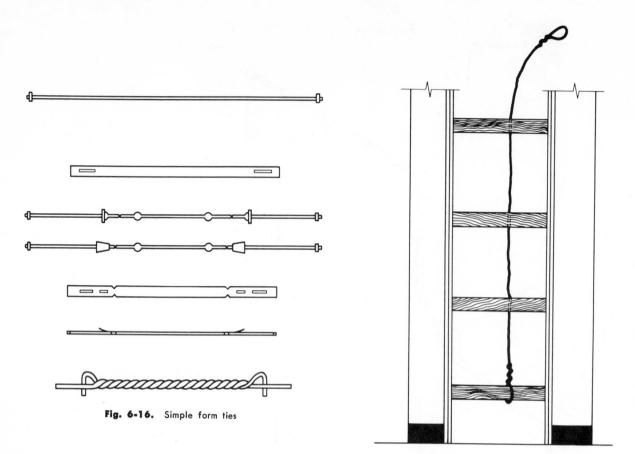

Fig. 6-16. Simple form ties

Fig. 6-18. Recovering spreaders from form

Fig. 6-17. Some typical form tie installations

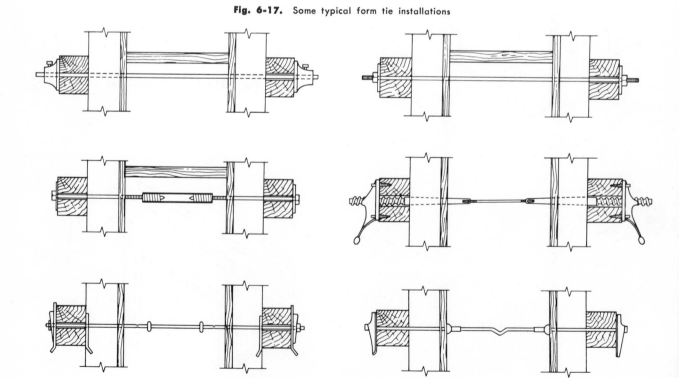

Fig. 6-19. Wale brackets. (Courtesy Jahn Concrete Forming)

Fig. 6-20. Braced wall form. (Courtesy Jahn Concrete Forming)

Braces should extend from the wales to solid support (see Fig. 6-20). They may act in compression only, in tension only, or in both—as when forms are braced on one side only. Heavy wire or cable is suitable for tension bracing.

Plumbing is the final operation of building a wall form. Many bracing systems have some means of adjusting the braces while the form is being plumbed, but if they do not, the wall must be plumbed as the braces are installed. If one wall is plumbed as soon as it is built, there is no need to plumb the opposite one. The second form will be plumbed automatically by the spreaders.

If the walls are thin and there is no room to work inside the form, steel is placed before the second form is erected. In this case, the second wall can be built in an inclined or flat position and tilted into place. Finally, the ties are tightened. Where through-the-wall tying is impossible or not allowed, external bracing must be provided to securely support both walls.

The use of prefabricated panels for formwork has recently been on the increase. These panels can be reused many times and reduce the time and labor required for erecting forms on the site.

Many types of prefabricated form panels are in use. Contractors sometimes build their own panels from wood framing covered with plywood sheathing. A standard size is 2′ by 8′, but panels can be sized to suit any particular situation. Figure 6-21 illustrates a typical 2′ by 8′ panel with metal straps at the corners. Note the grooves in the outside edges to allow ties to pass through. A simple bolt and wedge device for holding adjacent panels tightly together is shown in Fig. 6-22.

Panels made with a metal frame and plywood sheathing are also in common use and are available in a variety of sizes. Special sections are produced to form inside corners, pilasters, etc. Panels are held together by patented panel clamps. Flat bar ties (which lock into place between panels) eliminate the need for spreaders. Forms are aligned by using one or more doubled rows of 2″ by 4″s, secured to the forms by a special device which is attached to the bar ties.

Form panels made completely of steel are also available. 24″ by 48″ is a standard size, but various other sizes are also manufactured. Inside and outside corner sections are standard and insert angles allow odd-sized panels to be made up as desired.

Large projects requiring mass concrete placement are often formed by the use of giant panels or ganged, prefabricated forms. Cranes usually raise and place these large sections, so their size is limited only by available equipment. These large forms are built or

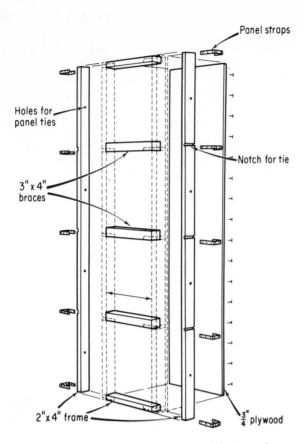

Fig. 6-21. Typical prefabricated wood form panel

Fig. 6-22. Bolt and wedge panel clamp

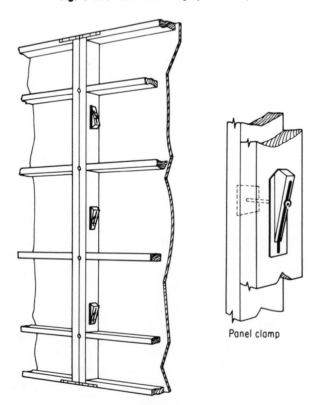

Panel clamp

Fig. 6-23. Giant curved form in place. (Courtesy Jahn Concrete Forming)

assembled on the ground, and their only basic difference from regular forms is the extra bracing required to withstand handling. Figure 6-23 shows an example of a giant form in place (notice the adjustable ends on the braces).

Special attention must be given to corners when forms are being erected. These are weak points because the continuity of sheathing and wales is broken. Forms must be pulled tightly together at these points to prevent leakage of concrete. One method of doing this is illustrated in Fig. 6-24. Another system involves the use of corner brackets and tie rods, as shown in Fig. 6-25. Vertical rods running through a series of metal eyes fastened to the sheathing panels are also used to secure forms at the corners (see Fig. 6-26). Another way of making a tight corner is to overlap the wales at the corner and to provide a vertical kick strip for each group of wale ends. Wedges behind each wale tighten the corner.

Openings in concrete walls are made by setting *bucks* into the form at the required position. Bucks are

Fig. 6-24. Producing tight corners (Courtesy Jahn Concrete Forming)

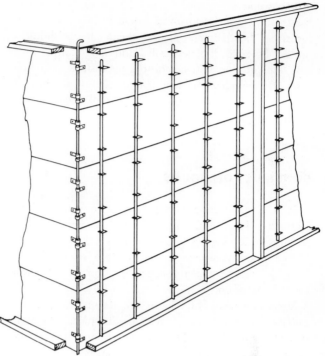

Fig. 6-26. Corner rods and eyes

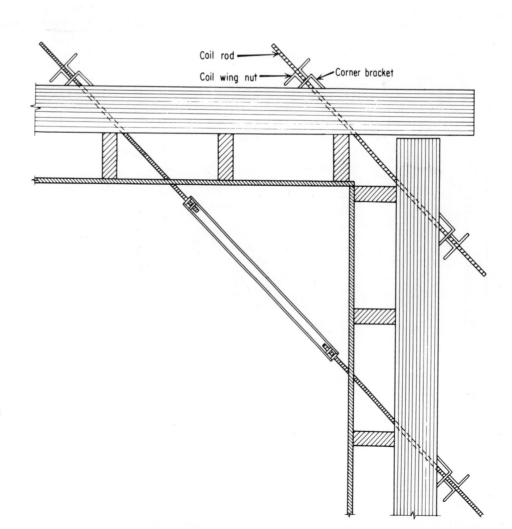

Coil rod

Coil wing nut

Corner bracket

Fig. 6-25. Corner brackets and tie rods

simply wooden or steel frames which are set between the inner and outer forms and held in place so that the forms can be tightened against them. Bucks should be braced horizontally, vertically, and diagonally so that concrete pressure will not distort their shape. In some cases, the window or door frame itself is set into the form. Care must be taken that proper anchorage is provided so that the frame will not move in the opening.

CONSTRUCTION JOINTS

It is often necessary to pour long or high walls in sections. This results in a vertical joint (where two sections of a long wall meet), or in a horizontal joint (when high walls are poured in two or more lifts). Such joints are called *construction* joints and require special attention.

Vertical construction joints are formed by placing a *bulkhead* in the form. It may be one piece of material placed vertically in the form or a number of short pieces placed horizontally. The latter is preferable when horizontal reinforcing bars project beyond the bulkhead, because the pieces can be cut to fit around the bars. In Fig. 6-28, the bulkhead is held in place by vertical strips nailed to the inside faces of the forms. Another method of securing the bulkhead is shown in Fig. 6-29.

It is usually desirable to provide a key between ad-joining sections to prevent lateral movement. One method of doing this is to attach a tapered strip to the inside face of the bulkhead, as shown in Fig. 6-29. Another type of key consists of a 6 in. strip of corrugated copper or galvanized iron to bridge the joint. The strip is bent into a right angle and fastened to the inside face of the bulkhead, as shown in Fig. 6-30. When the bulkhead is removed, the bent half is straightened out and projects into the adjacent pour. The metal also acts as a *waterstop*, to prevent passage of water through the joint.

Many types of waterstop are used, most of them made of rubber, neoprene, or some composition material. Two typical waterstops and their methods of installation are illustrated in Figs. 6-31 and 6-32.

Two important factors are involved when making horizontal construction joints. One is the necessity of having the two concrete pours bond at the joint, and the other, in certain cases, is the requirement that the joint be invisible or as inconspicuous as possible.

When the form for the first lift is built, a row of bolts is placed near the top of the lift. After this pour has set, the forms are stripped and raised as required for the next lift and supported on bolts placed in the top holes previously cast. A row of ties should be placed about 6 in. above the joint between the lifts to prevent leakage and help make the joint inconspicuous.

Hiding of horizontal construction joints is often accomplished by the use of *rustication strips*. These are narrow strips of various shapes (see Fig. 6-33) nailed

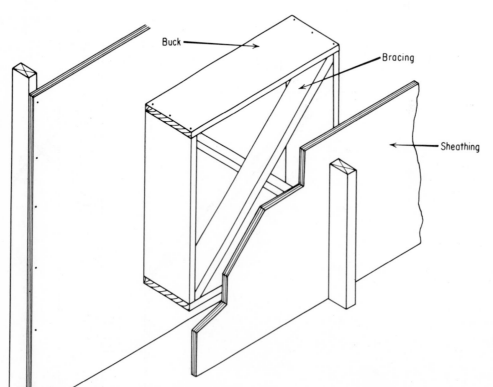

Fig. 6-27. Simple buck in form

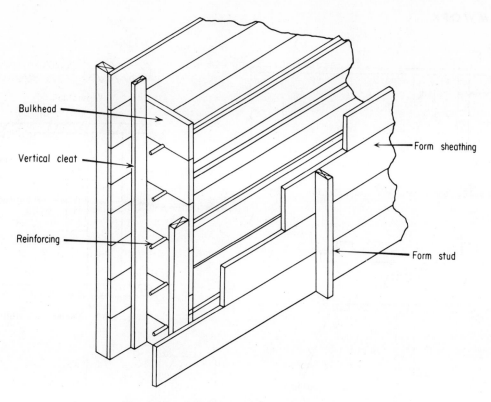

Fig. 6-28. Bulkhead made with horizontal pieces

Bulkhead

Vertical cleat

Reinforcing

Form sheathing

Form stud

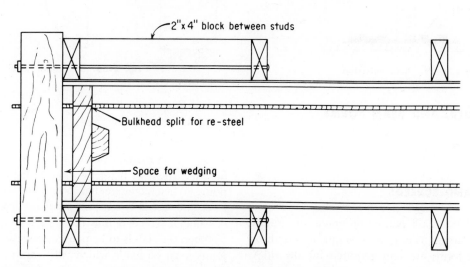

2"x 4" block between studs

Bulkhead split for re-steel

Space for wedging

Fig. 6-29. One method of securing a bulkhead

to the inside face of the form at the level of the joint. Concrete is poured to a height slightly above that required and then cut back to it.

CONTROL JOINTS

Control joints in concrete are those which are made to control cracking by expansion and contraction. They are formed by fastening a beveled insert of wood, metal, rubber, etc., to the inside face of the form. This insert produces a groove in the concrete which will control surface cracking. After the concrete has set, the insert may be removed and the joint can be caulked. Rubber inserts may be left in place. Figure 6-34 illustrates the forming of control joints. When a waterstop is required at a control joint, a rubber stop like that shown in Fig. 6-32 is often used.

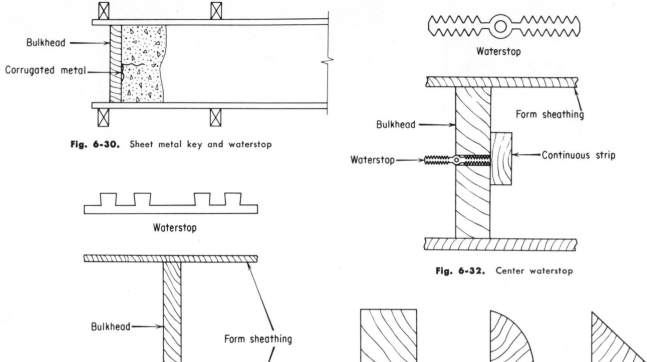

Fig. 6-30. Sheet metal key and waterstop

Fig. 6-31. Side waterstop

Fig. 6-32. Center waterstop

Fig. 6-33. Rustication strips

COLUMN, GIRDER, AND BEAM FORMS

See Chapter 9

SLAB FORMS AND SCREEDS

Forms for concrete slabs poured on grade are usually quite simple. Concrete is cast on a compacted earth or gravel base and forms are only required for the sides. Plywood, planks, or metal edge forms are commonly used. Wood forms are held in place by iron or wooden stakes. Metal edge forms (Fig. 6-35) are commonly used for large jobs and highway work.

Plastic sheets are often laid over a compacted base to act as moisture barriers. Welded wire mesh is laid down as slab reinforcement (Fig. 6-36), and the slab is poured.

It is often necessary to lay down temporary guides—*screeds*—in the slab area to bring it to the correct grade. One method of doing this is to set a 2″ by 4″ on edge (held in place by stakes) in the required position. When concrete has been poured to the correct level, the screed is removed and the depression is filled. A wooden screed is illustrated in Fig. 6-37.

When the slab is to be poured in sections, *construction* joints must be made which will transmit shear between adjacent sections. The simplest form for making such a joint is shown in Fig. 6-38. Metal forms like the one shown in Fig. 6-39 are also available.

Forms for *contraction* joints may be made in several ways. One common method is to insert a wood or metal strip into the slab, top or bottom, to form a plane of weakness. Figure 6-40 illustrates another method of providing a contraction joint—by sawing part-way through the slab with a carborundum blade. A construction joint may also act as a contraction joint.

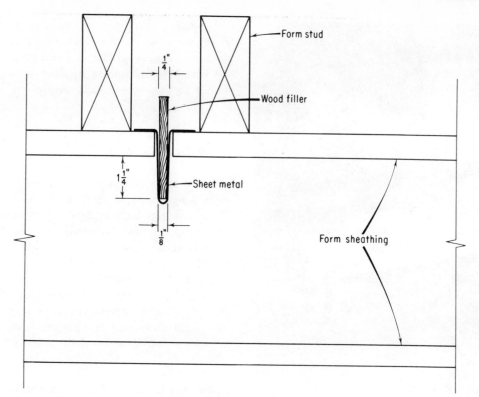

Fig. 6-34. Control joint form

Fig. 6-35. Steel slab edge form

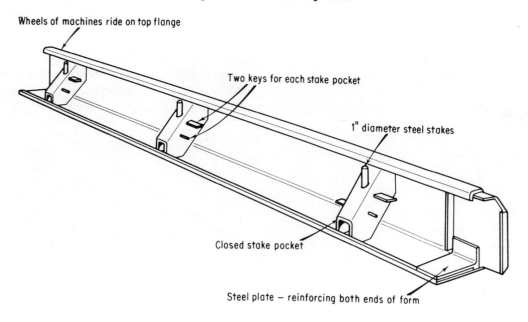

Fig. 6-36. Wire mesh slab reinforcement

Expansion joints are necessary in slab construction. They may be formed around walls, columns, and machine bases by placing a wood or metal strip along the base. Joints similar to those shown in Fig. 6-42 should be used where expansion joints will be crossed by traffic.

FORM ACCESSORIES

A vast array of products is currently available to aid in making forms stronger and erecting them faster. These products include items which have already been mentioned in this chapter, such as *ties, spreaders, wedges, corner brackets, waler clips,* etc. They also include *snap ties* for special conditions, *rock anchors, beam hangers, waterstops* and *keys, masonry ties, column clamps, shores, form rods, concrete inserts, sleeves, slab pans,* and many others. Detailed information on the uses of all these may be obtained from brochures and catalogues published by their manufacturers.

FORM TREATMENT, CARE, AND REMOVAL

In nearly all types of building construction, formwork

Fig. 6-37. Wooden slab screed

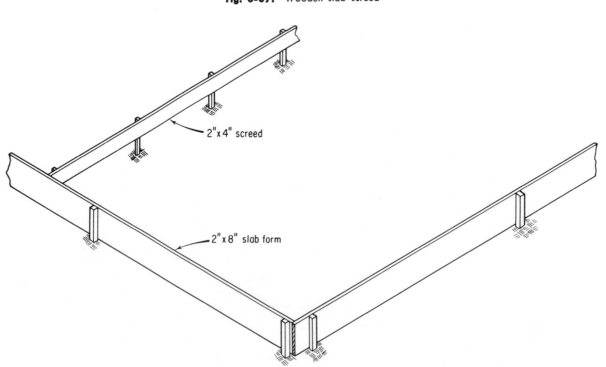

2" x 4" screed

2" x 8" slab form

Fig. 6-38. Simple construction joint form for slab

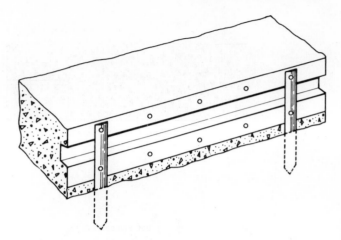

Fig. 6-39. Metal construction joint form

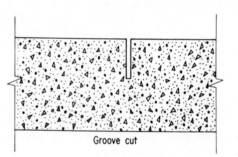

Groove cut

Slab contracted

Fig. 6-40. Sawed contraction joint

Fig. 6-41. Expansion joint at wall or column

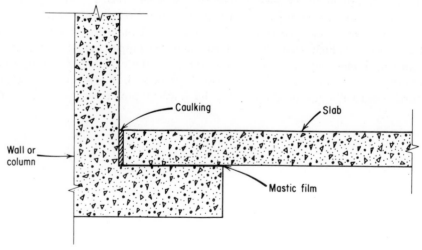

Wall or column

Caulking

Slab

Mastic film

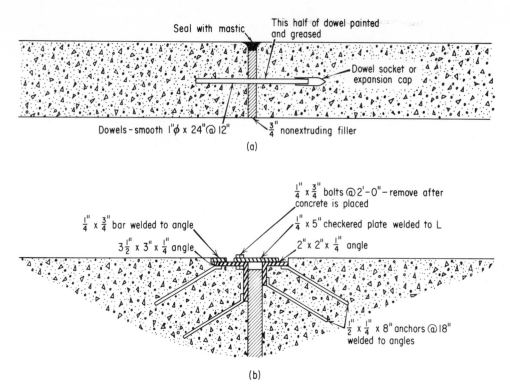

Fig. 6-42. Expansion joints in traffic area

constitutes a significant part of the cost of the building. In order to keep this cost at a minimum, forms are often made reusable, either wholly or in part. They must therefore be designed so that removal is simple and can be accomplished without damage to the form sections. Care must be taken in handling and storing these units so they will not be broken or damaged and will be available for reuse.

In order to facilitate removal, form faces must be treated to prevent concrete from adhering to them. A number of materials are available for this purpose, usually consisting of liquids which are to be brushed or sprayed on the form. Wooden forms must be treated to minimize absorption of water. Oil is one material used for this purpose. Form sealers which coat the surface of the form with an impervious film are also used for this type of treatment.

Form removal must be carried out without damaging either the forms or the structure being stripped. Levers should not be used against the concrete to pry forms away because green concrete is relatively easy to damage. If levering action is necessary, pressure should be applied against a broad, solid base. Form panels being removed from a wall section should be pulled straight off over the tie rods.

The production of concrete structures of desired size, shape, and strength—yet pleasing to the eye—can be achieved if a number of important points are remembered. Forms must be properly *designed*, carefully *constructed*, and *erected*. They must receive the appropriate *surface treatment*. *Tying*, *bracing*, and *shoring* must be adequate for the particular job involved. There must be proper *handling*, *placing*, *consolidation*, and *curing* of the concrete, and *form removal* must be carried out in such a way that no damage is incurred by the finished product.

REVIEW QUESTIONS

1. What seven basic features must forms have to fulfill their function?

2. Give three reasons for not including the earth as part of a form.

3. What is meant by *rate of pour?*

4. List three factors used in determining the rate of pour.

5. List the four main factors determining the pressure on forms.

6. Give two basic reasons for treating forms before using them.

7. Give three common methods of providing support against lateral pressure to square or rectangular forms.

8. Differentiate between a *construction joint* and an *expansion joint.*

9. List four factors which determine when forms may be removed.

10. Define the following: (a) form clearance; (b) form accessories; (c) prefabricated forms; (d) slip form; (e) form buck.

CONCRETE WORK 7

The extensive use of concrete is ample proof of its outstanding characteristics as a building material. It is such a familiar material that we take for granted the remarkable process by which cement and water, mixed with a wide range of aggregate materials, are converted into a strong and durable material of almost any desired shape. The development of modern Portland cements which can set quickly, even under water, began over one hundred years ago when the raw materials and processes needed for their manufacture were first recognized. Today, hundreds of scientists, engineers, and technicians are engaged in studying these materials, attempting to understand and to improve them still further.

Many of the physical and chemical reactions which take place during the setting and aging of concrete are so complicated that they are not yet fully understood. This is due in part to the wide range of chemical substances that can exist, partly by design and partly by chance, in any given concrete mix. Additional factors may be introduced in the methods of manufacture, handling, and curing at the site. All of the changes that take place relatively rapidly in the new concrete do not cease at the end of the formal curing period. Some may continue over a long period of time, and some may only begin in the environment to which the concrete is subsequently exposed. Despite all these complications, concrete of predictable properties and performance can be produced—and this does not occur by chance.

It is fortunately unnecessary for the designer, specification writer, job engineer, or supplier to keep in touch with the whole field of concrete technology. There are a number of guides to good practice in the form of codes, standards, and specifications from sources such as the Canadian Standards Association, National Building Code, American Society for Testing Materials, and the American Concrete Institute. Nevertheless, it is highly desirable to have some idea of the general nature of the material and its more important properties.

CONCRETE DESIGN

Concrete results from the combination of cement and water paste with some type of aggregate. The paste surrounds the aggregate particles, and as it sets—returns to a limestone-like state—binds them together. At the same time, in order to form a dense concrete, the paste must fill the voids between the particles of aggregate (see Fig. 7-1).

For several reasons, it is desirable to use a maximum amount of aggregate when making concrete of any given strength. Among these reasons are the facts

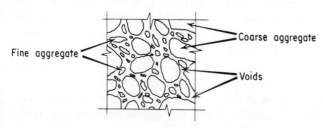

Fig. 7-1. Voids between aggregate particles

that cement is up to ten times more costly than aggregate, and that cement paste tends to shrink while setting and curing. The use of more paste than is necessary consequently produces excessive shrinking.

For the purpose of making concrete, natural aggregates—those formed from rock—are divided into two classes: fine aggregate (F.A.) and coarse aggregate (C.A.). Fine aggregate includes material that does not exceed $\frac{1}{4}$ in. in size, while coarse aggregate normally ranges from $\frac{3}{8}$ in. to 3 in., although sizes of up to 6 in. are used. Since aggregates form a considerable portion of the volume of a mix (from about 66% to 78%), it is important that they be of the best quality possible. It is therefore common practice to test concrete aggregates for cleanliness (the presence of excessive amounts of silt and/or fine organic matter), for density or specific gravity, for moisture content, and for proper distribution of particle sizes in a sample.

Silt clinging to the surface of coarse aggregates prevents proper bonding of the cement paste. In fine aggregates, the presence of too much very fine material means a significant increase in the surface area to be covered with paste. This results in either the use of more paste or the thinning out of that already used. The presence of silt on coarse aggregate can usually be detected visually, but in the case of fine aggregate, a *silt test* is used to determine the amount present. In making a silt test, proceed as follows:

Place 2 in. of the fine aggregate to be tested in a standard one quart glass jar. Fill the jar $\frac{3}{4}$ full of water, replace the cover, and shake well. Let the jar stand for several hours until the water has cleared. Upon settling, the fine silt will form a layer on top of the sand. If this layer exceeds $\frac{1}{8}$ in. in depth, the aggregate is unfit for making good concrete unless part of this material is removed.

The presence of small amounts of fine organic matter in a cement paste retards its setting action, sometimes so much so that a mix will dry out before setting properly. To test for the presence of harmful amounts of this organic matter in fine aggregate, a *colorimetric test* is used. The test is as follows:

Place 4 oz of the aggregate to be tested into a small jar or bottle. Then fill to $7\frac{1}{2}$ oz with a 3% solution of sodium hydroxide ($NaOH$). Shake well and allow to stand for 24 hr. The presence of organic matter will cause color changes in the clear solution varying from a very light straw color to a deep chocolate brown. If the color ranges from light to dark straw, the aggregate is suitable. If, on the other hand, the color is darker than this, too much organic matter is present and the aggregate is unsuitable for concrete work.

There are many methods of finding the specific gravity of a material, but one commonly used for finding the specific gravity of natural aggregates is carried out as follows:

Take a metal can which holds 48 fl oz and drill a small hole in its side, about 3 in. from the top. Insert a short piece of curved copper tubing into the hole and solder it in place as illustrated in Fig. 7-2. Fill the can with water, which will flow from the tube until its level reaches that of the hole. Set a graduated flask under the tube as shown in Fig. 7-3. Weigh out very carefully 1000 gr of the aggregate to be tested and pour it into the can. Water will overflow into the flask until it reaches its original level. The water in the flask is the amount displaced, and represents a volume equal to that of the aggregate. Read the volume in cu cm on the flask and divide 1000 by this figure. The result—usually in the neighborhood of 2.65—is the specific gravity of the aggregate. For example, suppose that the volume of the displaced water is 370 cu cm. The specific gravity of this particular sample will then be: $1000 \div 370 = 2.70$.

The proper gradation of particle sizes in the aggregate used to make concrete is essential for a number of reasons. It is apparent that the fewer the number of pieces required to fill any given volume, the smaller their total surface area becomes. This can be demonstrated with cubes or spheres, as in Fig. 7-4.

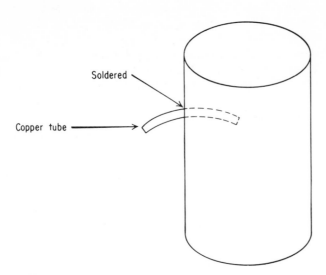

Soldered

Copper tube

Fig. 7-2. Can for measuring specific gravity of aggregates

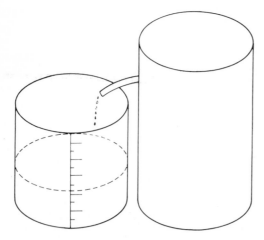

Fig. 7-3. Measuring displaced water

Since these pieces all have to be coated with cement paste, the smaller the surface area, the less paste required. In other words, the greater the maximum size of the aggregate, the more economical the job becomes.

But now let us take a small quantity of aggregate in which all the pieces are the same size. It is evident that no matter how these pieces are placed together there will always be spaces between them that cannot be filled, as shown in Fig. 7-5. If an aggregate of this type were used in making concrete, those spaces would have to be filled with cement paste, necessitating the use of a great deal more paste than would be required to simply coat the particles and bond them together. If smaller pieces of material were introduced, as illustrated in Fig. 7-6, a considerable portion of those spaces would be filled with aggregate. When still smaller pieces are used, more spaces are filled. This process can be continued until all the available particle sizes have been utilized. In other words, the proper gradation of particles, from the largest to the smallest, will effect an economy of paste.

Now let us go back to the situation in which all the pieces of aggregate were the same size and all the spaces were filled with paste. As previously mentioned, cement paste has a tendency to shrink as it sets. If the volumes of paste are relatively large, this shrinkage could result in the paste shrinking away from the aggregate, breaking their bonds, and leaving openings through which water can travel. Proper gradation can therefore affect the strength and watertightness of concrete. For these reasons, aggregates are tested to make sure that there is a proper gradation of sizes. This test is called a *fineness modulus test* and may be carried out on any aggregate.

Fig. 7-4. As particle size decreases per given volume, area increases

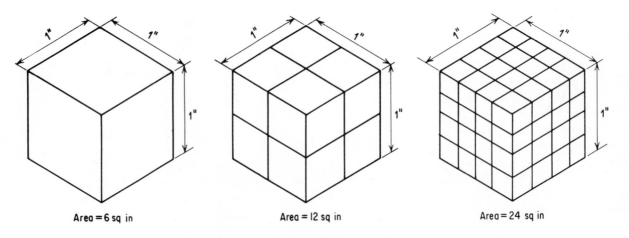

1" 1" 1"

Area = 6 sq in

1" 1" 1"

Area = 12 sq in

1" 1" 1"

Area = 24 sq in

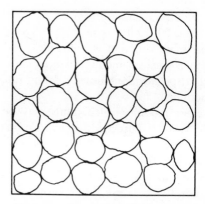

Fig. 7-5. Unavoidable spaces when size is uniform

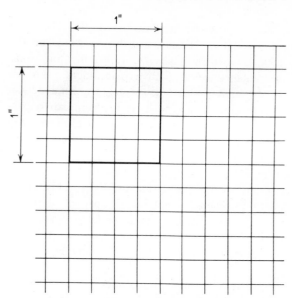

Fig. 7-7. #4 mesh screen

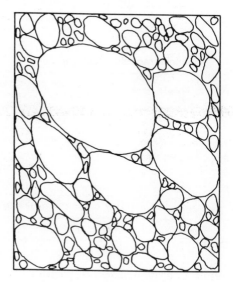

Fig. 7-6. Graded particle sizes

Fig. 7-8. Set of sand screens

When making a fineness modulus test on fine aggregate, a set of six standard wire screens is used, including a #4 sieve, having four wires per lineal inch or 16 openings per sq in., as illustrated in Fig. 7-7; a #8 sieve, with 64 openings per sq in.; a #16; a #30; a #50; a #100; and a pan to retain everything passing through the #100 sieve.

These sieves are stacked as shown in Fig. 7-8 so that aggregate placed in the top can pass through, to be held on any sieve with small enough mesh to retain that particular size. Very fine material passing the #100 sieve will be retained in the pan at the bottom.

Dry out a sample of the fine aggregate to be tested, very carefully weigh out 500 gr of it and place the sample in the top sieve (#4). The sieves may be shaken by hand or by a mechanical shaker. Shaking should continue for at least one minute. Weigh the material retained on each sieve, as illustrated in Fig. 7-9, and record the weights. Calculate the percentage of the total (500 g) which each size represents and total these percentages as cumulative percentages. This is done by beginning with the percentage retained on the #4 sieve and recording it as the cumulative percentage for that grade. The cumulative percentage for the next grade, (#8), is found by adding its percentage to the one above. Each grade is treated the same way. Now add these cumulative percentages together and divide the result by 100. This figure represents the fineness modulus number of that aggregate and is an indication of the relative fineness or coarseness of the material. Note than any material passing the #100 sieve is not included in the calculations.

Fineness modulus numbers for fine aggregate should range from 2.20 to 3.20 and any fine aggregate with a fineness modulus number falling within this range will generally be a suitable concrete aggregate, from a gradation standpoint.

The smaller numbers represent finer materials, aggregates with a greater proportion of fine particles, while larger numbers represent aggregates with a preponderance of large particles. Fine aggregate is classed as *fine, medium,* or *coarse*—depending on its fineness

Fig. 7-9. Weighing sand samples. (Courtesy Soiltest Inc.)

modulus. Fine sand ranges from 2.20 to 2.60, medium from 2.61 to 2.90, and coarse from 2.91 to 3.20. In cases where mass concrete is being designed, fine aggregate with a fineness modulus larger than 3.20 may be allowed. Specifications usually define the allowable fineness modulus.

The fineness modulus calculations may be recorded on a chart like that illustrated below. To better understand the procedure, let us go through a sample test. Suppose than a 500 gr sample has been put through the standard sieves and the results are as follows:

Retained on the #4 sieve, 12 gr; on the #8, 55 gr; on the #16, 100 gr; on the #30, 122 gr; on the #50, 118 gr; on the #100, 75 gr. Totaling these weights, it is found that 18 gr passed through to the pan below—weigh the contents of the pan to make sure. This information completes the chart as shown below.

Fineness Modulus Test for Sand

Sieve size	Weight retained	Percentage retained	Cumulative percentage
# 4	12 gr	2.4 %	2.4
# 8	55 gr	11.0 %	13.4
# 16	100 gr	20.0 %	33.4
# 30	122 gr	24.4 %	57.8
# 50	118 gr	23.6 %	81.4
# 100	75 gr	15.0 %	96.4
Pan	18 gr		Total = 284.8

Fineness modulus = 284.8 ÷ 100 = 2.85

The result indicates that this particular aggregate belongs in the medium sand category.

Fineness modulus is not an indication of whether there is the proper amount of each grade of sand in the sample, for a great number of gradings will give the same value for fineness modulus. However, it can be determined from the results of the test whether or not the sample contains the right proportion of each grade of sand.

This is done by plotting the percentages retained on each sieve on a graph such as that shown on this page. On this graph the solid line represents the ideal grading and the dotted lines show the maximum deviations. Consequently, when the test is plotted, the suitability of the sand is indicated. If necessary, recommendations may be made for blending in particular grades which the sample lacks.

Moisture content tests on aggregates, particularly fine aggregates, are carried out for two reasons. One is that the moisture content in a fine aggregate may necessitate adjusting the amount of water added to

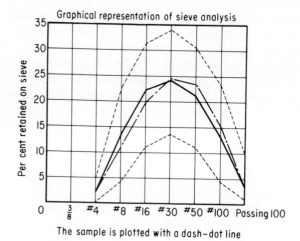

Graphical representation of sieve analysis

Per cent retained on sieve

$\frac{3}{8}$ #4 #8 #16 #30 #50 #100 Passing 100

The sample is plotted with a dash-dot line

the mix in order to produce a given strength. The other is that when water is present in certain proportions, a phenomenon known as *bulking* occurs. Volume increases considerably over that at a dry or saturated state because the particles are separated by a film of water. This means that when designing concrete mixes, it is much better to specify the amount of aggregate to be used by weight rather than by volume. It takes only a small compensation to make up for the difference in weight between dry and moist sand, while a large compensation is sometimes required if amounts to be used are specified by volume.

The amount of bulking varies with the fineness of the sand and the amount of moisture present—5% to 6% water, by weight—will produce maximum bulking and the condition is more pronounced in fine sand than

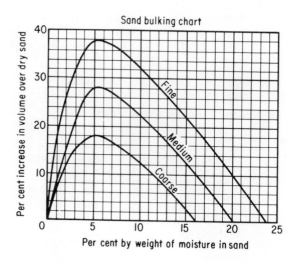

Sand bulking chart

Per cent increase in volume over dry sand

Fine

Medium

Coarse

0   5   10   15   20   25

Per cent by weight of moisture in sand

it is in coarse. The sand bulking chart below shows the percentage of increase in volume over dry sand for amounts of water varying from 0% to 25%, for fine, medium, and coarse sands.

The amount of water present in a sample is determined by carrying out a *moisture test*. Proceed as follows:

Weigh out a 500 g sample and spread it on the bottom of a flat metal pan about 12 in. in diameter and 1 in. deep. Set the pan over a heating unit and allow the sand to dry out, stirring continually. A change in the appearance of the sand can be noted as the moisture is driven off. When the material appears to be dry, weigh it again and record the weight. Dry once more and weigh again; it will probably have lost a little more weight this time. Continue this procedure until the weight remains constant. This is the dry weight. The total moisture content is found as follows:

$$\frac{\text{Loss in weight}}{\text{Dry weight}} \times 100 = \text{Percentage of moisture}$$

But a portion of the moisture driven off had been present in pores and cracks in the particles—adsorbed moisture—and was not available for reaction with cement. For average aggregates, it is assumed to be 1%. The free moisture—that which appears on the surface of the particles—is therefore found by subtracting 1 from the above result. In other words:

$$\frac{\text{Loss in weight}}{\text{Dry weight}} \times 100 - 1 = \text{Percentage of free moisture}$$

For example, if a 500 gr sample has a constant weight of 478 gr after drying, the loss in weight has been (500 − 478 =) 22 gr. The percentage of free moisture is then $\frac{22}{478} \times 100 - 1 = 3.6\%$

If this is the same sand which we previously tested for fineness modulus, we can tell by looking at the bulking chart that this medium sand, containing about 3½% free moisture, will increase by 24% over its dry volume.

There is cause for concern about the water present in aggregates used in making concrete. Concrete design is based on the theory that the strength of the concrete is regulated by the amount of water used per unit of cement, provided that the mix is plastic and workable. This is the water/cement ratio theory, which says that as the amount of water used per bag of cement is increased, the strength of the concrete will decrease. Table 7-1 gives the probable compressive strengths of concrete at 28 days, based on various water/cement ratios. Note that water quantities are given in pounds rather than gallons.

Table 7-1
Compressive Strengths for Various W/C Ratios

Water-cement ratio (lb per bag of cement)	Probable compressive strength at 28 days (in psi)	
	Plain concrete	Air-entrained concrete
66	2000	1600
60	2500	2000
54	3000	2400
50	3500	2800
44	4000	3200
40	4500	3600
36	5000	4000
33	5500	4400
30	6000	4800

Concrete design is also based on the assumption that sound coarse aggregate is absolutely essential to the production of high quality concrete. This being so, the best concrete is produced by using the largest size of aggregate and the greatest quantity of it, per given volume of concrete, that is compatible with job re-

quirements. However, there is a practical limit to the amount of coarse aggregate which can be used in any given situation, depending on the maximum size of the aggregate and the fineness modulus of the fine aggregate used with it. Table 7-2 gives the volume of coarse aggregate of various sizes that can be used per volume of concrete, for various fineness moduli of fine aggregate.

The largest size of coarse aggregate that can be used in any given situation depends on a number of things. Among them are: (1) the size of the unit being poured; (2) whether or not it is reinforced; and (3) the spacing of the reinforcement. Table 7-3 gives the recommended maximum sizes of coarse aggregate for various types of construction.

Another consideration in designing concrete is the desired plasticity or flowability of the mix. This will depend on the type of construction, the size of the unit being poured, and whether or not the unit is reinforced. This flowability is known as slump and is measured by testing with a slump cone in a pre-scribed manner (see page 122 for the description of a slump test). Table 7-4 gives recommended slumps for various types of construction.

Variations in slump for a given strength of concrete are produced by altering the amount of aggregate

Table 7-2
Volumes of C. A. to Be Used with Various F. M. of Sand

Maximum size of C. A.	Volume of dry rodded C.A. per unit volume of concrete for various F.M. of sand (%)										
	2.20–25	2.26–35	2.36–45	2.46–55	2.56–65	2.66–75	2.76–85	2.86–95	2.96–3.05	3.06–15	3.16–20
3/8 in.	0.48	0.47	0.46	0.45	0.44	0.43	0.42	0.41	0.40	0.39	0.38
1/2 in.	0.57	0.56	0.55	0.54	0.53	0.52	0.51	0.50	0.49	0.48	0.47
3/4 in.	0.67	0.66	0.65	0.64	0.63	0.62	0.61	0.60	0.59	0.58	0.57
1 in.	0.72	0.71	0.70	0.69	0.68	0.67	0.66	0.65	0.64	0.63	0.62
1-1/2 in.	0.78	0.77	0.76	0.75	0.74	0.73	0.72	0.71	0.70	0.69	0.68
2 in.	0.81	0.80	0.79	0.78	0.77	0.76	0.75	0.74	0.73	0.72	0.71
3 in.	0.86	0.85	0.84	0.83	0.82	0.81	0.80	0.79	0.78	0.77	0.76
6 in.	0.92	0.91	0.90	0.89	0.88	0.87	0.86	0.85	0.84	0.83	0.82

Table 7-3
Recommended Maximum Sizes of Aggregate for Various Types of Construction

Minimum dimension of section	Maximum size of aggregate			
	Reinforced walls, beams, and columns	Unreinforced walls	Heavily reinforced slabs	Lightly or unreinforced slabs
2-1/2 — 5 in.	1/2 — 3/4 in.	3/4 in.	3/4 — 1 in.	3/4 — 1-1/2 in.
6 — 11 in.	3/4 — 1-1/2 in.	1-1/2 in.	1-1/2 in.	1-1/2 — 3 in.
12 — 29 in.	1-1/2 — 3 in.	3 in.	1-1/2 — 3 in.	3 in.
30 in. or more	1-1/2 — 3 in.	6 in.	1-1/2 — 3 in.	3 — 6 in.

Table 7-4

Recommended Slumps for Various Types of Construction

	Slump	
	Maximum	Minimum
Reinforced foundation walls and footings	5 in.	2 in.
Plain footings, caissons, and substructure walls	4 in.	1 in.
Slabs, beams, and reinforced walls	6 in.	3 in.
Building columns	6 in.	3 in.
Pavements	3 in.	2 in.
Heavy, mass construction	3 in.	1 in.

used with that paste. However, experience has shown that in order to obtain a given slump, a fairly well fixed amount of water must be used per yard of concrete. This will vary, depending upon whether or not air entraining is used, and upon the maximum size of coarse aggregate used. Table 7-5 shows the approximate amount of water required for each yard of concrete under various conditions.

The amount of water used per bag of cement is influenced not only by the strength of concrete required but also by the climatic conditions to which the concrete will be subjected and by the thickness of the section and the location of the concrete—on land or in water. Table 7-6 gives the suggested water/cement ratio to be used under various conditions, depending on the thickness of the section and whether or not reinforcement is being used.

It has been stated earlier in this chapter that concrete is made by binding aggregates with cement paste

in such a way as to produce a strong, impervious material containing no voids in its bulk. In other words, a given quantity of concrete is made up of solid material—there are no air spaces involved. This product is made by mixing four ingredients, only one of which (water) contains no voids. The other three are made up of particles which have air spaces between them and, consequently, in a given volume of any of these, only part is actually usable. That part of the given volume which is actually cement or stone is known as the *absolute volume*—volume without voids. In order to get a true picture of the quantities of solid materials to be used to produce concrete, it seems reasonable to calculate these materials in terms of their absolute volume and then convert these to weights or actual volume. The absolute volume of a loose, dry material is found thus:

$$\text{Abs. vol.} = \frac{\text{Weight of loose, dry material}}{\text{Sp gr of material} \times \text{unit weight of water}}$$

For example, the absolute volume of a bag of cement 1 cu ft in actual volume, with a specific gravity of 3.15, will be:

$$\text{Abs. vol.} = \frac{87.5}{3.15 \times 62.4} = .45 \text{ cu ft}$$

In order to deal with aggregates in terms of absolute volume, it will be necessary to know the weights of the loose, dry materials. In the case of C.A., a 1 cu ft container should be used. It is filled in three layers, each rodded 25 times with a $\frac{5}{8}$ in. bullet-nosed rod. The top is struck off perfectly level and the net weight is found. This is the *dry rodded weight*. The value

Table 7-5

Approximate Mixing Water Requirements for Various Slumps and Maximum Sizes of C.A.

Slump	Water, lb per cu yd of concrete for indicated maximum sizes of C.A.							
	3/8"	1/2"	3/4"	1"	1-1/2"	2"	3"	6"
	Non-air entrained concrete							
1 to 2 in.	350	333	308	300	275	258	242	208
3 to 4 in.	383	367	342	325	300	284	267	234
6 to 7 in.	408	384	359	342	317	300	284	250
Approximate amount of entrapped air in %	3	2.5	2	1.5	1	.5	.3	.2
	Air entrained concrete							
1 to 2	308	300	275	258	242	225	209	184
3 to 4	342	325	300	284	267	250	234	200
6 to 7	359	342	317	300	284	267	250	217
Recommended average total air content in %	8	7	6	5	4.5	4	3.5	3

Table 7-6

Net Water/Cement Ratios for Various Types of Construction and Exposure Conditions

Type or location of structure	Severe or moderate climate, wide range of temperature, rain and long freezing spells or frequent freezing and thawing				
	Thin sections, 8 in. max. thickness, lb/sack		Moderate sections, 24 in. max. thickness, lb/sack		Heavy and mass sections, over 24 in. thick, lb/sack
	reinforced	plain	reinforced	plain	
1. At the water line in hydraulic or waterfront structures where complete saturation or intermittent saturation is possible, but not where the structure is continuously submerged:					
a. In seawater	40	42.5	42.5	47	47
b. In fresh water	42.5	47	47	50	50
2. Portions of hydraulic or waterfront structures some distance from the water line, but subject to frequent wetting:					
a. By seawater	42.5	47	47	47	47
b. By fresh water	47	50	50	50	50
3. Ordinary exposed structures, buildings, and portions of bridges not under above	47	50	50	55	55
4. Complete continuous submergence:					
a. In seawater	47	50	50	55	55
b. In fresh water	50	55	55	60	60
5. Concrete deposited through water	—	—	42.5	42.5	42.5
6. Base pavement slabs on ground	50	55			
Wearing slabs	42.5	74			

for 1 cu ft of sand is found without rodding, making sure that it is dry—in its SSD condition—(saturated surface dry).

With all this information, a concrete mix of given strength for a specific set of conditions can be designed. Follow the steps outlined below, record the information, and work out the solution on a worksheet like that illustrated in Table 7-7.

1. (a) Ascertain the maximum size of C.A. required for the job; (b) the specific gravity of the C.A. to be used; (c) free moisture in the C.A.; (d) the dry rodded weight of C.A. per cu ft.
2. Test F.A. to used for: (a) fineness modulus; (b) specific gravity; (c) free moisture; (d) weight per cu ft, SSD condition.
3. Decide on the W/C ratio for the specified concrete from Tables 7-1 and 7-6. If there is a difference between the amounts of water required per bag, choose the lesser ratio.
4. Check the maximum slump from specifications or take the recommendation from Table 7-4.
5. Find the amount of air expected (trapped or entrained) from specifications or Table 7-5.
6. Calculate the weight per cu ft, absolute volume of the C.A., and the F.A. by multiplying the specific gravity of each by 62.4, the unit weight of water.
7. Calculate the absolute volume of 1 cu ft of dry rodded C.A. by using the absolute volume formula.
8. Find the water required per yd of concrete and the expected amount of air from Table 7-5.
9. Calculate the cement factor—the number of sacks of cement required per yd of concrete, by dividing the water required per yd by the water required per sack, in lb.
10. Find the absolute volume of cement required per yd by multiplying the cement factor by 0.45.
11. Find the volume of water required per yd by dividing the weight of water per yd by the unit weight of water, 62.4 lb per cu ft.

12. Find the space per yd occupied by air, by multiplying the air percentage by 27.
13. Add the answers to 10, 11, and 12 to find the volume of the paste.
14. The absolute volume of aggregates required per yd of concrete will be 27 minus volume of paste.
15. Calculate the absolute volume of C.A. required per yd by multiplying the C.A. volume factor from Table 7-2 by the absolute volume of 1 cu ft of C.A. by 27.
16. Find the absolute volume of F.A. required per yd by subtracting the combined absolute volumes of C.A. and paste from 27.

Table 7-7

Mix Design Worksheet

Data:

Max. size C.A. =   in.; sp. gr. of C.A. =   ; free moisture in C.A. =   %; dry rodded wt/cu ft of C.A. =   lb; F.M. of F.A. =   ; spec. grav. of F.A. =   ; free moisture in F.A. =   %; wt/cu ft SSD condition =   lb; W/C ratio for concrete specified =   lb/sack; max. slump =   in.; air entrainment =   %.

Solution:

Wt/cu ft abs. vol. of F.A. = 62.4 × _____	=	lb
Wt/cu ft abs. vol. of C.A. = 62.4 × _____	=	lb
Abs. vol. of 1 cu ft dry rodded C.A. = ___ ÷ ___	=	cu ft
Water required/yd of concrete (from Table 7–5)	=	lb
Expected amount of air (from Table 7–5)	=	lb
Cement factor = _____ ÷ _____	=	sacks/yd
Abs. vol. of cement/yd of concrete = .45 × ___	=	cu ft
Vol. of water/yd of concrete = _____ ÷ 62.4	=	cu ft
Vol. of air = _____ × 27	=	cu ft
Vol. of paste/yd of concrete	=	cu ft
Abs. vol. of aggregates = 27 −	=	cu ft
C.A. vol. factor (from Table 7–2)	=	
Abs. vol. of C.A./cu yd = ___ × ___ × 27	=	cu ft
Abs. vol. of F.A./cu yd = 27 − (_____ + _____)	=	cu ft
Wt of dry F.A./yd of concrete = _____ × _____	=	lb
Wt of dry C.A./yd of concrete = _____ × _____	=	lb
Wt of moisture/yd of F.A. = _____ × _____	=	lb
Wt of moisture/yd of C.A. = _____ × _____	=	lb
Wt of moist F.A. req'd/yd = _____ + _____	=	lb
Wt of moist C.A. req'd/yd = _____ + _____	=	lb
Wt of added water req'd/yd = ___ − ___ − ___	=	lb

Mix design for 1 yd of concrete:
___ bags cement; ___ lb water; ___ lb C.A.; ___ lb F.A.

Mix design for 1 sack trial batch:
1 bag cement; ___ lb water; ___ lb C.A.; ___ lb F.A.

Estimated quantities:

Total volume of concrete req'd		=	yd
Cement req'd	= _____ × _____	=	sacks
F.A. req'd	= $\dfrac{\_\_ \times \_\_}{\_\_ \times 27}$	=	yd
C.A. req'd	= $\dfrac{\_\_ \times \_\_}{\_\_ \times 27}$	=	yd

17. The weights of dry F.A. and C.A. required per yd are found by multiplying their respective absolute volumes by their weight per cu ft, absolute volume.
18. Find the weights of moisture in F.A. and C.A. by multiplying the moisture percentage of each by the weight per yd of each.
19. The weights of moist F.A. and C.A. are then found by adding the weights of moisture to their respective dry weights.
20. The amount of water to be added per yd of the mix is found by subtracting the moisture in the F.A. and C.A. from the water required per yd.

Now the quantities of all the materials required to make a cu yd of concrete are known, and can be listed as shown in Table 7-7. But a trial mix, based on one sack of cement, will normally be required for test purposes. This is calculated by dividing each of the quantities mentioned by the cement factor.

Finally, an estimate of the amount of cement, F.A. and C.A., required for a specific job can be obtained as soon as the total number of yards of concrete involved are calculated. The amount of cement will be found by multiplying the number of yards of concrete required by the cement factor. The yards of fine aggregate required may be found by:

$$\frac{\text{Dry F.A./yd} \times \text{yds of concrete} \times \text{bulking factor}}{\text{Wt/cu ft} \times 27}$$

The coarse aggregate required will be calculated similarly:

$$\frac{\text{Dry C.A./yd} \times \text{yds of concrete}}{\text{Wt/cu ft} \times 27}$$

An alternative method of designing a concrete mix uses a prescribed percentage of sand in the total aggregate absolute volume as a basis for determining F.A. and C.A. quantities. Table 7-8 outlines the various percentages of sand to be used, depending on the fineness modulus of the sand, on whether the coarse aggregate is rounded or angular, on the maximum size of the C.A., and on the amount of water to be used per sack of cement.

The steps in designing a mix are the same as those outlined above up to and including step 14. The C.A. volume factor from Table 7-2 is not required in this method. From step 14, proceed as follows:

15. Calculate the absolute volume of the sand in the total aggregates by multiplying the figure found in the appropriate line in column 3 of Table 7-8 —sand, % of total—by the absolute volume of aggregate required per yd, from step 14.

Table 7-8

Suggested Trial Mixes for Concrete of Medium Consistency (3 in. Slump*)

With Fine Sand—Fineness Modulus 2.20-2.60

Max. size of coarse aggregate, in.	Water, gal per sack of cement	Using rounded coarse aggregate									Using angular coarse aggregate									
		Sand, % of total	Per sack cement		Per cu yd of concrete					Yield, cu ft concrete per sack cement	Sand, % of total	Per sack cement		Per cu yd of concrete					Yield, cu ft concrete per sack cement
			sand, lb	stone, lb	water lb	water gal	cement, sacks	sand, lb	stone, lb			sand, lb	stone, lb	water lb	water gal	cement, sacks	sand, lb	stone, lb	
3/4	4	41	165	230	310	31	7.75	1255	1805	3.48	46	160	190	335	33.5	8.37	1355	1595	3.23
1	4	36	150	260	300	30	7.50	1120	1985	3.60	41	150	225	325	32.5	8.13	1230	1760	3.32
1½	4	32	145	310	280	28	7.00	1025	2175	3.86	37	150	255	305	30.5	7.62	1140	1940	3.55
2	4	29	140	340	270	27	6.75	940	2300	4.00	34	145	280	295	29.5	7.37	1060	2050	3.67
3/4	4½	42	190	265	310	31	6.88	1315	1820	3.92	47	190	215	335	33.5	7.45	1420	1600	3.63
1	4½	37	175	300	300	30	6.67	1170	1995	4.05	42	180	250	325	32.5	7.22	1285	1775	3.74
1½	4½	33	170	350	280	28	6.22	1070	2180	4.34	38	175	290	305	30.5	6.78	1195	1955	3.98
2	4½	30	165	385	270	27	6.00	990	2310	4.50	35	170	315	295	29.5	6.56	1115	2070	4.12
3/4	5	43	220	290	310	31	6.20	1365	1815	4.36	48	220	240	335	33.5	6.70	1475	1600	4.03
1	5	38	205	330	300	30	6.00	1225	1995	4.50	43	210	275	325	32.5	6.50	1350	1775	4.16
1½	5	34	200	390	280	28	5.60	1125	2180	4.82	39	205	320	305	30.5	6.10	1245	1950	4.43
2	5	31	195	430	270	27	5.40	1040	2310	5.00	36	200	350	295	29.5	5.90	1165	2070	4.58
3/4	5½	44	250	320	310	31	5.64	1430	1790	4.79	49	250	260	335	33.5	6.10	1525	1590	4.43
1	5½	39	230	365	300	30	5.46	1265	1990	4.94	44	235	300	325	32.5	5.91	1390	1765	4.57
1½	5½	35	230	425	280	28	5.09	1170	2170	5.31	40	230	350	305	30.5	5.55	1295	1940	4.86
2	5½	32	220	470	270	27	4.92	1080	2300	5.49	37	225	385	295	29.5	5.37	1215	2060	5.03
3/4	6	46	290	340	310	31	5.17	1495	1760	5.23	50	280	280	335	33.5	5.58	1575	1575	4.94
1	6	41	270	390	300	30	5.00	1345	1940	5.40	45	265	325	325	32.5	5.41	1435	1755	4.99
1½	6	37	270	455	280	28	4.67	1250	2120	5.78	41	260	380	305	30.5	5.08	1340	1930	5.32
2	6	34	260	500	270	27	4.50	1160	2250	6.00	38	255	420	295	29.5	4.91	1260	2055	5.50
3/4	6½	47	320	365	310	31	4.77	1540	1740	5.67	51	315	300	335	33.5	5.16	1625	1560	5.23
1	6½	42	300	420	300	30	4.62	1390	1930	5.85	46	295	350	325	32.5	5.01	1480	1740	5.39
1½	6½	38	300	490	280	28	4.31	1290	2100	6.27	42	295	410	305	30.5	4.69	1385	1915	5.76
2	6½	35	290	535	270	27	4.16	1200	2230	6.49	39	285	450	295	29.5	4.54	1300	2040	5.94

With Medium Sand—Fineness Modulus 2.60-2.90

Max. size	Slump	1	2	3	4	5	6	7	8	9	10	11	12	13	14	15	16	17	18
3/4	4	43	170	225	310	31	7.75	1315	1740	3.48	48	170	185	335	33.5	8.37	1415	1535	3.23
1	4	38	155	260	300	30	7.50	1180	1930	3.60	43	160	210	325	32.5	8.13	1285	1700	3.32
1½	4	34	155	300	280	28	7.00	1090	2120	3.86	39	160	250	305	30.5	7.62	1200	1880	3.55
2	4	31	150	330	270	27	6.75	1005	2240	4.00	36	150	270	295	29.5	7.37	1125	1995	3.67
3/4	4½	44	200	255	310	31	6.88	1380	1755	3.92	49	200	205	335	33.5	7.45	1480	1540	3.63
1	4½	39	185	290	300	30	6.67	1235	1930	4.05	44	185	240	325	32.5	7.22	1345	1710	3.74
1½	4½	35	180	350	280	28	6.22	1140	2120	4.34	40	185	280	305	30.5	6.78	1260	1890	3.98
2	4½	32	175	370	270	27	6.00	1060	2240	4.50	37	180	305	295	29.5	6.56	1180	2000	4.12
3/4	5	45	230	280	310	31	6.20	1430	1750	4.36	50	230	230	335	33.5	6.70	1540	1540	4.03
1	5	40	215	320	300	30	6.00	1290	1930	4.50	45	215	260	325	32.5	6.50	1400	1710	4.16
1½	5	36	220	380	280	28	5.60	1190	2120	4.82	41	215	310	305	30.5	6.10	1310	1885	4.43
2	5	33	205	415	270	27	5.40	1100	2240	5.00	38	210	340	295	29.5	5.90	1230	2000	4.58
3/4	5½	46	260	310	310	31	5.64	1470	1740	4.79	51	260	250	335	33.5	6.10	1590	1530	4.43
1	5½	41	245	350	300	30	5.46	1340	1620	4.94	46	250	290	325	32.5	5.91	1450	1710	4.57
1½	5½	37	255	400	280	28	5.09	1300	2040	5.31	42	245	340	305	30.5	5.55	1360	1870	4.86
2	5½	34	255	435	270	27	4.92	1250	2130	5.49	39	240	370	295	29.5	5.37	1280	1995	5.03
3/4	6	48	300	330	310	31	5.17	1560	1690	5.23	53	300	265	335	33.5	5.58	1670	1485	4.94
1	6	43	285	375	300	30	5.00	1420	1880	5.40	48	280	305	325	32.5	5.41	1535	1660	4.99
1½	6	39	280	440	280	28	4.67	1315	2060	5.78	44	280	360	305	30.5	5.08	1440	1830	5.32
2	6	36	270	485	270	27	4.50	1230	2180	6.00	41	275	400	295	29.5	4.91	1360	1950	5.50
3/4	6½	49	340	350	310	31	4.77	1610	1675	5.67	54	335	285	335	33.5	5.16	1720	1465	5.23
1	6½	44	315	405	300	30	4.62	1460	1860	5.85	49	315	330	325	32.5	5.01	1580	1640	5.39
1½	6½	40	315	470	280	28	4.31	1360	2040	6.27	45	315	390	305	30.5	4.69	1485	1815	5.76
2	6½	37	305	520	270	27	4.16	1270	2160	6.49	42	310	430	295	29.5	4.54	1400	1940	5.94

With Coarse Sand—Fineness Modulus 2.90-3.20

Max. size	Slump	1	2	3	4	5	6	7	8	9	10	11	12	13	14	15	16	17	18
3/4	4	45	180	220	310	31	7.75	1375	1680	3.48	50	175	175	335	33.5	8.37	1475	1475	3.33
1	4	40	165	250	300	30	7.50	1240	1865	3.60	45	165	205	325	32.5	8.13	1340	1645	3.32
1½	4	36	165	290	280	28	7.00	1150	2050	3.86	41	165	240	305	30.5	7.62	1265	1820	3.55
2	4	33	160	320	270	27	6.75	1070	2180	4.00	38	160	260	295	29.5	7.37	1185	1935	3.67
3/4	4½	46	210	245	310	31	6.88	1440	1690	3.92	51	205	200	335	33.5	7.45	1540	1480	3.63
1	4½	41	195	280	300	30	6.67	1300	1870	4.05	46	195	230	325	32.5	7.22	1410	1650	3.74
1½	4½	37	195	330	280	28	6.22	1200	2050	4.34	42	195	270	305	30.5	6.78	1320	1825	3.98
2	4½	34	190	360	270	27	6.00	1120	2180	4.50	39	190	295	295	29.5	6.56	1240	1940	4.12
3/4	5	47	240	270	310	31	6.20	1500	1690	4.36	52	240	220	335	33.5	6.70	1600	1475	4.03
1	5	42	225	310	300	30	6.00	1350	1870	4.50	47	225	255	325	32.5	6.50	1460	1650	4.16
1½	5	38	225	365	280	28	5.60	1260	2050	4.82	43	225	300	305	30.5	6.10	1375	1825	4.43
2	5	35	215	400	270	27	5.40	1170	2180	5.00	40	220	330	295	29.5	5.90	1295	1940	4.58
3/4	5½	48	275	295	310	31	5.64	1550	1675	4.79	53	270	240	335	33.5	6.10	1650	1470	4.43
1	5½	43	255	340	300	30	5.46	1400	1860	4.94	48	260	280	325	32.5	5.91	1515	1640	4.57
1½	5½	39	260	405	280	28	5.09	1320	2060	5.31	44	255	330	305	30.5	5.55	1420	1815	4.86
2	5½	36	250	440	270	27	4.92	1220	2160	5.49	41	250	360	295	29.5	5.37	1340	1930	5.03
3/4	6	49	310	320	310	31	5.17	1590	1660	5.23	55	310	255	335	33.5	5.58	1735	1420	4.94
1	6	44	290	370	300	30	5.00	1450	1840	5.40	50	295	295	325	32.5	5.41	1595	1595	4.99
1½	6	40	290	430	280	28	4.67	1350	2020	5.78	46	295	350	305	30.5	5.08	1505	1770	5.32
2	6	37	280	475	270	27	4.50	1260	2150	6.00	43	290	385	295	29.5	4.91	1420	1875	5.50
3/4	6½	50	340	340	310	31	4.77	1640	1640	5.67	56	350	270	335	33.5	5.16	1785	1400	5.23
1	6½	45	320	395	300	30	4.62	1490	1825	5.85	51	330	315	325	32.5	5.01	1640	1580	5.39
1½	6½	41	330	470	280	28	4.31	1410	2020	6.27	47	330	370	305	30.5	4.69	1550	1750	5.76
2	6½	38	315	510	270	27	4.16	1310	2130	6.49	44	320	415	295	29.5	4.54	1470	1870	5.94

*Increase or decrease water content 3% for each increase of 1 in. in slump. For stone sand, increase percentage of sand by about 3 and water content by about 15 lb per cu yd of concrete. For less workable concrete, as in pavements, decrease percentage of sand by about 3 and water content by 8 lb per cu yd of concrete.

16. Find the absolute volume of C.A. required per yard by subtracting the combined absolute volumes of F.A. and paste from 27.

From this point on, the method is the same as previously described.

In addition to supplying data for designing a concrete mix, Table 7-8 has other useful information. It suggests trial mixes based on one sack of cement and it gives the amounts of material required for one cu yd of concrete under various conditions as outlined above. It also gives the amount of concrete that can be expected from each of the various trial mixes based on one sack of cement.

The presence of air in a concrete mix, either incidental or purposeful, has been noted in Table 7-5. Air is added intentionally in the form of millions of tiny bubbles which serve a number of useful purposes. Air-entrained concrete has greater flowability than plain concrete of similar composition. In other words, the water content can be reduced, thus increasing strength while retaining the same amount of slump. Air-entrained concrete is also more resistant to freezing and thawing cycles than plain concrete. Air is entrained into the concrete by the addition of *air entraining agents* into the mix. These agents are one of a series of additives commonly used in concrete design today.

One type of additive is called an *accelerator*, a chemical which speeds up the initial set of concrete. The most common material for this purpose is calcium chloride, used at the rate of not more than 2 lb per bag of cement. Another additive is used as a *dispersal agent*—a material which acts to separate individual particles of cement, thus allowing each one to come in full contact with water and hydrate completely. The cement can thus develop its full potential of strength.

Other additives act as *retarders*, and slow up the initial set of cement. This action is important when pouring deep girders in hot weather, for example. The first pour tends to set up before the next one can be placed, thus making it difficult to integrate the two and produce a monolithic member. A retarder used in the concrete placed at the bottom of the girder will delay its initial set until the remainder of the concrete has been poured. As a result, the set will be uniform throughout.

Additives are also available for use as hardeners and waterproofers. It is a good idea to contact the manufacturer or his agent and obtain full details on the proper use of these particular products prior to initial usage.

Regardless of tests made on materials which go into the making of concrete and of the care taken in designing a mix, tests are carried out on the concrete itself to make sure that it conforms to specifications. These tests normally consist of a *slump test*, a *compression test*, and sometimes a *flexure test*.

A slump test is made to insure that the concrete has the flowability required for placing. A slump or slump range will usually be stipulated in specifications. The test is carried out as soon as a batch of concrete is mixed, and a standard slump cone and tamping rod are required to carry it out. The cone is made of sheet metal, like that in Fig. 7-10, 4 in. in diameter at the top, 8 in. in diameter at the bottom, and 12 in. high. The rod is a ⅝ in. bullet-nosed rod about 24 in. long. The cone is filled in three equal layers, each tamped 25 times with the rod. After the third layer is in place and has been tamped, the concrete is struck off level, the cone is lifted carefully and set down beside the slumped concrete, and the rod is laid across the top. The distance from the underside of the rod

Fig. 7-10. Slump cone diagram

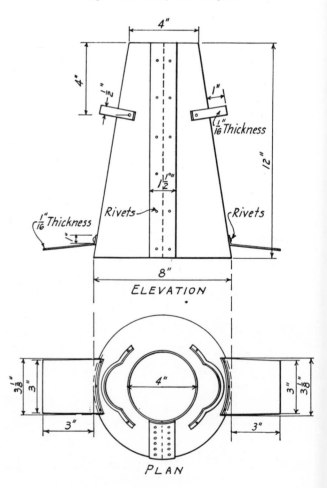

diameter and 12 in. high. One commonly used type of container is made of stiff waxed cardboard with a metal bottom and cardboard top.

The cylinder is filled in three equal layers, each layer having been tamped 25 times with the standard tamping rod. The top is struck off level, the cap is placed on, and the specimen is weighed (see Fig. 7-11). It is then set aside for 24 hr. Several specimens (at least 4) should be taken of each mix to be tested. Two test cylinders can set under actual conditions and two can be taken to a laboratory for curing under ideal conditions.

After 24 hr, those cylinders to be cured in the lab will be removed from the containers and placed in warm, moist conditions—preferably a curing cabinet—to cure for the designated period. Those cylinders left to cure under job conditions may be left in their containers, but should preferably be removed when the forms are taken off or, in the case of slabs, after 24 hr —to simulate job conditions as closely as possible.

At the end of the curing period the cylinders are weighed again and capped with a thin layer of capping compound usually made of a sulphur-base material. Caps should be plane to within 0.002 in.

After a two hour period to allow the caps to harden, each cylinder is placed in a compression testing machine and broken, as illustrated in Fig. 7-13. A dial registers the total load required to break the cylinder and this is converted into psi's of ultimate strength. The chart shown above illustrates a method of recording all the information required of each specimen during the test period.

Flexure tests are sometimes made to determine the bending strength of a particular concrete. Forms used must provide a beam with a length at least 2 in. greater than 3 times its depth as tested. This minimum cross-sectional dimension must be at least 3 times the maximum nominal size of the coarse aggregate used, but in no case less than 6 by 6 in. After proper curing, the beam is tested for flexural strength by third-point or center-point loading.

USE OF FAST-SETTING CEMENTS

It is sometimes necessary to use concrete in situations when it is impossible to wait the required period for concrete made with normal Portland cement to set and strengthen. In these situations it is possible to use a high early strength Portland cement. The difference in early strength is illustrated in Fig. 7-14.

It is also possible to use aluminous cement, which gains its strength in a very short time compared to

Compression tests

Specimen number	Water cement ratio	Aggregate proportions	Slump	Size of cylinder	Method of curing	Tested wet or dry	Weight when made	Weight when tested	Number of specimen	Date made	Date tested	Compressive strength in psi	Remarks

Portland cement. Concrete made with Portland cement will gain about 10% of its 28-day strength in one day at a temperature of about 65°F. On the other hand, concrete made with aluminous cement attains the 28-day strength of that made from Portland cement in approximately 24 hr, at the same temperature. At 36°F, concrete made with normal Portland cement will have gained very little—if any—of its 28-day strength, while under similar conditions, concrete made with aluminous cement will have gained about 50% of the 28-day strength of Portland cement concrete.

This fast-setting feature makes aluminous cement particularly valuable when concrete must be placed in cold weather. A considerable amount of heat is generated during the hydration process, and that heat is usually sufficient to insure the continuation of the hardening process if the concrete is protected from freezing for the first 6 hr.

PREPARATION FOR POURING CONCRETE

Before placing concrete, the subgrade must be properly prepared and forms and reinforcing must be erected according to specifications. Subgrades must be

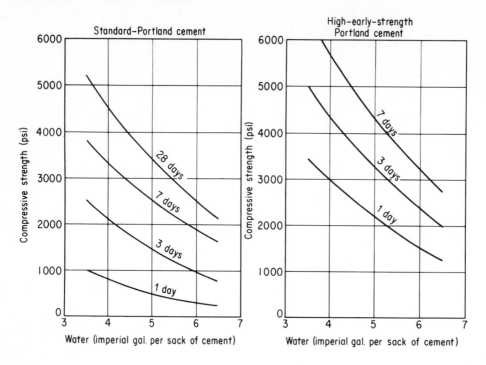

Fig. 7-14. Early strength of normal Portland and high early strength cements.

trimmed to specific elevation and should be moist when the concrete is placed. A moist subgrade is particularly important to prevent overly rapid extraction of water from concrete when flat work—such as floors

and pavements—are being poured in hot weather. When concrete is being poured on a rock foundation, all loose material should be removed before it is placed. If rock has to be cut, the rock faces should be vertical or horizontal, not sloping.

Forms must be made of material that will impart the desired texture to the concrete, and should be clean, tight, and well braced. They should be oiled, or treated with some type of form seal that will prevent them from absorbing water from the concrete and will facilitate form removal. Care must be taken to see that sawdust, nails, or other debris are removed from the bottom of the forms. Column and tall wall forms should have "windows" at the bottom to facilitate debris removal. It is also important that reinforcing steel be clean and free from scales or rust.

When fresh concrete is to be placed on hardened concrete, it is important to secure a good bond and a watertight joint. The hardened concrete should be fairly level, rough, clean, and moist. Some of the aggregate particles should be exposed by cutting away part of the existing surface by sand blasting, by cleaning with hydrochloric acid, or using a wire brush. Any laitance or soft layer of mortar must be removed from the surface.

When concrete is to be poured on a hardened concrete surface or on rock, a layer of mortar should be placed on the hard surface first. This provides a cushion on which the new concrete can be placed and stops aggregate from bouncing on the hard surface and

Table 7-9

Effect of Temperature on the Strength of Concrete

Crushing strength of 1:2:4 concrete expressed as a percentage of 28-day strength of normal Portland cement concrete.

Type of cement	Age (days)	Low temperature (36°F)	Normal temperature (64°F)
Normal Portland cement	1	0	10
	3	10	37
	7	25	64
	14	55	80
	28	92	100
	56	108	110
Rapid hardening Portland cement	1	0	20
	3	12	59
	7	37	93
	14	70	107
	28	118	126
	56	135	135
High alumina cement	1	54	146
	3	164	188
	7	188	197
	14	197	212
	28	207	218
	56	222	229

forming stone pockets. The mortar should be about 2 in. deep, with the same water content as the concrete being placed and a slump of 5 to 6 in.

Preparations must also include the building of adequate runways for wheelbarrows or buggies. Runways should be reasonably smooth, and stiff enough to prevent the wheelbarrows or buggies from bouncing or jarring as they travel. Some means of pouring concrete from the wheelbarrow, buggy, or bucket into the forms must also be provided. This may consist of a baffle board, hopper, downspout, or chute. These will be discussed in another section.

MIXING CONCRETE

Concrete should be mixed until it is uniform in appearance and consistency. The time required for mixing depends on the volume and stiffness of the mix and, to some extent, on the size of the C.A. and the fineness of the sand. Specifications usually require a minimum of one minute for mixers of up to 1 cu yd capacity, with an increase of at least 15 sec for every ½ cu yd (or fraction thereof) of additional capacity. If mixes are stiff, additional time will be required, and the same is true for mixes containing fine sand or small C.A. The mixing time begins when all materials are in the mixer drum.

Batch mixers are available in sizes varying from 1½ cu ft to 4 cu yd capacity. For general construction work, standard mixers are rated at 3½, 6, 11, 16, and 28 cu ft of mixed concrete. For larger jobs and central mixing plants, mixers of 2 to 8 cu yd capacity are used.

Mixers may be tilting or nontilting with either high or low loading skips. High loading skips are suitable when the skip is being charged from a bin batcher, but the low loading type is preferable if the skip has to be charged by shovel or wheelbarrow. Nontilting mixers may be equipped with a swinging discharge chute. Many mixers are provided with timing devices so that they can be set for a given mixing period and cannot be opened until the designated mixing time is up.

Mixers should not be loaded beyond their rated capacity and should not be operated at speeds other than those for which they were designed. Overloading or running either too fast or too slowly prevents the proper mixing action from taking place. When increased output is required, a larger mixer or additional ones should be used.

Under usual conditions, no more than about 10% of the mixing water should be placed in the drum

Fig. 7-15. 6 cu ft concrete mixer. (Courtesy Muller Machinery Co.)

before the dry materials are added. Water should then be added uniformly with the dry materials, leaving about 10% to be added after all the dry materials are in. If heated water is used during cold weather, this order may have to be changed. In this case, addition of cement should be delayed until most of the aggregate and water are mixed in the drum. This is done to prevent a flash set of the paste, a set brought about by too much heat when the water and cement combine.

The initial set of cement paste does not usually take place until 2 to 3 hr after it is mixed. Freshly mixed concrete that is left standing tends to dry out and stiffen somewhat before the paste sets. Concrete such as this may be used if, upon remixing, it becomes plastic enough to be properly consolidated in the forms. However, water should not be added, for this lowers the quality of the concrete.

MACHINERY FOR TRANSPORTING CONCRETE

Concrete may be mixed on the job site or brought to it from a mixing plant. In either case, a variety of methods may be used to transport the concrete from mixer to form and one of the prime considerations—regardless of method—is the prevention of segregation. Segregation is the separation of coarse aggregate from the mortar or of water from the other ingredients.

Concrete mixed on the job is transported to the

Fig. 7-16. Placing concrete by wheelbarrow. (Courtesy Gar-Bro. Mfg. Co.)

forms by *wheelbarrows, push-buggies, power-operated buggies, chutes,* and by crane-hoisted *buckets.*

On small jobs, concrete is transported by wheelbarrows (see Fig. 7-16), and the important thing is to provide smooth runways for their travel. Bouncing results in segregation in the wheelbarrows, thus causing concrete to be placed in a separated state.

Push carts and power buggies are made in a variety of sizes, from about 3½ to 11 cu ft capacity, and are today equipped with pneumatic tires for smoother operation (see Fig. 7-17). They must also be provided with smooth and rigid runways to minimize segregation.

Chutes may be used to carry concrete directly from mixer to forms or from a hopper conveniently situated

Fig. 7-17. Concrete power buggy. (Courtesy Whiteman Mfg. Co.)

to allow chuting. Chutes should be metal or metal-lined, with rounded bottoms, and of sufficient size to guard against overflow. They should be designed so that concrete will travel fast enough to keep the chute clean but not fast enough to cause segregation. It is generally recommended that the slope of chutes should be between 3 to 1 and 2 to 1, although steeper chutes may be used to carry stiff mixes.

Buckets lifted and moved about by crane or cable are commonly used where concrete has to be placed at a considerable height above ground level or where forms are in otherwise inaccessible locations.

Fig. 7-18 Concrete bucket. (Courtesy Gar-Bro. Mfg. Co.)

Buckets vary in size from about ½ to 8 cu yd capacity and may be circular or rectangular in cross section (see Fig. 7-18). The load is released by opening a gate which forms the bottom of the bucket. Gates which can regulate the flow and close when only part of the load has been discharged are preferred where sections are small and it is not desirable to place a full load in one location.

Care should be taken to prevent jarring or shaking buckets while they are in transit. This will cause

Fig. 7-19. Transit mix truck. (Courtesy White Motor Co.)

segregation, particularly if the concrete has a relatively high rate of slump.

When concrete is brought to the job from a mixing area some distance away, any of a number of methods may be used. They include *dump trucks, transit mix trucks, agitator trucks, rail cars,* and *pipelines*.

Dump trucks should have a body of special shape, with rounded and sloping front and rounded bottom. The rear end should taper to a discharge gate to facilitate delivery of the load.

A transit mix truck is essentially a heavy-duty truck chassis and motor on which is mounted a large, drum-type concrete mixer. It is equipped with a water tank and auxiliary engine which operates the mixer (see Fig. 7-19). The dry ingredients for a concrete mix are charged into the truck from a batching plant. If

the distance to be traveled from batching plant to job site can be covered within initial setting time of the cement paste, water may also be added at the batcher. The concrete is then mixed and agitated en route. But when long distances are involved, the driver must add the water at the appropriate time along the way.

Transit mix trucks are available in sizes ranging from 1 to 12 cu yd capacity. Each batch of concrete should be mixed not less than 50 nor more than 100 revolutions of the drum or blades at the prescribed rate of rotation. Any additional mixing should be done at the designated agitating speed. Concrete should be delivered and discharged from the truck mixer within 1½ hr after the introduction of water to cement and aggregate.

An agitator truck is similar to a transit mix truck, except that it carries no water tank. This means that the complete mix is made up at the batching plant and charged into the truck drum. The truck simply keeps the concrete agitated until it is delivered. As a result, the distance that may be traveled is limited to that which can be covered within the initial setting time of the paste. In extremely hot weather, it may be necessary to use ice to keep the temperature down. This is done to prevent the initial set of concrete from taking place before it can be delivered.

Rail cars especially designed for transporting concrete are used only on large projects. Some are tilted to discharge through side or end gates while others discharge through bottom gates. Concrete is normally dumped into a large hopper from which short chutes or downspouts direct it to the forms. It is essential to

Fig. 7-20. Concrete batching plant

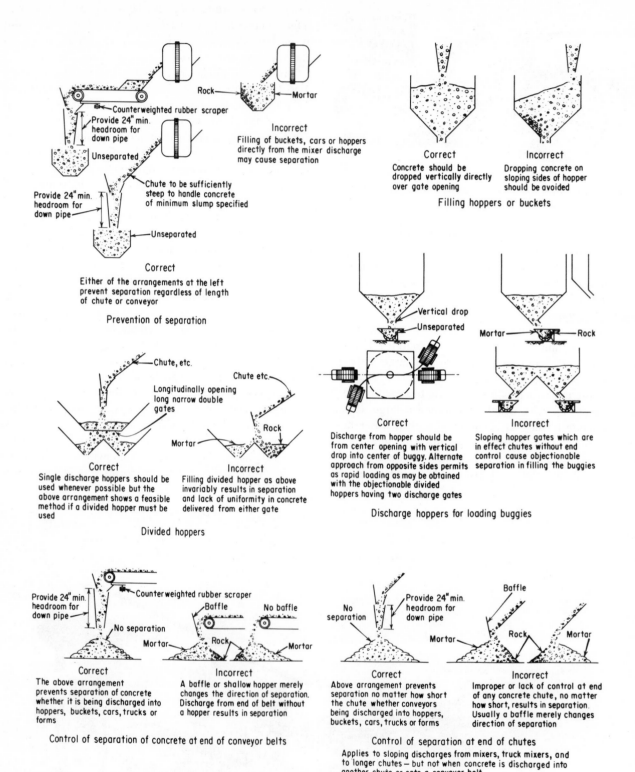

Fig. 7-21. Correct and incorrect methods of handling concrete. (Courtesy Portland Cement Co.)

closely supervise this operation in order to prevent segregation.

Concrete being transported by pipeline can be propelled by one of two methods. One is to use a heavy duty, horizontal piston-type pump and the other is to use compressed air. In either case, the concrete is delivered to a large hopper which feeds a constant flow of material to the pipeline. Best results are obtained when the slump is 3 in. or more, but concrete with considerably less slump has been pumped successfully.

A 6, 7, or 8 in. diameter pipe, with 45° or 90° bends if necessary, and vertical as well as horizontal runs is generally used. Vertical distances are calculated on the basis of 1 ft of vertical equaling 8 ft of horizontal. A 90° degree bend is equivalent to 40 ft of horizontal pipe and a 45° bend to 20 ft. Concrete can be transported up to 2000 ft of straight horizontal pipe by this method. Figure 7-21 illustrates correct and incorrect procedures in handling and transporting concrete.

PLACING CONCRETE

Concrete should be placed as nearly as possible in its final position. It should not be placed in large quantities in one position and allowed to flow or be worked over a long distance in the form. The mortar will tend to flow ahead of the coarser materials, thus causing stone pockets and sloping work planes.

Concrete poured in forms should *never* be allowed to drop freely more than 3 or 4 ft. When drops exceed this, rubber or metal chutes should be used. Figure 7-22 illustrates a metal drop chute to be used in narrow forms. These chutes should be provided in sections which can be coupled so that the length can be adjusted as required. When it is impractical to reach the bottom of narrow forms by means of drop chutes, concrete may be deposited through openings in the sides of forms, known as *windows*. Figure 7-23 illustrates the proper construction of such a "window," which allows the concrete to overflow into the forms rather than allowing it to enter at an angle.

When concrete is poured on a sloping surface, placing should begin at the bottom of the slope. This system will not only improve the compaction of the concrete as placing progresses, but will prevent the flowing out of mortar which would occur if pouring had begun at the top of a slope.

Placing of concrete for a slab should begin against a wall or against previously placed concrete. Dumping away from previously poured concrete allows the coarse aggregate to separate from the mortar. Figure 7-23 illustrates this.

Fig. 7-22. Using a drop chute in narrow form. (Courtesy Portland Cement Ass'n.)

Concrete should be placed in wall forms in relatively thin layers or *lifts*, 12 to 18 in. deep, each layer poured the full length of the form before the next lift is begun. This operation must take place so that each lift is poured in time to integrate easily and completely with the one below. This time factor will be determined by the kind of cement used in making the concrete, by the richness of the mix, by the presence or absence of accelerators, by the temperature of the concrete, and by atmospheric conditions at the time of placing. In addition, the first batches of each lift should be placed at the ends of the form section or in corners, and placing should then proceed towards the center. This is done to prevent the trapping of water at the ends of the sections, in corners, and along form faces. The integration of each lift with the one below is done with the aid of puddling spades or vibrators.

Concrete being poured in columns and walls should be allowed to stand for about two hours before placing the concrete for monolithic girders, beams, and slabs. This allows the concrete in the walls or columns to settle, and thus prevents cracking due to settlement, which would occur if all members were poured at one time.

The correct placing of concrete includes proper consolidation to insure that no pockets or spaces remain unfilled and that the face of the formed concrete has been made as smooth as required by specifications. The compacting or consolidation is done by means of *puddling spades* or *vibrators*. A puddling spade is simply a flat piece of metal attached to a handle, which is worked up and down in the freshly poured concrete. Vibrators may be either *internal* (see Fig. 7-24), or *external*. Internal vibrators should always be inserted vertically into the poured concrete and should be used for consolidation only—not to move concrete

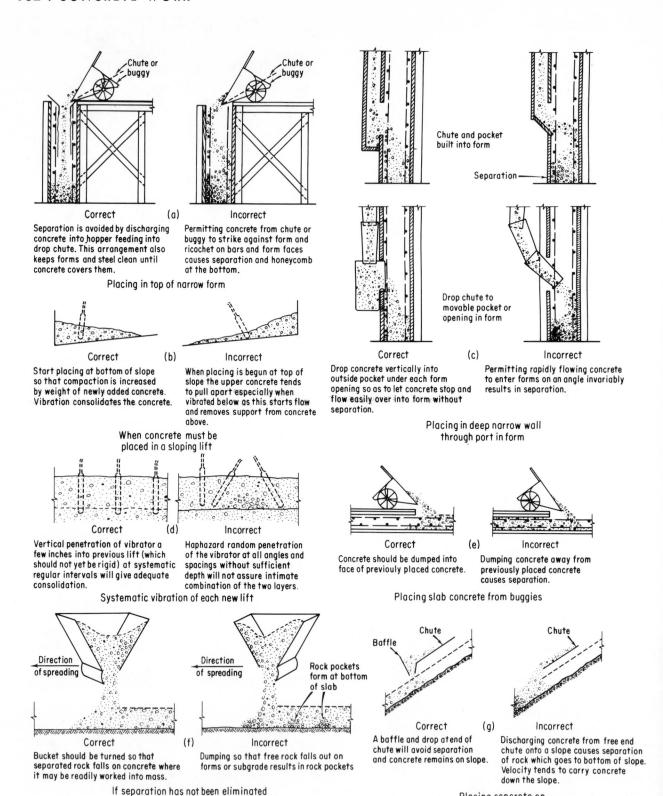

Chute or buggy

Chute and pocket built into form

Separation

Correct   (a)   Incorrect

Separation is avoided by discharging concrete into hopper feeding into drop chute. This arrangement also keeps forms and steel clean until concrete covers them.

Permitting concrete from chute or buggy to strike against form and ricochet on bars and form faces causes separation and honeycomb at the bottom.

Placing in top of narrow form

Drop chute to movable pocket or opening in form

Correct   (b)   Incorrect

Start placing at bottom of slope so that compaction is increased by weight of newly added concrete. Vibration consolidates the concrete.

When placing is begun at top of slope the upper concrete tends to pull apart especially when vibrated below as this starts flow and removes support from concrete above.

When concrete must be placed in a sloping lift

Correct   (c)   Incorrect

Drop concrete vertically into outside pocket under each form opening so as to let concrete stop and flow easily over into form without separation.

Permitting rapidly flowing concrete to enter forms on an angle invariably results in separation.

Placing in deep narrow wall through port in form

Correct   (d)   Incorrect

Vertical penetration of vibrator a few inches into previous lift (which should not yet be rigid) at systematic regular intervals will give adequate consolidation.

Haphazard random penetration of the vibrator at all angles and spacings without sufficient depth will not assure intimate combination of the two layers.

Systematic vibration of each new lift

Correct   (e)   Incorrect

Concrete should be dumped into face of previouly placed concrete.

Dumping concrete away from previously placed concrete causes separation.

Placing slab concrete from buggies

Direction of spreading

Rock pockets form at bottom of slab

Correct   (f)   Incorrect

Bucket should be turned so that separated rock falls on concrete where it may be readily worked into mass.

Dumping so that free rock falls out on forms or subgrade results in rock pockets

If separation has not been eliminated in filling placing buckets
(A tempory expedient until correction has been made)

Baffle   Chute   Chute

Correct   (g)   Incorrect

A baffle and drop at end of chute will avoid separation and concrete remains on slope.

Discharging concrete from free end chute onto a slope causes separation of rock which goes to bottom of slope. Velocity tends to carry concrete down the slope.

Placing concrete on a sloping surface

Fig. 7-23. Correct and incorrect methods of placing concrete

from one place to another within a form. External vibrators are used against the outside of forms and are most effective in producing smooth surfaces against the form faces.

Puddling or vibrating eliminates stone pockets and air bubbles and consolidates each layer of concrete with the one below. The process should also bring enough mortar to the surface or the form face to ensure the proper finish. It must be remembered that excessive vibration causes segregation because coarse aggregate is forced away from the vibrator and pockets of mortar form around it. It should also be remembered that vibrating tends to increase the pressure of concrete against the forms and that special care must be taken to see that forms are strong and tight enough to withstand the additional pressure.

Placing concrete under water requires special techniques. Of course, it cannot be dropped through the water, but must be conducted to its final position. A number of methods are used to place concrete for underwater structures, among them the use of a *tremie*, an *underwater bucket*, a *concrete pump*, or *grouted aggregate*.

The use of a tremie is probably the most popular method of placing concrete under water. It consists of a pipe, often 10 in. in diameter, fitted with a hopper at the top and a valve at the bottom. It must be long enough to reach from the surface to its lowest placing position.

Placing is begun by filling the tremie with its valve closed and lowering it to the starting position. The valve is opened and a constant flow of concrete is poured into the hopper as long as the valve is open. This forces concrete out the bottom into position. The tremie is raised slowly as concreting progresses, but the bottom end must be kept submerged in concrete at all times, as illustrated in Fig. 7-26. Where large areas are involved, several tremies are used together, the concrete from each flowing into a common mass. In most cases, tremies should not be more than 20 to 25 ft apart.

An underwater bucket has bottom gates which cannot be opened until the bucket is resting on the bottom or on previously placed concrete. This operation allows depositing the concrete and removing the bucket without disturbing the concrete or unduly agitating the water. A canvas cover prevents the swirling action of water from disturbing the concrete while the bucket is being lowered.

Using a concrete pump to place under water is similar to using a tremie. The lower end of the line must be kept submerged in concrete, and is then slowly

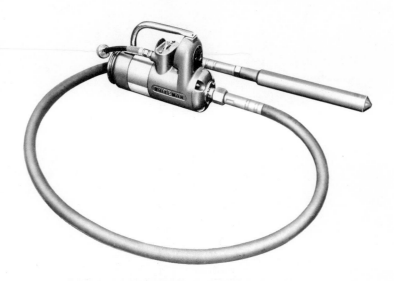

Fig. 7-24. Electrically driven internal vibrator. (Courtesy Whiteman Mfg. Co.)

raised to prevent the pressure from overcoming the pump as pouring progresses.

Using grouted aggregate involves first placing a series of small vertical pipes in the form, reaching from the bottom to a level above that which the concrete is to reach. The forms are then filled with the required coarse aggregate. Finally, grout (thin mortar) is pumped through the pipes, forcing the water out of

Fig. 7-25. Gas powered internal vibrator. (Courtesy Whiteman Mfg. Co.)

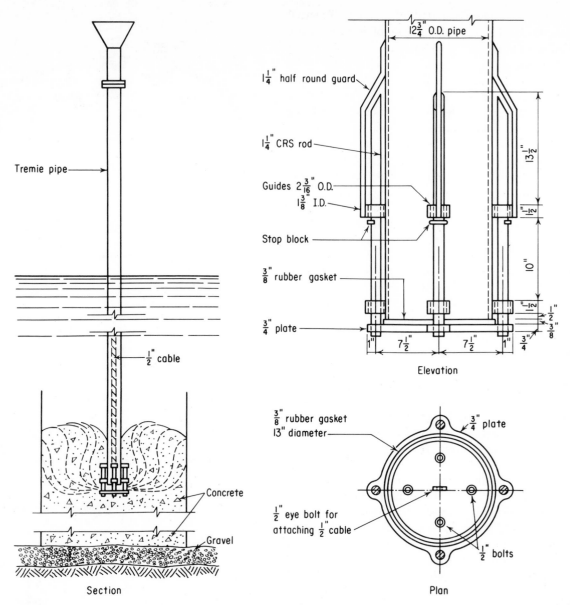

Fig. 7-26. Diagram of tremie

the forms and filling the spaces between the particles of aggregate. The pipes are slowly withdrawn as grouting proceeds, but their lower ends must be kept below the level of grout already in the form.

CONCRETE JOINTS

See Chapter 6

FINISHING AND CURING CONCRETE

The treatment of exposed concrete surfaces to produce the desired appearance, texture, or wearing quali-

ties is known as *finishing*. The procedure to follow depends primarily on whether the surface is horizontal or vertical. Horizontal surfaces are usually exposed, and must be finished before the concrete has hardened. Timing is a very important factor in this operation. Finishing must be done when the concrete is neither too hard to be worked nor so soft that it will fail to retain the desired finish.

The concrete must first be struck off level as soon as it has been placed. This is done by the use of *strike-off bars* worked against the top edge of *screeds* previously set to the proper height (see Fig. 7-27). These bars are operated either by hand or by power, the latter

Fig. 7-27. Power operated strike-off bars. (Courtesy Whiteman Mfg. Co.)

acting as vibrators as well as strike-off bars. Striking off removes all humps and hollows, leaving a true and even surface.

Further finishing is then delayed until the surface is quite stiff but still workable. Any water appearing on the surface should be removed with a broom, burlap, or other convenient means. Do not sprinkle cement or a mixture of cement and fine aggregate on the surface to take up excess water. This forms a layer that will dust and wear easily, or develop a great many fine cracks due to shrinkage. A short wood *float* produces an even surface, with all larger particles of aggregate embedded in mortar. This should be followed by a long wood float (see Fig. 7-29), which removes the marks left by the short one and produces a gritty non-skid surface.

If a scored surface is required, it can be produced by drawing a stiff, coarse broom across the surface, as shown in Fig. 7-30.

When a smooth surface is required, it is produced by using a steel trowel, illustrated in Fig. 7-31. Finishing can also be done by the use of power floats and

power trowels. These are commonly used on large projects and are operated as in Fig. 7-32.

Trimmed edges and joints are made by using edging tools such as those in Fig. 7-33. Special hard surfaces are applied and finished as described in Chapter 11.

When vertical surfaces have to be given a smooth finish, a different technique is used. First, the forms must be removed after the concrete is sufficiently strong. The tie holes must then be filled with mortar, or the snap ties must be broken off, and all depressions must be patched. All rough fins and protrusions must be removed. This can be done by rubbing the surface with a flat emery stone. Next, the surface is washed to remove all loosened material and at the same time dampen the concrete.

Grout is then applied to the surface with a stiff brush and rubbed in with a piece of burlap or a cork float. This will fill all the pores and small holes. After the grout has set sufficiently so that it will not rub out of the holes easily, the surface must be rubbed down with clean burlap to remove all excess material.

It has been shown that the strength, watertightness,

Fig. 7-28. Short wood float

Fig. 7-29. Long wood float

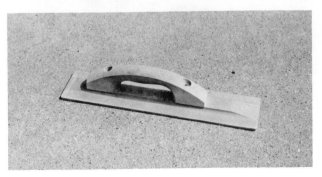

Fig. 7-30. A broomed surface. (Courtesy Portland Cement Ass'n.)

Fig. 7-31. Steel trowel

Fig. 7-32. Power trowel in operation. (Courtesy Whiteman Mfg. Co.)

and durability of concrete improve with age as long as conditions are favorable for continued hydration of the cement. The improvement in strength is rapid at the early stages, but continues more slowly for an indefinite period. The conditions required are sufficient moisture and temperatures preferably in the 65° to 70° range.

Fresh concrete contains more than enough water for complete hydration, but under most job conditions, much of it will be lost through evaporation unless certain precautions are taken. In addition, hydration proceeds at a much slower rate when temperatures are low, and practically ceases when they are near freezing. Thus, in order for concrete to develop its full potential, it must be protected against loss of moisture and low temperatures, particularly during the first seven days.

Concrete can be kept moist in several ways, such as by leaving forms in place, by sprinkling with water, by covering with water or a waterproof cover, and by sealing the surface with a wax coating.

When forms are left on, the top surfaces should be covered to prevent evaporation. In hot weather, it may be necessary to sprinkle water on wooden forms to prevent them from drying out and taking moisture from the concrete.

Where concrete is to be kept moist by sprinkling, care should be taken not to allow the surfaces to dry out between applications. One method of doing this is to cover the concrete with burlap or canvas.

Fig. 7-33. (a) Jointing tool; (b) Edging tool

(a)

(b)

Fig. 7-34. Heating water for concrete. (Courtesy Portland Cement Ass'n.)

Flat surfaces can be covered with water, damp sand, or waterproof material such as waxed paper or polyethylene film. Sprinkling may also be used, but it must be constant enough to prevent the concrete from drying out. A wax film applied as a spray is commonly used to seal a concrete surface.

Providing suitable temperatures for the proper curing of concrete involves the prevention of high temperatures as well as low ones. High temperatures promote fast setting, sometimes to the extent that proper placing and finishing cannot be accomplished. High temperatures may also result in cracking caused by shrinkage when the concrete cools, particularly in mass work.

Cool water and cooled aggregates help to keep the temperature of the concrete down. Long water lines may be cooled by covering them with burlap which is kept moist. Aggregates sprinkled with water are also cooled by evaporation.

In cold weather construction it is often necessary to heat the water, aggregates, or both; to cover the fresh concrete; and to provide a heated enclosure. During hydration, concrete generates some heat so that the temperature of the concrete at placing time depends on circumstances. In massive structures, such as dams, the concrete should have a placing temperature of at least 40° F, while in ordinary reinforced structures such as buildings, the temperature of the concrete should be about 70° F.

Water is the most convenient ingredient to heat, but should not be heated above 165° to 175°F because of the possibility of a *flash* set. When water tempera-

ture will not produce concrete of the desired temperature, the aggregates have to be heated. This may be done by running steam pipes through the piles, by injecting live steam into the aggregates, or by piling them over a pipe in which a fire has been built. Particularly in the latter case, the aggregate must be turned over frequently to prevent overheating of one section of the pile.

After concrete is in place, it must be kept warm enough so that hydration can proceed. This may be done by providing a heated enclosure, by covering the concrete with tarpaulins or a layer of straw, or by using blanket insulation.

When an enclosure is used, heat may be provided by oil or gas burning salamanders, by oil-fired heaters with blowers, like that shown in Fig. 7-35, or by live steam. Steam is an excellent method because it provides moisture as well as heat.

Too-rapid cooling of the concrete at the end of the protection period should be avoided. If the surface cools rapidly while the interior is still warm, stresses may be set up which will crack the concrete. A cooling rate of 20°/24 hr is satisfactory.

DESIGN OF LIGHTWEIGHT CONCRETE

Concrete made with stone aggregate weighs, on the average, about 150 lb per cu ft. Lighter concrete can be produced by using aggregates made from other materials. These include *expanded vermiculite, clay, shale, pumice,* and *blast furnace slag.* Sand is sometimes used as part of the fine aggregate to improve the

Fig. 7-35. Space heater. (Courtesy Kelley Machine Div., Wiesner-Rapp Co. Inc.)

workability of the mix. Concrete varying in weight from 40 to 120 lb per cu ft may be obtained, depending on the type of aggregate used.

Structural lightweight concrete will have a unit weight of 85 to 120 lb per cu ft, and a great deal of it is made using expanded shale or clay as the aggregate. Whereas concrete made from stone aggregate usually has a water content of from 270 to 320 lb per cu yd, lightweight concrete may have as much as 500 lb per cu yd. This difference is mainly in the water absorbed by the aggregates. While the water-cement ratio rule still holds true, the amount of water absorbed by the aggregates can only be estimated, and the calculation of a mix design based on a water-cement ratio is impractical. The common practice is therefore to design lightweight concrete mixes on the basis of cement content, taking into account the moisture in these aggregates, the proportion of fine to coarse that will produce the required workability, and the air content of the concrete. It appears that when the aggregates are pre-wetted to between 60% to 75% saturation, they are in the best condition for mix designing. This condition is reached after about 24 hr of pre-wetting For best results, air entrainment is recommended for all lightweight mixes.

There are three methods by which lightweight mixes may be designed, namely: *volumetric* method, *absolute volume* method, and specific *gravity factor* method. The absolute volume method, commonly used for normal weight concrete design, does not seem to be very reliable for lightweight concrete. It is based on the apparent specific gravity of the aggregates in a saturated, surface dry condition, and since the determination of absorption and apparent specific gravity are not simple, the method becomes too involved for common use and will not be discussed here.

The Volumetric Method of Design

A trial mix is calculated by this method either from loose, dry weights or from loose, damp weights of the aggregates as they come from the stockpile. When using loose, dry weights, the moisture contents are measured and the mix corrected from the results to produce a workable concrete with air content and slump as specified.

Suppose that it is required to produce a lightweight concrete having a cement content of 567 lb (approximately 6 bags, American or 6½ bags, Canadian) per cu yd, approximately 5% air content, and approximately 3 in. of slump.

Upon weighing the damp, loose aggregates it is found that the fine weighs 64 lb per cu ft and the coarse weighs 50 lb per cu ft. Assume that the total volume of aggregates required for a cu yd of concrete will be 32 cu ft (most lightweight aggregates vary from 31 to 33 cu ft per yd) and that a ratio of fine to coarse of 1 to 1 will give a satisfactory mix.

The weight of fine aggregate required for 1 cu yd batch would be $16 \times 64 = 1024$ lb.

The weight of coarse aggregate required would be $16 \times 50 = 800$ lb.

A trial batch of approximately 1 cu ft would then require:

Cement: $\dfrac{567}{27} = 21.0$ lb

F.A.: $\dfrac{1024}{27} = 37.9$ lb

C.A.: $\dfrac{800}{27} = 29.6$ lb

Water: $\qquad\qquad$ 13.0 lb (to produce a 3 in. slump)
Total weight $= 101.5$ lb

The wet unit weight is found to be 97 lb per cu ft and the air content test indicates 2.5% entrapped air.

The yield $= \dfrac{101.5}{97} = 1.047$ cu ft. The quantities required per cu yd of concrete are now calculated by multiplying the trial batch quantities by $\dfrac{27}{1.047} = 25.8$. Thus:

Cement $= 21.0 \times 25.8 = 542$ lb
F.A. $\quad= 37.9 \times 25.8 = 978$ lb
C.A. $\quad= 29.6 \times 25.8 = 764$ lb
Water $\;= 13.0 \times 25.8 = 335$ lb

Add the amount of air entraining agent specified for 3%. This may allow some reduction (usually 2% to 3% for each 1% of entrained air) in the water content.

Specific Gravity Factor Method

By this method a cement content is selected, aggregate proportions are assumed, and water is added to produce the required slump. The moisture contents of the aggregates are measured, as are the unit weight of the concrete and the air content of the mix. The batch weights are converted to a dry basis and the absolute volume of the aggregates is determined. A specific gravity factor is then calculated from the known dry weights. The batch is corrected to give the desired yield, cement content, and fine-to-coarse proportions.

Use the example chosen for the volumetric method. Suppose that, on testing, the moisture content of the fine aggregate is found to be 8% and that of the coarse aggregate, 10%. Then, from the quantities required for a cu yd of concrete, from above:

Water in F.A. = 72 lb approx.
Water in C.A. = 69 lb approx.
Total = 141 lb
Total water in batch = 335 + 141 = 476 lb
Weight of dry F.A. = 978 − 72 = 906 lb
Weight of dry C.A. = 764 − 69 = 695 lb

Now, to find the specific gravity factor, proceed as follows:

$$\text{Abs. volume of cement} = \frac{542}{3.15 \times 62.4} = 2.71 \text{ cu ft}$$

$$\text{Volume of water} = \frac{476}{62.4} = 7.63 \text{ cu ft}$$

$$\text{Volume of air} = .055 \times 27 = 1.48 \text{ cu ft}$$
$$\text{Total} = 11.82 \text{ cu ft}$$

$$\text{Abs. volume of aggregate} = 27 - 11.82 = 15.18 \text{ cu ft}$$

Since the fine and coarse aggregates were used in equal parts by volume, we assume that the absolute volume of each $= \frac{15.18}{2} = 7.59$ cu ft.

$$\text{Specific gravity factor of F.A.} = \frac{906}{62.4 \times 7.59} = 1.91$$

$$\text{Specific gravity factor of C.A.} = \frac{695}{62.4 \times 7.59} = 1.46$$

When designing further mixes with the *same aggregate* in the *same moisture conditions*, this specific gravity factor may be used as though it were the apparent specific gravity. The quantity of *coarse aggregate* is maintained constant and the water content is assumed to remain the same.

REVIEW QUESTIONS

1. Give two reasons why as much aggregate as possible should be used when designing a concrete mix of any given strength.

2. What is the purpose of the following aggregate tests: (a) silt test; (b) specific gravity test; (c) fineness modulus test; (d) colorimetric test?

3. Explain how a fineness modulus test may be used to determine whether the various sizes of aggregate in a sample

Suppose that it is required to design a mix using 750 lb of cement per yd of concrete, with 5% air entrainment and 3 in. of slump. Proceed as follows:

$$\text{Abs. volume of cement} = \frac{750}{62.4 \times 3.15} = 3.81 \text{ cu ft}$$

$$\text{Volume of water} = \frac{476}{62.4} = 7.63 \text{ cu ft}$$

$$\text{Abs. volume of C.A.} = \frac{695}{62.4 \times 1.46} = 7.63 \text{ cu ft}$$

$$\text{Volume of air} = .05 \times 27 = 1.35 \text{ cu ft}$$
$$\text{Total} = 20.42 \text{ cu ft}$$

$$\text{Abs. volume of F.A.} = 27 - 20.42 = 6.58 \text{ cu ft}$$

Weight of F.A. = $6.58 \times 62.4 \times 1.91 = 784$ lb

(The water content may still require a minor adjustment.)

A paddle-type mixer, similar to those used for mixing mortar, usually gives better results than a standard concrete mixer.

Lightweight concrete has much greater insulating qualities than stone concrete. This is particularly true of concrete made with expanded vermiculite aggregate. This feature makes it especially useful for non-bearing fire walls, for roof slabs, and as a base for floor slabs to be covered with stone concrete for wearing ability. Concrete made with burnt clay aggregate develops much greater strength than that made from vermiculite, and is often used for precast structural units such as roof slabs, floor joists, etc.

A lightweight concrete may also be made by adding aluminum powder to a standard mix made with stone concrete. The lightness is produced by a swelling action that leaves the concrete filled with air cells. The strength is lowered substantially, but concrete of this type is usually used for floor and roof fills where strength is not an important factor. Because the swelling occurs after the concrete is in place, allowance must be made for an increase in volume. Concrete made in this manner normally weighs about 50 lb per cu ft.

are present in desired proportion.

4. Differentiate between the *adsorbed moisture* and the *free moisture* in an aggregate.

5. Design a one-sack trial mix for interior reinforced columns. The concrete is to have 4″ slump, should contain 3% entrained air, and must withstand 4000 psi in 28 days. C.A. has a maximum size of 1½ in., sp gr = 2.67, free moisture = 0%, dry-rodded weight = 101 lb/cu ft. F.A. has a fineness modulus of 2.72, sp gr = 2.70, free moisture = 3%, 1 cu ft (SSD condition) weighs 112 lb. If each

column measures 12″ by 13″ by 10′ and 24 columns are to be poured, what are the requirements of cement, F.A., and C.A.?

6. Prepare a seven-point checklist to be used when preparing to pour concrete.

7. List eight rules to follow when placing concrete in forms.

8. Describe the purpose of each of the following when finishing a concrete slab: (a) screed; (b) strike-off bar; (c) float; (d) trowel; (e) broom or drag.

9. Explain briefly: (a) what is meant by a *flash set* of cement; (b) why it may be necessary to heat both water and aggregate in very cold weather; (c) why the placing temperature of concrete is lower for massive structures than it is for ordinary reinforced structures.

STRUCTURAL TIMBER FRAME

8

Building the structural frame of a multistory building from wood members is one of the oldest methods of construction used in North America. Many old wood-frame buildings are still in satisfactory condition and are still being used.

Originally, buildings made with a heavy timber frame were structures of two or more stories intended primarily for industrial and storage purposes. The earliest of these buildings used whole logs of various diameters as structural members. The next step was the use of sawn timbers for the structural frame, and more recently, timber members have been built from a number of small pieces, nailed, bolted, or glued together.

Heavy timber framing has now been expanded from the original industrial purpose to include schools, churches, auditoriums, gymnasiums, apartment buildings, supermarkets, etc.

There are a number of important factors which have contributed to the more efficient use of timber in modern building construction. One is the development and refinement of stress-graded timber, both solid and glue-laminated. This has made it possible to apply precise structural design procedures to heavy timber framing, resulting in a completely engineered structure.

The production of modern types of timber connectors has made it possible to develop the full strength of wood when stresses are being transferred from one member to another. It is no longer necessary to provide much larger sections in order to accommodate the fastenings formerly used to transfer stresses from member to member.

Full recognition of the fire resistivity of large timber sections has helped in the growth of timber building. Extensive tests have been successfully carried out to determine the ability of timber to withstand fire. The use of smooth surfaces and rounded edges has improved the ability of timber to oppose the inroads of fire.

Another important development in wood technology has been the use of preservative materials to help timber withstand the deteriorating effects of moisture, disease, and insects. Pressure treatment with these preservatives—including creosote, Wolman salts, and solutions of copper compounds—has given deep penetration and long-lasting effects.

Probably the most important achievement of all is the development of techniques of producing heavy timbers by glue-laminating. This aspect of timber building is dealt with more completely in Chapter 13.

Heavy timber construction means that type of wood construction in which a degree of fire endurance is obtained by limiting the minimum sizes of structural members and the minimum thickness and composition of wood floors and roofs. All wood parts are arranged in heavy, solid masses and smooth, flat surfaces so as to avoid thin sections, sharp projections, and concealed or inaccessible spaces.

The basic components of structural timber frame buildings may be classified as columns, girders, beams, and decking or planking. The size of each used in any specific case will depend on the load, the span of girders, beams, and planks, the unsupported height of columns, and the species and grade of timber being used. Complete data on allowable working stresses for species of timber used in construction and grades within a species are available from such sources as the Canadian Institute of Timber Construction, the American Institute of Timber Construction, the Southern Pine Association, the National Lumber Manufacturers Association, or the West Coast Lumberman's Association.

WOOD COLUMNS

Wood columns for heavy timber construction are made from timber or glue-laminated lumber and must be at least 8 in. nominal in least dimension when supporting floor loads and not less than 6 in. nominal in width and 8 in. in depth when supporting roof and ceiling loads only. Columns may be continuous throughout the entire height or superimposed at various levels and connected by means of reinforced concrete or metal caps, wood splice plates, or metal straps.

The first consideration in erecting a structural timber frame is the method to be employed in anchoring the columns to the foundation. This may be done in several ways, three of which are illustrated in Figs. 8-1 to 8-3. Notice that in Fig. 8-2 *shear plates* are set into the column behind the straps.

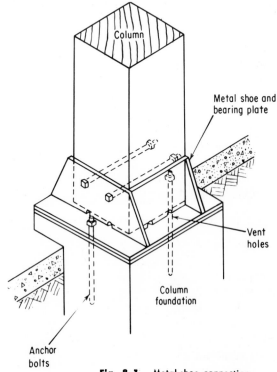

Fig. 8-1. Metal shoe connection

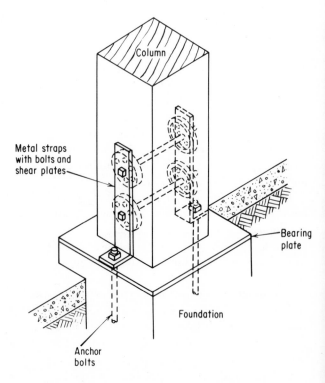

Fig. 8-2. Metal strap and shear plate connection

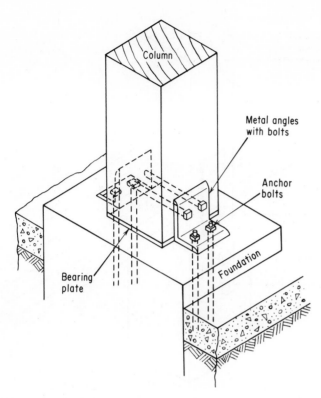

Fig. 8-3. Metal angle connection

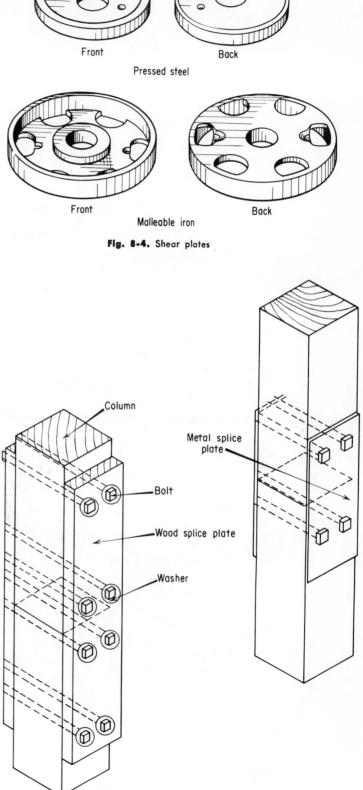

Fig. 8-4. Shear plates

Fig. 8-5. Column splices

Shear plates (see Fig. 8-4) are intended primarily for steel strap-to-wood connections. They may also be used in pairs, in wood-to-wood connections, where the connection is to be dismountable.

Noncontinuous columns may remain the same size throughout the full height of the building or may be reduced in size in the upper stories. In any case, they must be connected end to end, and a number of methods are used for doing this. One of the simplest is shown in Fig. 8-5, where columns of the same dimensions are connected by wood or metal splice plates. When column dimensions change at a connection, this change should be made at floor level so the decking hides the connection and also serves to center the smaller column on the larger one. Figure 8-6 illustrates such a connection. Bent steel straps and shear plates are used to tie the two together.

Another method of connecting two columns together is to use a metal column cap and *pintle*, as illustrated in Fig. 8-7. The pintle is the metal stem connecting the top and bottom caps. Notice that this type of connection allows for connecting girders or beams to columns at the same time.

Fig. 8-6. Joining columns of two different sizes

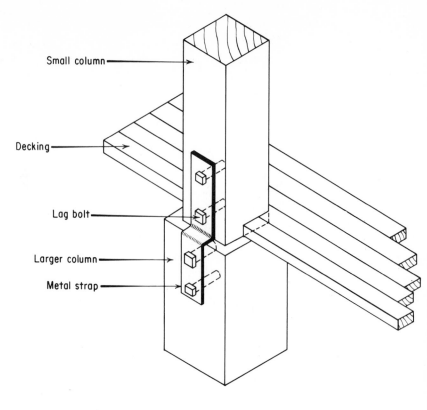

Small column

Decking

Lag bolt

Larger column

Metal strap

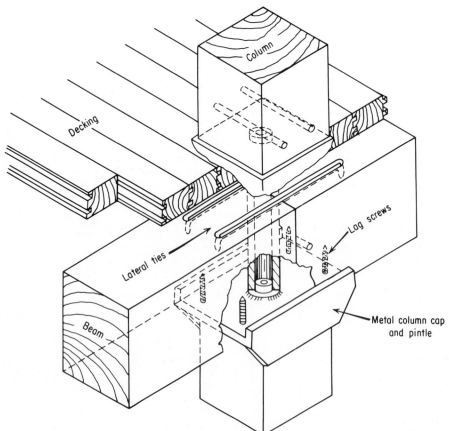

Column

Decking

Lateral ties

Beam

Lag screws

Metal column cap
and pintle

Fig. 8-7. Column cap and pintle

Fig. 8-8. Metal column cap connection

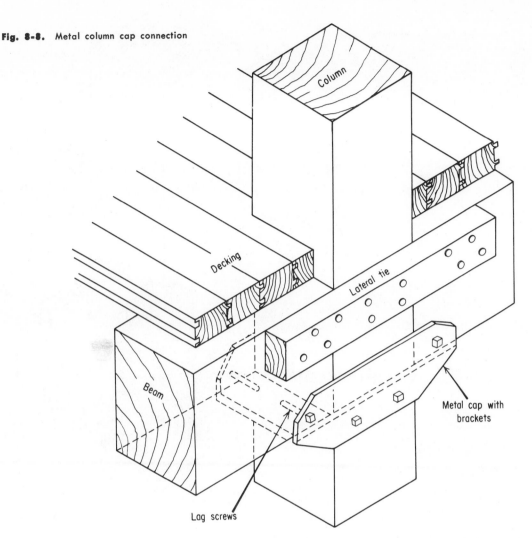

Another type of connection is shown in Fig. 8-8. Here a metal cap is secured by bolts to the top of a column and the upper column sits on the cap. Metal brackets attached to the cap allow girders or beams to be attached as shown. These girders and the lateral ties help to hold the upper column in position.

Precast reinforced concrete column caps are also used to connect columns and to allow attachment of beams to the column. This method is illustrated in Fig. 8-9.

WOOD GIRDERS AND BEAMS

Girders and beams which support floors are either of sawn timber or made by the glue-laminating process. They must be at least 6 in. nominal in width and not less than 10 in. in depth.

Three methods of connecting girders and beams to columns have been illustrated in Figs. 8-7, 8-8, and 8-9.

In addition to these, girder ends may be carried at the column by means of bearing blocks, as shown in Fig. 8-10. The bearing blocks are connected to the column by bolts and *split rings*.

Split ring connectors are steel rings with a tongue and groove split in the band. The ring fits into precut grooves in the pieces to be connected and a bolt holds the pieces together. Grooves are cut with a special grooving tool.

Two other methods of connecting girders and beams to columns are illustrated in Figs. 8-11 and 8-12. In Fig. 8-11, metal brackets fastened to a continuous column with bolts and shear plates carry the girders. Notice that the girder ends are tied together with lateral ties across the column. Figure 8-12 shows a special type of metal cap with brackets to accommodate four joining floor members. It is used with a non-continuous column.

Roof beams and girders are normally carried on top of the column and joints in the beam or girder will fall

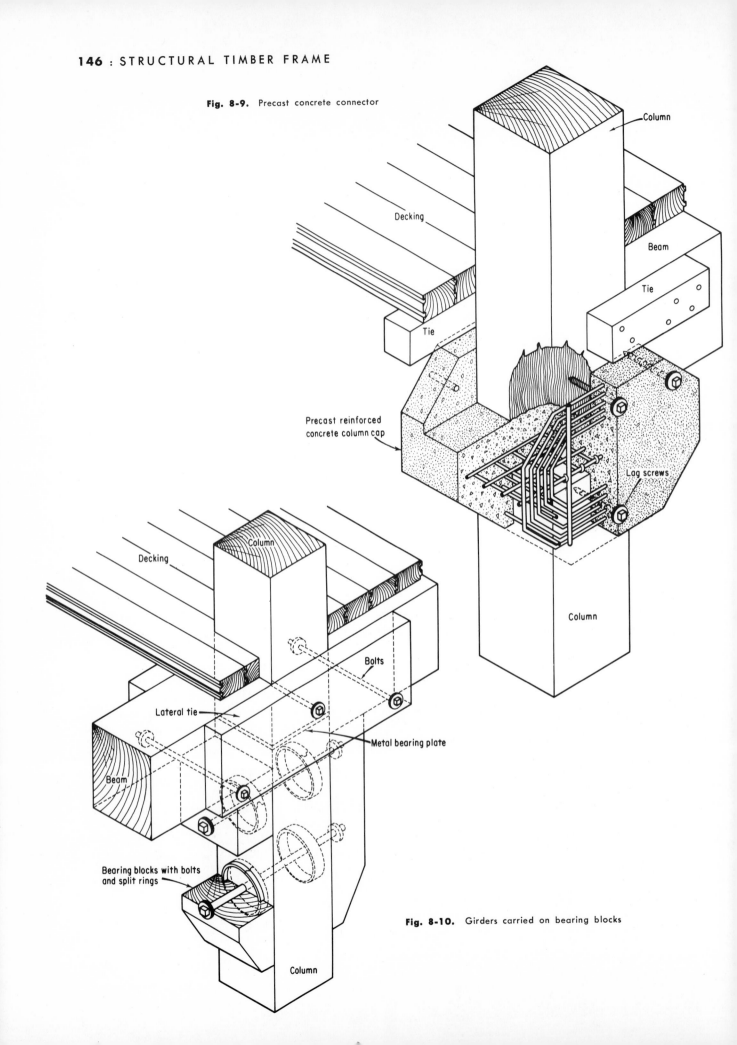

Fig. 8-9. Precast concrete connector

Column

Decking

Beam

Tie

Tie

Precast reinforced
concrete column cap

Lag screws

Column

Column

Decking

Bolts

Lateral tie

Metal bearing plate

Beam

Bearing blocks with bolts
and split rings

Column

Fig. 8-10. Girders carried on bearing blocks

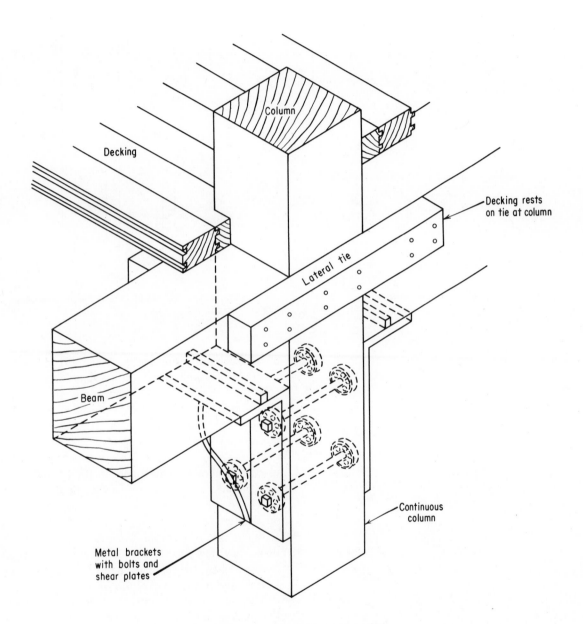

Fig. 8-11. Metal bracket girder connector

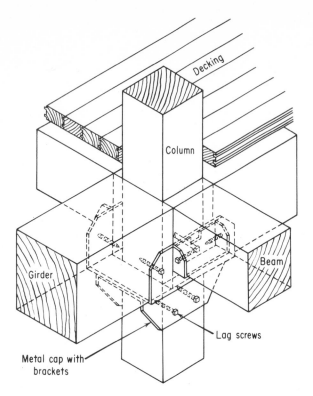

Fig. 8-12. Four-way metal bracket

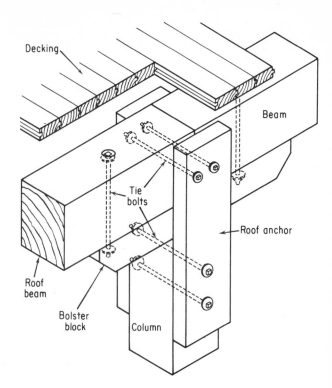

Fig. 8-14. Bolster block with wood splice plate

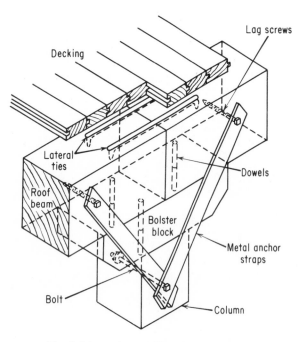

Fig. 8-13. Bolster block with metal straps

on the column. Figures 8-13 and 8-14 illustrate two methods of using wood *bolster blocks* on top of the column to carry the ends of the roof members. Metal straps on wood splice blocks tie the beams down to the column and, where metal straps are used, metal lateral ties hold the beam ends together.

Figures 8-15 and 8-16 show two kinds of metal caps used to anchor roof members to the columns. In Fig. 8-16, metal straps are again used to tie the beams down. In Fig. 8-15, the beams are tied down by the brackets on the cap.

Where intermediate beams are used to support a floor, they may rest on top of the girders, as illustrated in Fig. 8-17. In this case metal angles are being used to hold the beams in position on the girder.

The wasted space between floors can be reduced if the girders and beams can be arranged so that their top surfaces are flush with one another. One method of doing this is to carry the beam ends on ledgers fastened to the sides of the girder with split rings and bolts, as shown in Fig. 8-18.

Another method used is illustrated in Fig. 8-19. Here metal hangers are secured to the girder and to the beam ends with shear plates and bolts. Metal

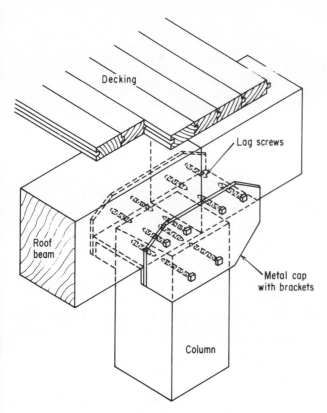

Fig. 8-15. Metal cap with brackets

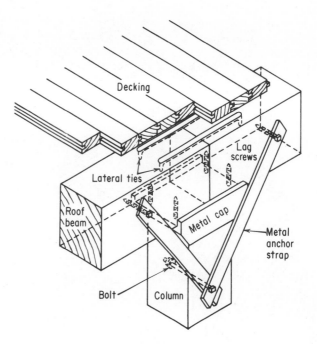

Fig. 8-16. Metal cap with straps

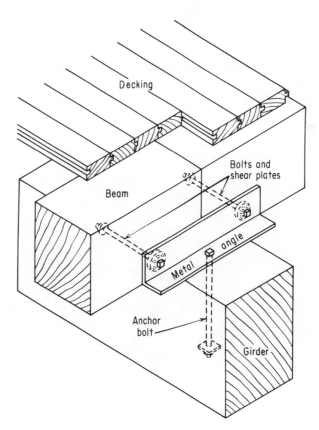

Fig. 8-17. Beams carried on girder

hangers are also used in Fig. 8-20. In all cases where angles or hangers are used, beam ends must be closely fitted between the metal sides.

Heavy timbers are sometimes used for the interior structural frame while masonry bearing walls carry the loads at the perimeter of the building. If this is the case, the outer ends of floor girders, beams, and header beams must be connected to the bearing wall.

Figure 8-21 demonstrates one method of connecting a header beam to a bearing wall. In this illustration, the beam is carried on a wall shelf, but a corbel (a wall offset) may be used as a bearing (see Fig. 8-25). In Fig. 8-22, an I beam is built into the wall and beam hangers are bolted or welded to its web. Pockets may be built into the face of the wall and bearing plates with anchor lugs set into the pockets. The ends of girders or beams are then supported as shown in Fig. 8-23. Another method consists of building hanger boxes into the wall and fastening the end of a wood member into each box with lag screws (see Fig. 8-24).

The method used to connect roof beams to exterior bearing walls depends on whether there is a parapet wall extending beyond the roof deck or whether the roof deck covers the top of the wall. In the former

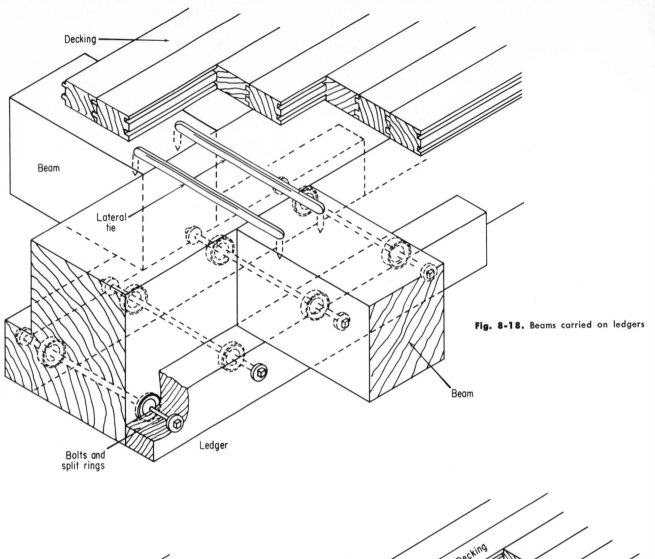

Fig. 8-18. Beams carried on ledgers

Decking

Beam

Lateral tie

Bolts and split rings

Ledger

Beam

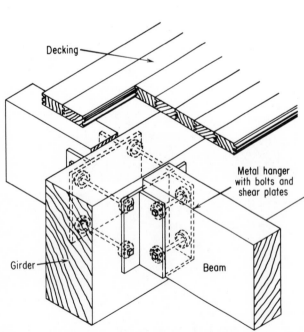

Fig. 8-19. Metal beam hangers

Decking

Metal hanger with bolts and shear plates

Girder

Beam

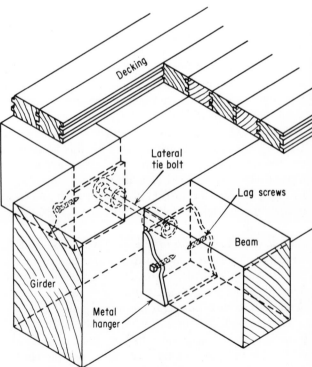

Fig. 8-20. Bolt-through beam hanger

Decking

Lateral tie bolt

Lag screws

Beam

Girder

Metal hanger

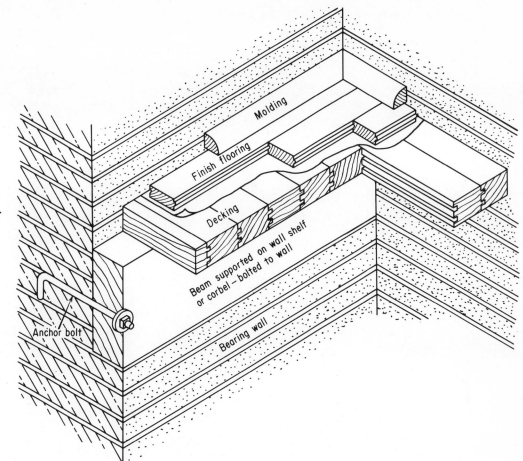

Fig. 8-21. Header beam supported on wall shelf

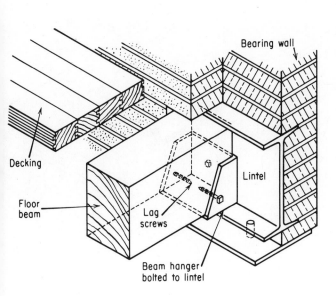

Fig. 8-22. Beam supported by hanger and I beam

case, beams are supported by the same methods as are described above for floor beams. Figures 8-25 and 8-26 illustrate two methods in common use. Note that in both cases anchor bars are used to tie the beams to the wall below. This anchorage is provided against uplift by wind. When the roof decking caps the wall, methods like those shown in Figs. 8-27 and 8-28 are used. A fascia is required along the outside top edge of the wall to provide solid backing for fastening down the roof flashing. When a party wall or a fire wall is involved in heavy timber construction, framing members can tie into it from both sides, as in Fig. 8-29.

FLOOR AND ROOF DECKS

Floors and roof decks in heavy timber frame buildings are constructed with planking which may be laid either flat or on edge. Floor planks laid flat are solid or glue-laminated, splined or tongue-and-grooved (see Fig. 8-30). The plank is at least 3 in. nominal in thickness and is covered with 1 in. thick nominal tongue-and-groove flooring laid crosswise or diagonally. Floor planks laid on edge are not less than 4 in. nominal in

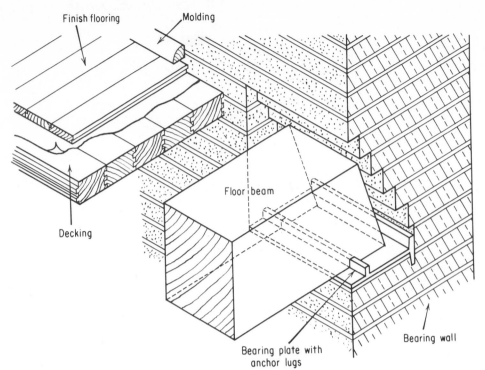

Fig. 8-23. Beam supported on bearing plate

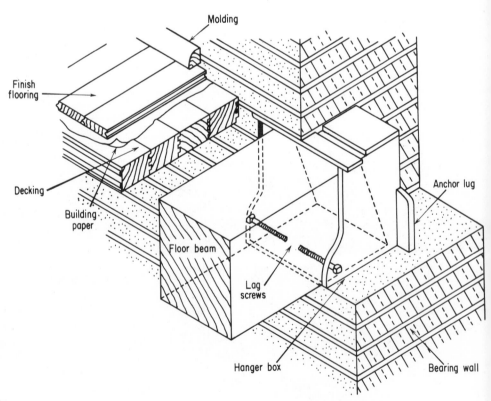

Fig. 8-24. Beam supported in hanger box

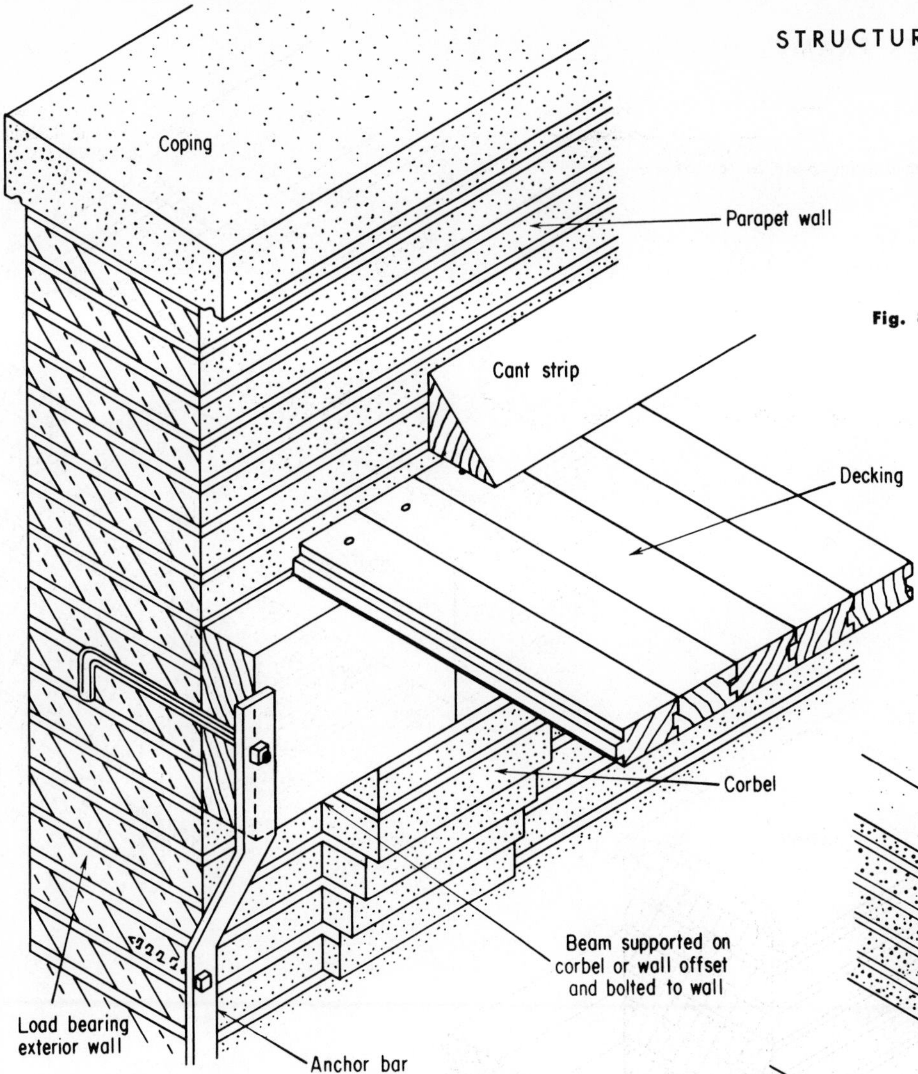

Coping

Parapet wall

Cant strip

Decking

Fig. 8-25. Roof beam supported by corbel

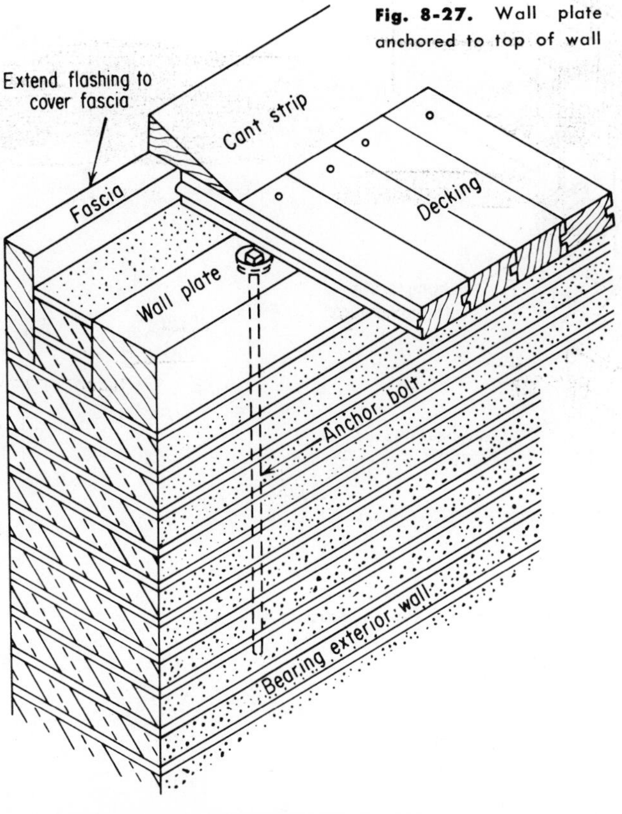

Corbel

Beam supported on
corbel or wall offset
and bolted to wall

Load bearing
exterior wall

Anchor bar

Coping

Parapet wall

Cant strip

Decking

Bearing
plate

Roof beam

Load-
bearing
exterior
wall

Anchor bar
bolted to
wall below

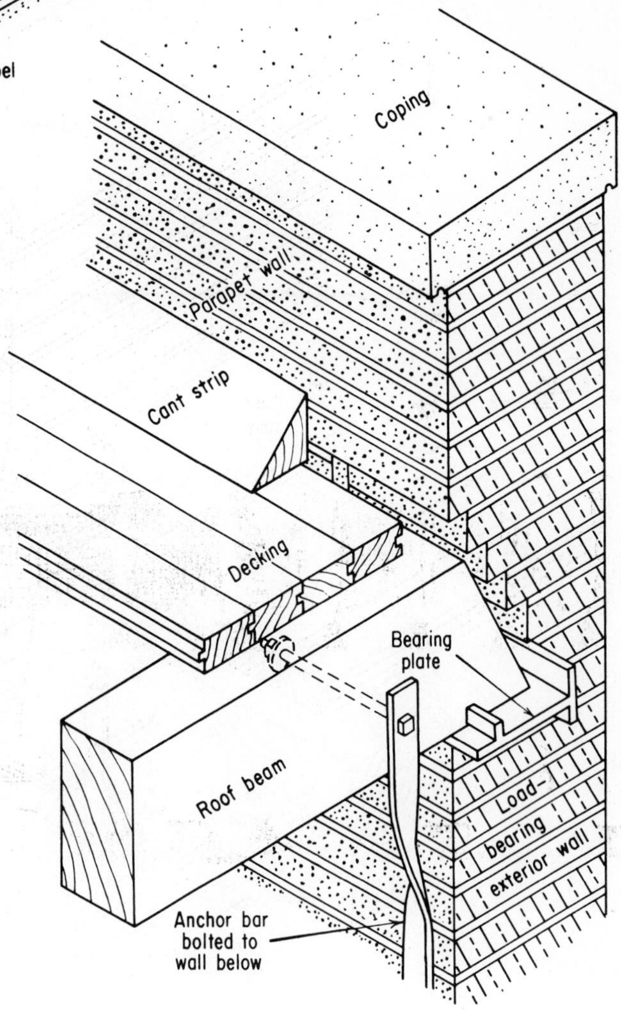

Fig. 8-26. Roof beam supported on bearing plate

Fig. 8-27. Wall plate
anchored to top of wall

Extend flashing to
cover fascia

Cant strip

Fascia

Decking

Wall plate

Anchor bolt

Bearing exterior wall

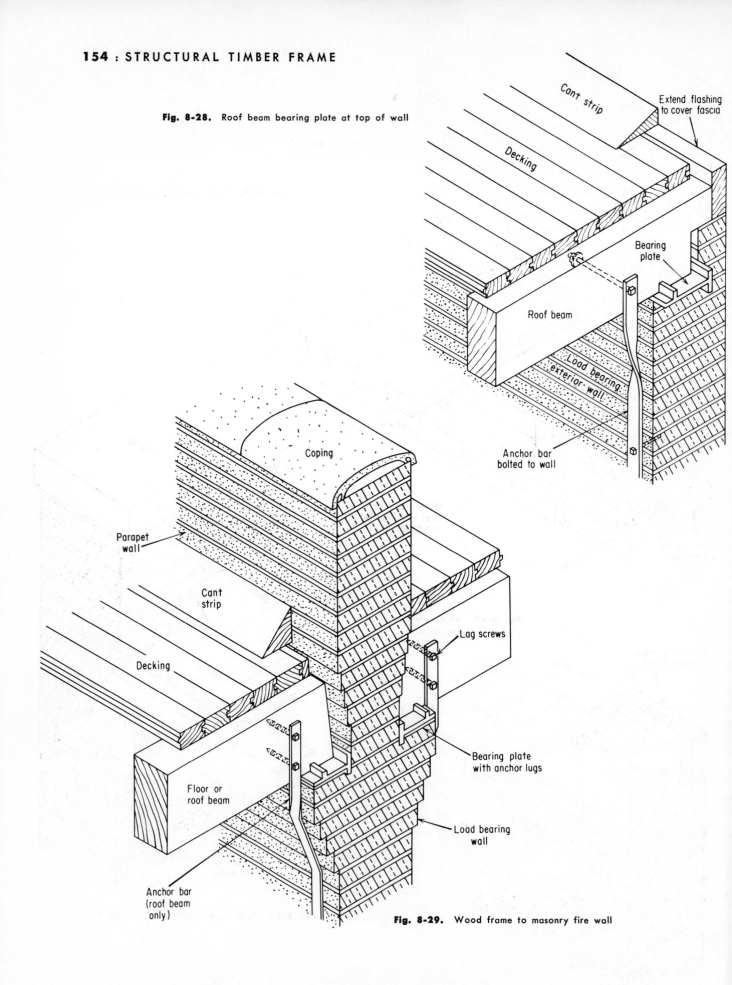

Fig. 8-28. Roof beam bearing plate at top of wall

Fig. 8-29. Wood frame to masonry fire wall

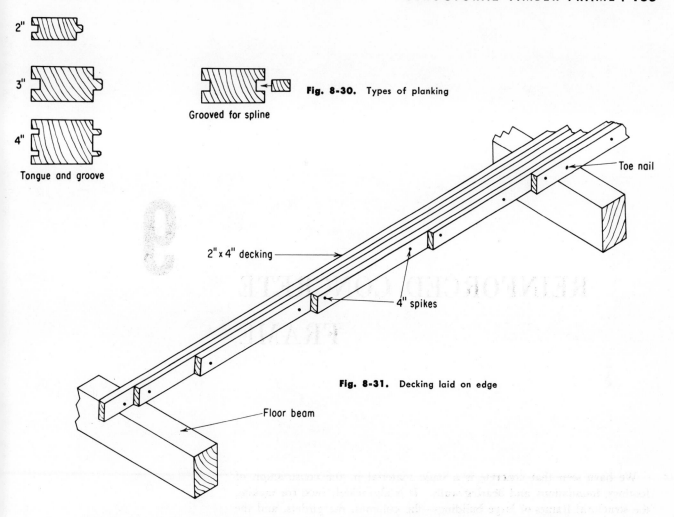

2"

3"

4"

Tongue and groove

Grooved for spline

Fig. 8-30. Types of planking

2" x 4" decking

Toe nail

4" spikes

Fig. 8-31. Decking laid on edge

Floor beam

width, well spiked together, and covered with 1 in. flooring. Roof planks on the flat must be not less than 2 in. nominal in thickness, while roof planks on edge are not less than 3 in. nominal in width.

Planks must be laid so that no continuous line of joints will occur except over supports. Planking should be kept ½ in. from walls, to allow for expansion, but the space should be covered at either the top or bottom to avoid flue action.

HEAVY TIMBER TRUSSES AND ARCHES

In addition to uses in the types of building components described in the foregoing paragraphs, timber and glue-laminated units are used in the construction of a great variety of roof trusses and wood arches.

The construction and erection of roof trusses is described in Chapter 12 while that of arches is discussed in Chapter 13.

REVIEW QUESTIONS

1. Outline five factors which have contributed to the more efficient use of timber in modern building construction.

2. Give four methods used to anchor wood columns to foundations.

3. What is the purpose of: (a) a pintle; (b) a bearing block; (c) a lateral tie?

4. Why must changes in wood column dimensions be made at floor level?

5. (a) Why is wood decking kept ½ in. back from the face of masonry walls? (b) How is this space concealed?

6. (a) What is a spline? (b) What is its purpose? (c) What is an alternative to the use of splines?

7. Describe the following: (a) scupper; (b) fascia; (c) parapet; (d) corbel.

9

REINFORCED CONCRETE
FRAME

We have seen that concrete is a basic material in the construction of footings, foundations, and bearing walls. It is also widely used for making the structural frames of large buildings—the columns, the girders, and the beams. Since these members are subjected to tensile stresses and concrete is weak in resisting tension, steel is added to the member—hence the term "reinforced concrete."

A reinforced concrete building frame may be erected by either of two methods. The members may be *cast-in-place* or the frame may be assembled from *precast* members. In the first case, forms are built and erected to form the shape of the frame and concrete is placed on the job. Precast members, on the other hand, are formed, cast, and cured in a plant and are subsequently brought to the building site ready for assembly.

CAST-IN-PLACE REINFORCED CONCRETE STRUCTURAL FRAME

There are two basic considerations in the erection of a cast-in-place structural frame. One of these is the actual building and erecting of forms of the size, shape, and strength required, and the other is the proper placing of the steel rods needed for reinforcement.

The size and shape of the members to be formed are indicated on the building plans, while the size and amount of material necessary to make the forms strong enough are based on the loads and pressures involved. The size, shape, and amount of steel required are also indicated on the plans in the form of column, girder, and beam *schedules*.

COLUMN FORMS

Column forms are often subjected to much greater lateral pressure than wall forms because of their comparatively small cross section and relatively high rates of placement. It is therefore necessary to provide tight joints and strong tie support. Some means of accurately locating column forms, anchoring them at their base, and keeping them in a vertical position are also prime considerations. Wherever possible, a *cleanout* opening should be provided at the bottom of the form so that debris may be removed before pouring begins (see Fig. 9-3). *Windows* are often built into one side of tall column forms to allow the placing of concrete in the bottom half of the form without having to drop it from the top.

Columns may be square, rectangular, round, or irregular, and forms may be of wood, steel, or fiberboard.

Fig. 9-1. (a) Fiberboard column forms; (b) Fiberboard form removed

(a)

(b)

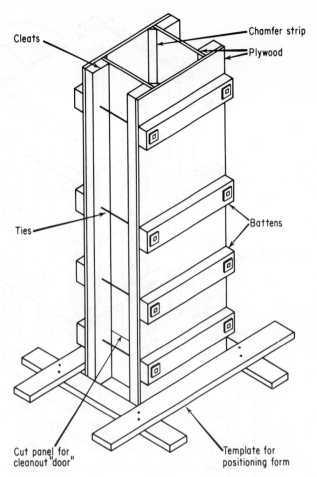

Fig. 9-2. Light column form

Wood—boards or plywood—is commonly used for square or rectangular forms and may also be used for irregular or round ones. However, most round columns are formed by the use of steel or fiberboard tubes of various diameters (see Fig. 9-1). Steel forms are also available for square or rectangular columns.

There are many ways to build square or rectangular wood column forms, depending on column size and height and on the type of tying equipment to be used. Figure 9-2 illustrates a simple method of making a form for a light column, up to about 12 in. by 12 in. The sheathing is generally plywood, with wood battens and steel rods used as a tying system.

As column sizes increase, either the thickness of the sheathing must be increased or vertical stiffeners must be added to prevent sheathing deflection. In Fig. 9-3 vertical stiffening is used. Also notice the adjustable metal clamps which tie the form together. Several methods of tying column forms are available, and some are illustrated in Fig. 9-4. Ties of this type are generally referred to as *yokes*.

Large columns require heavy yokes and a strong

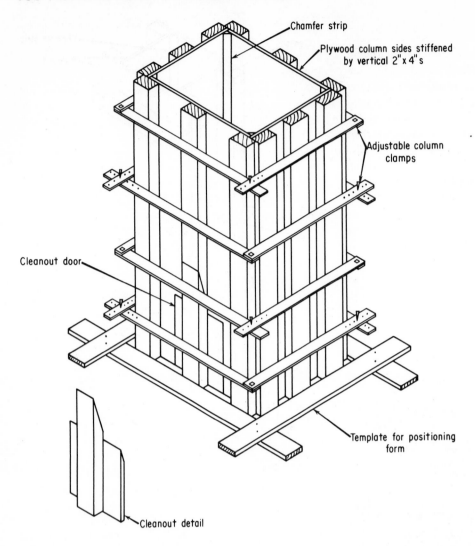

Chamfer strip

Plywood column sides stiffened by vertical 2" x 4"s

Adjustable column clamps

Cleanout door

Template for positioning form

Cleanout detail

Fig. 9-3. Heavier column form

tying system. In Fig. 9-5, the yokes are made from 2" by 4"s on edge, and the tighteners are patented U clamps and wedges.

Another method of tying columns involves the use of steel strapping (normally made in three widths: ¾ in., 1¼ in., and 2 in.) for column banding. The ¾ in. band is made in two thicknesses—.028 in. and .035 in., with approximate breaking strengths of 2300 lb and 3100 lb, respectively. The 1¼ in. width is made in thicknesses of .035 in. and .050 in. with approximate breaking strengths of 5000 lb and 7000 lb. The 2 in. band is .050 in. thick and has an approximate breaking strength of 11,000 lb.

Strapping may be used either with horizontal yokes (see Fig. 9-6) or with vertical stiffeners, as in Fig. 9-7. In either case, bands should not be bent at a 90° angle. The metal has a tendency to fracture under those conditions, and there may be danger of form failure caused by cracked bands (see Fig 9-6).

The band is tightened by a special tool, after which a metal clip is placed over the ends of the band and clamped in place by a crimping tool.

The first step in building a column form is to select the proper type and thickness of sheathing. Boards may be used, but plywood is more frequently employed because of its greater resistance to splitting and warping. It may be ½, ⅝, ¾, or 1 in. thick, depending on the size and height of the column. Table 6-7 may be used to determine the spacing of yokes, based on lateral pressures indicated in Table 6-3. It will be assumed that the first tie will be as close to the bottom of the form as is practical—within 6 or 8 in.—and that the top tie will be at or near the top. Yokes or bands must be checked to insure that they withstand bending and shear, and that deflection will not exceed ⅟₁₆ in.

One pair of form sides can be cut the exact width of one column dimension. The other pair must be made wider, depending on the method of form assembly. In Fig. 9-3, for example, the second pair of sides will be wider by twice the thickness of the sheathing. On the other hand, in Fig. 9-2, extra allowance must be made for the width of the cleats.

Lay out on the wide sides the position of chamfer strips by drawing lines parallel to the edge of the board. The distance between these lines will be the second dimension of the column (see Fig. 9-8). Fasten the chamfer strips in place with nails and glue.

If yokes or bands are to be used to tie the column, mark the location of each on the side of the form. If vertical stiffeners are used, tack them in place on the column sides and mark the position of the clamps or bands on a stiffener. When bands are used to tie the column, the yoke pieces can be tacked in place on each side before assembly. With other tying systems, any possible parts should be tacked in place before the form is assembled.

The form can now be assembled on a temporary basis. All four sides can sometimes be put together before erection, while in other situations it is preferable to put three sides together, set the partially completed form in place, and add the fourth side later. This would probably be done in setting column forms for a job like that shown in Fig. 9-11, where the reinforcement is already in position.

Round wood columns are usually made of 2 in. *cribbing*, as shown in Fig. 9-10. The edges of each piece of cribbing must be beveled so that they will form a circle when fitted together. The amount of bevel on each one will depend on the diameter of the column and the number of pieces used to make the form.

In order to locate column forms accurately, templates such as the one illustrated in Fig. 9-2 must be made. These are carefully located by chalk line or other convenient means and anchored in position (see Fig. 9-11).

Fig. 9-4. Light column ties

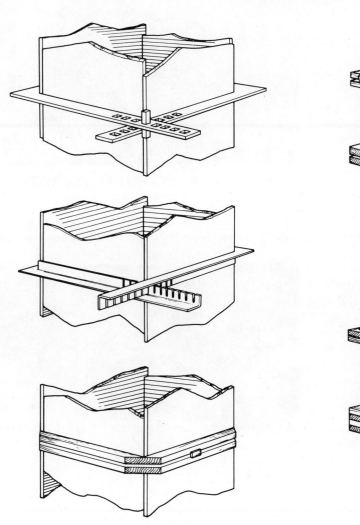

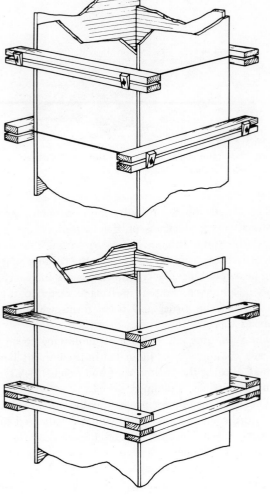

Fig. 9-5. Horizontal column form stiffeners. (Courtesy Jahn Concrete Forming.)

Fig. 9-6. Banding a plywood column form. (Courtesy Plywood Mfg. Ass'n. of B. C.)

The length of the column form is determined by subtracting the thickness of the bottom of the girder form which the column is to carry from the column height indicated on the plans or in the column schedule (see below). Once the column forms are in place, they must be plumbed, braced, and made ready to support the ends of the girder and beam forms which will be built to them.

The type, amount, and size of reinforcing to be used in each column will be indicated in a column schedule. It may also list the column sizes and heights. A typical column schedule is outlined below.

The column reinforcing is usually assembled as a unit on the job site, using the material indicated in the schedule. Wire is used to hold the vertical bars and lateral ties together. The unit is placed in position and fastened in place by tying to the dowels which project from the base surface (see Fig. 9-11). Notice

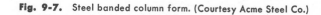

Fig. 9-7. Steel banded column form. (Courtesy Acme Steel Co.)

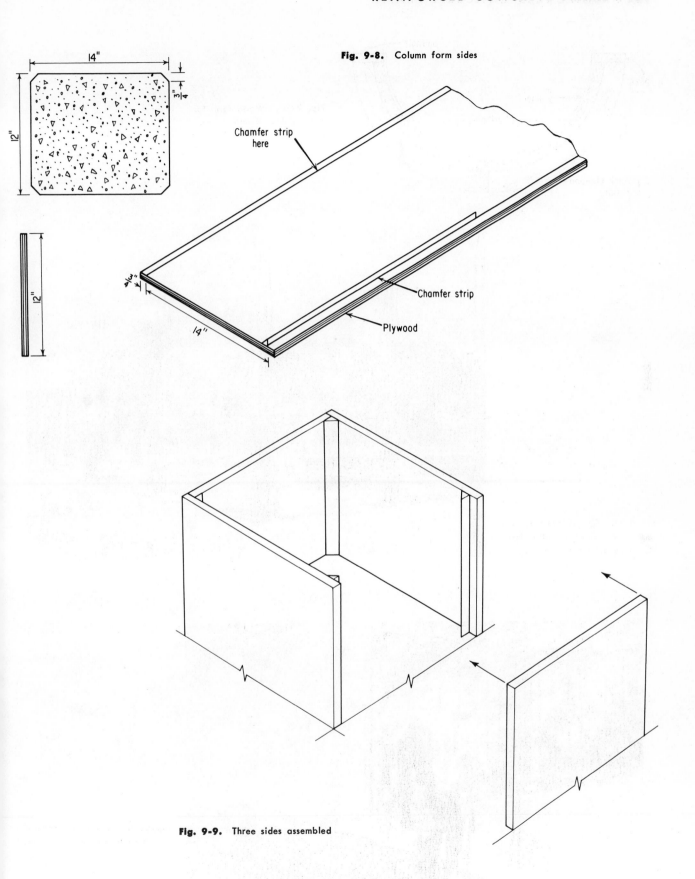

14"

12"

3"/4

12"

3"/4"

14"

Fig. 9-8. Column form sides

Chamfer strip here

Chamfer strip

Plywood

Fig. 9-9. Three sides assembled

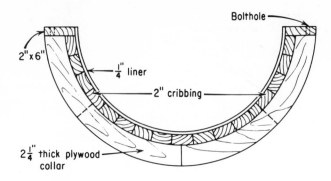

Fig. 9-10. Wood form for round column.(Courtesy American Concrete Institute.)

Fig. 9-11. Column form templates and column reinforcement in place. (Courtesy Bethlehem Steel Co.)

Fig. 9-12. Spiral reinforcement. (Courtesy Jahn Concrete Forming.)

that the vertical bars are cut long enough for their upper ends to act as dowels for the columns on the floor above.

Columns may be reinforced with spiral reinforcement as well as vertical bars. Spiral reinforcement consists of a continuous rod formed into a spiral of a given diameter. Rods of various sizes are used for this purpose, depending on the diameter of the spiral. The loops of the spiral are kept properly spaced—maintained at the proper *pitch*—by spacer bars, usually three per spiral. Vertical bars are generally used in addition to spirals, spaced evenly around their inside circumference as specified by the schedule.

GIRDER AND BEAM FORMS

Columns, girders, and beams on each floor of a reinforced concrete frame structure are usually poured bottom and column. Chamfer strips with beveled ends are nailed to the girder bottom, flush with the outside edge. Notice that the girder bottom rests on the narrow side of the column form.

The girder must be supported between columns by some type of shoring. T head shores are a frequent choice, their number depending on the load and carrying capacity of each shore. Stringers supported by adjustable metal posts or metal scaffolding (see Fig. 9-16) may also be used to support girder bottoms.

Girder sides overlap the bottom and rest on the shore heads and the sides of the column form (see Fig. 9-14). They are held in place by ledger strips nailed to the shore heads with double-headed nails. By removing these ledger strips and the *kickers* (see Fig. 9-17), girder form sides may be removed without disturbing the bottom. The bottom and its supports must remain in place until the beam concrete has gained a major portion of its design strength. Full concrete

Typical Column Schedule

Reinforced Concrete Column Schedule

Column #	Column size	Vertical reinforcement	Lateral ties	Top elevation	Bottom elevation
1, 5, 20	20 by 18 in.	4-#6	#3 @11 in. o.c.	98.67 ft	87.33 ft
2	34 by 18 in.	4-#8	#3 @12 in. o.c.	97.50 ft	87.33 ft
3	26 by 18 in.	4-#7	#3 @12 in. o.c.	97.50 ft	87.33 ft
4	24 by 16 in.	4-#7	#3 @12 in. o.c.	98.00 ft	87.33 ft
6	18 by 17 in.	4-#6	#3 @11 in. o.c.	98.67 ft	87.33 ft
7, 8, 9	18 by 18 in.	4-#6	#3 @11 in. o.c.	96.50 ft	87.67 ft
10	20 by 20 in.	4-#7	#3 @12 in. o.c.	96.00 ft	87.33 ft
11, 12, 13	36 by 18 in.	4-#8	#3 @12 in. o.c.	97.00 ft	87.33 ft
14, 15, 16, 17	20 by 20 in.	4-#7	#3 @12 in. o.c.	98.67 ft	87.33 ft
18	36 by 18 in.	6-#6	#3 @12 in. o.c.	97.67 ft	87.67 ft
19	36 by 18 in.	6-#6	#3 @12 in. o.c.	97.67 ft	85.50 ft
20	20 by 18 in.	4-#6	#3 @11 in. o.c.	98.00 ft	85.50 ft

monolithically. This means that all the forms must frame into one another. It is also important to remember that some parts of these forms may be removed before others. For example, the beam and girder sides may be removed first, followed later by the column forms, and finally by the beam and girder bottoms. It is therefore necessary to construct the girder and beam forms so that each part can be removed without disturbing the remainder of the form.

The first step in building a girder or beam form is to set the form bottom. Make its width exactly that of the member being formed and its length equal to the distance between columns. The two ends of the form bottom are cut at a 45° angle, as shown in Fig. 9-14, to produce a chamfer at the junction of the girder

strength will not be attained for 28 days. For larger girders, the side forms will have to be provided with vertical stiffeners to prevent buckling.

Beam forms are constructed in the same manner as girder forms. They may frame into either columns or girders (see Fig. 9-13) and they must be framed in such a way that form removal is as simple as possible.

A beam pocket is cut into the girder or column form (see Fig. 9-14) of sufficient size to receive the end of the beam form. Cut the ends of the side forms for the beam at a 45° angle (see Fig. 9-20). The beam bottom length should be such that its end is flush with the outside of the girder or column form. The end is supported by a block resting on girder ledger strips (see Figs. 9-18 and 9-20). Cut 45° beveled ends on

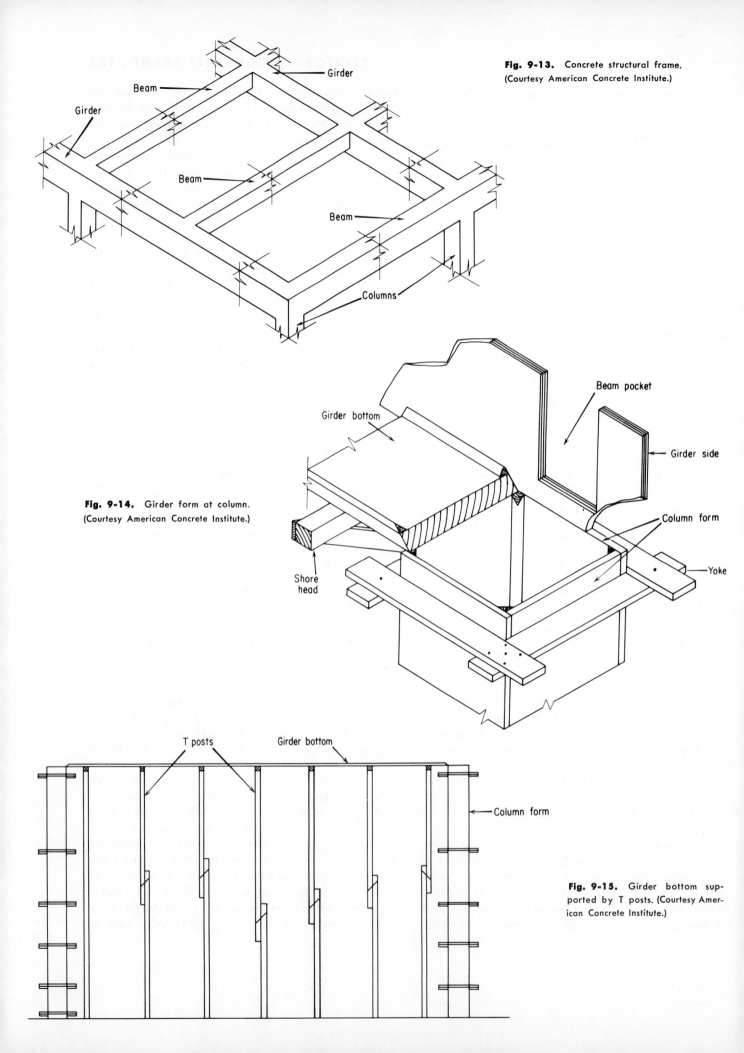

Fig. 9-13. Concrete structural frame. (Courtesy American Concrete Institute.)

Girder

Beam

Girder

Beam

Beam

Columns

Girder bottom

Beam pocket

Girder side

Column form

Yoke

Shore head

Fig. 9-14. Girder form at column. (Courtesy American Concrete Institute.)

T posts

Girder bottom

Column form

Fig. 9-15. Girder bottom supported by T posts. (Courtesy American Concrete Institute.)

Fig. 9-16. Scaffolding supports girder form

Fig. 9-17. Girder form details

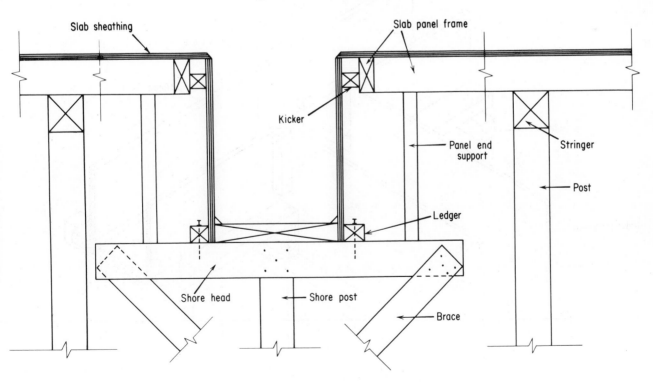

Slab sheathing

Slab panel frame

Kicker

Panel end support

Stringer

Post

Ledger

Shore head

Shore post

Brace

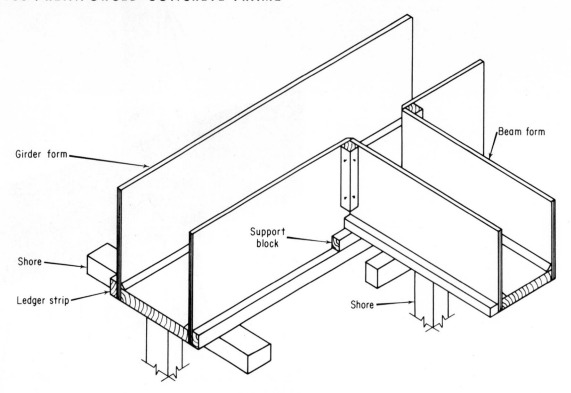

Fig. 9-18. Girder and beam form

Fig. 9-19. Column, girder, and beam forms.
(Courtesy American Concrete Institute.)

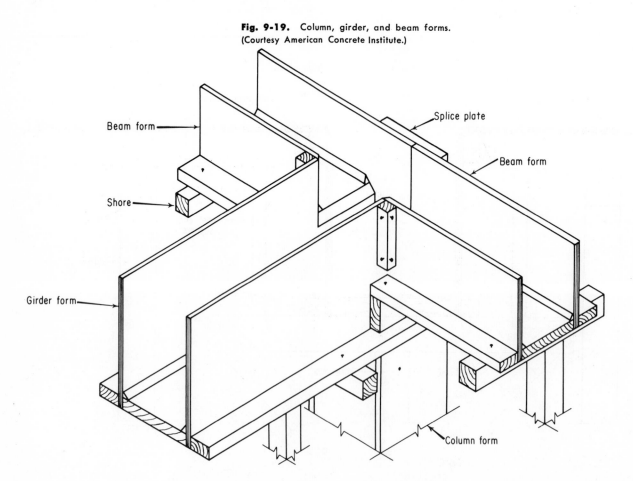

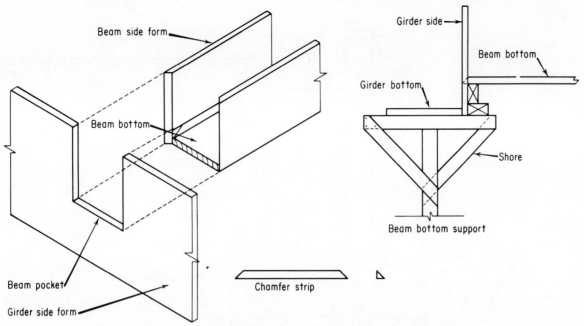

Fig. 9-20. Beam end to girder form

a length of chamfer strip and nail it to the bottom edge of the beam pocket so that the ends fit against the beveled edges of the beam sides.

Forms for girders and beams which frame into round columns require some special attention. Fiberboard column forms have relatively thin shells, and a yoke or collar is needed around the top of the form to support the girder bottom and sides. The girder bottom is cut the width of the column diameter and a half circle of the same diameter is cut in the ends. The girder bottom rests on the column collar, as shown in Fig. 9-22, and is supported by shores. Beam sides rest on the shores and on the column collar and are held in place by ledgers.

SPANDREL BEAM FORMS

Forms for spandrel beams—deep beams which span openings in outer walls—need to be very carefully

Fig. 9-21. Round column form with top collar

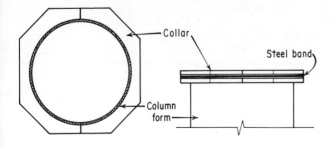

formed. Form alignment must be accurate to produce an attractive wall. Shore heads are often extended on the outside to accommodate the knee braces which are used to keep the forms in alignment. The extended shore head also frequently supports a catwalk for workmen.

Reinforcing for girders and beams is in the form of bars, straight or bent, and loops or *stirrups*. The bars

Fig. 9-22. Girder form to round column. (Courtesy American Concrete Institute.)

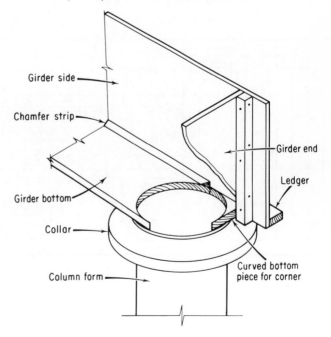

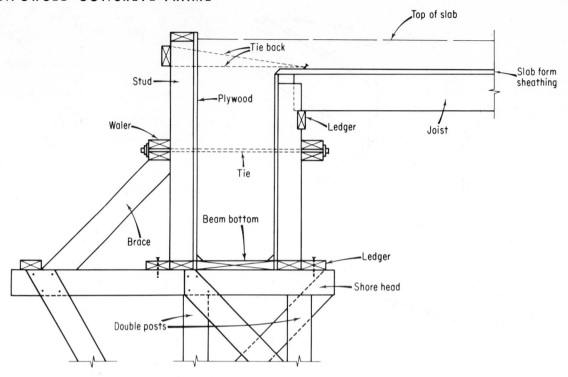

Fig. 9-23. Spandrel beam form

are used to resist tension in the member and the stirrups resist a combination of shear and tension known as *diagonal tension*. The bars rest on *chairs* set on the form bottom, and the stirrups hang from the top steel or from *loop bars* (see beam schedule below).

The details of the reinforcing for each girder and beam in a building are given in a *beam schedule*. Part of a typical reinforced concrete girder and beam schedule is shown below.

PRECAST CONCRETE STRUCTURAL FRAMES

Precast structural members are of three types. They may be *normally reinforced*, *prestressed pretensioned*, or *prestressed post-tensioned*. Reinforced precast members are normally designed according to common reinforced concrete practice. However, as a result of factory control, high strength concrete is produced whether required or not, for it is actually more eco-

Beam No.	Bars					Stirrups					Section	Elevation
	No.	Size	Length Ft	Length Ins	Mark	No.	Size	Length Ft	Length Ins	Mark		
1	2	6φ	25	0	1ₐ	12	3	5	6	S₁ₐ		
	2	6φ	20	0	Str							
2	2	7φ	19	6	2ₐ	8	4	5	6	S₂ₐ		
	2	6φ	12	6	2_B							

nomical to design reinforced concrete for higher strengths in the range of 5000 psi or better.

The members of a precast structural frame are often prestressed; that is, the tensile reinforcement has been placed under tension before the member is erected. Pretensioning is a technique in which the reinforcement is placed in the forms and stretched against fixed abutments; concrete is then poured around the wires or cables. Pretensioned members are made several at a time in a long bed (see Fig. 9-24), and the major requirements are therefore simplicity and quantity.

Post-tensioning involves first forming and pouring the member with ducts through its length. After the concrete is cured, reinforcement is placed in the ducts and anchored at one end. It is stretched against the concrete by means of jacks such as the one illustrated in Fig. 9-25. The *tendons* are gripped and tension is maintained by various patented gripping devices which fit into the end of the member. Post-tensioning is economical if the member is long or large. Both

Fig. 9-25. Hydraulic tensioning jack. (Courtesy Portland Cement Ass'n.)

weight and cost may generally be reduced by post-tensioning units longer than 45 ft or weighing over 7 tons.

Normally reinforced members (which include nearly all columns) are individually made, and this makes possible the production of special shapes to suit a particular situation. In Fig. 9-26, the columns include seats to support the girders. Figure 9-27 illustrates two other column shapes just as readily produced by precast members. In Fig. 9-29 still another specialized column shape is shown.

Precast girder and beam shapes have become standardized to a considerable degree, but it is possible to produce a special shape if required. In Fig. 9-28, a number of beam shapes in common use are shown. One great advantage in the use of these precast members is the possibility of erecting long free spans. In Fig. 9-29, for example, the single T girders shown have a span of 75 ft, and much greater spans are quite common.

Precast concrete joists are widely used to support concrete floor and roof slabs in many types of buildings. They are small, normally reinforced units, usually made in depths of 8, 10 and 12 in. (see Fig. 9-30) and in lengths of from 10 to 20 ft. A series of steel loops or stirrups is cast into the top edge to provide anchorage for the floor slab. These joists are normally used with conventional poured-in-place or concrete block walls, set up as indicated in Fig. 9-31 on centers of 20, 24, 27, 30, or 33 in. Slab forms are set as shown in Fig. 9-32, and for spans of over 16 ft, cast-in-place bridging should be used at midspan. A method of forming for this type of bridging is illustrated in Fig. 9-33.

Fig. 9-24. Precast, pretensioned beams. (Courtesy Portland Cement Ass'n.)

Fig. 9-26. Precast, prestressed concrete structural frame. (Courtesy Portland Cement Ass'n.)

I beam

Wide flange I

Modified I   Inverted T

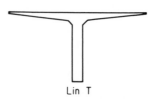

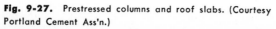
Lin T

Fig. 9-28. Precast girder shapes. (Courtesy American Concrete Institute.)

Fig. 9-27. Prestressed columns and roof slabs. (Courtesy Portland Cement Ass'n.)

Fig. 9-29. Single T prestressed girders. (Courtesy Portland Cement Ass'n.)

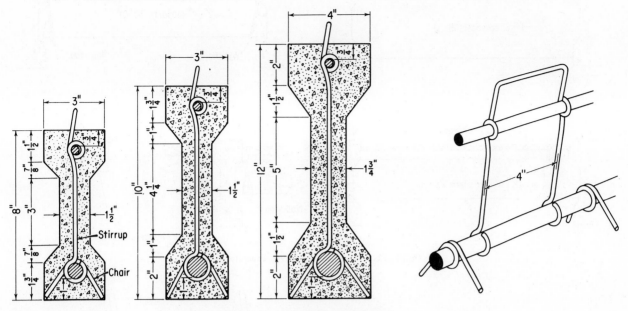

Fig. 9-30. Precast concrete joist sizes

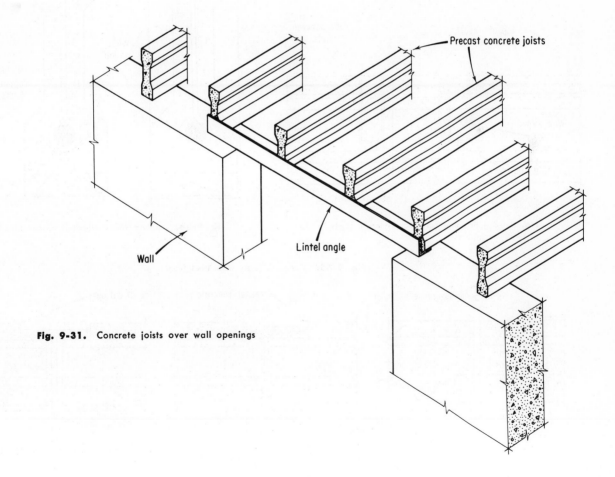

Fig. 9-31. Concrete joists over wall openings

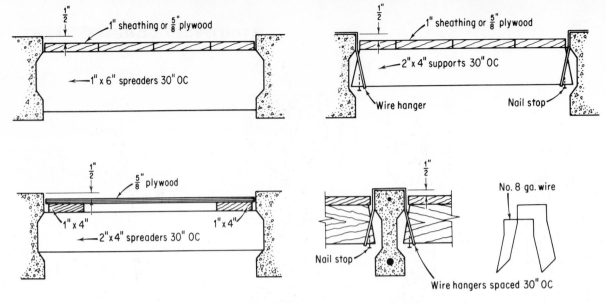

Fig. 9-32. Forms for slab over concrete joists

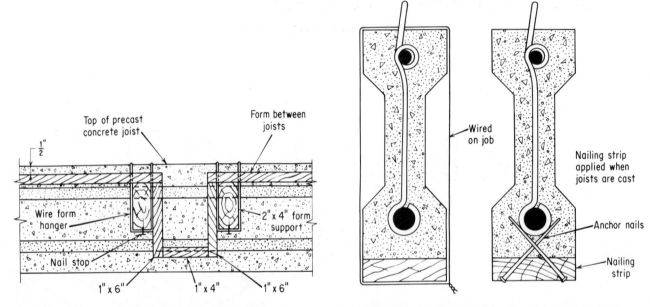

Fig. 9-33. Bridging form for concrete joists

Fig. 9-34. Nailing strips attached to concrete joists

Fig. 9-35. Concrete joists with steel frame

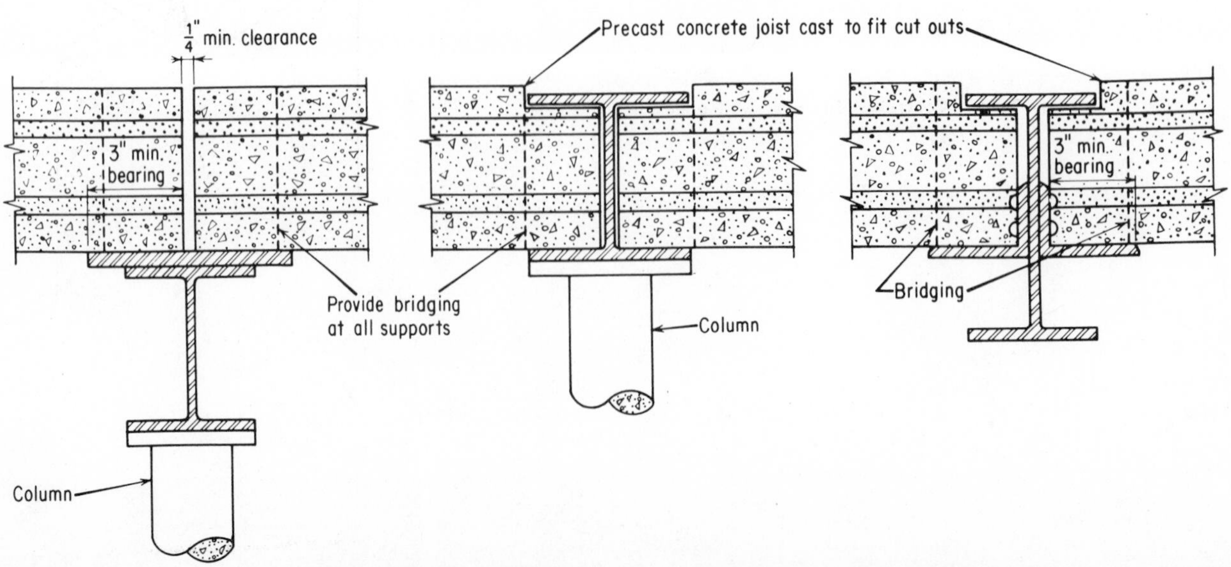

Fig. 9-36. Column-to-footing connections. (Courtesy Portland Cement Co.)

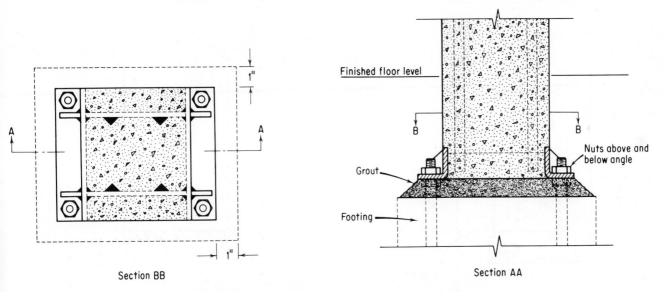

Section BB

Finished floor level

Grout

Footing

Nuts above and below angle

Section AA

Fig. 9-37. Column base connection at independent footing

Flat ceilings can be securely fastened to the bottom of concrete joists by means of wood nailing strips. These may be attached to the joists during casting (see Fig. 9-34) or attached by wire after the joists are in place.

Precast concrete joists may also be used with a structural steel frame. In some cases the regular joists may be used, while in others joists can be cast with special ends to fit steel framing members.

The first step in the erection of a precast structural frame is the preparation of the column footings. Since the columns must be mechanically attached to them, anchor bolts have to be set very accurately into the footing (see the section in Chapter 6 on dowel templates). Each column foot has anchor plates (Fig. 9-36) cast into it so that the column can be bolted to the footing.

A nut is turned onto each anchor bolt before the

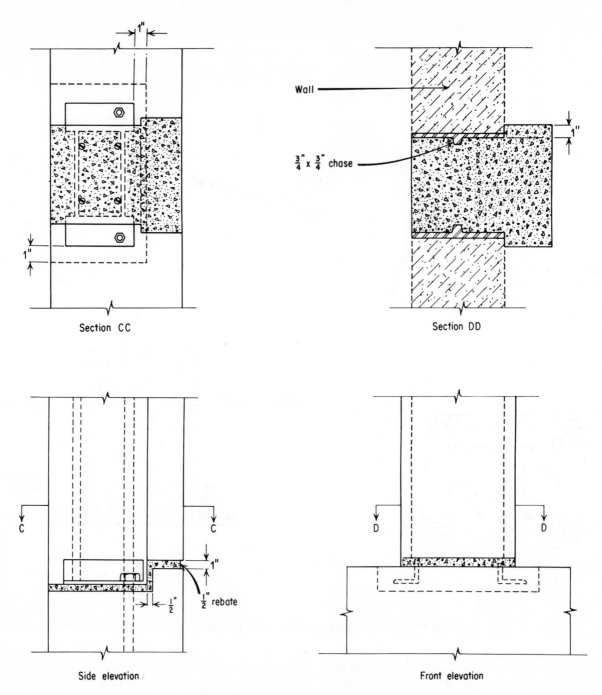

Fig. 9-38. External column base connection

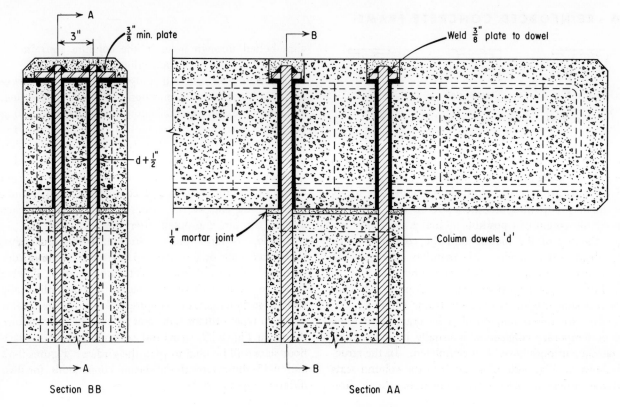

Section BB

Section AA

Fig. 9-39. Rigid column-beam connection

Fig. 9-40. Simply supported column-beam connection

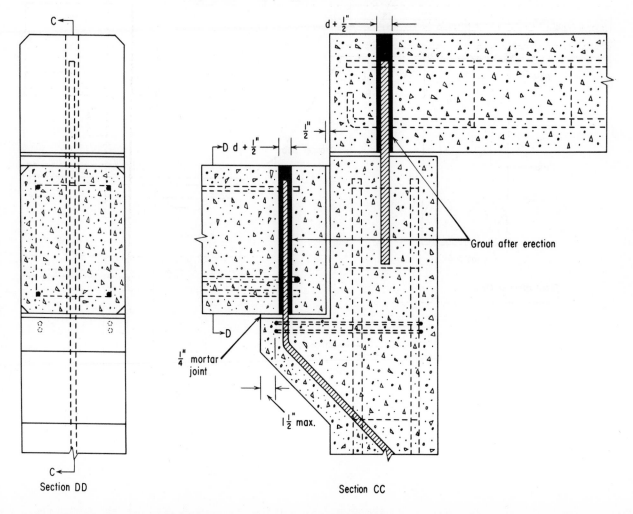

Section DD

Section CC

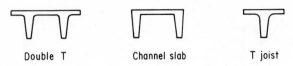

Double T   Channel slab   T joist

Fig. 9-41. Common precast roof slab shapes

column is set over them. After erection, the column is plumbed—using guy wires if necessary (see Fig. 9-26), and the nuts are adjusted until the column rests firmly over them. Top nuts are then put on and tightened to hold the column in position. Finally, the space between the top of the footing and the column is filled with grout—often made with metallic aggregate—to provide even pressure over the entire area.

In Fig. 9-38, a typical external column-to-wall connection is shown with its concrete frame exposed.

Girders are raised into position by crane, and some type of temporary connection is usually provided until the permanent ones have been completed. In the structure shown in Fig. 9-26, pins cast into the column seats hold the girders in place during erection. Angle iron

clips bolted through holes in the columns restrain the girders until the final connections can be made.

Connections may be either *rigid frame* or *simply supported*. Rigid frame connections are made by welding, and simply supported connections are made by inserting pins from one member to another. In Fig. 9-24, the beam shown has a steel plate cast into its ends so that a welded connection may be made between it and a plate or bar cast into the column. In simply supported connections, pins cast into the column seats project into holes in the end of the girder or beam. The space around the pin is grouted after erection.

Finally, in most precast structural frame designs, prestressed floor or roof slabs span from girder to girder or from wall to wall to complete the structure. These slabs are really floor or roof beams cast monolithically with a section of slab. Figure 9-41 illustrates a few common types of floor slabs now in use. In the structure shown in Fig. 9-29, structural concrete poured-in-place floor slabs will be used to span the girders. Figures 9-42 and 9-43 show typical slab-beam connections for two different types of slabs.

Fig. 9-42. Channel slab-beam connection

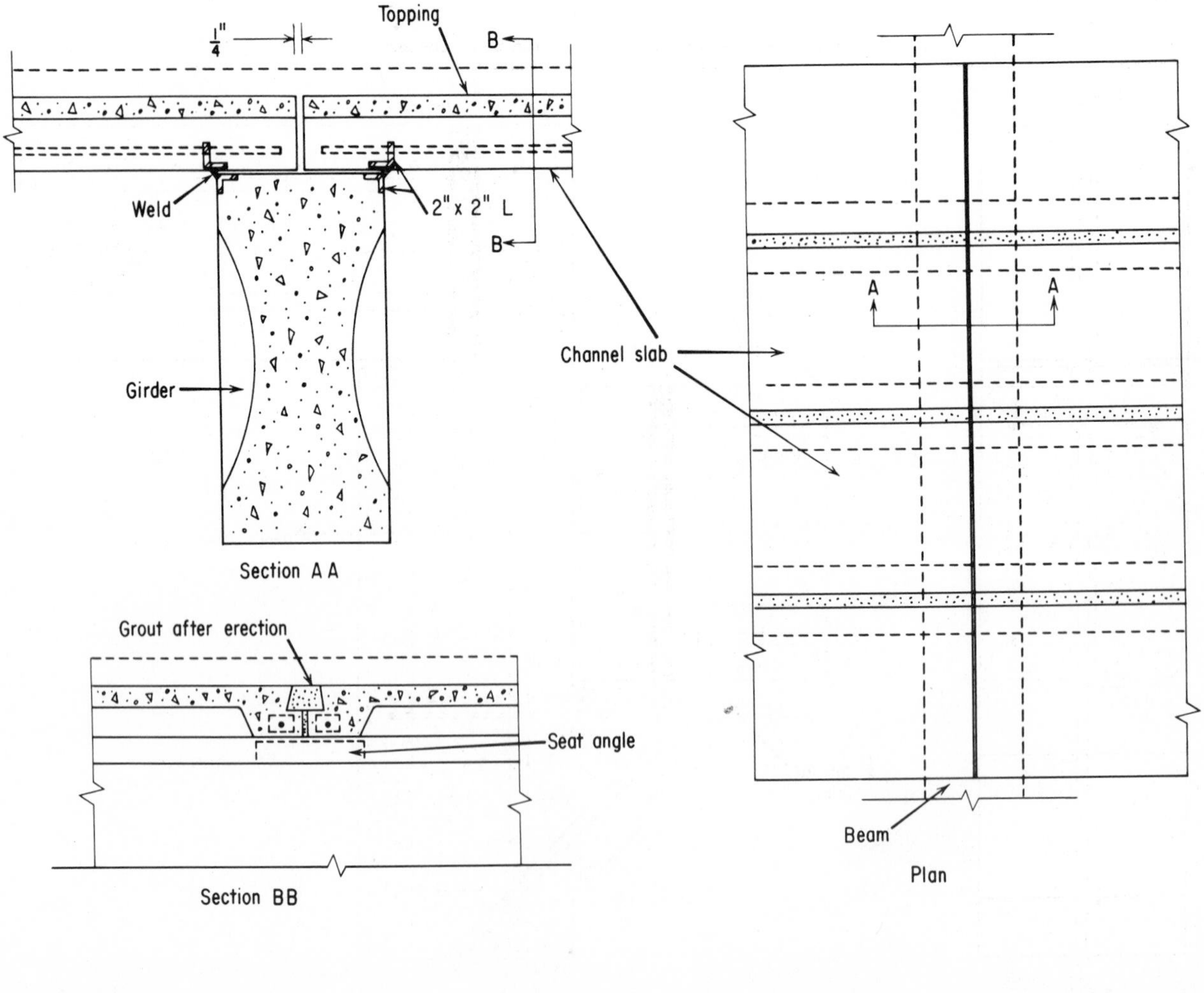

Topping

$\frac{1}{4}''$ B

Weld

2" x 2" L   B

Girder

Section A A

Grout after erection

Seat angle

Section BB

Channel slab

A   A

Beam

Plan

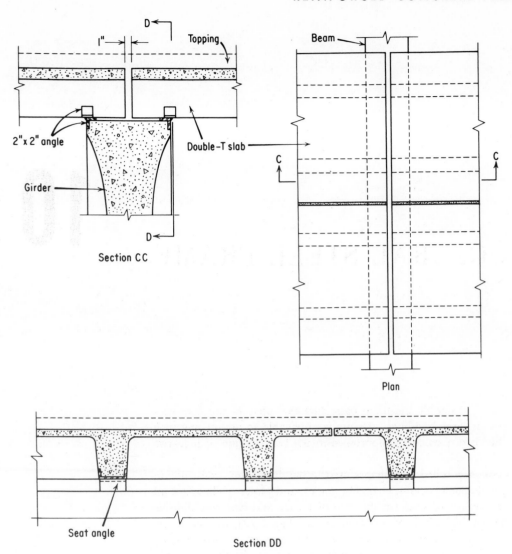

Fig. 9-43. Double T slab-beam connection

REVIEW QUESTIONS

1. What is the primary purpose of reinforcement in: (a) concrete girders and beams? (b) concrete columns?

2. What is the reason for including a window in a column form?

3. 24 pieces of 2″ by 6″ are to be used as cribbing to make a circular wooden form. How much bevel should there be on the edges of the cribbing pieces?

4. What is the purpose of the following items used in beam and girder forming: (a) T-head shore; (b) ledger strip; (c) kicker; (d) vertical stiffener?

5. What is a spandrel beam?

6. What is the purpose of the following items used to reinforce beams or columns: (a) stirrups; (b) chairs; (c) lateral ties?

7. Differentiate between: (a) *normal reinforcing* and *prestressing;* (b) *pretensioning* and *post-tensioning.*

8. What factors are usually considered to determine whether a prestressed member will be pretensioned or post-tensioned?

9. Outline three major advantages of using precast structural members instead of a cast-in-place concrete frame.

10. Differentiate between *rigid* and *simply supported* connections when joining precast structural members.

STRUCTURAL STEEL FRAME $\mathbf{10}$

Structural steel is one of the three basic methods used in the construction of frames for large buildings. Its use is applicable to almost any type of building, but is of particular importance in the construction of high-rise buildings.

The most common rolled steel shapes used in building frame construction are I beams, wide flange beams, channels, angles, and plates. These are all available in a number of sizes (in the case of beams and channels the size represents the nominal depth of the member; see Fig. 10-2), and each size is produced in several weights per lineal foot. Differences are produced by altering the width of flanges and the thickness of webs in the case of I beams, the width and thickness of flanges and the thickness of webs in the case of wide flange members, the thickness of channel webs, and the thickness of the legs of angles. Consult a steel manual for complete listings of the sizes and weights of various rolled shapes.

A great deal of detailing work is necessary before a steel frame can be erected. Each member is given an *erection mark* which it carries through the detailing stage and which is used on the job to identify the member and its position in the frame. The erection mark is usually placed on the left end of horizontal members to eliminate the possibility of trying to place the member end for end or upside down.

Studies must be made during the detailing stage to make sure that it is possible to place each member with the types of connections that have been designated for each end. Girders or beams are sometimes swung into place from the side and are sometimes lowered from above. The type of connection used at one end of a beam must not conflict with the type used at the other.

Two methods are used for raising the members of a steel frame into place. One is the use of *mobile cranes* which operate around the outside of the building, as in Fig. 10-3. But erection is limited by the height and

Fig. 10-1. High-rise office building. (Courtesy Columbia Fireproofing Co.)

any specific situation depends on such questions as: (a) Are shop or field connections involved? (b) What type of steel is in the framing members? (c) Are skilled workmen available? (d) What is the location of the building?

There are usually three steps in the completion of a finished structural frame. The first step is performed by the *raising* crew. These men work with the derrick or crane, raising the members into place, lining up holes with *drift pins*, and inserting temporary connections to hold them together. A *fitting* crew then plumbs the frame by hanging plumb bobs at the columns and adjusting the members by the use of diagonal cables equipped with turnbuckles. They also insert any shims, blocks, etc., that are required for proper alignment, and put in and tighten enough bolts at each connection to hold it until the permanent connection can be completed.

The final connections are made by riveting, bolting, or welding crews, depending on the situation. Riveting involves the use of button-head rivets which are heated and inserted into the holes while still hot. A riveting hammer forms a head on the blank end of the rivet while the other end is *bucked up* by a heavy metal *dolly*. The hot rivet shank is expanded by hammering until it fills the hole completely, and, as it cools and con-

reach of the boom, and *guyed derricks* (Fig. 10-4) resting on the building frame are used for tall buildings. A guyed derrick consists of a mast tied to the building frame and a boom anchored to the mast at one end. *Hairpin anchors* (see Fig. 10-5) cast into the concrete foundations at designated points hold the guy cables from the *spider* at the top of the derrick mast. This spider and a rotating base on the mast allow it to be turned through a complete circle without interfering with the cables.

Cranes are normally used to erect the first *lift* of columns and beams and to raise the derricks to their first position. Special beams, known as *dunnage* beams, are added to the frame at these positions to support the load of the derricks. Two floors are usually erected from one derrick setting, and when this has been completed, the derricks are *jumped* to the next position. This is done by first unpinning the boom and using the mast as a *gin pole* to raise it to the new level. The boom is then temporarily anchored and used as a gin pole to raise the mast.

There are three methods by which the components of a steel frame may be fastened together: *riveting*, *bolting*, and *welding*. The method to be employed in

Fig. 10-2. Typical rolled shapes

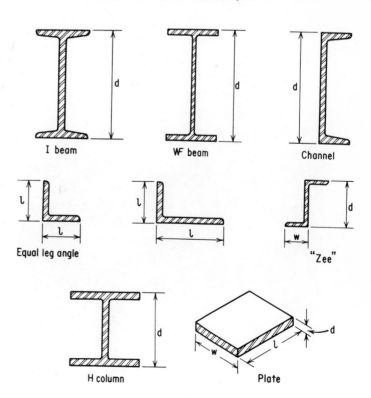

I beam

WF beam

Channel

Equal leg angle

"Zee"

H column

Plate

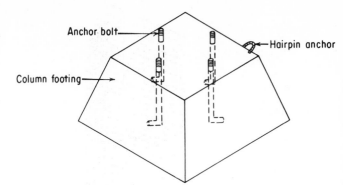

Fig. 10-5. Anchor bolts and hairpin anchors

Fig. 10-3. Crane used for steel erection

Fig. 10-4. Guyed derricks used for steel erection. (Courtesy Bethlehem Steel Co.)

tracts, pulls the two parts of the connection tightly together. Thus, part of the load is supported by friction and part of it by the resistance of the rivets to shear and tension.

Two types of bolt are used in connections. One type (which may be either *ribbed* or *turned*) fits very snugly in the hole and when tightened relies to a great extent on resistance to shear and tension to carry the load. The other type (known as a *high-strength* bolt) is made from treated carbon steel, which permits it to be placed under high tension. Pneumatic impact wrenches are used to tighten the nuts, introducing high clamping forces in the bolts and high friction between the connected parts.

Welded connections are most often made by *arc* welding, and most welded joints are either *butt* or *lap* joints. Figure 10-6 illustrates a few butt and lap welding techniques.

ANCHOR BOLTS

Anchor bolts (see Fig. 10-5) are cast into the concrete foundation and hold the first members of a steel frame to be placed—the column *bearing plates*. These anchor bolts must be positioned very carefully according to plan so that the bearing plates will be lined up accurately.

BEARING PLATES

The column bearing plates are steel plates of various thicknesses in which holes have been drilled to receive the anchor bolts. The holes are slightly larger than the bolts, so that some lateral adjustment of the bearing plate is possible. The angle connections by which the columns will be attached to the bearing

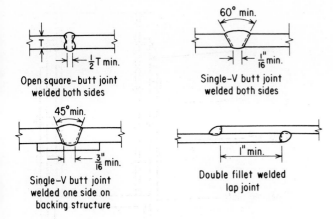

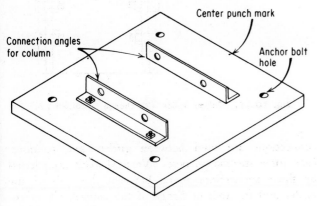

Fig. 10-6. Typical welded joints

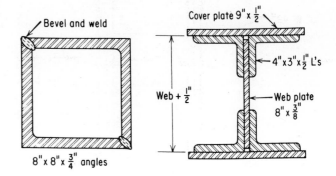

Fig. 10-7. Column bearing plate

A simple wood form is placed around the bearing plate about 2 in. away from its edges. Grout is poured or pumped into the space until it is completely filled. Large bearing plates have grout holes drilled near the center to make sure that no air becomes trapped under them. When grout can be seen in these holes, it indicates that the space has been filled.

COLUMNS

First-tier columns are the next group of members to be erected. They are often two stories long, or in any case, the same size for at least two stories. Column lengths are such that joints—splices—will come 1½ to 2 ft above the floor levels. This is done to prevent splice connections from interfering with girder or beam-to-column connections. Column ends are milled to exactly the right length and to make sure that column loads will be evenly distributed over the entire bearing area.

Wide flange members, as nearly square in cross

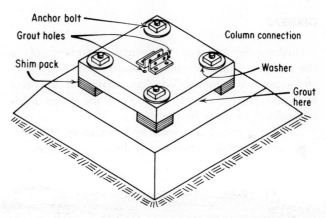

Fig. 10-8. Leveled bearing plate

Fig. 10-9. Built-up column sections

plates are bolted or welded on them. Plates are marked on the axis lines of their four edges to allow positioning by a survey instrument, used to line them up accurately.

Shim packs are set under the four corners of each bearing plate as it is placed. These are 3 to 4 in. metal squares of thicknesses ranging from ¹⁄₁₆ to ¾ in. which are used to bring all the bearing plates to the correct grade level and to level each on its own base. The bearing plates are first leveled individually by adjusting the thickness of the shim packs. They are then brought to the proper grade by raising or lowering each by the same amount at all four corners. Finally, they are lined up in both directions by adjusting each on its anchor bolts as necessary.

After all bearing plates have been set and aligned, they must be *grouted*. This is done by completely filling the space between the bearing plate and the top of the concrete with mortar, preferably a non-shrinking type made with metallic aggregate.

section as possible (see Fig. 10-2), are often chosen for columns. Large diameter pipe may also be used, though a column of this type often presents connecting problems. Columns may also be *built-up* by welding or bolting a number of other rolled shapes—usually angles and plates—into a single unit.

COLUMN SPLICES

Columns sections are joined together by *splice plates* which are bolted, riveted, or welded to the column flanges or, in special cases, to the webs as well. If the sections are the same size, it is common practice to butt one end directly to the other and fasten the splice plates over the joint, as illustrated in Fig. 10-10. When bolts are used, heads are placed to the outside so that bolts will not interfere with the fireproofing.

When the column size is reduced at a joint, a plate is used between the two ends to provide bearing, and filler plates are used between the splice plates and the smaller column flanges (Fig. 10-11).

GIRDERS

Girders—the primary horizontal members of a frame—span from column to column (see Fig. 10-3) and support the intermediate floor beams. They carry wall and partition loads as well as the point loads transmitted to them by the beams.

Regular rolled shapes such as I beams or WF sections are normally used for girders. Two types of

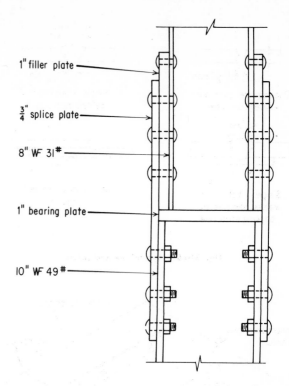

Fig. 10-11. Column splice with change in column size

connections are used between girders and columns, each for a specific purpose. Vertical loads are carried by shear connections made between the web of the girder and the web or flange of the column. Connections are normally made by angles, as in Fig. 10-12, the number of rivets or bolts used depending on the load and the allowable shear stress.

Wind pressure causes lateral loads which vary from floor to floor. At the top of the building, the total force causing lateral movement is the actual force of the wind in psf. The force increases at each floor because of the cumulative effect of forces on each floor above. These forces are resisted by wind bracing or *moment* connections which are generally largest on the lower floors. These connections are made between the flanges of the girder and the flange or web of the column by using angles with one leg extended along the girder flange and the other against the column (see Fig. 10-13). The moment connection to the lower flange of a girder is called a *seated* connection, and the angle-to-column portion of it is usually made in the shop. The *seats* thus provide the means by which the raising crew positions the girders during erection. The vertical legs of moment connections also act as reinforcement for the shear connection, or may in some cases be the only shear connections.

Where heavy loads are involved, the seated connec-

Fig. 10-10. Column splice with no size change

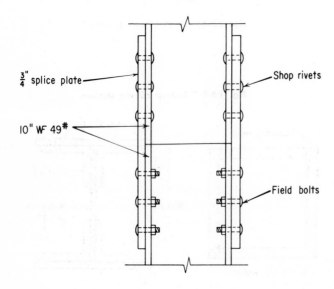

tion may be fabricated as a *reinforced seat*. This may be done by backing two angles together and welding a piece of plate to their top edges, as illustrated in Fig. 10-14.

Split beams are sometimes used for making moment connections (Fig. 10-15) and brackets are frequently used where they will not interfere with architectural features. They may be bolted, riveted (Fig. 10-16), or welded (as in Fig. 10-4).

Most connections have been standardized, and the tables in steel manuals give allowable loads for various sizes of connections, stiffened or unstiffened.

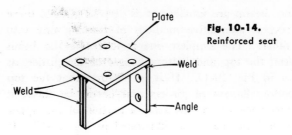

Fig. 10-14.
Reinforced seat

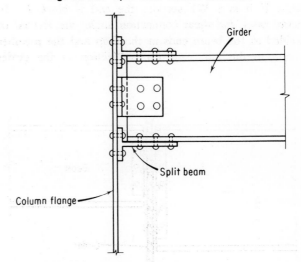

Fig. 10-15. Split beam moment connection

Fig. 10-16. Bracket type moment connections

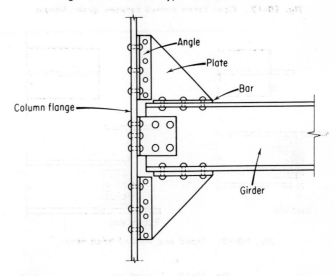

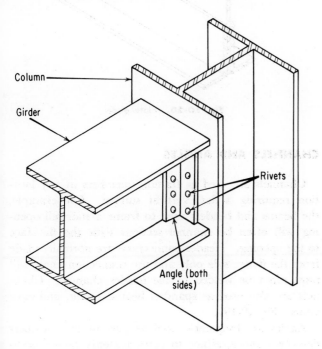

Fig. 10-12. Shear connection

Fig. 10-13. Moment connections

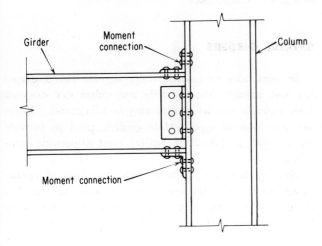

BEAMS

Beams, generally smaller than girders, may be connected either to a column or to a girder. Beam connections at a column are similar to the girder-to-column connections. In beam-to-girder connections, the main consideration is the shear connection, since the beams are considered to be carrying the floor loads and transferring them to girders as vertical loads.

Since beams are usually not as deep as girders, there are several alternative methods of framing one into the other. The simplest one is to frame the beam between the top and bottom flanges of the girder, as shown in Fig. 10-17. If it is required that the top or bottom flanges of girders and beams be flush, it becomes necessary to cut away a portion of the upper or lower beam flange, as illustrated in Fig. 10-18. If the girder is an I beam, the end of the beam is *coped*, while if it is a WF section, the end is *blocked*. In many cases, the shear connection angles are riveted or welded to the beam ends in the shop and the member comes to the job ready for connection to the girder web.

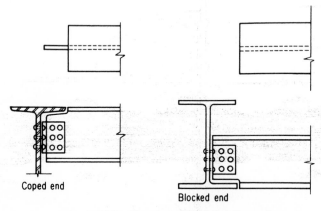

Fig. 10-17. Floor beams framed between girder flanges

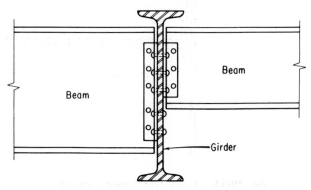

Fig. 10-18. Coped and blocked beam ends

Fig. 10-19. Channel uses

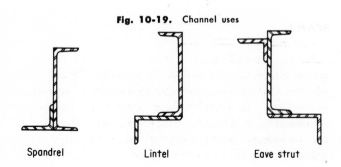

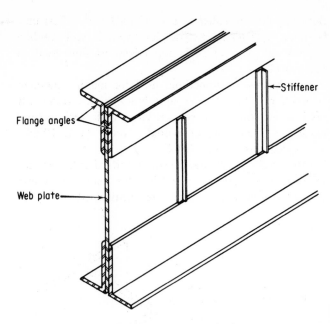

Fig. 10-20. Plate girder

CHANNELS AND ANGLES

Channels are used as framing members in any location requiring a flat, vertical surface. For example, the beams and headers used to frame a stairwell opening will often be channel sections with the flat face to the opening. Header connections are normally made from the flange side only and the connection angle will most often be welded to the header channel. Channels are also used as spandrel beams, lintels, and eave struts (Fig 10-19).

Angles are frequently used as part of the members described above, either to carry masonry facing or to complete the required shape. Angles are also used as diagonal wind bracing, as in Fig. 10-4. Notice that *gusset* plates are used here to simplify angle-to-column-and-girder connections.

SPECIAL GIRDERS

In particular situations where regular rolled shapes are not suitable because they are either not deep or wide enough, special girders may be fabricated. There are two general types—*plate girders*, used to provide extra depth, and *built-up girders*, used to provide extra width.

Plate girders are made by using a plate of appropriate width and thickness for the web, and angles, riveted or welded at the top and bottom edges for flanges. Deep plate girders often require vertical stif-

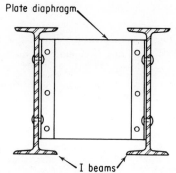

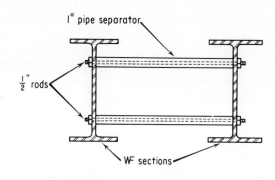

Fig. 10-21. Built-up girder

Fig. 10-22. Steel raising operations. (Courtesy Dominion Steel and Coal Co.)

feners, in the form of angles welded to the web. In Fig. 10-4, a plate girder made from plate and channels and with vertical stiffeners is being hoisted into place as a spandrel beam.

Built-up girders are made by joining two or more regular rolled shapes side by side by means of plates or pipes known as *separators*.

As soon as one tier is erected, the derrick is raised to the next level. While this is being done, the fitting crew is completing work on the last tier. Columns are plumbed, shims are placed if necessary, and if the connections are bolted, all the bolts are inserted. If the frame is to be riveted, only those bolts needed to hold the connections tight are used. They will be replaced with rivets later.

The erection of steel requires skill, thoughtfulness, and constant attention to rules of safety. Some general safety rules to observe are as follows:

1. Do not attempt steel erection on rainy days. It is dangerous to work on wet steel.
2. Wear shoes with sewn leather or rubber soles.
3. Do not allow anyone to stand beneath a loaded boom.
4. Do not allow anyone to ride a load.
5. Wear heavy gloves which do not have loose cuffs.
6. Do not wear loose clothing which could easily catch on projections or swinging objects.
7. Use shackles instead of hooks.
8. Use cable slings instead of chains for lifting steel.
9. Make sure that the brakes on hoisting drums are inspected daily.
10. Keep a constant lookout for frayed or broken strands in cables and repair or replace them if necessary.

REVIEW QUESTIONS

1. (a) What is the purpose of placing erection marks on structural steel members? (b) Where is the erection mark placed on a beam?

2. (a) What is a hairpin anchor? (b) What is it used for? (Give two uses.)

3. (a) What is the difference between the operation of a *mobile crane* and that of a *guyed derrick*? (b) What is the purpose of a *dunnage beam*?

4. What are *shim packs* and what are they used for?

5. How does one allow for the lining-up of column billets after placement?

6. Outline the function of a fitting crew.

7. Provide explanations for the following: (a) column splices are made above floor level; (b) column ends are milled in the shop; (c) it is sometimes necessary to use plates in column connections.

8. (a) Give the two primary types of girder- or beam-to-column connections. (b) What purpose does each type serve? (c) Describe each type briefly.

9. How are columns plumbed after erection?

10. What is meant by *coping* and *blocking* in steel framing?

11. What is the difference between plate girders and built-up girders?

12. What is meant by *jumping* a derrick?

11

FLOOR SYSTEMS AND INDUSTRIAL FLOORING

The erection of the structural frame marks the completion of a phase in the construction of a building. The next step involves the installation of floors and is usually done in two operations—first a base, or *subfloor* is built; and second, the application of *finish flooring*.

Subfloors may be made of wood, concrete, or a combination of concrete and steel. The type used in any particular situation depends to a great extent on the type of structural frame present. When a reinforced concrete frame is involved, the base slab is usually also concrete and the installation of floors is not really a separate phase since both frame and floor are poured monolithically. If timber or steel frames are used, the structural supports are erected prior to the start of all floor construction.

WOOD FLOORS

Wood floors are almost always used with timber frames, but may be used with steel frames.

Wood subfloors may be constructed in two ways. One method involves the use of 2″ by 4″s or 2″ by 6″s laminated on edge and at right angles to the floor beams. The pieces are spiked together side by side and no attempt is made to make the end joints meet over a support (although some of them should and, of course, the starting course end joints must do so).

When the floor frame is composed of wood beams, the laminations may be toenailed to the beams. In the case of a steel floor frame, a wooden pad is first fastened to the top flange of the beams (Fig. 11-2) and the subfloor is then toenailed to the pad.

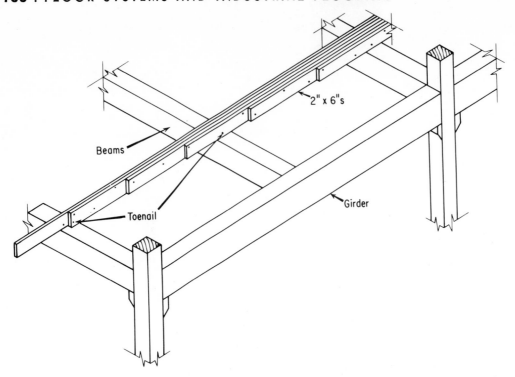

Fig. 11-1. Laminated wood deck on timber frame

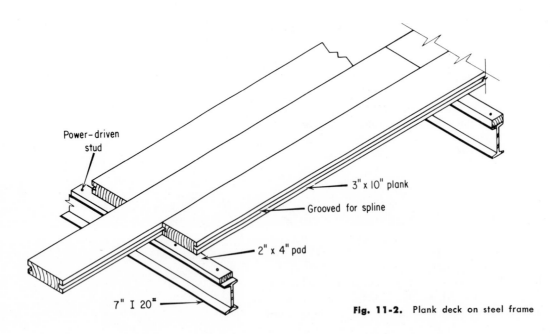

Fig. 11-2. Plank deck on steel frame

The other type of wood floor consists of heavy planks, thick enough to carry their load without excessive deflection, laid across the beams and spiked to them. Planks are usually tongue-and-grooved or *splined* for greater rigidity. End joints in these planks will come over a beam, as in Fig. 11-2.

CONCRETE FLOORS

Concrete is used for floors laid directly on the ground (*slab-on-grade*) and for floors supported by the structural frame. Slab-on-grade floors may be poured before any other part of the building has been built, as in Fig. 11-3, or on a leveled and compacted grade after the rest of the building has been erected. In the first case, side forms of wood or metal are placed, leveled, and staked, and screed strips are placed at convenient intervals to provide guides in leveling the concrete. In Fig. 11-3, note the vibrating straight edge and drag used to level the slab. Figure 11-4 depicts another type of construction in which the slab is poured before the erection of a structural frame.

A single course slab poured on grade after the walls have been erected is a common occurrence in industrial and commercial buildings. A reasonably standard procedure may be followed in making such a floor.

1. Backfill all ditches and trenches within the walls with granular fill. Compact it thoroughly, preferably with some type of mechanical equipment such as that shown in Fig. 11-5.
2. Isolate all columns from the floor slab by boxing

Fig. 11-3. Slab-on-grade concrete floor

them with square wood or metal forms, or with round fiberboard forms. Forms should be set to the level of the top of the slab (Fig. 11-6).
3. Set screed strips at the same elevation at convenient intervals throughout the area to be concreted. Provide a keyway form on each screed strip.
4. Isolate the walls from the slab by fastening strips of asphalt-impregnated fiberboard or other joint material not more than ½ in. thick around the walls, level with the top of the slab.

Fig. 11-4. Subbasement floor for office building. (Courtesy Bethlehem Steel Co.)

Fig. 11-5. Compacting machine

Fig. 11-6. Leveling screed stakes

5. Prepare any changes in slab thickness, as at doorways, to be as gradual as possible and at slopes of not more than 1 in 10.

6. Use a template with legs the length of the slab thickness to check the grade (see Fig. 11-6).

7. Oil the screed strips.

8. Cover the grade with a polyethylene moisture barrier, allowing generous lap between strips.

9. Place the reinforcement—mesh or rod—as specified in plans.

10. Place the concrete as close to its final position as possible. Consolidate with an internal vibrator, especially at corners, walls, and bulkheads.

11. Straight-edge the concrete to the level of the screed strips.

12. Smooth the surface with a long handled float or a darby (Fig. 11-7) to remove the high and low spots. Cover with damp burlap until ready for the next operation.

13. Float the surface with hand or mechanical floats as soon as the concrete supports the weight of a man.

14. If specified, apply metallic aggregate hardener (see directions for applying hardener, p. 200).

Fig. 11-7. Darbying a concrete slab. (Courtesy Portland Cement Ass'n)

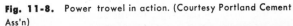

Fig. 11-8. Power trowel in action. (Courtesy Portland Cement Ass'n)

Fig. 11-9. Sawing control joints

floor, shown in Fig. 11-10. Here the slab is supported by a series of parallel beams. Another type is known as a *flat slab* floor. There are no beams in this type of construction but the slab is supported by thickened sections over the columns known as *drop panels*. Increased support is provided at the column by enlarging its top end into what is known as a *column capital*. A third type is a *ribbed slab*. It consists of a series of concrete joists or ribs, containing the reinforcement, cast monolithically with a relatively thin slab. The ribs, in turn, frame into supporting girders. The main purpose of using a ribbed slab floor is to reduce the dead load by concentrating the reinforcement in the ribs and leaving out most of the concrete between them. A variation of the ribbed slab is made by running ribs in two directions, at right angles to one another, thus producing what is commonly referred to as a *waffle* floor.

Another method of reducing the weight of floors is

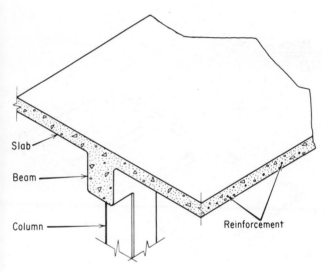

Fig. 11-10. Beam-and-slab floor

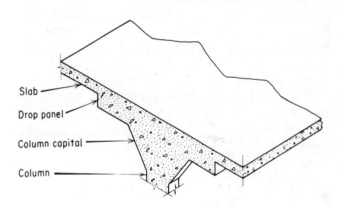

Fig. 11-11. Flat slab floor

15. Trowel to a hard, dense surface with hand or power trowels (Fig. 11-8).
16. Cure by covering with: (a) waterproof curing paper; (b) two coats of curing compound; (c) burlap kept moist at all times; or (d) a layer of damp sand.
17. Remove the forms around columns and attach joint material to the vertical faces of the slab and the base of the columns. Fill with concrete, edge, and finish.
18. Cut control joints to a depth of at least ⅕ the slab thickness with a power saw every 20 to 25 ft in both directions (Fig. 11-9).
19. Caulk the joints with mastic joint filler.
20. Cure for at least 7 days before allowing regular traffic on the floor.

Concrete floors supported by a concrete frame are of several different types. One is a *beam-and-slab*

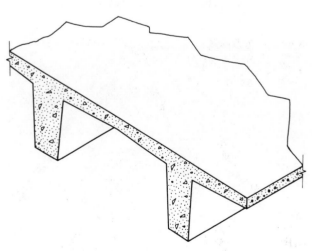

Fig. 11-12. Ribbed slab

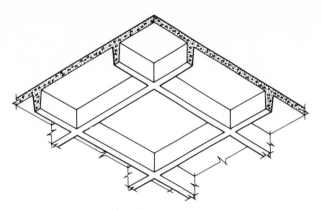

Fig. 11-13. Two-way ribbed slab

to produce a series of voids. This may be done by laying cardboard tubes with sealed ends in rows as in Fig. 11-14, by using egg-crate type cardboard core forms, or by using a type of lightweight block, laid in rows, to replace concrete.

Forms for a beam-and-slab floor consist of slab forms and the shores which support them, beam forms and the T shores which support them, *kickers* between slab and beam forms (see Fig. 9-18), and supports for the edges of the slab form over the T shores.

The slab forms should be made first. The frames are of 2″ by 4″s in any required size, but one edge of the sheathing should be beveled at 45° and extended about 2¼ in. beyond the frame on panels which will meet the beam form.

The column forms are next erected, plumbed, and braced. The T shores are set up between each pair of columns (see Fig. 9-16), using a chalk line from one column top to another as a guide. If a camber

Fig. 11-14. Forms for floor voids

is required in the beam, raise the center shore the required amount, run the chalk line over it, and set the remainder of the shores to the line.

The beam form may now be built on the shore heads and the slab form panels can be raised and supported. It is important to see that the *kickers* are in place between the beam sides and the edges of the slab forms. These kickers prevent the beam sides from being pushed out by the pressure of the concrete and allow easy removal of beam sides when the concrete has cured sufficiently.

The first step in the erection of formwork for a flat slab floor is to erect the shores and brace them temporarily. Stringers are then placed on the shores and joists laid across the stringers, leaving openings wher-

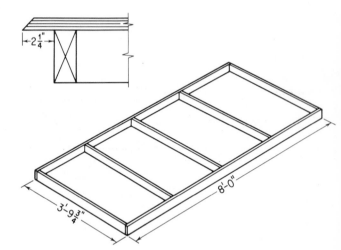

Fig. 11-15. Frame for slab form panel

ever there are to be drop panels. This framework is leveled by wedging or adjusting the length of the shores, and sheathing is finally laid over the joists. Where sheathing meets a drop panel, the edge is beveled and extended over the top of the drop panel in the same way that slab form sheathing extends over beam side forms.

Drop panels are built separately and are supported on separate shores or on sections of steel scaffolding set up to form a square supporting structure. Figure 11-17 illustrates one method of forming the drop panel. The sheathing must be cut to fit the column capital which will be part of the column form.

Ribbed slab floors are formed by the use of pre-fabricated metal or plastic forms—called *pans* or *tile* ——held in position and supported in any one of several ways. Pans for one-way ribs are usually made

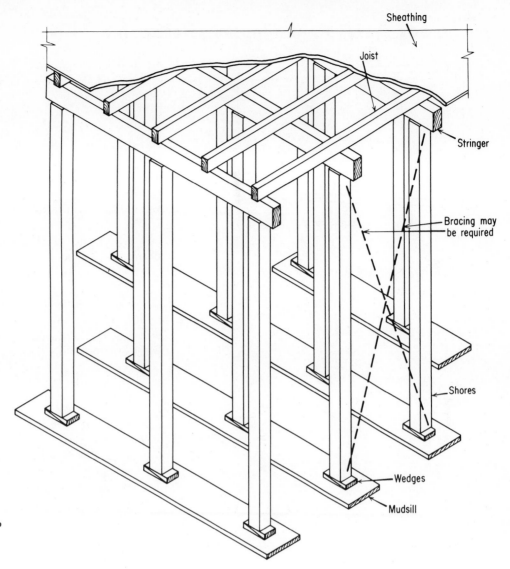

Fig. 11-16. Typical flat slab formwork

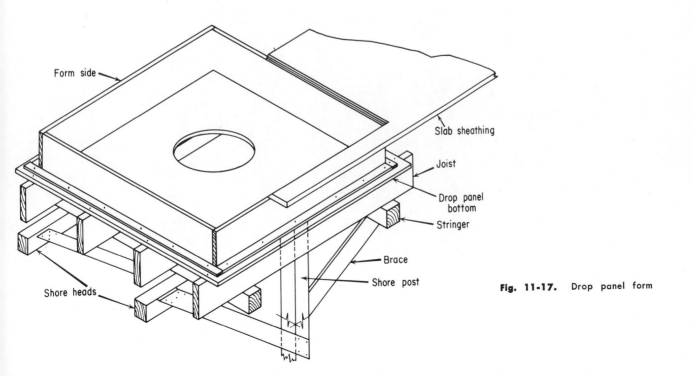

Fig. 11-17. Drop panel form

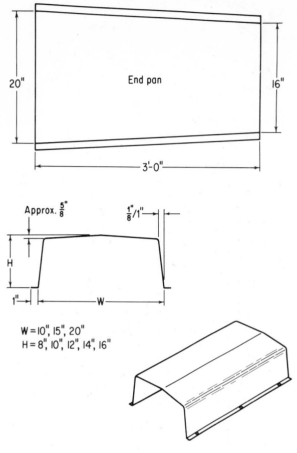

Fig. 11-18. Bent leg metal pan

from sheet metal, but those used to form two-way ribs—a *waffle* floor—may be either sheet metal or plastic.

Pans for one-way ribs are made in two ways. One type has the ends of its legs turned out flat, as illustrated in Fig. 11-18, so that the pan may rest on a flat surface, while the other has straight legs (see Fig. 11-22) which must be fastened to the sides of supports. The *bent-leg* type is made in several widths and depths while the straight-leg type is usually made in 20 in. widths. Both are made in 3 ft sections, with tapered end sections to provide greater width of rib at the beam. Both types have sheet metal end caps.

The bent-leg pans may be used in two ways. In the nail-down system, the pans are placed and nailed to a series of *soffit boards* supported on stringers and shores (Fig. 11-19). The depth of the ribs is determined by that of the pans. When this system is used, the procedure for setting up pans is as follows:

1. Erect and support soffit boards as required.
2. Nail the end caps to the soffit boards at each end of a bay.
3. Place the first pan—usually a tapered one—over the end cap.
4. Place the next pan over the first and lap at least two in.
5. Continue setting pans with at least two in. laps until they meet at the center. The middle pan must always be placed last.

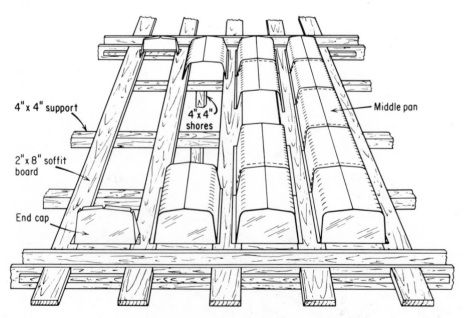

Fig. 11-19. Metal pans in nail-down system

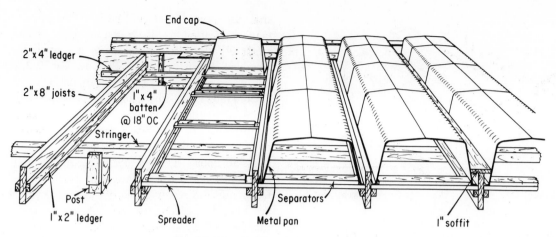

Fig. 11-20. Metal pans in adjustable system

The other system of using bent-leg pans—known as the adjustable system—is illustrated in Fig. 11-20. Here the depth of ribs may be altered, within limits, according to the position of the ledger strips on the joists. The procedure for setting up pans this way is as follows:

1. Set up and level stringers as required.
2. Nail ledger strips to the joists at the specified level.
3. Set joists on the stringers on the required centers.
4. Cut spreaders to length (face to face of joists) and separators 2¼ in. shorter, with ends cut to the slope of the pans. Tack separators to spreaders.
5. Set the spreaders on the ledger strips, two per pan section.
6. Place end caps on spreaders at each end of bay.
7. Place metal pans on spreaders, using the same sequence as outlined above.
8. Cut soffit pieces from 1 in. material, wide enough to fit between pans and rest on the top of joists. The ends of these soffits must be widened to compensate for the taper on the end pans.

Pans for a waffle floor may be set on a solid deck or on soffit boards. In Fig. 11-21, soffit boards are used to support the *dome* pans, and a plywood deck form is used where a solid section of slab is required.

Straight-leg pans are supported by nailing them to the sides of the joists with double-headed nails (Fig. 11-22). Three or more sets of nail holes are drilled in the legs and the depth of ribs is altered by adjusting the position of the legs against the joists and using the appropriate set of holes. Joists to be used with this type of pan are usually built to form a standard rib width. The ends of the joists are widened to com-

pensate for the tapered end pans (Fig. 11-23).

Positive reinforcement in ribbed floors is concentrated in the ribs, with temperature reinforcement being placed over the pans. Figure 11-24 shows a typical ribbed floor being poured. Notice that the exterior walls, beams, and floor are being poured monolithically. Notice also the column dowels for second floor columns and the runways used to carry concrete buggies over the pans.

Forms for all these concrete floors must have some type of adjustable support. This is usually provided by posts or by sections of steel scaffolding. One-piece wood posts are adjusted by wedges under the bottom

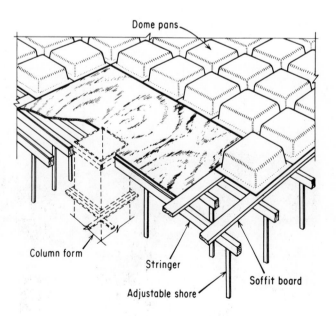

Fig. 11-21. Dome pans for waffle floor

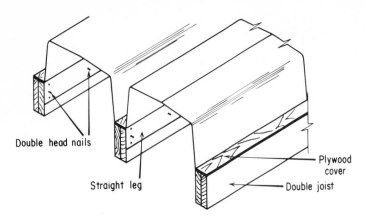

Fig. 11-22. Straight leg pans on double joists

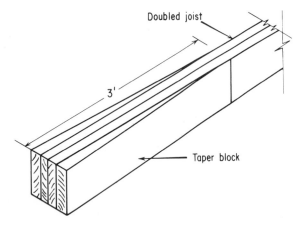

Fig. 11-23. Joist ends widened

end, as shown in Fig. 11-16. Two-piece posts are made and used as illustrated in Fig. 11-25. Several kinds of adjustable metal posts are available, one of which is shown in Fig. 11-26. In Fig. 9-8, steel scaffolding is being used as form support.

Concrete floors supported by a steel frame are often simple flat slabs. However, in some cases, concrete fireproofing for the beam may be incorporated with the slab, in which case the structure becomes a beam-and-slab floor. Though the forms shown in Fig. 11-27 are supported from below, the steel frame itself is frequently utilized to support the forms. Steel *hangers* are placed over the top web of the beams and carry the ends of wood joists spanning from beam to beam. Plywood sheathing laid on the joists provides the base for the slab.

Hangers are available in a number of styles and lengths. Long *loop* hangers, such as those used in Fig. 11-28, allow the top flange and the upper portion of the beam webs to be encased by the slab. *Coil* hangers (Fig. 11-29) make it possible to keep the sheathing up tight under the top flanges, so that the entire slab is above the beams.

Combination concrete and steel floors consist of a sheet steel base covered with a concrete slab. The base may be made of corrugated sheet metal laid over a steel or concrete floor frame or it may be one of several styles of specially formed steel decking. Illustrated in Fig. 11-31 is a *cellular* type deck, but other types consist only of the upper, folded sheet.

Decking of this kind is fastened to a steel frame by

Fig. 11-24. Combination floor and wall pour

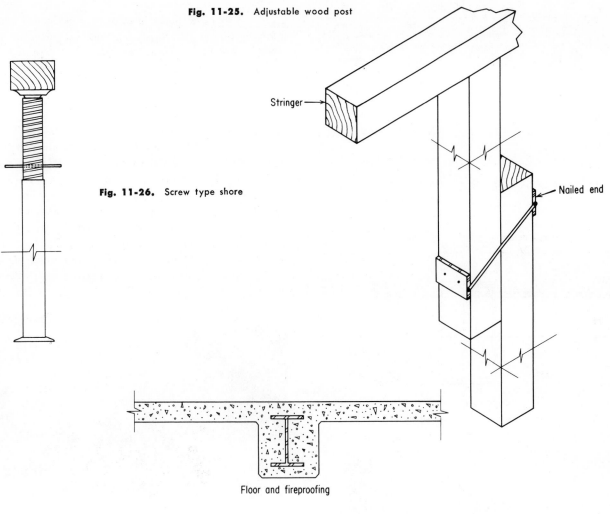

Fig. 11-25. Adjustable wood post

Stringer

Nailed end

Fig. 11-26. Screw type shore

Floor and fireproofing

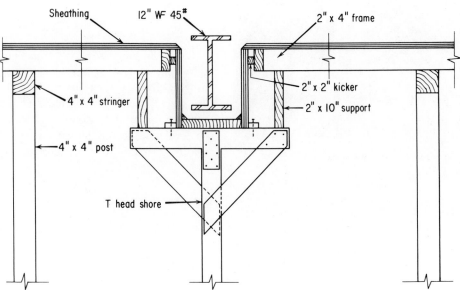

Sheathing

12" WF 45#

2" x 4" frame

4" x 4" stringer

2" x 2" kicker

2" x 10" support

4" x 4" post

T head shore

Fig. 11-27. Forming for floor slab and fireproofing

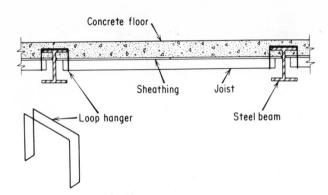

Fig. 11-28. Floor form suspended by loop hangers

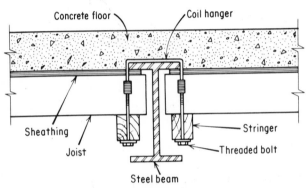

Fig. 11-29. Floor form suspended by coil hangers

Fig. 11-30. Corrugated sheet metal decking. (Courtesy Bethlehem Steel Co.)

spot welding (Fig. 11-32), by plug welding, or by self-tapping screws—for which holes must be predrilled. Connections to a concrete frame may be made by welding to cast-in connection strips or by the use of powder-driven pins. Notice in Fig. 11-30 that the studs which fasten the decking to the frame will also act as anchors to the concrete slab.

INDUSTRIAL FLOORING

The structural floors previously described generally require some type of *finish floor*. It may be *wood* (block or strip flooring), *concrete, terrazzo, terra cotta tile, mastic flooring,* or *resilient tile.*

Wood Floors

Strip flooring for industrial use is made from both hardwood and softwood in thicknesses of from 2 to 4 in. Widths of strips vary from 1½ in. for hardwood flooring to 12 in. for heavy softwood flooring. Strips may be single or double tongue-and-grooved, or grooved on both edges for *splines*. Strip flooring may be laid over plank or laminated wood subfloors by direct nailing, or over a concrete subfloor by nailing to *sleepers* which are laid in asphalt or partially cast into concrete.

Fig. 11-31. Cellular steel decking. (Courtesy Bethlehem Steel Co.)

Block flooring is made from both hardwood and softwood, in edge grain blocks of various dimensions ranging from 1 to 4 in. thick. The softwood blocks are usually heavily creosoted and laid over a concrete subfloor in asphalt mastic. The concrete base must be level and reasonably smooth to achieve satisfactory results with this type of flooring.

Concrete Floors

Concrete finish floors are widely used in industrial and commercial buildings and may consist of a single, finished slab or of a base and topping slab.

A two-course slab is sometimes specified in order to produce a harder, denser, more durable surface. If this is the case, the base slab should be left about 1 in.

below the finish grade. Just before the concrete sets, the surface should be roughened with a stiff broom to provide a better bond with the topping.

The topping mix should be made from the hardest, densest aggregates available, with a high design strength and a very low slump (not exceeding 1 in.). Just prior to the application of the topping, the base slab should be washed, and a coat of cement paste applied with a stiff brush. The topping mix is spread over the surface, raked, leveled, and tamped (preferably with a power tamper). Notice in Fig. 11-36 that in spite of the dry mix, the machine is bringing enough moisture to the top to produce a smooth surface. Final floating and troweling is best accomplished when done by power machinery.

A very durable surface may be produced on a concrete floor slab by the introduction of metallic aggregate into the topping. Metallic aggregate is composed of iron particles which have been size-graded to within the range of #4-100 mesh sieves, specially processed

Fig. 11-32. Spot-welding steel deck. (Courtesy Bethlehem Steel Co.)

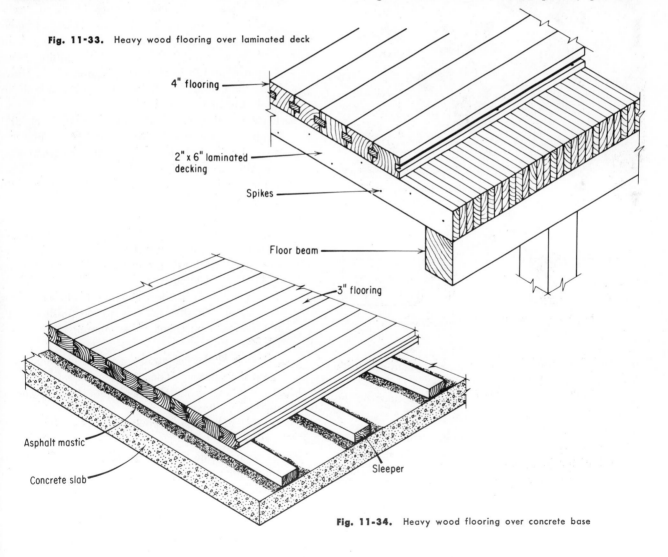

Fig. 11-33. Heavy wood flooring over laminated deck

4" flooring

2" x 6" laminated decking

Spikes

Floor beam

3" flooring

Asphalt mastic

Concrete slab

Sleeper

Fig. 11-34. Heavy wood flooring over concrete base

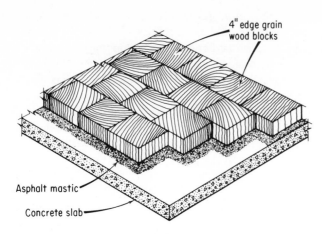

Fig. 11-35. Wood blocks over concrete base

Fig. 11-36. Power tamper and float. (Courtesy Portland Cement Ass'n)

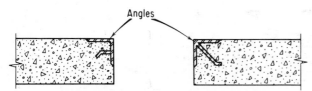

Fig. 11-37. Reinforcing for expansion joints

for ductility, and mixed with a cement-dispersing agent, calcium lignosulfonite.

A series of operations for producing a floor of this type follows:

1. Provide expansion joints around columns and at least every 50 ft in both directions. Reinforce the top of the joints with angle iron (see Fig. 11-37).
2. Design the base concrete for at least 3500 psi.
3. Set the screeds for the base slab 1 in. below the finish grade, pour the slab, and leave the surface with a raked finish.
4. Clean and saturate the base slab. It should be saturated from 4 to 6 hr before placing the topping.
5. Set the *screed level pats* for the topping a few hours before the topping slab is to be poured. These are small mounds of mortar set over the surface at frequent intervals with their tops leveled off to the finish grade.
6. For old or hard base coats, a slush bond coat should be brushed into the surface just before pouring the topping. This may be made up of 100 lb of expanding metallic aggregate to one bag of cement, mixed with water to form a slurry (about 16 lb of the metallic aggregate will cover 100 sq ft).
7. Design the topping mix. A good design consists of 1 sack of cement, enough water (in lb/sack) to produce the specified strength of concrete, and a sufficient quantity of clean, well-graded F.A. and ¾ in. maximum C.A. in equal amounts to produce a mix with not more than 1 in. of slump. This will usually require about 1½ cu ft or 150 lb each of F.A. and C.A. However, there must be enough moisture available to apply the metallic aggregate.
8. Place the topping mix. Rake, screed, level, and tamp. A grill-type tamper is preferred (Fig. 11-38). Remove the level pats as placing progresses, and fill the holes.
9. Immediately after tamping, float the surface to bring moisture to the top.
10. First metallic aggregate shake. Mix 1 sack of Portland cement and 2 sacks of metallic aggregate together dry and shake evenly over the surface at the following rates: for light duty floors —45 lb per 100 sq ft; for moderate duty floors— 75 lb per 100 sq ft; for heavy duty floors—90 lb per 100 sq ft. If the floor is to be finished with mechanical equipment, these amounts may be increased.
11. After the shake has absorbed the surface moisture, tamp the surface. Then follow with a wood float.
12. Apply a second metallic aggregate shake as above, tamp, and float.
13. Immediately after floating, trowel the floor with a steel trowel.
14. As soon as the surface becomes hard enough to ring under it, burnish with a steel trowel to a hard, dense finish.
15. Cure the finished floor as required.

Fig. 11-38. Consolidating and leveling concrete floor. (Courtesy Portland Cement Ass'n)

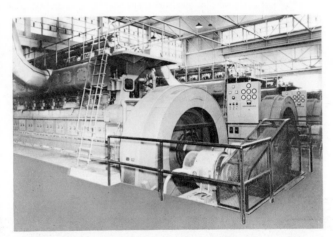

Fig. 11-39. A well-finished metallic aggregate floor. (Courtesy Master Builders Ltd.)

When a non-slip concrete floor is specified, it may be produced by the addition of an aggregate which is composed of ceramically bonded *aluminum oxide abrasive* to the leveled surface. The following procedure is recommended:

1. Allow the leveled concrete surface to set until it will bear some weight.
2. Soak the abrasive aggregate in water for 10 min. before applying.
3. Shake the aggregate evenly over the surface at the rate of ¼ lb per sq ft.

Fig. 11-40. Colored concrete walk

4. Float the aggregate into the surface but do not trowel smooth.

A colored surface may be produced by the addition of a prepared coloring material. It consists of a synthetic mineral oxide of a given color, mixed with fine silica sand or silicon carbide. The coloring procedure is as follows:

1. As soon as the slab is poured, float the surface with a wood float.
2. Shake the coloring material evenly over the surface at the rate of $\frac{1}{4}$ lb per sq ft.
3. Float the surface until the color is evenly distributed and worked into the topping.
4. Immediately apply another shake at the same rate.
5. Float again until the color has been worked into the surface to a depth of approximately $\frac{1}{4}$ in.
6. When the concrete has set sufficiently, trowel smooth as required.

Terrazzo Floors

Terrazzo is produced by laying a concrete topping mix containing marble chips or other aggregates of the desired color over a concrete base slab. Additional aggregate is rolled into the fresh topping when necessary so that 70% to 85% of the finished surface will consist of aggregate. Coloring may be added to produce a mix of almost any shade or color desired, and white Portland cement may be used if clarity of color is important. After the topping has hardened for several days, it is ground and polished to a very smooth surface.

The floor area is usually sectioned by dividing strips of brass, aluminum, plastic, or other suitable material. They are used to separate colors into a desired pattern and to prevent shrinkage cracks.

The terrazzo course may be bonded to the base course to obtain what is known as a *bonded finish*, or it may be separated from the base by a $\frac{1}{4}$ in. sand cushion and a layer of asphalt-impregnated paper called a *broken bond finish*. The use of the latter method insures that structural cracks which may occur in the base slab will not penetrate the terrazzo topping.

A bed of dry mortar about $1\frac{1}{2}$ in. thick in the proportion of 1 part cement to 4 parts sand is laid either over the base slab or the paper and is brought to a level of not less than $\frac{1}{2}$ nor more than $\frac{3}{4}$ in. below the finish grade. When the mortar has stiffened sufficiently, the dividing strips are installed as planned to a level slightly above the finish grade.

The terrazzo mixture, consisting of 1 part cement to 2 parts aggregate mixed as dry as possible, is placed in the spaces formed by the dividing strips. It is struck off to the level of the dividing strips and compacted with heavy rollers. Extra aggregate may be rolled into the surface if required. Immediately after rolling, the surface is floated and troweled so that the edges of the strips show at the surface.

When the terrazzo has hardened, it is wet-ground with machine grinders to a smooth, even surface. It is then washed, and a grout of cement and water, colored if necessary, is applied to fill any voids. The grouting is removed after about 3 days, and the surface is polished by machine to a satisfactory finish.

Terra Cotta Tile

Tile flooring consists of a layer of some type of ceramic tile, from $\frac{1}{4}$ to 1 in. thick, laid over a concrete base slab. The tile is laid in a mortar bed spread evenly over the surface, and the spaces between tiles are filled with grout.

The procedure for laying terra cotta tile is as follows:

1. Wash and saturate the base slab. If the concrete is old or hard, apply a slush bond coat of cement and water with a stiff brush.
2. Stretch two lines across the floor at right angles to one another so that the area is divided into four equal parts.
3. Mix the bedding mortar in the proportion of 1 part cement to 3 parts sand, with enough water to make a plastic, workable mix.
4. Start at the intersection of the two lines, apply a layer of mortar, and lay the first row of tiles to

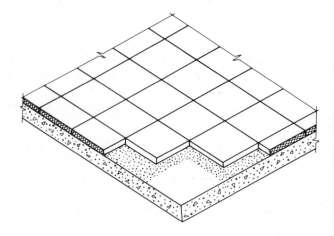

Fig. 11-41. Quarry tile floor

the line. Tap each one firmly so that it is well bedded in mortar.

5. Lay a second row at right angles to the first, along the second line.

6. Lay the remainder of the tiles in that quarter, keeping them as level as possible, and maintaining an even spacing between tiles.

7. Repeat in the opposite quarter and then lay the other two quarters.

8. When the tiles are set, prepare a grouting mix using the same proportions of cement and sand, but make the mortar a little more fluid. Pour some over a section of tiled surface and rub it into the spaces between tiles with a piece of heavy burlap.

9. Rub off the excess grout and when it has set sufficiently so as not to pull out of the spaces, clean the surface of the tiles thoroughly.

Mastic Floors

Mastic flooring materials are applied to the base floor in a stiff plastic state by spreading, rolling, and troweling. Three types of material are commonly used: *magnesite, asphalt,* and *epoxy resin* compounds.

Magnesite flooring is composed of calcined *magnesium oxide* and *magnesium chloride,* mixed with water to form a stiff plaster. The material is applied in two coats, each about $\frac{1}{4}$ in. thick. It may be installed over either wood or concrete; when used over a wood subfloor, metal lath is laid first to provide a better bond.

The first coat of magnesite should contain some fibrous material such as asbestos or nylon to give it greater strength. The second coat—which may contain color, fine marble chips, or an abrasive aggregate—is placed as soon as the base coat has set. It is screeded, compacted, and troweled in much the same way as concrete topping.

Asphalt flooring consists of emulsified asphalt containing asbestos fiber mixed with Portland cement and stone aggregates to form a stiff plastic material. It is spread over the base floor and rolled smooth and level. Asphalt flooring may be laid over either wood or concrete bases, though the application is somewhat different in each case. For a wood base, a layer of 15 lb asphalt-saturated felt is laid first with 4 in. laps. Stucco wire is laid over the paper and nailed down, followed by a coat of asphalt primer.

A fill mix is then applied to level the surface and cover the stucco wire. It consists of 1 part Portland cement, 1 part emulsified fibrated asphalt, and 5 parts of clean, coarse sand. The final coat is the same as that used over a concrete floor.

A concrete base slab should first be coated with asphalt primer thinned with equal parts of mineral spirits. When it is dry, a slurry coat consisting of 1 gal Portland cement, 1 gal emulsified asphalt primer, and 15 gal water is painted over the surface. The flooring mix consists of 1 part Portland cement, 2 parts emulsified fibrated asphalt, $2\frac{1}{2}$ parts clean coarse sand, $4\frac{1}{2}$ parts $\frac{1}{8}$ to $\frac{3}{8}$ in. pea gravel, and not more than 1 part water. This mixture is spread, leveled, compacted, and rolled (to a depth of from $\frac{5}{8}$ to $\frac{3}{4}$ in.) to a smooth finish.

Epoxy resin is a synthetic now used for several purposes in construction. It may be used as a basic ingredient of floor topping. It is made of two components—a liquid resin and a curing agent. These must be mixed in prescribed proportions when the topping mixture is made.

Two types of floor topping can be made with this plastic. Kiln-dry, salt-free sand and Portland cement may be mixed with it to produce a smooth floor topping. The mix is made up of $182\frac{1}{2}$ lb liquid resin, $17\frac{1}{2}$ lb curing agent, 160 lb Portland cement, and 640 lb 30-50 mesh sand. The topping may be colored by adding pigments to the liquid portion. The surface is first primed with an epoxy prime coat and the mix is then spread over the floor, floated, and troweled smooth to a depth of from $\frac{1}{8}$ to $\frac{1}{4}$ in. Mixes should be limited to 100 lb batches because of the limited pot life of the mixed topping.

A terrazzo topping may be prepared by mixing marble chips with liquid plastic. Coloring pigment may also be added. These ingredients are mixed in the following ratios: 160 lb liquid plastic, 87 lb calcium silicate, 35 lb rutile titanium dioxide paste, and 18 lb of hardener per 700 lb of marble chips. The surface must again be primed and the mix must be applied and troweled to a depth of from $\frac{3}{16}$ to $\frac{1}{4}$ in. After 24 hr, the surface is ready for grinding and polishing.

Resilient Tile

Resilient tile flooring includes a number of products such as asphalt, linoleum, cork, vinyl or vinyl-asbestos, and rubber. All require a smooth surface—either wood or concrete—and a special mastic. Asphalt and vinyl-asbestos tiles are particularly suited for concrete slabs on grade, since both are laid in moisture-proof asphalt mastic. Laying should in all cases begin at a line stretched across the center of the floor.

REVIEW QUESTIONS

1. Briefly describe two main types of wood subfloors.

2. List four basic types of concrete floors used in industrial construction and describe how each is supported.

3. Briefly state the reasons for the following: (a) isolating columns from a concrete floor around them; (b) providing a keyway form at the edge of a concrete slab section; (c) covering the grade with a moisture barrier before pouring a concrete slab.

4. List three methods of providing concrete floor slabs in a structural steel building frame.

5. How is strip flooring fastened to a concrete subfloor?

6. What advantages does metallic aggregate bring to a concrete floor topping?

7. What are the advantages of *block flooring* over *strip flooring*?

8. How are *nonskid* concrete floors produced?

9. (a) Of what does a terrazzo floor topping consist? (b) What is the purpose of using dividing strips in a terrazzo floor? (c) What is the difference between a *bonded* and a *broken bond* terrazzo topping?

10. What is *mastic* flooring?

11. What precaution must be taken when selecting a resilient tile that is to be laid over a slab-on-grade concrete floor?

12

ROOF FRAMES AND
INDUSTRIAL ROOFING

The primary purpose of a roof is to protect a building's interior, but it may also be used to contribute to a building's exterior appearance.

The completed roof consists of several components, including the *roof frame, roof deck, vapor barrier, insulation, waterproof roofing material, flashing* and *drains, construction* and *control joints, walks, parapets, gravel stops*, etc.

A great many factors enter into the design of a roof, such as weather, appearance, height, area, and style of the frame. As a result, many roofing systems have been designed, some used very frequently, others less so.

FLAT ROOF

The simplest system is the *flat* roof, framed in wood, steel, or reinforced concrete. This frame supports a roof deck which is in turn covered with a waterproof roofing material.

In heavy timber frame construction, the roof members for a flat roof are framed to columns as outlined in Chapter 8. A positive roof anchoring system must be employed to protect against displacement by wind. Figures 8-27, 28, 29, and 30 illustrate methods of attaching roof beams to masonry exterior bearing walls. Roof anchors are again used. Note the *lugs* on bearing plates (Fig. 8-28) to hold roof beams in place. The framing of roof members in steel or reinforced concrete frame structures is essentially the same as that used for floors.

In place of regular roof beams, *joists* may be used to frame a flat roof.

Fig. 12-1. Steel frame building with flat roof

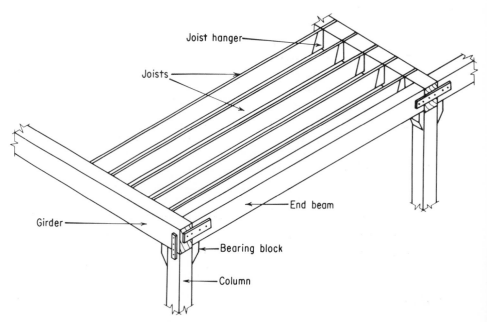

Fig. 12-2. Wood joist roof frame

Wood joists, 12 or 16 in. o.c., span from girder to girder or from one bearing wall to another. Spans will generally be limited to about 24 ft.

Open web steel joists up to 96 ft in length and 4 ft in depth, spaced 12 to 30 in. o.c., span from girder to girder (as shown in Fig. 12-3) or from one bearing wall to another. Joist ends may be welded to a steel girder or to a connection plate cast into the top of a concrete girder or wall, bolted to a wood or concrete wall, or built into pockets—*chases*—in a brick wall.

Precast concrete joists (see Fig. 9-32) are made in depths of 8, 10, and 12 in., with a maximum span of 24 ft. They may be spaced 20, 24, 27, 30, or 33 in. o.c., depending on their length and load. They normally span from one bearing wall to another and the spaces between their ends on the wall are filled with masonry.

The roof frame supports a roof deck of wood, concrete, steel, gypsum, or lightweight cellular concrete. A wood deck may be of planks laid on the flat, 2 in.

Fig. 12-3. Open web stool joists. (Courtesy Bethlehem Steel Co.)

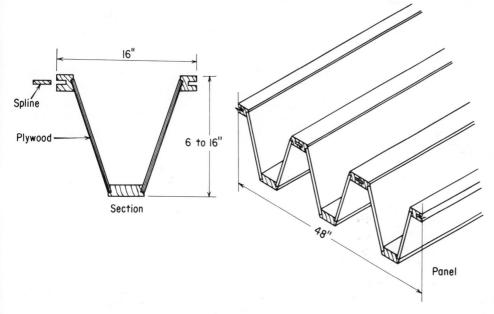

Fig. 12-4. Prefabricated wood decking

material laminated on edge, or prefabricated units as illustrated in Fig. 12-4. The units are 16 in. wide, vary in depth from 6 to 16 in., and have a maximum length of about 30 ft. Units may be handled singly or in panels 32 or 48 in. wide.

Solid wood decks should be kept back ½ in. from parapet walls (Fig. 8-28) or from the fascia where a flush deck is used (Fig. 8-29), with a cant strip to cover the gap. In the case of a flush deck, the cant strip also acts as a gravel stop.

A concrete deck may be poured over removable wood forms, steel deck forms laid on the roof frame, or paper-backed wire mesh laid over a joist frame.

A steel deck is most frequently used in conjunction with a steel frame and is laid and covered as shown in Fig. 12-5.

Gypsum decks are made from poured-in-place gypsum or precast gypsum planks. To use poured-in-place gypsum, the roof frame is made of structural T's spaced 33 in. o.c.; ½ in. gypsum board 32 in. wide

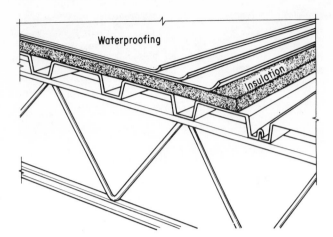

Fig. 12-5. Steel deck on open web joists

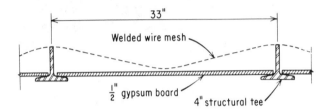

Fig. 12-6. Form for gypsum deck

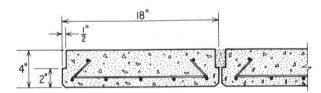

Fig. 12-7. Cellular concrete roof slab

lengths of up to 100 ft or more, depending on the type of slab used. Connections to the girder are usually made by welding between plates in the slab and a connection plate cast into the girder. Joints between adjoining slabs are grouted and the deck is ready for roofing.

Provisions must be made for draining a flat roof. This may be done by installing roof drains at various places and sloping the roof surface toward them. The roof may also be left perfectly flat with a parapet all around so that it retains water. Roof drains must then project several inches above the surface so that excess water may drain. The roof is sometimes sloped in one direction so that water may flow into a collecting gutter. Another method is to provide drainage outlets through parapet walls. These outlets are called *scuppers,* and their installation is illustrated in Fig. 12-9.

TRUSS ROOF

Another method of framing the roof of a building is by the use of trusses. These are framed structures designed to carry the roof loads and transmit them to

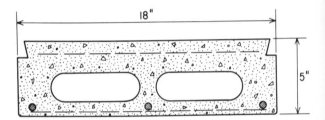

Fig. 12-8. Precast hollow core roof slab

is then laid over the flanges of the steel members (Fig. 12-6). Welded wire mesh is draped over the T's, and freshly mixed gypsum is poured and screeded to the proper level.

Gypsum planks are *plain* or *metal edged*. Both are supported on steel roof framing members, but in the case of metal edged planks it is not necessary for the ends to rest on a beam.

Cellular concrete is used for roof decks as precast slabs 18 in. wide, 4 in. thick, and up to 10 ft in length. Slabs may be used over any type of roof frame and are fastened with nails, bolts and washers, galvanized metal clips, or power-driven steel pins. Grooves between slabs are later filled with grout.

A flat roof may also be made from precast, prestressed concrete roof slabs such as those shown in Fig. 9-42, or from precast hollow-core slabs such as those in Fig. 12-8. These units are actually a combination of joist and slab, and span from girder to girder in

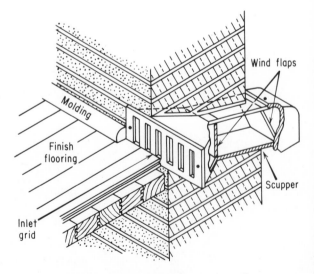

Fig. 12-9. Scupper through parapet wall

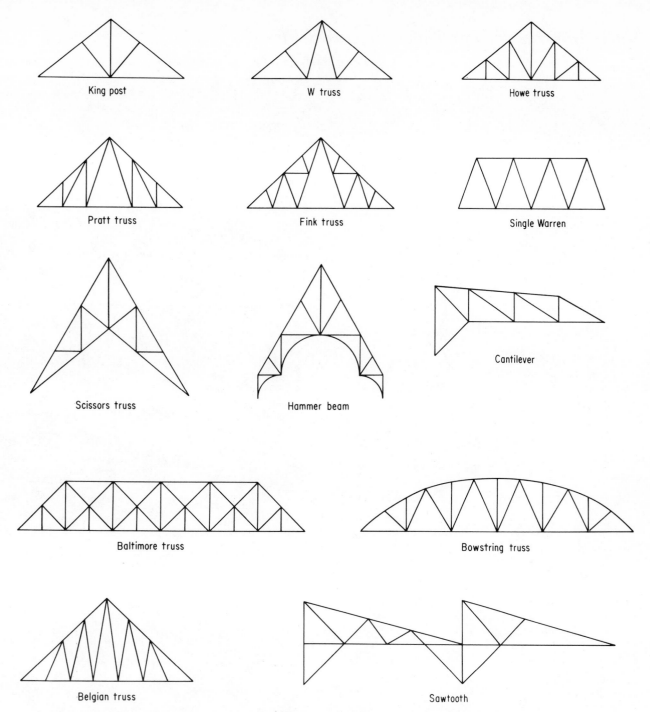

Fig. 12-10. Truss types

the bearing walls on which they rest. They are generally made of straight members arranged and fastened together in triangular form, so that the stresses in the members caused by loads at the *panel points* are either compressive or tensile. A number of truss styles have been designed and Fig. 12-10 illustrates some of them.

Trusses consist basically of upper and lower *chords*, tension and compression *webs*, and the devices used to fasten the members together. Two methods are used to connect the members of a wooden truss. If members are butted to one another, a wood or steel *gusset plate* is fastened over the joint with glue and nails or with bolts. If the members overlap one another, *split rings* and bolts are used to connect them. The split rings are set in circular grooves cut in the meeting faces Fig. 12-13, and a bolt through the assembly holds the two members tightly together. Grooves are cut to a predetermined depth by a special tool which drills the bolt hole at the same time.

Roof sheathing may be applied directly to trusses,

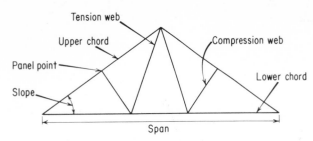

Fig. 12-11. Parts of a truss

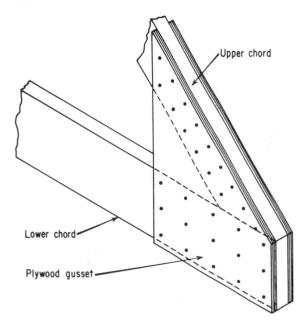

Fig. 12-12. Gusset joint

Fig. 12-13. Cutting grooves for split rings

but is more often supported by *purlins* which span from truss to truss at panel points or by joists resting on the upper chord (Fig. 12-14).

LAMELLA ROOF

A *lamella* roof is a curved roof similar in shape to one formed by the use of bowstring trusses, but without the framework of webs and lower chords found in a truss roof. It does, however, provide clear spans of great width. It is formed by framing together a series of intersecting arches made up of relatively short members (called lamellas). They are made of 2 in. material, 12 to 16 ft in length, beveled, bored with two holes at each end, and bolted together as shown in Fig. 12-15.

A lamella roof may be erected over a curved form made the width of the building and the depth of one bay, carried on movable scaffolds. The erection of

Fig. 12-14. Bowstring trusses with joists

the framework is begun from both sides at the sills and completed at the center. Figure 12-16 shows a plan view of a completed frame. The horizontal thrust developed in this type of roof must be taken

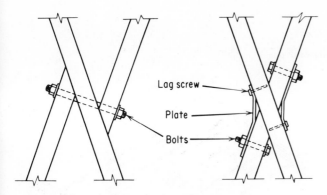

Fig. 12-15. Lamella joints

care of by tie rods (Fig. 12-17), wooden ties, buttressed walls, or wall columns. The usual length of individual members is 12, 14, or 16 ft with arch spacings of approximately 4, 4½, and 5 ft, respectively. The angle between intersecting lamellas should not exceed 45° and should preferably be between 38° and 40°. Decking may be applied directly over the framework of the roof.

FOLDED PLATE ROOF

A *folded plate* roof (Fig. 12-18) is another type in which the roof slab has been formed into a thin,

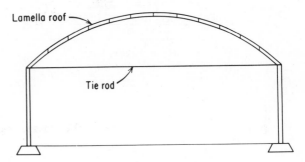

Fig. 12-17. Tie rod for lamella roof

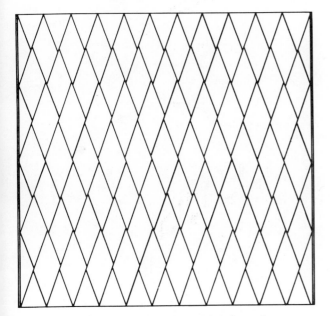

Fig. 12-16. Plan view of lamella roof

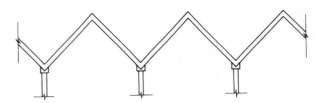

Fig. 12-18. Folded plate roof shape

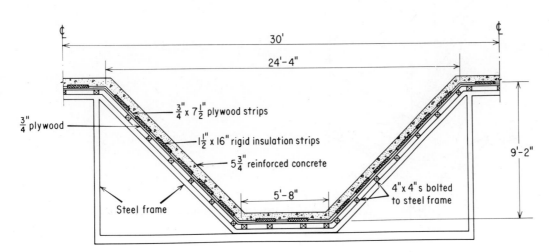

Fig. 12-19. Form for concrete folded plate

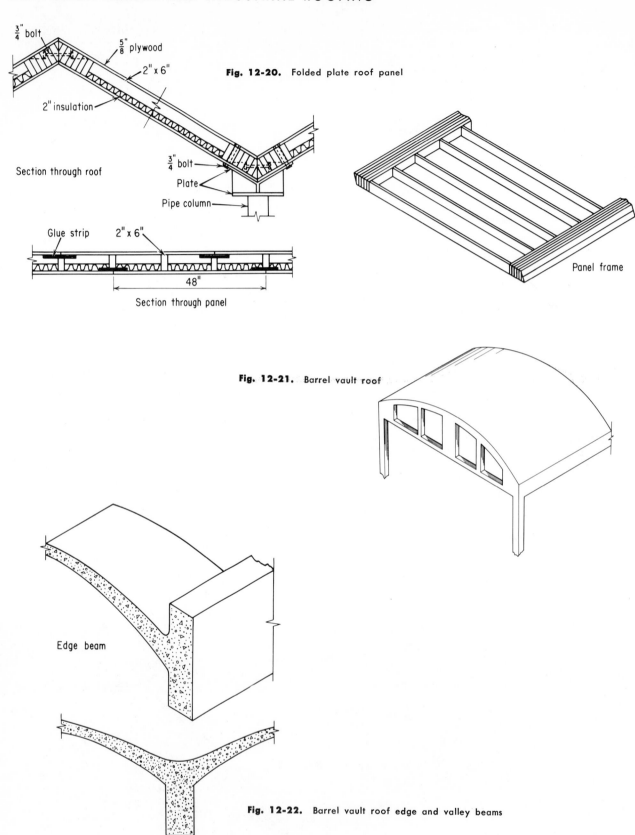

Fig. 12-20. Folded plate roof panel

$\frac{3}{4}$" bolt

$\frac{5}{8}$" plywood

2" x 6"

2" insulation

Section through roof

$\frac{3}{4}$" bolt

Plate

Pipe column

Glue strip

2" x 6"

48"

Section through panel

Panel frame

Fig. 12-21. Barrel vault roof

Edge beam

Valley beam

Fig. 12-22. Barrel vault roof edge and valley beams

self-supporting structure, usually made either of wood or concrete.

A concrete roof of this type can be made with precast panels or may be poured in place. Figure 12-19 shows details of typical formwork for a poured-in-place concrete folded plate roof.

A wood folded plate roof is made up of panels bolted together to form a complete roof structure. The top and bottom chords of each panel are usually laminated members, and the ribs are 2″ by 4″s, 2″ by 6″s, or 2″ by 8″s, as the case may be, 16 in. o.c., with a plywood skin on both sides of the panel. Figure 12-20 shows details in the construction of a typical panel.

BARREL VAULT ROOF

A *barrel vault* roof (Fig. 12-21) is a curved, thin-shell concrete roof, normally reinforced. Posttensioning is sometimes introduced into the shell and transverse beams to allow a reduction in shell thickness. Edge and valley longitudinal beams are shaped as in Fig. 12-22. Forms for the vaults consist of a series of light bowstring trusses of the proper span and height, supported on shores or metal scaffolding, and sheathed over the top with plywood.

HYPERBOLIC PARABOLOID ROOF

A *hyperbolic paraboloid* roof is a warped surface of thin-shell concrete or wood construction designed to derive its strength from its shape rather than its mass. The doubly-curved surface (which might be called a warped parallelogram) allows the transfer of loads to supports entirely by direct forces, so that all parts of the shell are uniformly stressed.

A great many shapes are possible with this type of roof. A simple method of forming most is to build them with straight steel members welded at the joints, as shown in Fig. 12-24. Note the permanent and temporary supports. The surfaces are outlined by stretching cables from member to member and placing them under light tension. The tension can be applied by a tool similar to the one shown in Fig. 12-25, and cables may be anchored by welding or by wedges.

The surface is produced by covering the cables with a layer of rigid material, usually foamed plastic insulation, over which is poured a thin layer of concrete (Fig. 12-26).

Reinforcement (in the form of wire mesh, or rods laid as shown in Fig. 12-27) is placed, and the surface is built with lightweight concrete to the top of the steel frame. After the concrete has cured sufficiently, the temporary supports can be removed, and the exposed parts of the steel frame and roof surface may be finished as required.

MOLDED SHELL ROOF

Another method of constructing a shell-type roof is to form it over a mold. The dome-shaped roof in Fig. 12-29 is an example of this method of construction.

The first step in the construction of a roof by this method is to pour footings and set up a series of columns around the perimeter of the roof so that the roof extension will project beyond them. An iron

Fig. 12-23. Hyperbolic paraboloid roof

Fig. 12-24. Roof frame with cables

Fig. 12-25. Tensioning roof cables

Fig. 12-26. Insulation board deck

Fig. 12-27. Roof reinforced

Fig. 12-28. Roof complete

Fig. 12-29. Dome-shaped shell roof

collar such as that illustrated in Fig. 12-30 is dropped over each column.

The mold is made next—a mound of earth which is formed and compacted to the shape of the roof (Fig. 12-31). A layer of rigid insulation is spread over the mold, out under the column collars, and to the edge of the roof. Two-way reinforcement is then placed over the insulation.

Concrete is poured over the mold to the specified depth, completely surrounding the collar at the base of each column. In Fig. 12-32, note the little form used around each column to prevent concrete from getting into the collar.

After the concrete has properly cured, the roof is ready to be lifted into position. Note the plate welded to each column to indicate the final position of the collars (Fig. 12-33). Hydraulic jacks are placed on each column and two heavy, threaded rods extended from each jack to engage in the holes in the collars. When the jacks are operated simultaneously, the rods are drawn through them, and the entire roof is raised as the collars slide up the columns (Fig. 12-34).

When the roof has reached the proper height, steel blocks are welded to the columns (under the collars) to hold them in position. The rods and jacks are removed, and the tops of the columns are cut off at roof level. The earth mound can now be removed and the building may be finished according to plans.

INDUSTRIAL ROOFING

As indicated earlier in the chapter, the final operation in the construction of a roof is the application of the *roofing*. It is probably the most important element in a building, for it must protect the structure and its occupants while exposed to a wide variety of climatic conditions.

There are many types of roofing from which to choose—the type selected for a particular building will depend on a number of factors. These factors include: (1) the basic design and suitability of materials for that design; (2) the location and type of vapor barrier to be used; (3) the characteristics of the particular insulation to be used; (4) the probable expansion, contraction, and deflection of the roof deck; (5) the durability of roofing to be selected; (6) the fire resistance of the roofing; (7) the value of the roofing as a decorative feature.

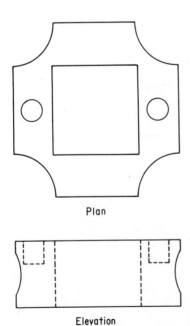

Plan

Elevation

Fig. 12-30. Lifting collar

Fig. 12-31. The roof mold

Fig. 12-32. Concreting the dome

Fig. 12-33. Jacks in place ready for lifting

Fig. 12-34. Roof half-way up

Fig. 12-35. Roof in position

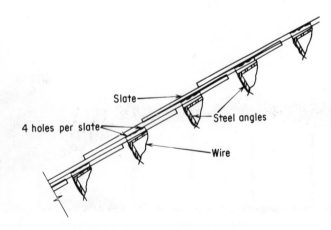

Fig. 12-36. Slate supported on steel angles

Roofing materials include *shingles and shakes, terra cotta tile, slate, sheet metal, asbestos-cement boards, built-up roofing, monoform roofing,* and *liquid envelope roofing.* The first three materials are used primarily in residential construction and will not be discussed here.

SLATE ROOFING

Slate roofing consists of rectangular slates 10 to 24 in. long and 6 to 14 in. wide, in thicknesses ranging from $3/16$ to 2 in. They are laid like shingles over nailable concrete, gypsum, wood decks, or steel angles running the length of the roof (Fig. 12-36). When slates are to be laid over a solid deck, a layer of 15 to 65 lb

Fig. 12-37. Corrugated sheet metal siding and roofing. (Courtesy Dominion Foundry and Steel Co.)

felt paper (depending on the slate thickness) is placed over the deck and each slate is secured by two flat-head copper wire nails. When slates are to be laid over steel angles, they require four holes each for wiring.

SHEET METAL ROOFING

Various methods are used to make roofing sheets, but two basic types of sheet are generally made—corrugated and flat. Galvanized steel, aluminum, and Galbestos are all used to make corrugated roofing sheets of varying width, depth and pattern of corrugation, and allowable span, depending on the gauge and material used.

Corrugated sheet metal roofing sheets are normally supported on wood or steel purlins, properly spaced according to the gauge of the metal and the roof load involved. Table 12-1 indicates maximum purlin spacings for galvanized corrugated steel roofing sheets of various gauges.

There are two common laying orders for roofing

sheets, as illustrated in Fig. 12-38. When laying according to order (B), be sure to tuck the corner of the #3 sheet under #2, that of #5 under #4, etc. Laying should start at the leeward end of the building so that side laps will have better protection from wind-driven rain. The top edges of eave sheets should extend at least 1½ in. beyond the back of

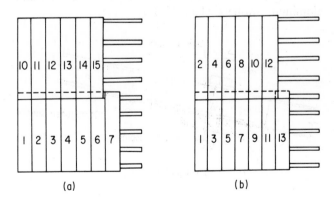

Fig. 12-38. Sheet laying orders

Table 12-1

Maximum Permissible Purlin Spacing for Galvanized Corrugated Sheet Metal

	Superimposed load in psf									
	10		15		20		25		30	
	Pitch of roof									
Gauge	3″/ft	5″/ft	3″/ft	5″/ft	3″/ft	5″/ft	3″/ft	5″/ft	3″/ft	5″/ft
14	11′3″	15′9″	10′0″	14′3″	9′3″	13′3″	8′9″	14′0″	8′3″	(11′9″)
16	10′6″	15′0″	9′6″	13′6″	8′9″	12′6″	8′3″	11′0″	7′9″	(10′6″)
18	9′9″	14′0″	8′9″	(12′3″)	8′0″	(10′9″)	7′6″	(10′0″)	(7′3″)	(9′3″)
20	9′3″	(12′9″)	(8′3″)	(10′9″)	(7′3″)	(9′6″)	(6′6″)	(8′6″)	(6′0″)	(8′0″)
22	9′0″	(11′3″)	(7′6″)	(9′9″)	(6′6″)	(8′6″)	(6′0″)	(7′9″)	(5′6″)	(7′0″)
24	8′0″	(10′6″)	(6′9″)	(8′9″)	(5′9″)	(7′6″)	(5′3″)	(6′9″)	(4′9″)	(6′3″)
26	(7′3″)	(9′6″)	(6′0″)	(8′0″)	(5′3″)	(6′0″)	(4′9″)	(6′3″)	(4′3″)	(5′9″)

Note: Figures enclosed in parentheses are governed by stress values; the remainder are governed by deflection values.

steel purlins and 3 in. beyond the center line of timber purlins. At side laps (where the edge corrugation of adjacent sheets is opposite in direction), the under lapping side should finish with an upturned edge and the overlapping side with a downturned edge.

Sheets should extend at least one corrugation over the gable and there should be 3 in. of overhang at the eaves. End laps between sheets should generally be 6 in. and side laps 1½ corrugations, but these may be increased to 9 in. and 2 corrugations for extreme conditions. For low-pitched roofs, it is good practice to seal the laps with a suitable caulking compound.

Special nails with a ring or screw-type shank should be used for fastening corrugated sheets to wood purlins. They should be zinc coated, with a lead underhead, and long enough to provide adequate holding power. Nails should be driven at the top of corrugations, but care must be taken not to drive them so far as to flatten the corrugations—thus preventing the next sheet from fitting properly. Sheets are fastened to steel purlins with stainless steel self-tapping screws and aluminum washers (Fig. 12-39).

Flat sheets of metal—terne plate, galvanized iron, copper, lead, zinc, aluminum, monel metal, or stainless steel—are applied over solid backing on either a flat deck or a pitched roof. Sheets are applied in strips which run up the slope of pitched roofs and are locked together by one of three types of joints (called *seams*) in common use. These seams allow the metal to expand without buckling. Figure 12-40 illustrates these three types of seams.

ASBESTOS-CEMENT ROOFING

Roofing sheets of asbestos-cement are made in several designs, four of which are shown in Fig. 12-41. Corrugated board and transitile are used on sloping roofs over wood or steel purlins, and are laid with 6 in. end lap and 1 corrugation side lap. Various types of fasteners are available for attaching these corrugated boards to the frame, and some are illustrated in Fig. 12-42.

There should be expansion joints in transitile roofing

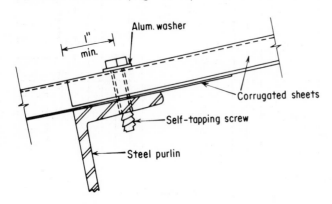

Fig. 12-39. Corrugated roofing over steel purlins

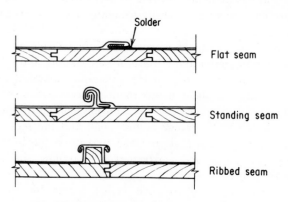

Fig. 12-40. Seams for sheet metal roofing

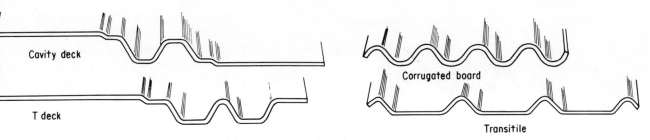

Fig. 12-41. Asbestos-cement roofing sheets

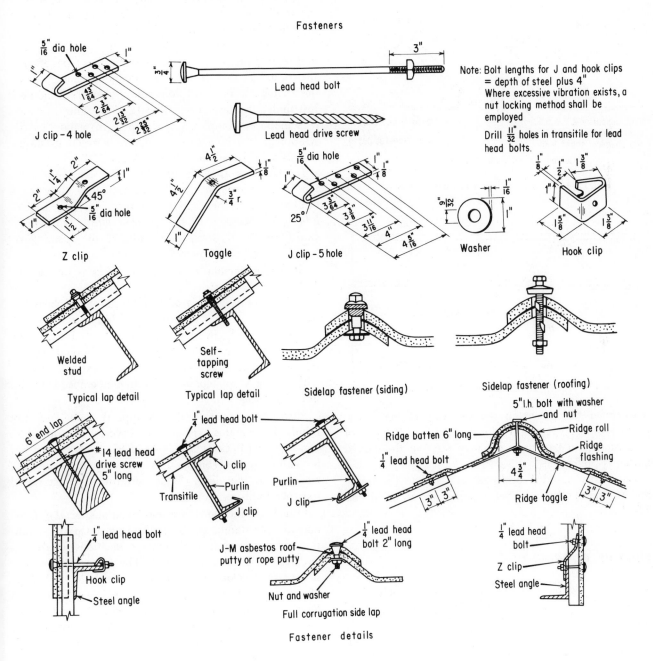

Fig. 12-42. Fasteners for asbestos-cement roofing

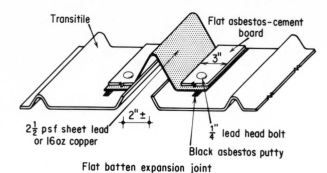

Flat batten expansion joint

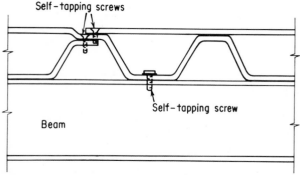

Curved batten expansion joint

Fig. 12-43. Expansion joints in transitile roofing

Fig. 12-44. Attaching asbestos-cement decking to roof frame

—wherever they occur in the structure or every 100 ft, if possible. Figure 12-43 illustrates two types of expansion joint battens in common use, but the curved batten is preferable.

Cavity decks and T decks are attached to the frame and to one another with self-tapping screws, as in Fig. 12-44.

BUILT-UP ROOFING

Built-up roofing is probably the most widely used material for flat or nearly flat roofs. It consists of layers of roofing felt bonded with tar or asphalt. It is laid down to conform and bond to the roof deck and to seal all angles formed by projecting surfaces,

and thus constitutes a single, flexible, waterproof membrane. The membrane is usually turned up to make a *base flashing* on vertical surfaces in order to form a large, watertight tray.

Insulation and vapor barriers are a part of most built-up roofing installations. The use of a vapor barrier is essential wherever insulation is part of the roof structure. The proper design and installation of a vapor barrier is particularly important in northern regions. Without it, moisture vapor from within the building will penetrate the insulation, condense, destroy the insulating value, and eventually result in blistering or other damage to the roof covering.

The vapor barrier may be located at various points in the roof assembly, depending on the type of construction. It may be over a suspended ceiling, under the roof deck, or, most commonly, over the roof deck just under the insulation (Fig. 12-45). The insulation is sometimes completely enveloped in vapor barrier wrapping, in which case the joints between insulation boards must be adequately sealed.

Insulation is applied over the vapor barrier or over the deck by cementing it with asphalt. Roof deck insulation is of the rigid board type and may be *cellular glass* (see Fig. 12-45), *foamed plastic, glass fiberboard, corkboard, strawboard* (Fig. 12-46), *wood fiberboard,* or *cellular concrete.*

A five-ply membrane for wood decks is one of the earliest standard specifications to be developed for built-up roofing. It consists of a layer of sheathing paper and two plies of dry felt nailed to the deck to secure the roof covering and prevent bitumen from dripping through the wood joints. Additional plies of felt are applied alternately with layers of bitumen, with a heavy top coating of bitumen embedded with gravel or slag.

Sheathing paper and dry-applied felts are not required when this type of roof covering is applied to concrete roof decks. One layer of felt is eliminated but an extra layer of bitumen is necessary to secure the covering to the deck. This constitutes the standard four-ply built-up roofing.

Other specifications are modifications of the four- and five-ply standards, designed to meet varying conditions or to arrive at minimum specifications for roofing with reduced life expectancy. The factors to be considered in developing a specification include: (1) slope of the roof; (2) type of roof deck—single or assembled units; (3) nailability of the roof deck; (4) presence of insulation and vapor barriers; (5) life expectancy of the membrane; (6) type of bitumen to be used; (7) type of paper to be used.

Fig. 12-45. Foamglas rigid insulation. (Courtesy Pittsburgh-Corning Corp.)

Five basic types of membrane are recognized, depending on the types of paper and bitumen used. They are:

1. Asphalt felts, asphalt and gravel.
2. Tarred felts, pitch and gravel.
3. Asbestos felts, asphalt and asphalt smooth flood coat.
4. 17 or 19 in. Selvage roofing.
5. Cold process roofing.

The basic specifications for each of these membranes, based on a 100 sq ft wood deck without insulation, are as follows:

1. *Incline*: ½ to 2 in. per ft.
   Dry sheathing: 5 lb/100 sq ft.
   Felts: 2 layers, 15# asphalt impregnated, dry applied;
   2 layers, 15# asphalt impregnated, mopped on.

Fig. 12-46. Strawboard rigid insulation

Asphalt: 3 moppings, approx. 20 lb/mopping;
   topping, approx. 65 lb poured;
   for ⅛ to 1 in. slope—140° asphalt;
   for 1 to 2 in. slope—170° asphalt;
   if over 2 in. slope, use 210° asphalt.
Nails & Caps: 1 lb, 1¼ in. barbed nails; ½ lb flat caps.
Surfacing: 400 lb gravel *or* 300 lb slag, ¼ to ⅝ in. size, dry, well rounded, free of dust.

2. *Incline*: 0 to 1 in. per ft.
   Dry sheathing: 5# dry sheathing paper.
   Felts: 2 layers, 15# tarred, dry applied;
   3 layers, 15# tarred, mopped on.
   Pitch: standard roofing pitch, not heated over 400°F or mopped at less than 350°F, 3 moppings, approx. 25 lb/mopping;
   topping, 80 lb poured.
Nails & Caps: 1 lb, 1¼ in. barbed nails; ½ lb flat caps.
Surfacing: 400 lb gravel *or* 300 lb slag.

3. *Incline*: ½ to 8 in. per ft.
   Dry sheathing: 9# waxed Kraft.
   Base sheet: 25# asphalt felt.
   Felts: 2 layers, 15# perforated asphalt felt, mopped on;
   2 layers, 15# perforated asbestos felt, mopped on.
   Asphalt: 4 moppings, approx. 20 lb/mopping;
   flood coat, 25 lb/flooding;
   for ⅛ to 1 in. slope—140° asphalt;
   for 1 to 2 in. slope—170° asphalt;
   over 2 in. slope—210° asphalt.
Nails & Caps: ¾ lb, 1 in. barbed nails; ½ lb flat caps.
Surfacing: flood coat as above.

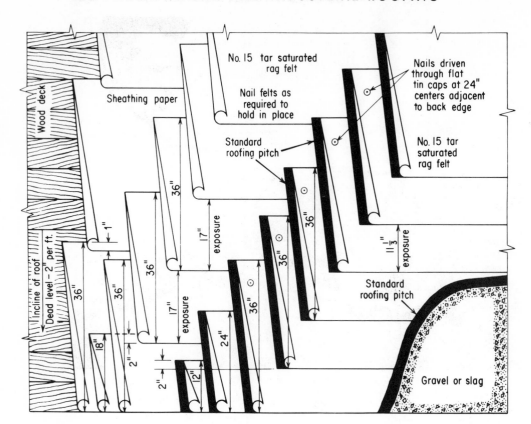

No. 15 tar saturated rag felt

Sheathing paper

Nail felts as required to hold in place

Nails driven through flat tin caps at 24" centers adjacent to back edge

No. 15 tar saturated rag felt

Standard roofing pitch

Wood deck

Incline of roof
Dead level – 2" per ft.

36"

36"

36"

36"

36"

36"

36"

17" exposure

17" exposure

1"

$11\frac{1}{3}$" exposure

18"

2"

2"

12"

24"

Standard roofing pitch

Gravel or slag

Fig. 12-47. Five-ply tar and gravel roof on a wood deck

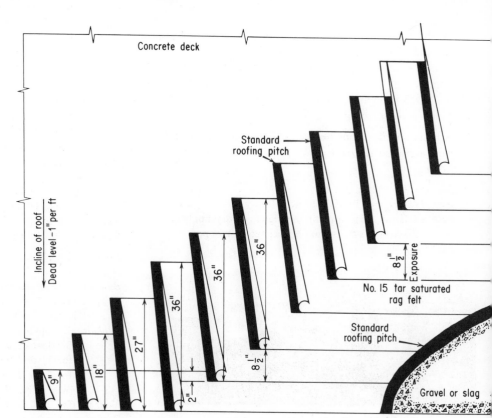

Concrete deck

Standard roofing pitch

Incline of roof
Dead level – 1" per ft

36"

36"

36"

27"

18"

9"

2"

$8\frac{1}{2}$" Exposure

$8\frac{1}{2}$"

No. 15 tar saturated rag felt

Standard roofing pitch

Gravel or slag

Fig. 12-48. Four-ply tar and gravel roof on concrete deck

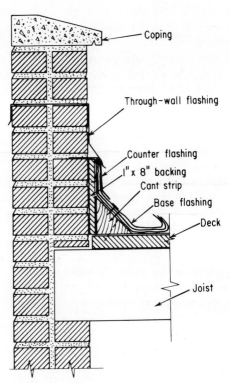

Fig. 12-49. Flashing at parapet wall

4. *Incline*: 2 to 8 in. per ft.
   Dry sheathing: 5# dry sheathing paper.
   Felts: 1 layer, 15# asphalt felt, dry applied;
   2 layers, 15# asphalt felt, mopped on;
   2 layers, 120#, slate surfaced, 19 in. or 17 in.
   Selvage, mopped on.
   Asphalt: 4 moppings, approx. 20 lb per mopping, 210°
   asphalt.
   Nails & Caps: 1½ lb, 1¼ in. barbed nails; ¾ lb flat caps.

5. *Incline*: ⅛ to 8 in. per ft.
   Felts: 3 layers, cold process, 53# felt, adhesive applied
   (backnailed and lap adhesion only).
   Adhesive: Approx. 2½ gal asphalt adhesive between
   laps.
   Nails & Caps: 2 lb, 1 in. flat head galvanized nails;
   1 lb flat caps.
   Surfacing: 4 gal Static Asphalt Fibrated Emulsion.

A double pour top coating is desirable on low-pitched roofs. It is accomplished by embedding approximately 200 lb of gravel in a top pour of 50 lb of bitumen, and later repeating the operation with 300 lb of gravel in 75 lb of bitumen on a second pour. This gives added protection against standing water and melting snow or ice. The second pour can be placed after all other phases of roof construction have been completed and provides an opportunity to check for possible damage.

Overheating bitumens during application must be avoided. The temperature range is 325° to 400°F for coal-tar pitch and 400° to 450°F for hot asphalt. If applied below these temperatures, the workability and cementing action is seriously reduced, while if poured above the maximum temperature, the material loses valuable oils by distillation, and forms only a thin film which cannot provide adequate cementing action.

Careful attention should be given to interruptions in the roof surface at parapets, penthouses, vents, pipes, chimneys, and drains. Bends in felt used to make base flashing must be supported with cant strips. Base flashing should extend a minimum of 8 in. above the level of the deck and should be protected at the top edge with metal counterflashing. Since there is danger of rupture caused by movements between horizontal and vertical surfaces, base flashing should not be fastened directly to vertical surfaces such as parapet walls. An 8 in. board should be placed behind the cant strip against the wall, but not fastened to it (Fig. 12-49). The base flashing can then be nailed and cemented to the board and the top edge of the board and the base flashing covered by the counterflashing attached to the wall. Through-wall flashing must be provided in masonry walls extending above the roof to act in conjunction with counterflashing.

The need for expansion joints in the roof will depend on the size and design of the building. Expansion joints in the building itself must be extended to the roof. An expansion joint should be provided at each junction of the main portion of the building with a wing, and on the main roof if any dimension exceeds 150 ft. It is also desirable to provide an expansion joint at each change of joist or roof direction.

MONOFORM ROOFING

Monoform roofing is a reinforced asphaltic membrane which is applied to a roof with a special type of spray applicator. The membrane consists of a specially formulated asphalt compound reinforced with glass fibers.

Base felts are applied as they are to any built-up roof. A special pressure gun is used to cut the glass fiber reinforcing into designated lengths and to spray out the fibers together with liquid asphalt. The result is a one-piece reinforced membrane of great strength and flexibility which is evenly spread over the entire surface. This method is particularly useful for contoured and steep-pitch roofs, to which a conventional built-up roof is sometimes difficult to apply.

The labels in the figure read: Coping, Through-wall flashing, Counter flashing, 1" x 8" backing, Cant strip, Base flashing, Deck, Joist

LIQUID ENVELOPE ROOFING

Liquid envelope roofing is a vinyl-based compound, available either clear or in a range of colors. It is sprayed on in enough applications to build up a 15 to 40 mil dry film which is impervious to moisture and humidity, flexible, and elastic through a wide range of temperatures. It may be applied on wood, concrete, steel, insulated surfaces, and on asphalt or tar if the surface is first coated with a suitable primer. A continuous film can be carried up the face of a parapet or over the edges of a roof to reinforce flashing.

REVIEW QUESTIONS

1. Differentiate between *roof decking* and *roofing*.

2. (a) List three types of joists which may be used to frame a flat roof. (b) Of the types listed above, which provides the greatest clear span?

3. How is a poured-in-place gypsum roof deck supported?

4. (a) List four types of precast concrete units used to form a roof deck. (b) Why are such long spans made possible by the use of precast units?

5. Briefly answer the following: (a) What are two basic features of a truss? (b) What is a panel joint? (c) When are split rings used in a truss assembly? (d) What is a purlin?

6. Explain what is meant by a *lamella*.

7. Outline the basic features of a folded plate roof.

8. Explain how: (a) To form a molded shell concrete roof; (b) to raise the shell into place.

9. (a) Why are flat metal roofing plates applied to a solid deck? (b) List three types of seams used to fasten flat metal roofing sheets together. (c) Why are metal sheets joined by seams rather than soldered or welded?

10. Why is a rigid board type of insulation used under built-up roofing?

11. What is meant by a *five-ply* built-up roof?

12. What is *cold process* roofing?

13. Differentiate between *monoform* and *liquid envelope* roofing.

CONSTRUCTION WITH LAMINATED TIMBER

Bonding wood with adhesives is an old art—examples of it have been found in Egyptian tombs. It was first used in Europe for constructional purposes in the early 1900's, where it gained ready acceptance. But not until the early 1930's was glued-laminated structural timber introduced in America. World War II and its heavy demand for military and industrial construction provided the impetus which made glued-laminated construction commercially important.

Architects and builders are finding glued-laminated timber the answer to some of their most pressing problems. Such timbers have proved to be extremely versatile and have allowed architects to develop shapes and sizes which would be difficult to obtain with solid timber, concrete, or steel.

MATERIALS USED

Laminated timbers are widely recognized as being among the finest permanent structural materials. They are made from kiln-dried stock, mostly *Douglas fir* and *Southern pine*, with some *western larch* and *western hemlock*. Both fir and pine are extremely strong, straight-grained, tough, resilient, and durable woods. The larch and hemlock are not quite as strong, but match the fir and pine quite closely in color and texture, and are used in the portions of the laminated timber where stresses will be lowest.

Tests have shown that adhesives can be made to develop the full strength of wood and that time alone does not affect the strength of the joint when the proper adhesive is used for given conditions. For laminated members which are protected from appreciable amounts of moisture and relatively

227

high humidity, *casein glue* is satisfactory. When laminated members are continuously immersed in water or subjected to intermittent wetting and drying, such as exterior exposures or in buildings where high humidities are encountered for long periods of time, highly water-resistant adhesives such as *phenol, resorcinol,* or *melamine* resin glues should be used.

The manufacture of glued-laminated timber begins with the selection and grading of the laminating lumber. The finished product will be only as good as the pieces which went into it, so the laminating stock must be of good quality. Of the materials available to the laminator, the highest quality is almost free of natural defects which restrict strength, and is used almost exclusively for face laminations where appearance, as well as strength, is a factor. The lower grades of laminating stock are almost equivalent to select structural, construction, and standard grades of joists and planks, with special additional limitations which qualify them for laminating purposes. One of these limitations relates to cross grain. Limitations in this aspect of material selection are more severe than commonly imposed by grading rules. They apply to only the outer 10% of the depth of a member stressed principally in bending but apply to all laminations of members under tension or compression. Working unit stresses must be modified to the slope of grain, as specified in Table 13-1.

Table 13-1

Strength Ratios Corresponding to Slope of Grain

Slope of grain	Maximum Strength Ratio	
	Fiber stress in bending or tension	Stress in compression parallel to grain
1 in 6	——	0.56
1 in 8	0.53	0.66
1 in 10	0.61	0.74
1 in 12	0.69	0.82
1 in 14	0.74	0.87
1 in 15	0.76	1.00
1 in 16	0.80	——
1 in 18	0.85	——
1 in 20	1.00	——

PREPARATION OF MATERIAL

The laminating stock must be dried to a moisture content as close as practicable to that which it will attain in service. It must, in any case, not be less than 7% nor more than 16%. There are two reasons for these limits. One is to provide the moisture conditions under which the best possible glue bonds may be obtained, and the other is to assure that there will be

Fig. 13-1. Measuring moisture content of laminating stock with electric moisture meter. (Courtesy Canadian Inst. of Timber Const.)

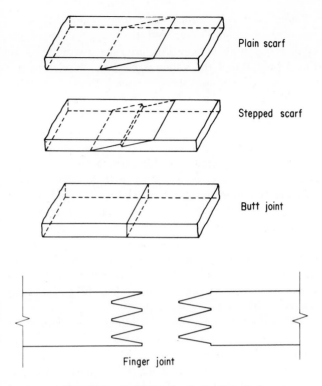

Plain scarf

Stepped scarf

Butt joint

Finger joint

Fig. 13-2. End joints for laminating stock

Butt joints are not recommended, especially in important structural members, but are sometimes used in members or portions of members subjected to compression only. If butt joints are used in the compression portion of a member subjected to bending, the cross-sectional area of all laminations containing butt joints at a particular cross section should be disregarded in computing the effective moment of inertia for that cross section. Butt joints in adjacent laminations should not be spaced closer than ten times the thickness of the lamination.

Every piece comprising a single lamination (as well as the completed end joint) must be of equal thickness to avoid gaps in the glue lines which will affect strength. For practical reasons, laminating plants maintain a constant thickness of all laminating stock. The standard thicknesses used by most manufacturers are 0.75 and 1.625 in., with a permissible tolerance of $\pm$ 0.0075 in. Figure 13-3 shows laminating stock being checked for thickness as it emerges from a surfacer.

ASSEMBLY OF MATERIAL

The first step in the assembly of a glued-laminated timber is the positioning and gluing of end joints. This must be done in such a way that the completed joint, after bonding, will be the same thickness as the lamination. End jointing may be a separate operation, but many manufacturers have devised systems of indexing scarf joints for gluing during the assembly operation. One is to bore a small hole at the time the scarf is made, so a dowel can be inserted during assembly to hold the two pieces in the right position. When used, the stepped scarf helps to position the two pieecs at a joint. Other methods of marking meeting points automatically—including hand pinning—are also employed. Finger joints do not require indexing prior to assembly.

Laminations are coated with adhesive by passing them through a mechanical glue spreader which controls the amount of adhesive applied. Scarf joints are coated and pinned during this operation, when the single operation assembly system is used. Finger joints are sprayed with adhesive, fitted together, and set electronically in a single operation. The entire lamination is then laid on edge in a jig or press made of steel frames, according to the shape of the member being formed. The position of each lamination is previously determined according to grade, either by assembling in a trial run or by showing the position of every piece on a drawing. Successive laminations are laid on edge next to the first until the full depth of the member has been reached.

as little dimensional change as possible once the member has been placed in service (Fig. 13-1).

Laminated timbers are often required to be longer than commercially available stock, and the individual pieces must accordingly be spliced end-to-end to make full length laminations. This is done in several ways, including *plain scarf joints, stepped scarf joints, finger joints*, and *butt* joints. Figure 13-2 illustrates all four.

Plain scarf joints are relatively easy to make and are used extensively in important structural members. When they occur in tension members or in the tension portion of a member subjected to bending, a reduction in allowable stress is necessary. The scarf is made by a machine which produces a smooth, sloping surface at one or both ends of each board.

A stepped scarf joint employs a mechanical as well as a glue bond, but is more difficult to make. In addition, when stepped scarf joints are used, the portion of the thickness of the lamination occupied by the step is disregarded in calculating the moment of inertia and the net effective area.

Finger joints are cut with special saws and are often used where the laminating stock is 3/4 in. material. Notice in Fig. 13-2 that each finger has a square end and that the bottom of each V has a flat surface. This eliminates the likelihood of the fingers splitting the end of the matching piece as the two halves of the joint are fitted together.

Fig. 13-3. Checking thickness of laminating stock with "go-no-go" gauge as it comes from surfacer. (Courtesy Canadian Inst. of Timber Const.)

Fig. 13-4. Tightening clamp bolts with air-operated impact wrench. (Courtesy Canadian Inst. of Timber Const.)

Clamping begins as soon as the final laminations have been placed in the jig. Steel bolts with wood or metal clamp blocks are commonly used to press the laminations together. Clamping begins at the middle and progresses towards the ends, tightening the nuts with an impact wrench set to produce a pressure of from 10 to 200 psi on the glue lines (Fig. 13-4). A torque wrench is used to check the tension on the clamp nuts (Fig. 13-5).

Some adhesives require a minimum glue line temperature of about 75°F, and the temperature of the laminations may be checked prior to assembly, as in Fig. 13-6. When the adhesive has set, the clamps are removed and the member is passed through a large double surfacer to remove irregularities (such as squeezed-out beads of glue) and to bring the member to its finished width. Irregular buildups are sawed to the required shape, ends are trimmed, and daps or other fabrication completed. Surface irregularities are corrected as necessary for the required appearance grade, and identification marks are placed on the ends of the member. Finally, it is given a coat of transparent moisture seal.

If necessary, finished members are wrapped before shipment to protect their appearance. Some manufacturers use a wrap of double-creped, impregnated paper, while others use an inner wrap of polyethylene covered with jute.

When dictated by service conditions, glued-laminated timbers may be pressure-treated for protection against decay or insect damage. Straight, or almost straight members to be accommodated in a pressure-treating cylinder may be treated after laminating. Creosote or Wolman salts are generally used for this purpose. If the shape of the member prevents it from being placed in the cylinder after fabrication, the laminations may be pressure-treated beforehand. Wolman salts are used in this case, since this preservative does not affect subsequent glue bonding.

PROPERTIES OF GLUED-LAMINATED TIMBERS

The standard finished widths of glued-laminated members and corresponding nominal widths of laminating stock are given in Table 13-2.

Table 13-2

Nominal and Finished Widths

Nominal width of laminating stock	Finished width of laminated members
4 in.	$3\frac{1}{4}$ in.
5 in.	$4\frac{1}{4}$ in.
6 in.	5 in.
6 in.	$5\frac{1}{4}$ in.
8 in.	7 in.
10 in.	9 in.
12 in.	11 in.
2 & 12; 4 & 10; 6 & 8 in.	$12\frac{1}{2}$ in.
4 & 12; 6 & 10; 8 & 8 in.	$14\frac{1}{2}$ in.

Reprinted by permission from *Timber Construction Manual*.

Table 13-4 is a section economy table. The most suitable section for a required section modulus may be selected from this table, which includes all sizes listed in Table 13-3. To use the table, find the value equal to or next larger than the calculated section modulus required. This section size and all those above it have a sufficient section modulus. The first section appearing in bold-faced type above the required section modulus is the most economical section. Depth limitations can be met by selecting from sizes of sufficient section

Fig. 13-5. Checking tension on clamp bolts with calibrated torque wrench. (Courtesy Canadian Inst. of Timber Const.)

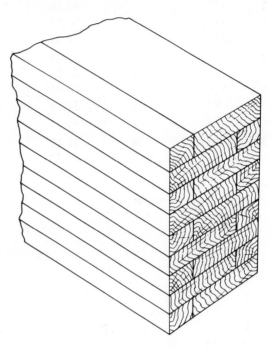

Fig. 13-7. Edge joints staggered

Fig. 13-6. Measuring core temperature of laminating stock. (Courtesy Canadian Inst. of Timber Const.)

Lamination widths greater than 11 in. are composed of two edge-glued boards. In successive layers of laminations such as this, the joints are staggered as in Fig. 13-7.

The properties of sections of glued-laminated structural timbers made with 1⅝ in. laminations are given in Table 13-3. They include the cross-sectional area, section modulus, moment of inertia, and weight per lineal foot.

modulus. It is necessary to make sure that the moment of inertia is adequate for deflection limitations and that the cross-sectional area is adequate for horizontal shear. The table assumes that adequate lateral support has been provided.

The properties of sections of glued-laminated structural timbers made with ¾ in. laminations are given in Table 13-5.

Table 13-6 is a section economy table for the sizes listed in Table 13-5. The same rules used for Table 13-4 apply here as well.

Douglas fir laminations, 1⅝ in. thick, may be bent to a minimum radius of 32 ft when the ends are tangent, or 40 ft when the member is curved throughout its length. Limiting radii for ¾ in. laminations are 9 ft 4 in. and 12 ft 6 in., respectively. When smaller curves are specified, laminations must be reduced in thickness, resulting in extra cost and an added waste of material.

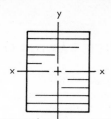

Table 13-3*

Properties of Sections

Laminations

$3\frac{1}{4} \times 1\frac{5}{8}$

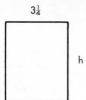

$3\frac{1}{4}$ / h

Actual size	Number of lams.	Area	Axis X-X		Axis Y-Y		Weight per foot†
			S	I	S	I	
in.		in.²	in.³	in.⁴	in.³	in.⁴	lb
b × h							
$3\frac{1}{4} \times 19\frac{1}{2}$	12	63.38	206.0	2,008.2	34.33	55.78	15.0
$17\frac{7}{8}$	11	58.09	173.1	1,546.8	31.47	51.14	13.7
$16\frac{1}{4}$	10	52.81	143.0	1,162.1	28.61	46.49	12.5
$3\frac{1}{4} \times 14\frac{5}{8}$	9	47.53	115.9	847.2	25.75	41.84	11.2
13	8	42.25	91.54	595.0	22.89	37.19	10.0
$11\frac{3}{8}$	7	36.97	70.09	398.6	20.02	32.54	8.7
$9\frac{3}{4}$	6	31.69	51.49	251.0	17.16	27.89	7.5
$8\frac{1}{8}$	5	26.41	35.76	145.3	14.30	23.24	6.2
$3\frac{1}{4} \times 6\frac{1}{2}$	4	21.13	22.89	74.38	11.44	18.59	5.0
$4\frac{7}{8}$	3	15.84	12.87	31.38	8.58	13.95	3.7
$3\frac{1}{4}$	2	10.56	5.72	9.30	5.72	9.30	2.5

*Reprinted from *Timber Construction Manual*.
†Based upon 34.0 lb per cu ft (Douglas fir).

Properties of Sections

Laminations

$4\frac{1}{4} \times 1\frac{5}{8}$

$4\frac{1}{4}$ / h

Actual size	Number of lams.	Area	Axis X-X		Axis Y-Y		Weight per foot*
			S	I	S	I	
in.		in.²	in.³	in.⁴	in.³	in.⁴	lb
b × h							
$4\frac{1}{4} \times 26$	16	110.5	478.8	6,224.8	78.27	166.3	26.1
$24\frac{3}{8}$	15	103.6	420.8	5,129.1	73.38	155.9	24.5
$4\frac{1}{4} \times 22\frac{3}{4}$	14	96.69	366.6	4,'70.2	68.49	145.5	22.8
$21\frac{1}{8}$	13	89.78	316.1	3,338.9	63.60	135.1	21.2
$19\frac{1}{2}$	12	82.88	269.3	2,626.1	58.70	124.7	19.6
$17\frac{7}{8}$	11	75.97	226.3	2,022.8	53.81	114.3	17.9
$16\frac{1}{4}$	10	69.06	187.0	1,519.7	48.92	104.0	16.3
$4\frac{1}{4} \times 14\frac{5}{8}$	9	62.16	151.5	1,107.9	44.03	93.56	14.7
13	8	55.25	119.7	778.1	39.14	83.16	13.0
$11\frac{3}{8}$	7	48.34	91.65	521.3	34.24	72.77	11.4
$9\frac{3}{4}$	6	41.44	67.34	328.3	29.35	62.37	9.8
$8\frac{1}{8}$	5	34.53	46.76	190.0	24.46	51.98	8.2
$4\frac{1}{4} \times 6\frac{1}{2}$	4	27.63	29.93	97.26	19.57	41.58	6.5
$4\frac{7}{8}$	3	20.72	16.83	41.03	14.68	31.19	4.9
$3\frac{1}{4}$	2	13.81	7.48	12.16	9.78	20.79	3.3

*Based upon 34.0 lb per cu ft (Douglas fir).

Properties of Sections

Laminations

$$5 \times 1\tfrac{5}{8}$$

Actual size	Number of lams.	Area	Axis X-X		Axis Y-Y		Weight per foot*
			S	I	S	I	
in.		in.^{2}	in.^{3}	in.^{4}	in.^{3}	in.^{4}	lb
b $\times$ h							
5 $\times$ 30$\frac{7}{8}$	19	154.4	794.4	12,263	128.6	321.6	36.4
29$\frac{1}{4}$	18	146.3	713.0	10,427	121.9	304.7	34.5
27$\frac{5}{8}$	17	138.1	636.0	8,784.1	115.1	287.8	32.6
26	16	130.0	563.3	7,323.3	108.3	270.8	30.7
24$\frac{3}{8}$	15	121.9	495.1	6,034.2	101.6	253.9	28.8
5 $\times$ 22$\frac{3}{4}$	14	113.8	431.3	4,906.1	94.79	237.0	26.9
21$\frac{1}{8}$	13	105.6	371.9	3,928.1	88.02	220.1	24.9
19$\frac{1}{2}$	12	97.50	316.9	3,089.5	81.25	203.1	23.0
17$\frac{7}{8}$	11	89.38	266.3	2,379.7	74.48	186.2	21.1
16$\frac{1}{4}$	10	81.25	220.1	1,787.9	67.71	169.3	19.2
5 $\times$ 14$\frac{5}{8}$	9	73.13	176.2	1,303.4	60.94	152.3	17.3
13	8	65.00	140.8	915.4	54.17	135.4	15.3
11$\frac{3}{8}$	7	56.88	107.8	613.3	47.40	118.5	13.4
9$\frac{3}{4}$	6	48.75	79.22	366.2	40.63	101.6	11.5
8$\frac{1}{8}$	5	40.63	55.01	223.5	33.85	84.64	9.6
5 $\times$ 6$\frac{1}{2}$	4	32.50	35.21	114.4	27.08	67.71	7.7
4$\frac{7}{8}$	3	24.38	19.80	48.27	20.31	50.78	5.8

*Based upon 34.0 lb per cu ft (Douglas fir).

Properties of Sections

Laminations

$$5\tfrac{1}{4} \times 1\tfrac{5}{8}$$

Actual size	Number of lams.	Area	Axis X-X		Axis Y-Y		Weight per foot*
			S	I	S	I	
in.		in.^{2}	in.^{3}	in.^{4}	in.^{3}	in.^{4}	lb
b $\times$ h							
5$\frac{1}{4}$ $\times$ 30$\frac{7}{8}$	19	162.1	834.1	12,877	141.8	372.3	38.3
29$\frac{1}{4}$	18	153.6	748.6	10,949	134.4	352.7	36.3
27$\frac{5}{8}$	17	145.0	667.7	9,223.3	126.9	333.1	34.2
26	16	136.5	591.5	7,689.5	119.4	313.5	32.2
24$\frac{3}{8}$	15	128.0	519.9	6,336.0	112.0	293.9	30.2
5$\frac{1}{4}$ $\times$ 22$\frac{3}{4}$	14	119.4	452.9	5,151.4	104.5	274.3	28.2
21$\frac{1}{8}$	13	110.9	390.5	4,124.5	97.04	254.7	26.2
19$\frac{1}{2}$	12	102.4	332.7	3,244.0	89.58	235.2	24.2
17$\frac{7}{8}$	11	93.84	279.6	2,498.7	82.11	215.6	22.2
16$\frac{1}{4}$	10	85.31	231.1	1,877.3	74.65	196.0	20.1
5$\frac{1}{4}$ $\times$ 14$\frac{5}{8}$	9	76.78	187.2	1,368.6	67.18	176.4	18.1
13	8	68.25	147.9	961.2	59.72	156.8	16.1
11$\frac{3}{8}$	7	59.72	113.2	643.9	52.25	137.2	14.1
9$\frac{3}{4}$	6	51.19	83.18	405.5	44.79	117.6	12.1
8$\frac{1}{8}$	5	42.66	57.76	234.7	37.32	97.98	10.1
5$\frac{1}{4}$ $\times$ 6$\frac{1}{2}$	4	34.13	36.97	120.1	29.86	78.38	8.1
4$\frac{7}{8}$	3	25.59	20.79	50.69	22.39	58.79	6.0

*Based upon 34.0 lb per cu ft (Douglas fir).

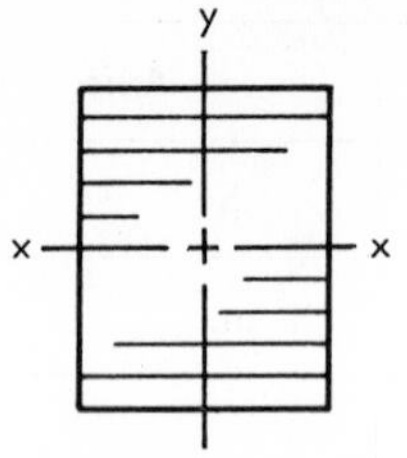

Properties of Sections

Laminations

$7 \times 1\frac{5}{8}$

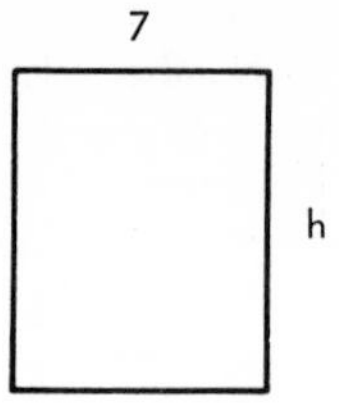

Actual size	Number of lams.	Area	Axis X-X		Axis Y-Y		Weight per foot*
			S	I	S	I	
in.		in.²	in.³	in.⁴	in.³	in.⁴	lb
b × h							
7 × 39	24	273.0	1,774.5	34,603	318.5	1,114.7	64.5
37⅜	23	261.6	1,629.7	30,455	305.2	1,068.3	61.8
35¾	22	250.3	1,491.1	26,653	292.0	1,021.9	59.1
34⅛	21	238.9	1,358.6	23,181	278.7	975.4	56.4
32½	20	227.5	1,232.3	20,025	265.4	929.0	53.7
7 × 30⅞	19	216.1	1,112.1	17,169	252.1	882.5	51.0
29¼	18	204.8	998.2	14,598	238.9	836.1	48.3
27⅝	17	193.4	890.3	12,298	225.6	789.6	45.7
26	16	182.0	788.7	10,253	212.3	743.2	43.0
24⅜	15	170.6	693.2	8,447.9	199.1	696.7	40.3
7 × 22¾	14	159.3	603.8	6,868.5	185.8	650.3	37.6
21⅛	13	147.9	520.6	5,499.3	172.5	603.8	34.9
19½	12	136.5	443.6	4,325.3	159.3	557.4	32.2
17⅞	11	125.1	372.8	3,331.6	146.0	510.9	29.5
16¼	10	113.8	308.1	2,503.1	132.7	464.5	26.9
7 × 14⅝	9	102.4	249.5	1,824.8	119.4	418.0	24.2
13	8	91.00	197.2	1,281.6	106.2	371.6	21.5
11⅜	7	79.63	151.0	858.6	92.90	325.1	18.8
9¾	6	68.25	110.9	540.7	79.63	278.7	16.1
8⅛	5	56.88	77.02	312.9	66.35	232.2	13.4
7 × 6½	4	45.50	49.29	160.2	53.08	185.8	10.7

*Based upon 34.0 lb per cu ft (Douglas fir).

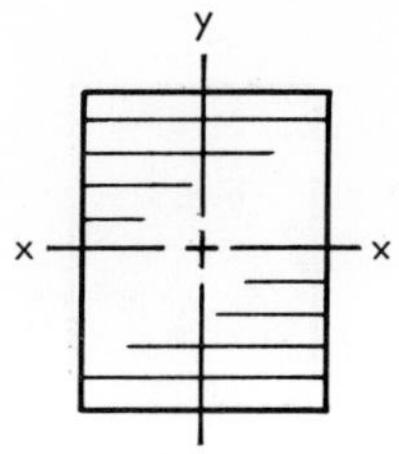

Properties of Sections

Laminations

$9 \times 1\frac{5}{8}$

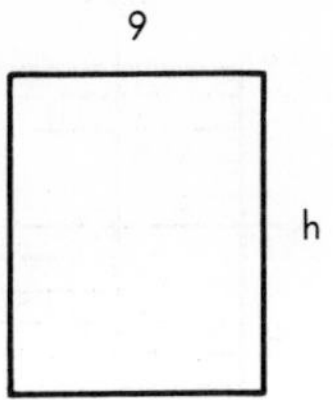

Actual size	Number of lams.	Area	Axis X-X		Axis Y-Y		Weight per foot*
			S	I	S	I	
in.		in.²	in.³	in.⁴	in.³	in.⁴	lb
b × h							
9 × 52	32	468.0	4,056.0	105,456	702.0	3,159.0	110
50⅜	31	453.4	3,806.5	95,875	680.1	3,060.3	107
48¾	30	438.8	3,564.8	86,893	658.1	2,961.6	104
9 × 47⅛	29	424.1	3,331.1	78,490	636.2	2,862.8	100
45½	28	409.5	3,105.4	70,647	614.3	2,764.1	96.7
43⅞	27	394.9	2,887.5	63,345	592.3	2,665.4	93.2
42¼	26	380.3	2,677.6	56,564	570.4	2,566.7	89.8
40⅝	25	365.6	2,475.6	50,285	548.4	2,468.0	86.3
9 × 39	24	351.0	2,281.5	44,489	526.5	2,369.3	82.9
37⅜	23	336.4	2,095.3	39,157	504.6	2,270.5	79.4
35¾	22	321.8	1,917.1	34,268	482.6	2,171.8	76.0
34⅛	21	307.1	1,746.8	29,804	460.7	2,073.1	72.5
32½	20	292.5	1,584.4	25,746	438.8	1,974.4	69.1
9 × 30⅞	19	277.9	1,429.9	22,074	416.8	1,875.7	65.6
29¼	18	263.3	1,283.3	18,769	394.9	1,776.9	62.2
27⅝	17	248.6	1,144.7	15,811	372.9	1,678.2	58.7
26	16	234.0	1,014.0	13,182	351.0	1,579.5	55.2
24⅜	15	219.4	891.2	10,862	329.1	1,480.8	51.8
9 × 22¾	14	204.8	776.3	8,830.9	307.1	1,382.1	48.3
21⅛	13	190.1	669.4	7,070.5	285.2	1,283.3	44.9
19½	12	175.5	570.4	5,561.2	263.3	1,184.6	41.4
17⅞	11	160.9	479.3	4,283.5	241.3	1,085.9	38.0
16¼	10	146.3	396.1	3,218.3	219.4	987.2	34.5
9 × 14⅝	9	131.6	320.8	2,346.1	197.4	888.5	31.1
13	8	117.0	253.5	1,647.8	175.5	789.8	27.6
11⅜	7	102.4	194.1	1,103.9	153.6	691.0	24.2
9¾	6	87.75	142.6	695.1	131.6	592.3	20.7
8⅛	5	73.13	99.02	402.3	109.7	493.6	17.3

*Based upon 34.0 lb per cu ft (Douglas fir).

Properties of Sections

Laminations

$11 \times 1\frac{5}{8}$

Actual size	Number of lams.	Area	Axis X-X		Axis Y-Y		Weight per foot*
			S	I	S	I	
in.		in.²	in.³	in.⁴	in.³	in.⁴	lb
b × h							
$11 \times 55\frac{1}{4}$	34	607.8	5,596.4	154,600	1,114.2	6,128.2	143
$53\frac{5}{8}$	33	589.9	5,272.0	141,356	1,081.4	5,947.9	139
52	32	572.0	4,957.3	128,891	1,048.7	5,767.7	135
$50\frac{3}{8}$	31	554.1	4,652.3	117,181	1,015.9	5,587.4	131
$48\frac{3}{4}$	30	536.3	4,357.0	106,203	983.1	5,407.2	127
$11 \times 47\frac{1}{8}$	29	518.4	4,071.4	95,932	950.4	5,227.0	122
$45\frac{1}{2}$	28	500.5	3,795.5	86,347	917.6	5,046.7	118
$43\frac{7}{8}$	27	482.6	3,529.2	77,422	884.8	4,866.5	114
$42\frac{1}{4}$	26	464.8	3,272.6	69,134	852.0	4,686.2	110
$40\frac{5}{8}$	25	446.9	3,025.7	61,460	819.3	4,506.0	106
11×39	24	429.0	2,788.5	54,376	786.5	4,325.8	101
$37\frac{3}{8}$	23	411.1	2,561.0	47,858	753.7	4,145.5	97.1
$35\frac{3}{4}$	22	393.3	2,343.1	41,883	721.0	3,965.3	92.9
$34\frac{1}{8}$	21	375.4	2,135.0	36,428	688.2	3,785.0	88.6
$32\frac{1}{2}$	20	357.5	1,936.5	31,467	655.4	3,604.8	84.4
$11 \times 30\frac{7}{8}$	19	339.6	1,747.7	26,979	622.6	3,424.6	80.2
$29\frac{1}{4}$	18	321.8	1,568.5	22,940	589.9	3,244.3	76.0
$27\frac{5}{8}$	17	303.9	1,399.1	19,325	557.1	3,064.1	71.7
26	16	286.0	1,239.3	16,111	524.3	2,883.8	67.5
$24\frac{3}{8}$	15	268.1	1,089.3	13,275	491.6	2,703.6	63.3
$11 \times 22\frac{3}{4}$	14	250.3	948.9	10,793	458.8	2,523.4	59.1
$21\frac{1}{8}$	13	232.4	818.2	8,641.7	426.0	2,343.1	54.9
$19\frac{1}{2}$	12	214.5	697.1	6,797.0	393.3	2,162.9	50.6
$17\frac{7}{8}$	11	196.6	585.8	5,235.4	360.5	1,982.6	46.4
$16\frac{1}{4}$	10	178.8	484.1	3,933.4	327.7	1,802.4	42.2
$11 \times 14\frac{5}{8}$	9	160.9	392.1	2,867.5	294.9	1,622.2	38.0
13	8	143.0	309.8	2,013.9	262.2	1,441.9	33.8
$11\frac{3}{8}$	7	125.1	237.2	1,349.2	229.4	1,261.7	29.5
$9\frac{3}{4}$	6	107.3	174.3	849.6	196.6	1,081.4	25.3

*Based upon 34.0 lb per cu ft (Douglas fir).

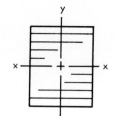

Properties of Sections

Laminations

$12\frac{1}{2} \times 1\frac{5}{8}$

$12\frac{1}{2}$

h

Actual size	Number of lams.	Area	Axis X-X		Axis Y-Y		Weight per foot*
			S	I	S	I	
in.		in.²	in.³	in.⁴	in.³	in.⁴	lb
b × h							
$12\frac{1}{2} \times 71\frac{1}{2}$	44	893.8	10,651	380,756	1,862.0	11,637	211
$69\frac{7}{8}$	43	873.4	10,172	355,381	1,819.7	11,373	206
$68\frac{1}{4}$	42	853.1	9,704.3	331,159	1,777.3	11,108	201
$66\frac{5}{8}$	41	832.8	9,247.7	308,064	1,735.0	10,844	197
65	40	812.5	8,802.1	286,068	1,692.7	10,579	192
$12\frac{1}{2} \times 63\frac{3}{8}$	39	792.2	8,367.5	265,145	1,650.4	10,315	187
$61\frac{3}{4}$	38	771.9	7,943.9	245,267	1,608.1	10,050	182
$60\frac{1}{8}$	37	751.6	7,531.3	226,409	1,565.8	9,786.0	177
$58\frac{1}{2}$	36	731.3	7,129.7	208,543	1,523.4	9,521.5	173
$56\frac{7}{8}$	35	710.9	6,739.1	191,643	1,481.1	9,257.0	168
$12\frac{1}{2} \times 55\frac{1}{4}$	34	690.6	6,359.5	175,681	1,438.8	8,992.5	163
$53\frac{5}{8}$	33	670.3	5,990.9	160,631	1,396.5	8,728.0	158
52	32	650.0	5,633.3	146,467	1,354.2	8,463.5	153
$50\frac{3}{8}$	31	629.7	5,286.7	133,160	1,311.8	8,199.1	149
$48\frac{3}{4}$	30	609.4	4,951.2	120,685	1,269.5	7,934.6	144
$12\frac{1}{2} \times 47\frac{1}{8}$	29	589.1	4,626.6	109,014	1,227.2	7,670.1	139
$45\frac{1}{2}$	28	568.8	4,313.0	98,121	1,184.9	7,405.6	134
$43\frac{7}{8}$	27	548.4	4,010.4	87,979	1,142.6	7,141.1	129
$42\frac{1}{4}$	26	528.1	3,718.9	78,561	1,100.3	6,876.6	125
$40\frac{5}{8}$	25	507.8	3,438.3	69,841	1,057.9	6,612.1	120
$12\frac{1}{2} \times 39$	24	487.5	3,168.8	61,791	1,015.6	6,347.7	115
$37\frac{3}{8}$	23	467.2	2,910.2	54,384	973.3	6,083.2	110
$35\frac{3}{4}$	22	446.9	2,662.6	47,595	931.0	5,818.7	106
$34\frac{1}{8}$	21	426.6	2,426.1	41,395	888.7	5,554.2	101
$32\frac{1}{2}$	20	406.3	2,200.5	35,758	846.4	5,289.7	95.9
$12\frac{1}{2} \times 30\frac{7}{8}$	19	385.9	1,986.0	30,658	804.0	5,025.2	91.1
$29\frac{1}{4}$	18	365.6	1,782.4	26,068	761.7	4,760.7	86.3
$27\frac{5}{8}$	17	345.3	1,589.9	21,960	719.4	4,496.3	81.5
26	16	325.0	1,408.3	18,308	677.1	4,231.8	76.7
$24\frac{3}{8}$	15	304.7	1,237.8	15,086	634.8	3,967.3	71.9
$12\frac{1}{2} \times 22\frac{3}{4}$	14	284.4	1,078.3	12,265	592.4	3,702.8	67.1
$21\frac{1}{8}$	13	264.1	929.7	9,820.2	550.1	3,438.3	62.3
$19\frac{1}{2}$	12	243.8	792.2	7,723.8	507.8	3,173.8	57.6
$17\frac{7}{8}$	11	223.4	665.7	5,949.3	465.5	2,909.3	52.8
$16\frac{1}{4}$	10	203.1	550.1	4,469.8	423.2	2,644.9	48.0
$12\frac{1}{2} \times 14\frac{5}{8}$	9	182.8	445.6	3,258.5	380.9	2,380.4	43.2
13	8	162.5	352.1	2,288.5	338.5	2,115.9	38.4
$11\frac{3}{8}$	7	142.2	269.6	1,533.1	296.2	1,851.4	33.6

*Based upon 34.0 lb per cu ft (Douglas fir).

Properties of Sections

$14\frac{1}{2} \times 1\frac{5}{8}$ Laminations

Actual size	Number of lams.	Area	Axis X-X		Axis Y-Y		Weight per foot*
			S	I	S	I	
in.		in.²	in.³	in.⁴	in.³	in.⁴	lb
b × h							
$14\frac{1}{2} \times 84\frac{1}{2}$	52	1,225.3	17,256	729,049	2,961.0	21,467	289
$82\frac{7}{8}$	51	1,201.7	16,598	687,792	2,904.1	21,055	284
$81\frac{1}{4}$	50	1,178.1	15,954	648,122	2,847.1	20,642	278
$14\frac{1}{2} \times 79\frac{5}{8}$	49	1,154.6	15,322	610,007	2,790.2	20,229	273
78	48	1,131.0	14,703	573,417	2,733.3	19,816	267
$76\frac{3}{8}$	47	1,107.4	14,097	538,320	2,676.3	19,403	261
$74\frac{3}{4}$	46	1,083.9	13,503	504,685	2,619.4	18,990	256
$73\frac{1}{8}$	45	1,060.3	12,923	472,481	2,562.4	18,578	250
$14\frac{1}{2} \times 71\frac{1}{2}$	44	1,036.8	12,355	441,677	2,505.5	18,165	245
$69\frac{7}{8}$	43	1,013.2	11,799	412,242	2,448.5	17,752	239
$68\frac{1}{4}$	42	989.6	11,257	384,145	2,391.6	17,339	234
$66\frac{5}{8}$	41	966.1	10,727	357,354	2,334.7	16,926	228
65	40	942.5	10,210	331,839	2,277.7	16,513	223
$14\frac{1}{2} \times 63\frac{3}{8}$	39	918.9	9,706.3	307,568	2,220.8	16,101	217
$61\frac{3}{4}$	38	895.4	9,214.9	284,510	2,163.8	15,688	211
$60\frac{1}{8}$	37	871.8	8,736.3	262,635	2,106.9	15,275	206
$58\frac{1}{2}$	36	848.3	8,270.4	241,910	2,049.9	14,862	200
$56\frac{7}{8}$	35	824.7	7,817.3	222,306	1,993.0	14,449	195
$14\frac{1}{2} \times 55\frac{1}{4}$	34	801.1	7,377.0	203,790	1,936.1	14,036	189
$53\frac{5}{8}$	33	777.6	6,949.5	186,333	1,879.1	13,624	184
52	32	754.0	6,534.7	169,901	1,822.2	13,211	178
$50\frac{3}{8}$	31	730.4	6,132.6	154,466	1,765.2	12,798	172
$48\frac{3}{4}$	30	706.9	5,743.4	139,994	1,708.3	12,385	167
$14\frac{1}{2} \times 47\frac{1}{8}$	29	683.3	5,366.8	126,456	1,651.3	11,972	161
$45\frac{1}{2}$	28	659.8	5,003.1	113,821	1,594.4	11,559	156
$43\frac{7}{8}$	27	636.2	4,652.1	102,056	1,537.5	11,147	150
$42\frac{1}{4}$	26	612.6	4,313.9	91,131	1,480.5	10,734	145
$40\frac{5}{8}$	25	589.1	3,988.4	81,015	1,423.6	10,321	139
$14\frac{1}{2} \times 39$	24	565.5	3,675.8	71,677	1,366.6	9,908.0	134
$37\frac{3}{8}$	23	541.9	3,375.8	63,086	1,309.7	9,495.2	128
$35\frac{3}{4}$	22	518.4	3,088.6	55,210	1,252.7	9,082.4	122
$34\frac{1}{8}$	21	494.8	2,814.2	48,018	1,195.8	8,669.5	117
$32\frac{1}{2}$	20	471.3	2,552.6	41,480	1,138.9	8,256.7	111
$14\frac{1}{2} \times 30\frac{7}{8}$	19	447.7	2,303.7	35,564	1,081.9	7,843.9	106
$29\frac{1}{4}$	18	424.1	2,067.6	30,239	1,025.0	7,431.0	100
$27\frac{5}{8}$	17	400.6	1,844.3	25,474	968.0	7,018.2	94.6
26	16	377.0	1,633.7	21,238	911.1	6,605.4	89.0
$24\frac{3}{8}$	15	353.4	1,435.8	17,499	854.1	6,192.5	83.5
$14\frac{1}{2} \times 22\frac{3}{4}$	14	329.9	1,250.8	14,228	797.2	5,779.7	77.9
$21\frac{1}{8}$	13	306.3	1,078.5	11,391	740.3	5,366.9	72.3
$19\frac{1}{2}$	12	282.8	918.9	8,959.6	683.3	4,954.0	66.8
$17\frac{7}{8}$	11	259.2	772.2	6,901.2	626.4	4,541.2	61.2
$16\frac{1}{4}$	10	235.6	638.1	5,185.0	569.4	4,128.3	55.6
$14\frac{1}{2} \times 14\frac{5}{8}$	9	212.1	516.9	3,779.8	512.5	3,715.5	50.1
13	8	188.5	408.4	2,654.7	455.5	3,302.7	44.5

*Based upon 34.0 lb per cu ft (Douglas fir).

Table 13-4*

Section Economy Table—1⅝″ Laminations

Section modulus	Size	Section modulus	Size	Section modulus	Size	Section modulus	Size
17,256	14½ × 84½	3,806.5	9 × 50⅜	1,112.1	7 × 30⅞	316.1	4¼ × 12⅛
16,598	14½ × 82⅞	3,795.5	11 × 45½	1,089.3	11 × 24⅜	309.8	11 × 13
15,954	14½ × 81¼	3,718.9	12½ × 42¼	1,078.5	14½ × 21⅛	308.1	7 × 16¼
15,322	14½ × 79⅝	3,675.8	14½ × 39	1,078.3	12½ × 22¾	279.6	5¼ × 17⅞
14,703	14½ × 78			1,014.0	9 × 26	269.6	12½ × 11⅜
14,097	14½ × 76⅜	3,564.8	9 × 48¾			269.3	4¼ × 19½
13,503	14½ × 74¾	3,529.2	11 × 43⅞	998.2	7 × 29¼	266.3	5 × 17⅞
12,923	14½ × 73⅛	3,438.3	12½ × 40⅝	948.9	11 × 22¾	253.5	9 × 13
12,355	14½ × 71½	3,375.8	14½ × 37⅜	929.7	12½ × 21⅛	249.5	7 × 14⅝
11,799	14½ × 69⅞			918.9	14½ × 19½	237.2	11 × 11⅜
11,257	14½ × 68¼	3,331.1	9 × 47⅛	891.2	9 × 24⅜	231.1	5¼ × 16¼
10,727	14½ × 66⅝	3,272.6	11 × 42¼				
		3,168.8	12½ × 39	890.3	7 × 27⅝	226.3	4¼ × 17⅞
10,651	12½ × 71½			834.1	5¼ × 30⅞	220.1	5 × 16¼
10,210	14½ × 65	3,105.4	9 × 45½	818.2	11 × 21⅛		
		3,088.6	14½ × 35¾			206.0	3¼ × 19½
10,172	12½ × 69⅞	3,025.7	11 × 40⅝	794.4	5 × 30⅞	197.2	7 × 13
9,706.3	14½ × 63⅜	2,910.2	12½ × 37⅜	792.2	12½ × 19½	194.1	9 × 11⅜
				788.7	7 × 26	187.2	5¼ × 14⅝
9,704.3	12½ × 68¼	2,887.5	9 × 43⅞	776.3	9 × 22¾	187.0	4¼ × 16¼
		2,814.2	14½ × 34⅛	772.2	14½ × 17⅞	178.2	5 × 14⅝
9,247.7	12½ × 66⅝	2,788.5	11 × 39			174.3	11 × 9¾
9,214.9	14½ × 61¾			748.6	5¼ × 29¼		
		2,677.6	9 × 42¼			173.1	3¼ × 17⅞
8,802.1	12½ × 65	2,662.6	12½ × 35¾	713.0	5 × 29¼	151.5	4¼ × 14⅝
8,736.3	14½ × 60⅛	2,561.0	11 × 37⅜	697.1	11 × 19½	151.0	7 × 11⅜
		2,552.6	14½ × 32½	693.2	7 × 24⅜	147.9	5¼ × 13
8,367.5	12½ × 63⅜			669.4	9 × 21⅛		
8,270.4	14½ × 58½	2,475.6	9 × 40⅝			143.0	3¼ × 16¼
		2,426.1	12½ × 34⅛	667.7	5¼ × 27⅝	142.6	9 × 9¾
7,943.9	12½ × 61¾	2,343.1	11 × 35¾	665.7	12½ × 17⅞	140.8	5 × 13
7,817.3	14½ × 56⅞	2,303.7	14½ × 30⅞	638.1	14½ × 16¼	119.7	4¼ × 13
7,531.3	12½ × 60⅛	2,281.5	9 × 39	636.0	5 × 27⅝		
7,377.0	14½ × 55¼	2,200.5	12½ × 32½	603.8	7 × 22¾	115.9	3¼ × 14⅝
		2,135.0	11 × 34⅛			113.2	5¼ × 11⅜
7,129.7	12½ × 58½			591.5	5¼ × 26	110.9	7 × 9¾
6,949.5	14½ × 53⅝	2,095.3	9 × 37⅜	585.8	11 × 17⅞	107.8	5 × 11⅜
		2,067.6	14½ × 29¼	570.4	9 × 19½	99.02	9 × 8⅛
6,739.1	12½ × 56⅞	1,986.0	12½ × 30⅞			91.65	4¼ × 11⅜
6,534.7	14½ × 52	1,936.5	11 × 32½	563.3	5 × 26		
				550.1	12½ × 16¼	91.54	3¼ × 13
6,359.5	12½ × 55¼	1,917.1	9 × 35¾	520.6	7 × 21⅛	83.18	5¼ × 9¾
6,132.6	14½ × 50⅜	1,844.3	14½ × 27⅝			79.22	5 × 9¾
5,990.9	12½ × 53⅝	1,782.4	12½ × 29¼	519.9	5¼ × 24⅜	77.02	7 × 8⅛
5,743.4	14½ × 48¾	1,774.5	7 × 39	516.9	14½ × 14⅝		
		1,747.7	11 × 30⅞			70.09	3¼ × 11⅜
5,633.3	12½ × 52	1,746.8	9 × 34⅛	495.1	5 × 24⅜	67.34	4¼ × 9¾
5.596.4	11 × 55¼	1,633.7	14½ × 26	484.1	11 × 16¼	57.76	5¼ × 8⅛
5,366.8	14½ × 47⅛			479.3	9 × 17⅞	55.01	5 × 8⅛
5,286.7	12½ × 50⅜	1,629.7	7 × 37⅜	478.8	4¼ × 26	51.49	3¼ × 9¾
		1,589.9	12½ × 27⅝	452.9	5¼ × 22¾	49.29	7 × 6½
5,272.0	11 × 53⅝	1,584.4	9 × 32½	445.6	12½ × 14⅝	46.76	4¼ × 8⅛
5,003.1	14½ × 45½	1,568.5	11 × 29¼	443.6	7 × 19½	36.97	5¼ × 6½
		1,491.1	7 × 35¾	431.3	5 × 22¾		
4,957.3	11 × 52	1,435.8	14½ × 24⅜			35.76	3¼ × 8⅛
4,951.2	12½ × 48¾	1,429.9	9 × 30⅞	420.8	4¼ × 24⅜	35.21	5 × 6½
		1,408.3	12½ × 26	408.4	14½ × 13	29.93	4¼ × 6½
4,652.3	11 × 50⅜	1,399.1	11 × 27⅝	396.1	9 × 16¼		
4,652.1	14½ × 43⅞			392.1	11 × 14⅝	22.89	3¼ × 6½
4,626.6	12½ × 47⅛	1,358.6	7 × 34⅛	390.5	5¼ × 21⅛	20.79	5¼ × 4⅞
		1,283.3	9 × 29¼	372.8	7 × 17⅞	19.80	5 × 4⅞
4,357.0	11 × 48¾	1,250.8	14½ × 22¾	371.9	5 × 21⅛		
4,313.9	14½ × 42¼	1,239.3	11 × 26			16.83	4¼ × 4⅞
4,313.0	12½ × 45½	1,237.8	12½ × 24⅜	366.6	4¼ × 22¾	12.87	3¼ × 4⅞
4,071.4	11 × 47⅛			352.1	12½ × 13		
4,056.0	9 × 52	1,232.3	7 × 32½	332.7	5¼ × 19½	7.48	4¼ × 3¼
4,010.4	12½ × 43⅞	1,144.7	9 × 27⅝	320.8	9 × 14⅝	5.72	3¼ × 3¼
3,988.4	14½ × 40⅝			316.9	4 × 19½		

*Reprinted from Timber Construction Manual.

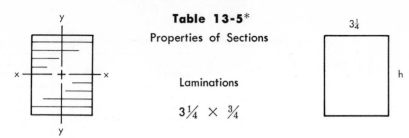

Table 13-5*

Properties of Sections

Laminations

$3\frac{1}{4} \times \frac{3}{4}$

Actual size	Area	Axis X-X		Axis Y-Y		Weight per foot†
		S	I	S	I	
in.	in.²	in.³	in.⁴	in.³	in.⁴	lb
b × h						
$3\frac{1}{4} \times 16\frac{1}{2}$	53.63	147.5	1,216.6	29.05	47.20	12.7
$15\frac{3}{4}$	51.19	134.4	1,058.1	27.73	45.06	12.1
$3\frac{1}{4} \times 15$	48.75	121.9	914.1	26.41	42.91	11.5
$14\frac{1}{4}$	46.31	110.0	783.7	25.09	40.76	10.9
$13\frac{1}{2}$	43.88	98.72	666.3	23.77	38.62	10.4
$12\frac{3}{4}$	41.44	88.05	561.3	22.45	36.47	9.8
$3\frac{1}{4} \times 12$	39.00	78.00	468.0	21.13	34.33	9.2
$11\frac{1}{4}$	36.56	68.55	385.6	19.80	32.18	8.6
$10\frac{1}{2}$	34.13	59.72	313.5	18.48	30.04	8.1
$9\frac{3}{4}$	31.69	51.49	251.0	17.16	27.89	7.5
$3\frac{1}{4} \times 9$	29.25	43.88	197.4	15.84	25.75	6.9
$8\frac{1}{4}$	26.81	36.87	152.1	14.52	23.60	6.3
$7\frac{1}{2}$	24.38	30.47	114.3	13.20	21.46	5.8
$6\frac{3}{4}$	21.94	24.68	83.29	11.88	19.31	5.2
$3\frac{1}{4} \times 6$	19.50	19.50	58.50	10.56	17.16	4.6
$5\frac{1}{4}$	17.06	14.93	39.19	9.24	15.02	4.0
$4\frac{1}{2}$	14.63	10.97	24.68	7.92	12.87	3.5
$3\frac{3}{4}$	12.19	7.62	14.28	6.60	10.73	2.9
$3\frac{1}{4} \times 3$	9.75	4.88	7.31	5.28	8.58	2.3

*Reprinted from *Timber Construction Manual.*
†Based upon 34.0 lb per cu ft (Douglas fir).

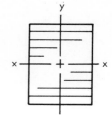

Properties of Sections

Laminations

$4\frac{1}{4} \times \frac{3}{4}$

Actual size	Area	Axis X-X		Axis Y-Y		Weight per foot*
		S	I	S	I	
in.	in.²	in.³	in.⁴	in.³	in.⁴	lb
b × h						
$4\frac{1}{4} \times 21$	89.25	312.4	3,279.9	63.22	134.3	21.1
$20\frac{1}{4}$	86.06	290.5	2,940.9	60.96	129.5	20.3
$19\frac{1}{2}$	82.88	269.3	2,626.1	58.70	124.7	19.6
$18\frac{3}{4}$	79.69	249.0	2,334.5	56.45	119.9	18.8
$4\frac{1}{4} \times 18$	76.50	229.5	2,065.5	54.19	115.1	18.1
$17\frac{1}{4}$	73.31	210.8	1,817.9	51.93	110.4	17.3
$16\frac{1}{2}$	70.13	192.8	1,591.0	49.67	105.6	16.6
$15\frac{3}{4}$	66.94	175.7	1,383.7	47.41	100.8	15.8
$4\frac{1}{4} \times 15$	63.75	159.4	1,195.3	45.16	95.96	15.1
$14\frac{1}{4}$	60.56	143.8	1,024.8	42.90	91.16	14.3
$13\frac{1}{2}$	57.38	129.1	871.4	40.64	86.36	13.5
$12\frac{3}{4}$	54.19	115.1	734.0	38.38	81.56	12.8
$4\frac{1}{4} \times 12$	51.00	102.0	612.0	36.13	76.77	12.0
$11\frac{1}{4}$	47.81	89.65	504.3	33.87	71.97	11.3
$10\frac{1}{2}$	44.63	78.09	410.0	31.61	67.17	10.5
$9\frac{3}{4}$	41.44	67.33	328.3	29.35	62.37	9.8
$4\frac{1}{4} \times 9$	38.25	57.38	258.2	27.09	57.57	9.0
$8\frac{1}{4}$	35.06	48.21	198.9	24.84	52.78	8.3
$7\frac{1}{2}$	31.88	39.84	149.4	22.58	47.98	7.5
$6\frac{3}{4}$	28.69	32.27	108.9	20.32	43.18	6.8
$4\frac{1}{4} \times 6$	25.50	25.50	76.50	18.06	38.38	6.0
$5\frac{1}{4}$	22.31	19.52	51.25	15.80	33.58	5.3
$4\frac{1}{2}$	19.13	14.34	32.27	13.55	28.79	4.5
$3\frac{3}{4}$	15.94	9.96	18.68	11.29	23.99	3.8

*Based upon 34.0 lb per cu ft (Douglas fir).

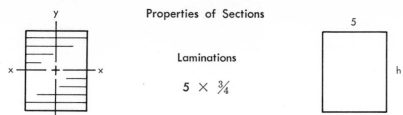

Properties of Sections

Laminations

$5 \times \frac{3}{4}$

Actual size	Area	Axis X-X		Axis Y-Y		Weight per foot*
		S	I	S	I	
in.	in.²	in.³	in.⁴	in.³	in.⁴	lb
b × h						
5 × 25½	127.5	541.9	6,908.9	106.3	265.6	30.1
24¾	123.8	510.5	6,317.0	103.1	257.8	29.2
5 × 24	120.0	480.0	5,760.0	100.0	250.0	28.3
23¼	116.3	450.5	5,236.7	96.87	242.2	27.4
22½	112.5	421.9	4,746.1	93.75	234.4	26.6
21¾	108.8	394.2	4.287.1	90.62	226.6	25.7
5 × 21	105.0	367.5	3,858.8	87.50	218.8	24.8
20¼	101.3	341.7	3,459.9	84.37	210.9	23.9
19½	97.50	316.9	3,089.5	81.25	203.1	23.0
18¾	93.75	293.0	2,746.6	78.13	195.3	22.1
5 × 18	90.00	270.0	2,430.0	75.00	187.5	21.2
17¼	86.25	248.0	2,138.7	71.88	179.7	20.4
16½	82.50	226.9	1,871.7	68.75	171.9	19.5
15¾	78.75	206.7	1,627.9	65.63	164.1	18.6
5 × 15	75.00	187.5	1,406.3	62.50	156.3	17.7
14¼	71.25	169.2	1,205.7	59.38	148.4	16.8
13½	67.50	151.9	1,025.2	56.25	140.6	15.9
12¾	63.75	135.5	863.6	53.13	132.8	15.1
5 × 12	60.00	120.0	720.0	50.00	125.0	14.2
11¼	56.25	105.5	593.3	46.88	117.2	13.3
10½	52.50	91.88	482.3	43.75	109.4	12.4
9¾	48.75	79.22	386.2	40.63	101.6	11.5
5 × 9	45.00	67.50	303.8	37.50	93.75	10.6
8¼	41.25	56.72	234.0	34.38	85.94	9.7
7½	37.50	46.88	175.8	31.25	78.13	8.9
6¾	33.75	38.00	128.1	28.13	70.31	8.0
5 × 6	30.00	30.00	90.00	25.00	62.50	7.1
5¼	26.25	22.97	60.29	21.88	54.69	6.2
4½	22.50	16.88	37.97	18.75	46.88	5.3

*Based upon 34.0 lb per cu ft (Douglas fir).

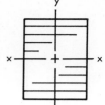

Properties of Sections

Laminations

$5\frac{1}{4} \times \frac{3}{4}$

$5\frac{1}{4}$

h

| Actual size | Area | Axis X-X | | Axis Y-Y | | Weight per foot* |
| | | S | I | S | I | |
in.	in.²	in.³	in.⁴	in.³	in.⁴	lb
b × h						
$5\frac{1}{4} \times 26\frac{1}{4}$	137.8	602.9	7,913.5	120.6	316.5	32.5
$25\frac{1}{2}$	133.9	569.0	7,254.3	117.1	307.5	31.6
$24\frac{3}{4}$	129.9	536.0	6,632.9	113.7	298.5	30.7
$5\frac{1}{4} \times 24$	126.0	504.0	6,048.0	110.3	289.4	29.7
$23\frac{1}{4}$	122.1	473.0	5,498.5	106.8	280.4	28.8
$22\frac{1}{2}$	118.1	443.0	4,983.4	103.4	271.3	27.9
$21\frac{3}{4}$	114.2	413.9	4,501.5	99.91	262.3	27.0
$5\frac{1}{4} \times 21$	110.0	385.9	4,051.7	96.47	253.2	26.0
$20\frac{1}{4}$	106.3	358.8	3,632.9	93.02	244.2	25.1
$19\frac{1}{2}$	102.4	332.7	3,244.0	89.58	235.1	24.2
$18\frac{3}{4}$	98.44	307.6	2,883.9	86.13	226.1	23.2
$5\frac{1}{4} \times 18$	94.50	283.5	2,551.5	82.69	217.1	22.3
$17\frac{1}{4}$	90.56	260.4	2,245.7	79.24	208.0	21.4
$16\frac{1}{2}$	86.63	238.2	1,965.3	75.80	199.0	20.5
$15\frac{3}{4}$	82.69	217.1	1,709.3	72.35	189.9	19.5
$5\frac{1}{4} \times 15$	78.75	196.9	1,476.6	68.91	180.9	18.6
$14\frac{1}{4}$	74.81	177.7	1,266.0	65.46	171.8	17.7
$13\frac{1}{2}$	70.88	159.5	1,076.4	62.02	162.8	16.7
$12\frac{3}{4}$	66.94	142.2	906.8	58.57	153.7	15.8
$5\frac{1}{4} \times 12$	63.00	126.0	756.0	55.13	144.7	14.9
$11\frac{1}{4}$	59.06	110.7	622.9	51.68	135.7	13.9
$10\frac{1}{2}$	55.13	96.47	506.5	48.23	126.6	13.0
$9\frac{3}{4}$	51.19	83.18	405.5	44.79	117.6	12.1
$5\frac{1}{4} \times 9$	47.25	70.88	318.9	41.34	108.5	11.2
$8\frac{1}{4}$	43.31	59.55	245.7	37.90	99.48	10.2
$7\frac{1}{2}$	39.38	49.22	184.6	34.45	90.44	9.3
$6\frac{3}{4}$	35.44	39.87	134.6	31.01	81.40	8.4
$5\frac{1}{4} \times 6$	31.50	31.50	94.50	27.56	72.35	7.4
$5\frac{1}{4}$	27.56	24.12	63.31	24.12	63.31	6.5
$4\frac{1}{2}$	23.63	17.72	39.87	20.67	54.26	5.6

*Based upon 34.0 lb per cu ft (Douglas fir).

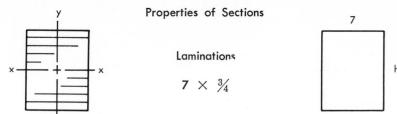

Properties of Sections

Laminations

7 × ¾

Actual size	Area	Axis X-X		Axis Y-Y		Weight per foot*
		S	I	S	I	
in.	in.²	in.³	in.⁴	in.³	in.⁴	lb
b × h						
7 × 27¾	194.3	898.4	12,465	226.6	793.2	45.9
7 × 27	189.0	850.5	11,482	220.5	771.8	44.6
26¼	183.8	803.9	10,551	214.4	750.3	43.4
25½	178.5	758.6	9,672.5	208.3	728.9	42.1
24¾	173.3	714.7	8,843.9	202.1	707.4	40.9
7 × 24	168.0	672.0	8,064.0	196.0	686.0	39.7
23¼	162.8	630.7	7,331.4	189.9	664.6	38.4
22½	157.5	590.6	6,644.5	183.8	643.1	37.2
21¾	152.3	551.9	6,002.0	177.6	621.7	35.9
7 × 21	147.0	514.5	5,402.3	171.5	600.3	34.7
20¼	141.8	478.4	4,843.9	165.4	578.8	33.5
19½	136.5	443.6	4,325.4	159.3	557.4	32.2
18¾	131.3	410.2	3,845.2	153.1	535.9	31.0
7 × 18	126.0	378.0	3,402.0	147.0	514.5	29.7
17¼	120.8	347.2	2,994.2	140.9	493.1	28.5
16½	115.5	317.6	2,620.4	134.8	471.6	27.3
15¾	110.3	289.4	2,279.1	128.6	450.2	26.0
7 × 15	105.0	262.5	1,968.8	122.5	428.8	24.8
14¼	99.75	236.9	1,688.0	116.4	407.3	23.6
13½	94.50	212.6	1,435.2	110.3	385.9	22.3
12¾	89.25	189.7	1,209.1	104.1	364.4	21.1
7 × 12	84.00	168.0	1,008.0	98.00	343.0	19.8
11¼	78.75	147.7	830.6	91.88	321.6	18.6
10½	73.50	128.6	675.3	85.75	300.1	17.4
9¾	68.25	110.9	540.7	79.63	278.7	16.1
7 × 9	63.00	94.50	425.3	73.50	257.3	14.9
8¼	57.75	79.41	327.6	67.38	235.8	13.6
7½	52.50	65.63	246.1	61.25	214.4	12.4
6¾	47.25	53.16	179.4	55.13	192.9	11.2

*Based upon 34.0 lb per cu ft (Douglas fir).

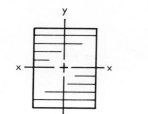

Properties of Sections

Laminations

9 × ¾

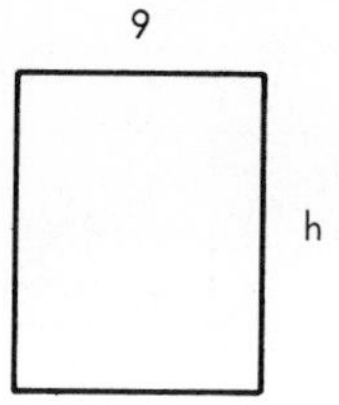

Actual size	Area	Axis X-X		Axis Y-Y		Weight per foot*
		S	I	S	I	
in.	in.²	in.³	in.⁴	in.³	in.⁴	lb
b × h						
9 × 36	324.0	1,944.0	34,992	486.0	2,187.0	76.5
35¼	317.3	1,863.8	32,850	475.9	2,141.4	74.9
34½	310.5	1,785.4	30,798	465.8	2,095.9	73.3
33¾	303.8	1,708.6	28,833	455.6	2,050.3	71.7
9 × 33	297.0	1,633.5	26,953	445.5	2,004.8	70.1
32¼	290.3	1,560.1	25,157	435.4	1,959.2	68.5
31½	283.5	1,488.4	23,442	425.3	1,913.6	66.9
30¾	276.8	1,418.3	21,807	415.1	1,868.1	65.3
9 × 30	270.0	1,350.0	20,250	405.0	1,822.5	63.7
29¼	263.3	1,283.3	18,769	394.9	1,776.9	62.2
28½	256.5	1,218.4	17,362	384.8	1,731.4	60.6
27¾	249.8	1,155.1	16,027	374.6	1,685.8	59.0
9 × 27	243.0	1,093.5	14,762	364.5	1,640.3	57.4
26¼	236.3	1,033.6	13,566	354.4	1,594.7	55.8
25½	229.5	975.4	12,436	344.3	1,549.1	54.2
24¾	222.8	918.8	11,371	334.1	1,503.6	52.6
9 × 24	216.0	864.0	10,368	324.0	1,458.0	51.0
23¼	209.3	810.8	9,426.1	313.9	1,412.4	49.4
22½	202.5	759.4	8,543.0	303.8	1,366.9	47.8
21¾	195.8	709.6	7,716.8	293.6	1,321.3	46.2
9 × 21	189.0	661.5	6,945.8	283.5	1,275.8	44.6
20¼	182.3	615.1	6,227.8	273.4	1,230.2	43.0
19½	175.5	570.4	5,561.2	263.3	1,184.6	41.4
18¾	168.8	527.3	4,943.8	253.1	1,139.1	39.8
9 × 18	162.0	486.0	4,374.0	243.0	1,093.5	38.2
17¼	155.3	446.3	3,849.7	232.9	1,047.9	36.7
16½	148.5	408.4	3,369.1	222.8	1,002.4	35.1
15¾	141.8	372.1	2,930.2	212.6	956.8	33.5
9 × 15	135.0	337.5	2,531.3	202.5	911.3	31.9
14¼	128.3	304.6	2,170.2	192.4	865.7	30.3
13½	121.5	273.4	1,845.3	182.3	820.1	28.7
12¾	114.8	243.8	1,554.5	172.1	774.6	27.1
9 × 12	108.0	216.0	1,296.0	162.0	729.0	25.5
11¼	101.3	189.8	1,067.9	151.9	683.4	23.9
10½	94.50	165.4	868.2	141.8	637.9	22.3
9¾	87.75	142.6	695.1	131.6	592.3	20.7
9 × 9	81.00	121.5	546.8	121.5	546.8	19.1
8¼	74.25	102.1	421.1	111.4	501.2	17.5

*Based upon 34.0 lb per cu ft (Douglas fir).

Properties of Sections

$11 \times \frac{3}{4}$ Laminations

Actual size	Area	Axis X-X		Axis Y-Y		Weight per foot*
		S	I	S	I	
in.	in.²	in.³	in.⁴	in.³	in.⁴	lb
b × h						
11 × 45	495.0	3,712.5	83,531	907.5	4,991.2	117
44¼	486.8	3,589.8	79,424	892.4	4,908.1	115
43½	478.5	3,469.1	75,453	877.3	4,824.9	113
42¾	470.3	3,350.5	71,618	862.1	4,741.7	111
11 × 42	462.0	3,234.0	67,914	847.0	4,658.5	109
41¼	453.8	3,119.5	64,339	831.9	4,575.3	107
40½	445.5	3,007.1	60,894	816.8	4,492.1	105
39¾	437.3	2,896.8	57,574	801.6	4,408.9	103
11 × 39	429.0	2,788.5	54,376	786.5	4,325.7	101
38¼	420.8	2,682.3	51,299	771.4	4,242.6	99.3
37½	412.5	2,578.1	48,340	756.3	4,159.4	97.4
36¾	404.3	2,476.0	45,497	741.1	4,076.2	95.5
11 × 36	396.0	2,376.0	42,768	726.0	3,993.0	93.5
35¼	387.8	2,278.0	40,150	710.9	3,909.8	91.6
34½	379.5	2,182.1	37,642	695.8	3,826.6	89.6
33¾	371.3	2,088.3	35,240	680.6	3,743.4	87.7
11 × 33	363.0	1,996.5	32,942	665.5	3,660.2	85.7
32¼	354.8	1,906.8	30,747	650.4	3,577.1	83.8
31½	346.5	1,819.1	28,651	635.3	3,493.9	81.8
30¾	338.3	1,733.5	26,653	620.1	3,410.7	79.9
11 × 30	330.0	1,650.0	24,750	605.0	3,327.5	77.9
29¼	321.8	1,568.5	22,940	589.9	3,244.3	76.0
28½	313.5	1,489.1	21,220	574.8	3,161.1	74.0
27¾	305.3	1,411.8	19,588	559.6	3,077.9	72.1
11 × 27	297.0	1,336.5	18,043	544.5	2,994.7	70.1
26¼	288.8	1,263.3	16,581	529.4	2,911.6	68.2
25½	280.5	1,192.1	15,200	514.3	2,828.4	66.2
24¾	272.3	1,123.0	13,897	499.1	2,745.2	64.3
11 × 24	264.0	1,056.0	12,672	484.0	2,662.0	62.3
23¼	255.8	991.0	11,521	468.9	2,578.8	60.4
22½	247.5	928.1	10,441	453.8	2,495.6	58.4
21¾	239.3	867.3	9,431.7	438.6	2,412.4	56.5
11 × 21	231.0	808.5	8,489.2	423.5	2,329.2	54.5
20¼	222.8	751.8	7,611.8	408.4	2,246.1	52.6
19½	214.5	697.1	6,797.0	393.3	2,162.9	50.6
18¾	206.3	644.5	6,042.5	378.1	2,079.7	48.7
11 × 18	198.0	594.0	5,346.0	363.0	1,996.5	46.7
17¼	189.8	545.5	4,705.2	347.9	1,913.3	44.8
16½	181.5	499.1	4,117.8	332.8	1,830.1	42.9
15¾	173.3	454.8	3,581.4	317.6	1,746.9	40.9
11 × 15	165.0	412.5	3,093.7	302.5	1,663.7	39.0
14¼	156.8	372.3	2,652.5	287.4	1,580.6	37.0
13½	148.5	334.1	2,255.3	272.3	1,497.4	35.1
12¾	140.3	298.0	1,899.9	257.1	1,414.2	33.1
11 × 12	132.0	264.0	1,584.0	242.0	1,331.0	31.2
11¼	123.8	232.0	1,305.2	226.9	1,247.8	29.2
10½	115.5	202.1	1,061.2	211.8	1,164.6	27.3

*Based upon 34.0 lb per cu ft (Douglas fir).

Table 13-6*

Section Economy Table—3/4″ Laminations

Section modulus	Size
3,712.5	11 × 45
3,589.8	11 × 44¼
3,469.1	11 × 43½
3,350.5	11 × 42¾
3,234.0	11 × 42
3,119.5	11 × 41¼
3,007.1	11 × 40½
2,896.8	11 × 39¾
2,788.5	11 × 39
2,682.3	11 × 38¼
2,578.1	11 × 37½
2,476.0	11 × 36¾
2,376.0	11 × 36
2,278.0	11 × 35¼
2,182.1	11 × 34½
2,088.3	11 × 33¾
1,966.5	11 × 33
1,944.0	9 × 36
1,906.8	11 × 32¼
1,863.8	9 × 35¼
1,819.1	11 × 31½
1,785.4	9 × 34½
1,733.5	11 × 30¾
1,708.6	9 × 33¾
1,650.0	11 × 30
1,633.5	9 × 33
1,568.5	11 × 29¼
1,560.1	9 × 32¼
1,489.1	11 × 28½
1,488.4	9 × 31½
1,418.3	9 × 30¾
1,411.8	11 × 27¾
1,350.0	9 × 30
1,336.5	11 × 27
1,283.3	9 × 29¼
1,263.3	11 × 26¼
1,218.4	9 × 28½
1,192.1	11 × 25½
1,155.1	9 × 27¾
1,123.0	11 × 24¾
1,093.5	9 × 27
1,056.0	11 × 24

Section modulus	Size
1.033.6	9 × 26¼
991.0	11 × 23¼
975.4	9 × 25½
928.1	11 × 22½
918.8	9 × 24¾
898.4	7 × 27¾
867.3	11 × 21¾
864.0	9 × 24
850.5	7 × 27
810.8	9 × 23¼
808.5	11 × 21
803.9	7 × 26¼
759.4	9 × 22½
758.6	7 × 25½
751.8	11 × 20¼
714.7	7 × 24¾
709.6	9 × 21¾
697.1	11 × 19½
672.0	7 × 24
661.5	9 × 21
644.5	11 × 18¾
630.7	7 × 23¼
615.1	9 × 20¼
602.9	5¼ × 26¼
594.0	11 × 18
590.6	7 × 22½
570.4	9 × 19½
569.0	5¼ × 25½
551.9	7 × 21¾
545.5	11 × 17¼
541.9	5 × 25½
536.0	5¼ × 24¾
527.3	9 × 18¾
514.5	7 × 21
510.5	5 × 24¾
504.0	5¼ × 24
499.1	11 × 16½
486.0	9 × 18

Section modulus	Size
480.0	5 × 24
478.4	7 × 20¼
473.0	5¼ × 23¼
454.8	11 × 15¾
450.5	5 × 23¼
446.3	9 × 17¼
443.6	7 × 19½
443.0	5¼ × 22½
421.9	5 × 22½
413.9	5¼ × 21¾
412.5	11 × 15
410.2	7 × 18¾
408.4	9 × 16½
394.2	5 × 21¾
385.9	5¼ × 21
378.0	7 × 18
372.3	11 × 14¼
372.1	9 × 15¾
367.5	5 × 21
358.8	5¼ × 20¼
347.2	7 × 17¼
341.7	5 × 20¼
337.5	9 × 15
334.1	11 × 13½
332.7	5¼ × 19½
317.6	7 × 16½
316.9	5 × 19½
312.4	4¼ × 21
307.6	5¼ × 18¾
304.6	9 × 14¼
298.0	11 × 12¾
293.0	5 × 18¾
290.5	4¼ × 20¼
289.4	7 × 15¾
283.5	5¼ × 18
273.4	9 × 13½
270.0	5 × 18

Section modulus	Size
269.3	4¼ × 19½
264.0	11 × 12
262.5	7 × 15
260.4	5¼ × 17¼
249.0	4¼ × 18¾
248.0	5 × 17¼
243.8	9 × 12¾
238.2	5¼ × 16½
236.9	7 × 14¼
232.0	11 × 11¼
229.5	4¼ × 18
226.9	5 × 16½
217.1	5¼ × 15¾
216.0	9 × 12
212.6	7 × 13½
210.8	4¼ × 17¼
206.7	5 × 15¾
202.1	11 × 10½
196.9	5¼ × 15
192.8	4¼ × 16½
189.8	9 × 11¼
189.7	7 × 12¾
187.5	5 × 15
177.7	5¼ × 14¼
175.7	4¼ × 15¾
169.2	5 × 14¼
168.0	7 × 12
165.4	9 × 10½
159.5	5¼ × 13½
159.4	4¼ × 15
151.9	5 × 13½
147.7	7 × 11¼

Section modulus	Size
147.5	3¼ × 16½
143.8	4¼ × 14¼
142.6	9 × 9¾
142.2	5¼ × 12¾
135.5	5 × 12¾
134.4	3¼ × 15¾
129.1	4¼ × 13½
128.6	7 × 10½
126.0	5¼ × 12
121.9	3¼ × 15
121.5	9 × 9
120.0	5 × 12
115.1	4¼ × 12¾
110.9	7 × 9¾
110.7	5¼ × 11¼
110.0	3¼ × 14¼
105.5	5 × 11¼
102.1	9 × 8¼
102.0	4¼ × 12
98.72	3¼ × 13½
96.47	5¼ × 10½
94.50	7 × 9
91.88	5 × 10½
89.65	4¼ × 11¼
88.05	3¼ × 12¾
83.18	5¼ × 9¾
79.41	7 × 8¼
79.22	5 × 9¾
78.09	4¼ × 10½
78.00	3¼ × 12
70.88	5¼ × 9
68.55	3¼ × 11¼
67.50	5 × 9

Section modulus	Size
67.33	4¼ × 9¾
65.63	7 × 7½
59.72	3¼ × 10½
59.55	5¼ × 8¼
57.38	4¼ × 9
56.72	5 × 8½
53.16	7 × 6¾
51.49	3¼ × 9¾
49.22	5¼ × 7½
48.21	4¼ × 8¼
46.88	5 × 7½
43.88	3¼ × 9
39.87	5¼ × 6¾
39.84	4¼ × 7½
38.00	5 × 6¾
36.87	3¼ × 8¼
32.27	4¼ × 6¾
31.50	5¼ × 6
30.47	3¼ × 7½
30.00	5 × 6
25.50	4¼ × 6
24.68	3¼ × 6¾
24.12	5¼ × 5¼
22.97	5 × 5¼
19.52	4¼ × 5¼
19.50	3¼ × 6
17.72	5¼ × 4½
16.88	5 × 4½
14.93	3¼ × 5¼
14.34	4¼ × 4½
10.97	3¼ × 4½
9.96	4¼ × 3¾
7.62	3¼ × 3¾
4.88	3¼ × 3

*Reprinted from *Timber Construction Manual.*

Fig. 13-8. Glued-laminated and sawed timber used together in a truss. (Courtesy Bondwood Structures, Alberta Ltd.)

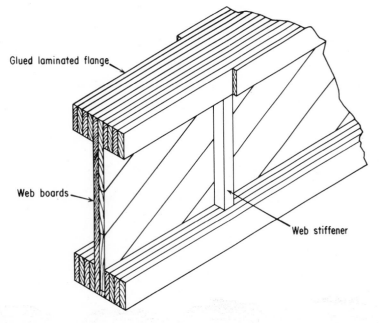

Glued laminated flange

Web boards

Web stiffener

Fig. 13-9. Combination glued-laminated and sawed timber beam

TYPES OF UNITS

Glued-laminated members may be used independently from or together with other materials in the construction of structural units. For example, trusses may be built with glued-laminated chords and sawed lumber web members (Fig. 13-8). Special beams may be made with flanges of glued-laminated timber and diagonal webs of sawed lumber or plywood (Fig. 13-9). Special units, such as folded plates or stressed-skin panels, may be combinations of glued-laminated timber and plywood. Figure 13-10 shows the cross section of a typical folded plate roof and Fig. 13-11 illustrates a stressed-skin panel.

The greatest use of glued-laminated timber is in the fabrication of beams and arches. Three basic types of beams are made: *straight, tapered,* and *curved* (Fig. 13-12). Straight and tapered beams are usually made with a slight camber to allow for normal deflection and to improve appearance. Figure 13-13 shows the manufacture of a large, straight beam.

The three-hinged arch (most commonly used) may be straight, circular, or of varying curvature. Straight arches are normally either *high V* or *low V*, as the V-type arch allows maximum utilization of enclosed space. High and low V arches are illustrated in Fig. 13-14. Circular arches are actually segments of a circle, as shown in Fig. 13-15. Arches of varying curvature may be parabolic or gothic in shape, or may be a combination of curve and straight line. Figure 13-16 illustrates some of these shapes.

The simplest types of glued-laminated arches are those made for light construction work—normally from 2 in. wide laminations. They are also available in a variety of shapes, the basic ones being the *gothic arch,* the *utility arch,* and the *shed rafter.* In the case of the gothic arch, the member is curved throughout. The utility arch has a short, straight portion, which maintains a 4 in 12 slope at the top, while the shed rafter is

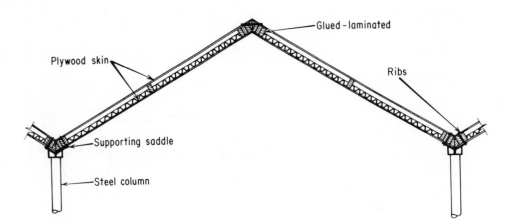

Plywood skin

Glued-laminated

Ribs

Supporting saddle

Steel column

Fig. 13-10. Folded plate roof

partly curved and partly straight, with the straight portion tangent to the curve. Light arches (ribs) are commonly used in spans of up to 80 ft, for 2 ft o.c. spacing. The number of laminations will vary from 4 to 12, depending on the span and the load.

ERECTION AND FASTENING OF BEAMS AND ARCHES

The method used to erect glued-laminated beams depends on their size, but is often done by crane or gin pole. Connection methods depend on whether the beam is being fastened to a wall, column, girder, or another beam. Steel angles and machine bolts form the normal connection of beam to masonry wall (Fig. 13-17). The same type of connection may be used when fastening a beam to a wooden wall, although dowels may be used if the connection must be hidden.

Beam-to-column connections may be made in several ways. If the beam is made up of laminations on edge, a rigid connection may be set up between laminated column and beam by interlocking the laminations, much as is done in a mortise-and-tenon connection. The center portion of the laminated column forms the tenon, while the mortise is created by leaving out part of the center laminations of the beam. Another method is to use a saddle, as in Fig. 13-18. The connection may be made by straps—Fig. 13-19—or by bent plate and lag bolts, Fig. 13-20. A beam-to-girder connection is usually made by means of hangers. Beams are often connected to one another end-to-end. This may be done over a column or wall (Fig. 13-18), or between columns, as a continuous beam (Fig. 13-21).

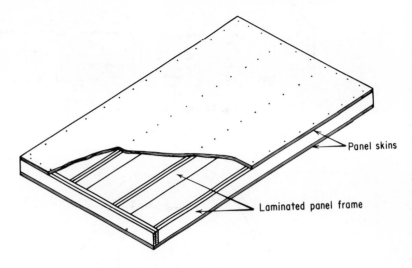

Fig. 13-11. Stressed skin panel

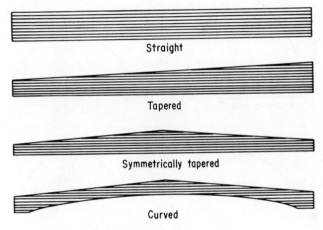

Fig. 13-12. Basic beam shapes

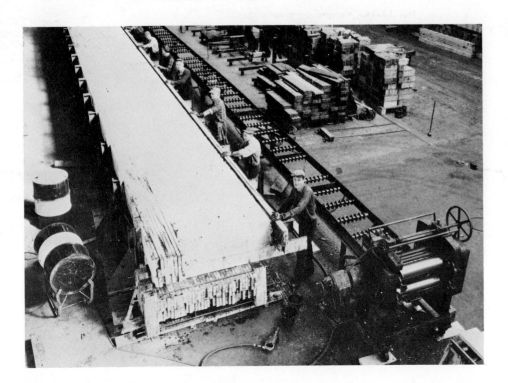

Fig. 13-13. Large glued-laminated beam. (Courtesy Canadian Inst. of Timber Const.)

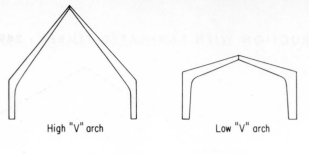

High "V" arch   Low "V" arch

Fig. 13-14. Straight arches

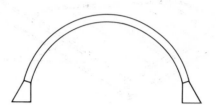

Fig. 13-15. Buttressed segmental arch

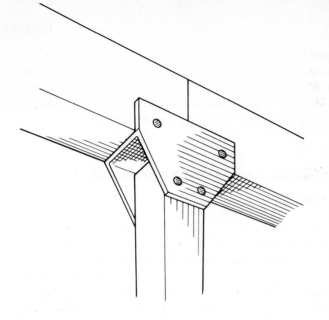

Fig. 13-18. Beam-to-column connection

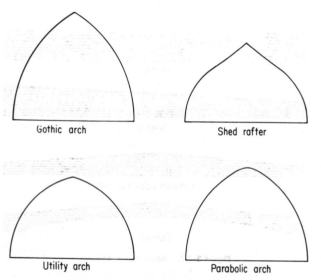

Gothic arch   Shed rafter

Utility arch   Parabolic arch

Fig. 13-16. Varying curvature arches

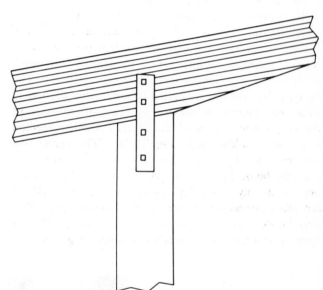

Fig. 13-19. Strap connection

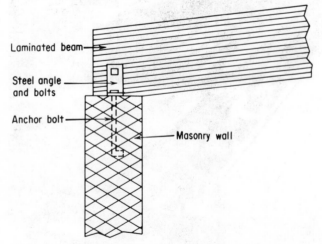

Laminated beam

Steel angle
and bolts

Anchor bolt

Masonry wall

Fig. 13-17. Beam-to-masonry wall connection

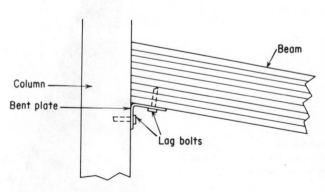

Column

Bent plate

Beam

Lag bolts

Fig. 13-20. Bent plate connection

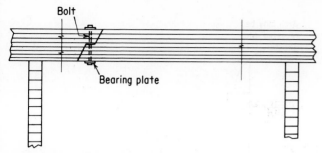

Fig. 13-21. Continuous glued-laminated beam joined between supports

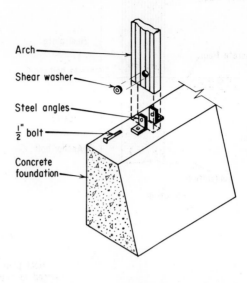

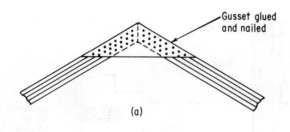

(a)

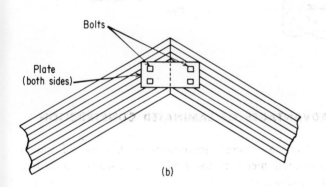

(b)

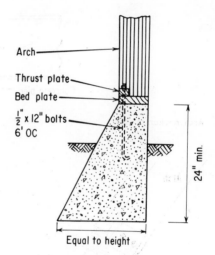

Fig. 13-23. Bottom connections for light arches

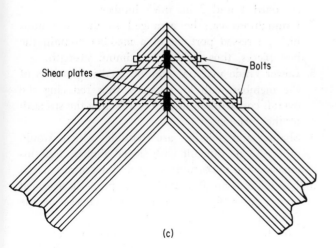

(c)

Fig. 13-22. Upper hinge connections

Methods of erecting arches depend on their size and weight. Light arches may be raised by hand, while others are erected by gin pole or by crane. The top—*upper hinge*—of arches may be fastened by bolts, plates, or gussets (Fig. 13-22). Light arches are normally connected with gussets, while heavier ones require bolts or plates, depending on their pitch.

The bottom—*lower hinge*—of light arches is generally anchored by one of the methods shown in Fig. 13-23. Figure 13-24 shows a typical anchor system for connecting heavier arches to a concrete foundation, although a similar arrangement may be used with a wood base. Figure 13-25 illustrates the bottom connection of a glued-laminated arch to a steel frame. Another type, used for barrel arches set on exterior piers, is illustrated in Fig. 13-26.

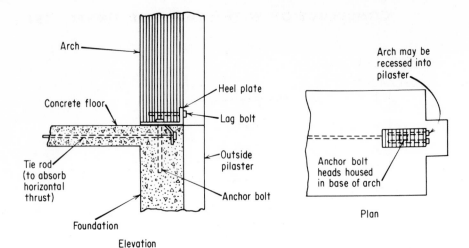

Fig. 13-24. Arch anchor to concrete foundation

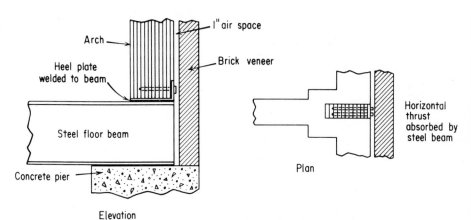

Fig. 13-25. Arch anchor to steel frame

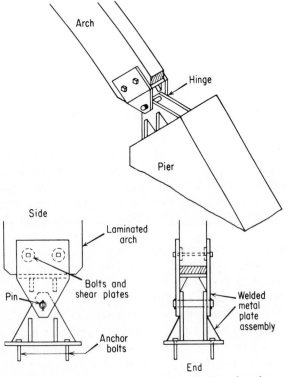

Fig. 13-26. Typical hinge connection for barrel arch on exterior pier

ADVANTAGES OF LAMINATED CONSTRUCTION

There are many advantages in the use of glued-laminated members for timber construction, including the following:

1. Large members can easily be produced from standard 1 and 2 in. thick lumber.
2. Laminations can be arranged so that the most highly stressed portions of a member contain the best pieces, thus insuring maximum strength.
3. Lower grade material may be used in portions of the member with low stresses, thus reducing the overall cost without adversely affecting the strength of the member.
4. Shapes and lengths are possible which would otherwise be difficult with sawed timber, thus increasing the opportunities for architectural variety.
5. Laminations are thin and can be properly seasoned before assembly, thus eliminating checks in the finished unit.
6. Members to be used in dry conditions may be designed on the basis of dry strength, which is considerably better than green or semi-dry strength.

7. Fire resistive qualities of large cross sections of timber are well known and can be utilized fully by building up large sections.

8. Large trees once required for the production of large sawn timber units, now increasingly difficult and expensive to obtain, are no longer essential since the advent of large glued-laminated units.

9. Units of varying cross-sectional size can now be designed in accordance with structural requirements.

10. Beams may be cambered to a predetermined shape to offset deflection, and the tops of roof beams can be shaped to provide the necessary slope for the roof.

However, there are also disadvantages and limitations in the use of glued-laminated structural members. Considerable labor is involved in handling and preparing lumber during the drying, gluing, and laminating processes, thus raising the cost of the product over that of solid, green lumber. Special plant facilities, special skills, and additional time are required in the production of glued-laminated timbers. A strict manufacturing code has been established and great care must be taken in each operation to insure a high-quality product.

REVIEW QUESTIONS

1. What are three primary advantages of using laminated timber instead of solid timber for construction purposes?

2. (a) When may casein glue be used to laminate structural members? (b) What type of glue would you recommend for laminated members that are to be continuously immersed in water?

3. (a) Why are there severe limitations to the use of cross-grained material in laminated members? (b) Why is the moisture content of laminating lumber closely controlled?

4. (a) How are end joints made for material used to build up a member which will be under tension? (b) Why is there a relatively small tolerance in the thickness of laminating material?

5. (a) Give two reasons for using a predetermined plan when placing laminations in a gluing jig.

6. (a) What are *arch ribs*? (b) What is their normal spacing in a building frame? (c) What is a *gin pole*?

7. What is a *three-hinged* arch?

8. List three ways of increasing the fire resistivity of timber.

MASONRY CONSTRUCTION

14

Building with masonry—stone, brick, etc.—involves two types of construction. In one type, the exterior walls are built first and the remainder of the building is framed into them in such a way that those walls transmit the loads of the building directly to the foundations. They are called *bearing walls*. In the other type, the load-bearing framework of a building is constructed of steel, concrete, or timber, and masonry may be utilized simply to close in the building; the walls are being used here as *curtain walls*.

Historically, *brick* and *stone* were the foremost masonry materials. *Clay tile*, *architectural terra cotta*, and *concrete blocks* of many kinds now also enjoy wide acceptance. All are unit masonry products and require mortar to bond them together. Whether in bearing walls or in curtain walls, the basic techniques involved in building with any type of masonry are similar, though the details of construction may depend on the type of unit used or the type of wall being built.

BUILDING WITH CONCRETE BLOCKS

The basic techniques used in building with concrete blocks have been illustrated and described in many books and manuals and need not be repeated here. The allowable height and minimum thickness of block bearing walls are specified by building codes and depend on the type of wall and its eventual use. Nonbearing walls may be 4 in. thinner than comparable bearing walls.

Concrete block bearing walls must be provided with horizontal or vertical supports at right angles to the face of the wall. Vertical support may be provided by cross walls, pilasters, or buttresses; horizontal support is provided by floors or the roof. The greatest distance separating supports is usually 20 times the nominal wall thickness for walls of solid units, 18 times the nominal thickness for walls of hollow blocks, and 18 times the combined thicknesses of inner and outer wythes for cavity walls.

In order to provide maximum stability and to increase the strength of block walls, the following practices are recommended:

1. Choose blocks of good dimensional stability.
2. Keep blocks dry at all times, particularly during site storage and laying operations.
3. Use horizontal joint reinforcement, especially around wall openings.
4. Provide control joints at appropriate locations.
5. Use bond beams where feasible.

Continuous horizontal joint reinforcement is provided by embedding specially fabricated wire reinforcement (Fig. 14-1) in the horizontal mortar joints. The reinforcement may be used continuously in every or every other joint throughout the building, but should in any case be used for two consecutive joints above and below openings (unless there are control joints) and should extend at least 24 in. beyond the opening.

Control joints are vertical joints which separate walls into sections and allow freedom of movement. They should occur at intervals in long, straight walls, where abrupt changes in wall thickness take place, at openings (Fig. 14-2), at intersections of main walls and cross walls, and at locations of structural columns or pilasters in main walls.

To produce a control joint, place building paper or a coat of asphalt paint on the ends of the blocks on one side of the joint. Fill the core with concrete or mortar

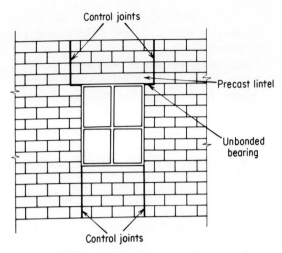

Fig. 14-2. Control joints at window

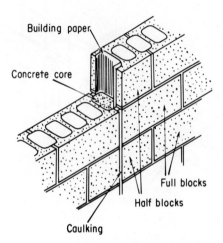

Fig. 14-3. Control joint in block wall

to provide lateral stability (Fig. 14-3). Single wire ties may also be used across the joint. Rake the mortar in the control joint to a depth of ¾ in. and caulk with a suitable compound. Caulking may be omitted on the interior face and the joint finished with a deep groove.

The primary purpose of bond beams is to act as continuous ties for exterior block walls where control joints are not required. They may also be used between control joints in larger buildings. Bond beams can also act as structural members, transmitting lateral loads to other structural members, and can provide bearing for beams or joists.

A bond beam is a continuous, cast-in-place, reinforced concrete beam running around the perimeter of a building or between control joints. It is formed by using standard lintel blocks, deeper bond beam blocks, or standard blocks with a large portion of the webs cut

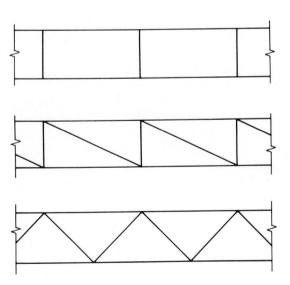

Fig. 14-1. Typical masonry reinforcement

out. In Fig. 14-4, the bond beam is being utilized as a lintel over an opening. Notice the shoring required in the opening.

Lintels over openings in block walls consist of precast concrete units, as in Fig. 14-5, or may be poured in place. In the latter case (illustrated in Fig. 14-6), lintel blocks are used again, and are supported by shoring. When greater strength is required, two-course lintels may be employed. In Fig. 14-7, standard blocks with cut-away webs are being used to form the lintel.

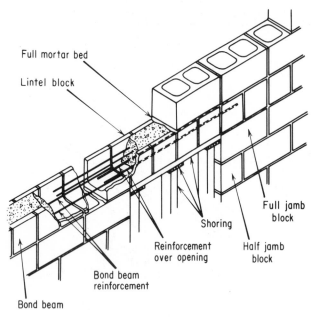

Fig. 14-4. Reinforced bond beam

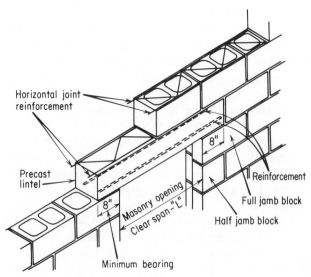

Fig. 14-5. Precast concrete lintel

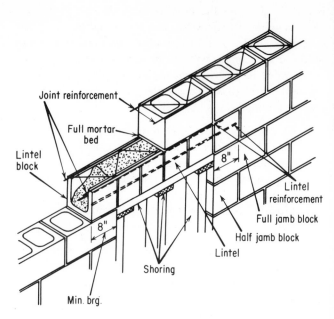

Fig. 14-6. Cast-in-place concrete lintel

The large number of shapes available makes a great variety of patterns possible for a block wall. Consult a concrete block manual for illustrations or patterns. In addition to the standard blocks, *screen* blocks are available to add to the variety or to build open walls which are to act as solar screens. Figure 14-8 illustrates three common solar screen shapes. Manufacturers' brochures are available which will provide a complete list of such units.

Concrete blocks are also used to build back-up walls for brick, tile, or stone facing. Various types of metal ties are used to bind the facing to the back-up, and the commonly used ones are illustrated in Fig. 14-9.

BRICK CONSTRUCTION

Building with brick may involve the construction of solid brick walls (Fig. 14-10), walls of reinforced brick (Fig. 14-15), brick cavity walls (Fig. 14-17), or brick veneer walls (Fig. 14-18). The terminology used in connection with various positions of brick in a wall (see Fig. 14-11) applies in all cases, and almost any of the numerous *pattern bonds* available may be used with any one of these walls. The structural bond involved will depend on the type of wall.

Different types of mortar may be used in laying brick masonry, and the kind used for a specific job may be designated by type or by compressive strength. Table 14-1 outlines the composition and strength of various

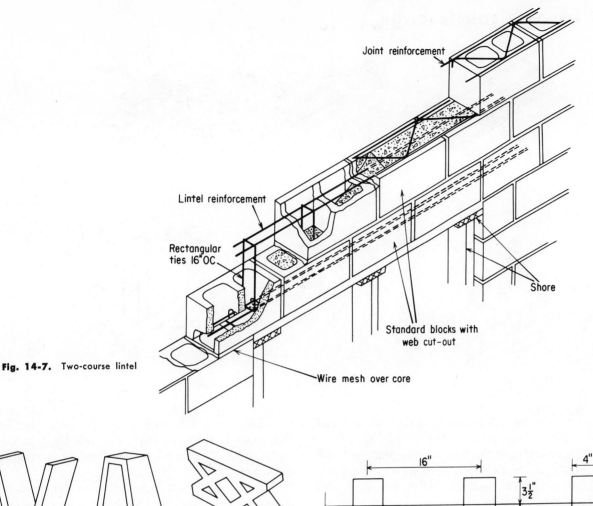

Fig. 14-7. Two-course lintel

Lintel reinforcement

Rectangular ties 16"OC

Joint reinforcement

Shore

Standard blocks with web cut-out

Wire mesh over core

Vee

Double vee

Double X

Fig. 14-8. Typical screen blocks

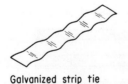

16"

$3\frac{1}{2}$"

4"

Variable

Continuous wire tie

Galvanized strip tie

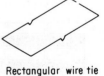

Rectangular wire tie

Fig. 14-9. Typical metal ties

8" Flemish bond

12" English bond

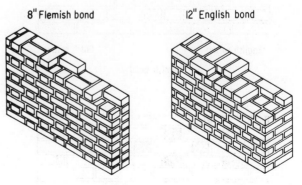

Fig. 14-10. Typical solid brick walls

mortars. Types O or K may not be used where masonry is to be in direct contact with the soil, where an isolated pier is being built, or where the wall is exposed to the elements on all sides—as in the case of a parapet.

The thickness of solid brick walls is governed by building codes which may vary somewhat from one area to another, but generally speaking, the minimum thickness is 8 in. for the top story of a wall not over 36 ft in height. An exception is made in the case of one-story buildings, which may have walls not less than 6 in. thick when built with SCR brick (Fig. 14-14).

When brick walls are required to have greater resistance to compressive, tensile, or shear forces than usual, they may be reinforced with steel rods as in Fig. 14-15. Two or three wythes of brick are laid, the

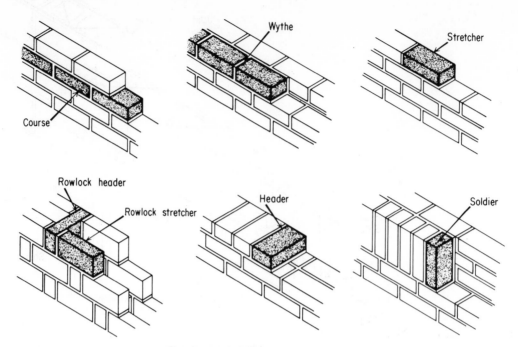

Fig. 14-11. Common terms used in brickwork

starting wythe to be built up not more than 16 in. ahead of the others. Metal ties connect each pair of wythes; reinforcing steel (½ in. for a two-wythe wall or ¼ in. for a three-wythe wall) is placed in the cavities, vertically and horizontally, and the cavities are filled with pea gravel grout. Depth of a pour should not exceed about 4 ft.

Brick walls may be further strengthened by the use of bond beams (Fig. 14-16). In the case of a three-

wythe wall, the two outside wythes act as the form. Side forms must be provided for a bond beam in a two-wythe wall. Vertical reinforcing should extend through the beam.

A brick cavity wall consists of two wythes of brick separated by a continuous air space not less than 2 in. wide. Metal ties are used to connect the two wythes. They should be spaced 36 in. o.c. horizontally with rows of ties spaced 16 in. o.c. vertically. The spacing should be staggered in alternate rows. The facing wythe is always a nominal 4 in. thick, while the interior one may be 4, 6, or 8 in. thick, depending on height, loads, etc.

Fig. 14-12. Two common brick pattern bonds

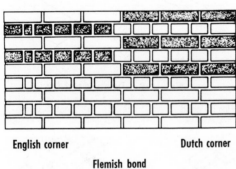

English corner   **Dutch corner**

Flemish bond

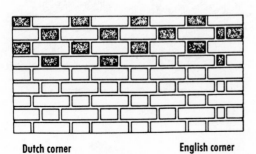

Dutch corner   **English corner**

English bond

Table 14-1

Mortar Types

Type of mortar	Parts by volume				Compressive strength (psi)
	Portland cement	Masonry cement	Lime	Aggregate	
M	1	1	—	Not less than 2 ¼ or more than 3 times the sum of volumes of cement and lime used.	2500
	1	—	¼		
S	½	1	—		1800
	1	—	¼ to ½		
N	—	1	—		750
	1	—	½ to 1¼		
O	—	1	—		350
	1	—	1¼ to 2½		
K	1	—	2½ to 4		75
	—	—	1		

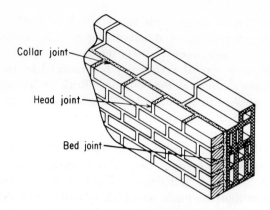

Fig. 14-13. Mortar joints

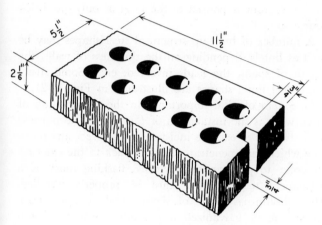

Fig. 14-14. SCR brick

If insulation is required in the wall, it is usually installed in the cavity, and 2 in. rigid insulation is normally used. Whether insulation is required or not, a vapor barrier in the form of an asphalt coating is usually applied to the cavity face of the inner wythe.

Care should be taken that *weep holes* are provided at the bottom of the outer wythe so that the cavity will drain. Oiled rods, sash cord, or rolled fiberglass insulation may be used in the vertical joints to form the drain holes. The sash cord or fiberglass need not be removed.

Brick veneer construction consists of applying a 4 in. wythe of brick as facing material over a back-up wall. The back-up wall may be of frame construction or a masonry wall of common brick, structural clay tile, concrete block, cellular concrete blocks, or poured-in-place concrete. In any case, the load-bearing properties of brick are not utilized.

Structural stability of the facing wythe is obtained by anchoring the veneer to the back-up with metal ties or by grouting it to the wall with a reinforced grout core, usually 1 in. thick.

The support of the masonry over openings in brick walls is an important consideration. That support may be provided either by an arch (Fig. 14-19) or by a lintel. The lintel may be a reinforced concrete unit, a reinforced brick structure, or a built-up structural steel member.

Arches must be built to a form which must be carefully set and supported until the arch itself has gained enough strength to carry the loads. Arches may be

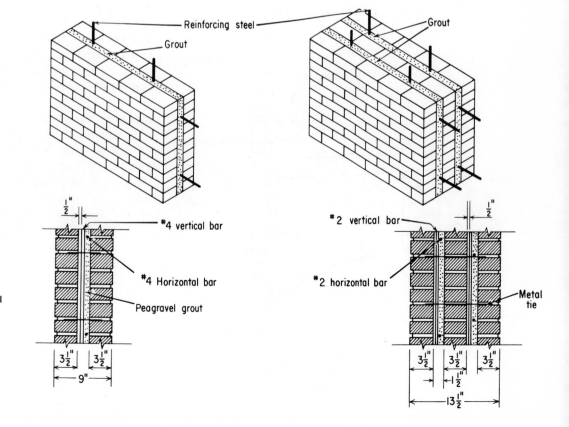

Fig. 14-15. Reinforced brick wall

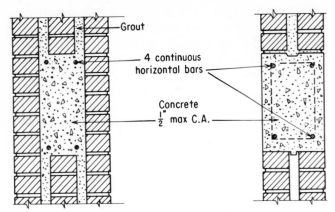

Fig. 14-16. Reinforced bond beams

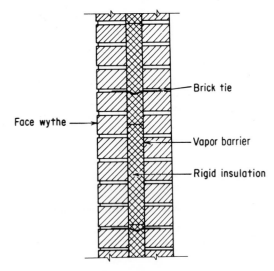

Fig. 14-17. Insulated cavity wall

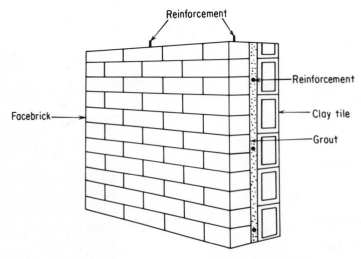

Fig. 14-18. Brick veneer bonded with reinforced grout core

made in special shapes with mortar joints of constant thickness, or may be of standard shapes with varying mortar joint thicknesses to obtain the desired curvature. In some cases, special shapes may be produced by cutting standard units at the job site. Brick arches are usually made with the units laid in soldier or rowlock header bond at the crown. In some instances, it is difficult to lay units in soldier bond and obtain completely filled mortar joints. If this is the case, it is preferable to use two or more rings of rowlock headers.

Reinforced brick lintels are similar to a bond beam. A support must be made on which to build the lintel, and the brick is laid in running bond with full bed and head joints. Horizontal reinforcing steel may be laid in the mortar joints as the units are laid, or the lintel may be built as illustrated in Fig. 14-20. In the latter case, the grout is poured to the level of only one brick course at a time.

A number of built-up structural steel shapes may be used as lintels, depending on the thickness of walls, the length of spans, the loads involved, etc. Some structural steel lintel shapes are illustrated in Fig. 14-21.

One item of vital importance in the construction of brick walls is the installation of *flashing*. The purpose of flashing is to exclude moisture or to direct any moisture which may penetrate the wall back to the exterior. In order to perform satisfactorily, flashing must be a permanent material and must be properly installed. Most flashing is made of sheet metal (copper, lead, aluminum, or galvanized iron), fabric saturated with asphalt, or pliable synthetic material. Copper and bituminous material are sometimes combined to form flashing material.

Two types of flashing are in common use, *external* and *internal*. External flashing prevents the penetration of water at points where walls intersect flat surfaces, such as roofs. Internal flashing is built into and usually concealed in the wall to control the spread of moisture and to direct it to the outside. This is sometimes called *through* flashing.

The points at which flashing should be installed are: (1) above grade in exterior walls; (2) under and behind window sills; (3) over lintels; (4) over spandrel beams; (5) at projections or recesses from the face of a wall; (6) under parapet copings; (7) at intersections of wall and roof; (8) at projections from the roof, such as ventilators, penthouses, etc.; (9) around chimneys and dormers.

External flashing for roof and wall intersections was described in Chapter 12 and illustrated in Fig. 12-49. Flashing at various vulnerable points in brick structures is shown in Fig. 14-22.

Expansion joints are needed in brick construction

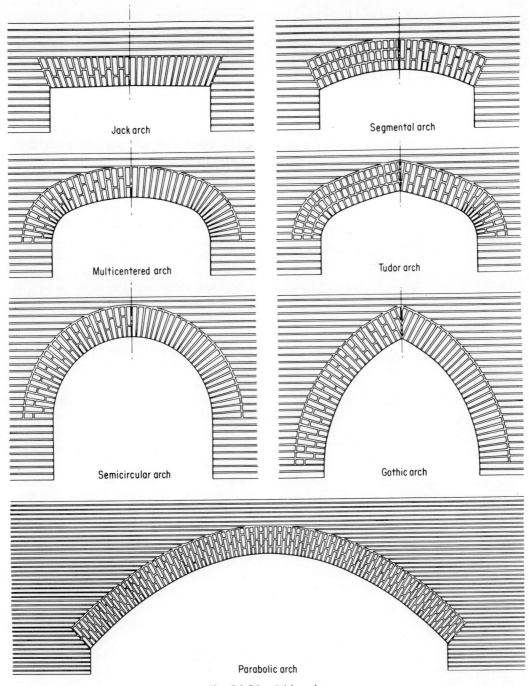

Jack arch

Segmental arch

Multicentered arch

Tudor arch

Semicircular arch

Gothic arch

Parabolic arch

Fig. 14-19. Brick arches

under certain conditions. Their purpose is to provide separations in a structure so as to relieve the stresses set up by changes in temperature and moisture conditions or caused by settlement. They should generally be located at offsets if the wall running into the offset is 50 ft or more in length, and at junctions in walls as in Fig. 14-23. Figure 14-24 illustrates typical expansion joints in combination brick and tile walls. Notice the molded copper water stop used in the vertical joint on the outer face. Caulking is later applied to seal the joint. A premolded expansion joint material is used to separate the sections of back-up wall, and the vertical joint on the face is covered with a metal plate which is fastened to one section only.

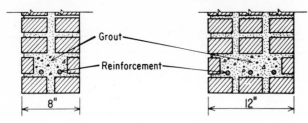

Fig. 14-20. Reinforced brick lintels

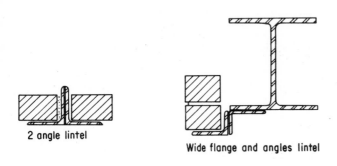

2 angle lintel

Wide flange and angles lintel

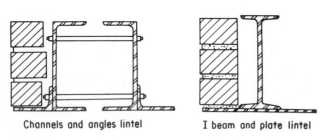

Channels and angles lintel

I beam and plate lintel

Fig. 14-21. Structural steel lintels

STRUCTURAL CLAY TILE CONSTRUCTION

Structural clay tiles are hollow units made from the same materials and by the same methods used to make brick. A number of types are made, each for a specific purpose: structural tile, back-up tile, facing tile, partition tile, fireproofing tile, and floor tile. Some are intended for load-bearing usage while others, such as partition and fireproofing tile, serve special purposes.

Tile may be laid in either *side* or *end* construction. In side construction, the tile are laid so that cells run horizontally, thus providing greater areas for bearing and mortar bond. In end construction, the bearing area is smaller but the unit compressive rating considerably higher. The same types of mortar are used for tile as are used for brick and block.

Figure 14-25 shows several methods of using tile as a back-up for brick. Notice the two basic shapes of back-up tile used.

Structural tile may be plain or glazed on one or both faces. Unglazed tile may be smooth, textured, or roughened to receive plaster or stucco. Thus a structural tile wall may be left exposed, be stuccoed or plastered, be covered by a veneer on the outside or be furred and finished on the inside.

Standard shapes of fireproofing tile, either whole or split, are used to fireproof columns, as shown in Fig. 14-26. Notice that the tile are used in end construction. Special shapes are made for fireproofing steel beams, as illustrated in Fig. 14-27. Notice that these are laid in side construction.

ARCHITECTURAL TERRA-COTTA FACING

Two types of architectural terra-cotta are produced, the *adhesion* type and the *anchor* type. The adhesion type, commonly called *ceramic veneer*, is fastened to the wall by the mortar bond between wall and veneer. It is limited to a thickness of 1¼ in. and a maximum face area of 540 sq in. Figure 14-28 shows the application of ceramic veneer to four different wall types. In the case of metal or wood stud walls, high-ribbed metal lath is first applied over the studs. A ½ in. scratch coat of mortar is then applied to the lath and allowed to set.

A ¾ in. mortar coat is used to bond the veneer to any of these walls, half of it applied to the wall surface and other half to the back of the veneer slab. The wall should be dampened before receiving the bond coat, and the veneer slabs should be water-soaked for about an hour and then allowed to surface-dry before mortar is applied to them. Each slab is tapped into place to eliminate air bubbles and must be supported at the bottom edge until the mortar sets. Joints are then grouted and pointed, and the surface is finally cleaned thoroughly.

Anchor type terra-cotta is larger and heavier than adhesion-type tile, and must have a more positive method of support. This is done by providing some kind of anchoring system between the terra-cotta and the back-up wall. *Pencil rods* are one means of providing this support. They are ¼ in. diameter steel rods running up the wall and held at least 1 in. away from the face by wire loops or metal eyes, as in Fig. 14-29. Loose copper wire anchors are then looped around the pencil rod, and bent ends are inserted into holes in the top edge of the slab.

Various types of round or flat metal anchors are also used to hold the slabs in place. One end of the anchor is fastened to the wall (as in Fig. 14-29) and

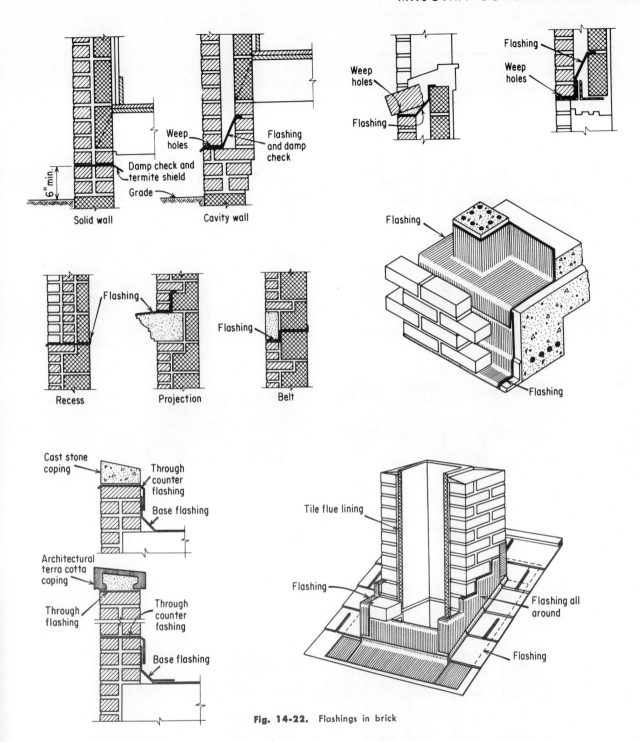

Fig. 14-22. Flashings in brick

the other end fits into a slot or holes in the edge of the terra-cotta slab.

When a course is completed, the space between it and the wall is filled with grout and wood wedges are set along the top edge to support the next course. After the mortar has set, the wedges are removed and the joints are grouted.

BUILDING WITH STONE

Although stone has been a major structural material in the past, modern builders use it almost always as a veneer or curtain wall material. As a veneer, stone is laid up to a masonry back-up wall in *ashlar* or *rubble* patterns. Ashlar patterns feature cut stone laid with

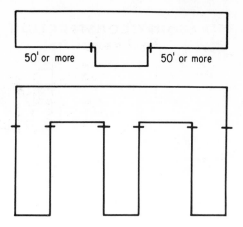

Fig. 14-23. Positions of expansion joints

well defined course lines while rubble patterns use uncut or semi-cut stone laid with few or no course lines. Stones for ashlar work are produced in thicknesses of from 2 to 8 in., in heights of from 1 to 48 in., and in lengths of from 1 to 8 ft.

Methods of bonding stone veneer to back-up walls vary somewhat, depending on the size of stones used. For small stones, ties similar to those used for brick and tile facing work are commonly used. For larger stones, and particularly when the back-up wall is non-bearing, a variety of anchor types are available (Fig. 14-31).

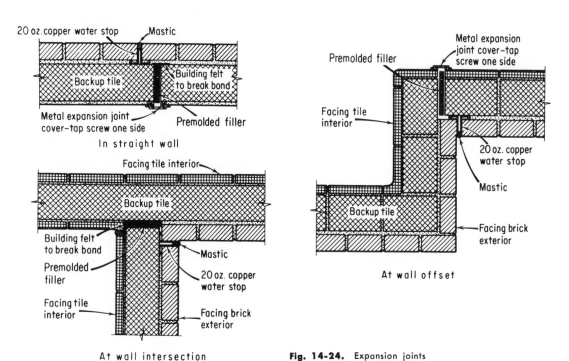

In straight wall

At wall intersection

At wall offset

Fig. 14-24. Expansion joints

Fig. 14-25. Structural clay tile with brick veneer

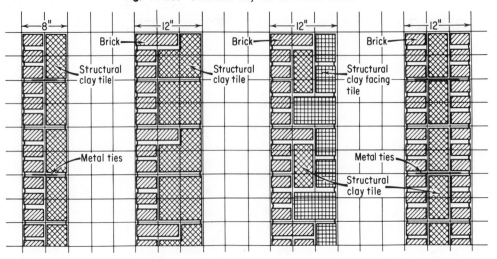

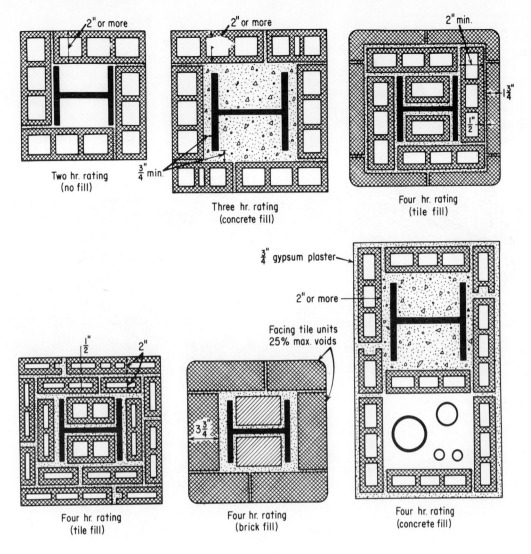

Two hr. rating
(no fill)

Three hr. rating
(concrete fill)

Four hr. rating
(tile fill)

Four hr. rating
(tile fill)

Four hr. rating
(brick fill)

Four hr. rating
(concrete fill)

Fig. 14-26. Fireproofing steel columns with clay tile

Two methods are used to support stone veneer on nonbearing walls. One method involves the use of shelf angles at the spandrel beams, as in Fig. 14-32. The stone is held in place on the shelf by a ½ in. rod welded to the horizontal leg of the angle or by dowels protruding through the horizontal leg. In the first instance, the rod lies in a groove cut in the bottom edge of the stone slab, and in the second, the dowel fits into a hole in the edge of the stone.

In the second method, *bond stones* rest on the spandrel beam and provide support for the rest of the veneer. Anchors are not required in the bond stones themselves, but are used between bond stones and regular veneer slabs and between veneer and the back-up wall. If the stones are not more than 30 in. in height, two anchors per stone should be supplied in the top bed only. If stones exceed 30 in. in height, anchors should be supplied in both the top and bottom beds.

Fig. 14-27. Detail of fireproofing steel beam with clay tile

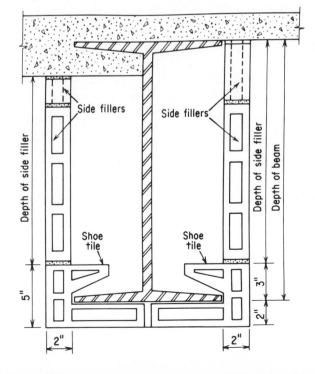

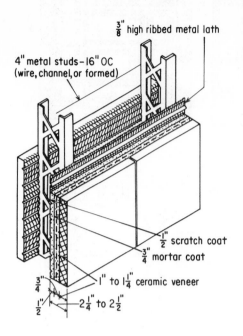

$\frac{3}{8}$" high ribbed metal lath

4" metal studs-16" OC
(wire, channel, or formed)

$\frac{1}{2}$" scratch coat

$\frac{3}{4}$" mortar coat

1" to 1$\frac{1}{4}$" ceramic veneer

$\frac{3}{4}$"

$\frac{1}{2}$"

2$\frac{1}{4}$" to 2$\frac{1}{2}$"

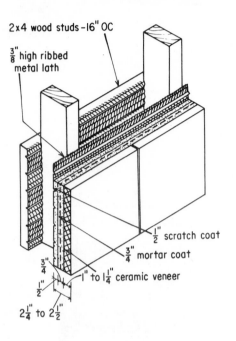

2x4 wood studs-16" OC

$\frac{3}{8}$" high ribbed
metal lath

$\frac{1}{2}$" scratch coat

$\frac{3}{4}$" mortar coat

1" to 1$\frac{1}{4}$" ceramic veneer

$\frac{3}{4}$"

$\frac{1}{2}$"

2$\frac{1}{4}$" to 2$\frac{1}{2}$"

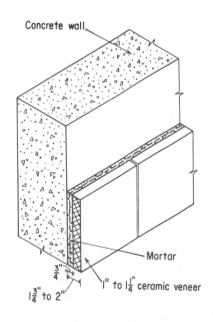

Concrete wall

Mortar

$\frac{3}{4}$"

1" to 1$\frac{1}{4}$" ceramic veneer

1$\frac{3}{4}$" to 2"

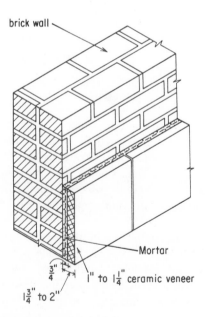

brick wall

Mortar

$\frac{3}{4}$"

1" to 1$\frac{1}{4}$" ceramic veneer

1$\frac{3}{4}$" to 2"

Fig. 14-28. Adhesion type architectural terra-cotta

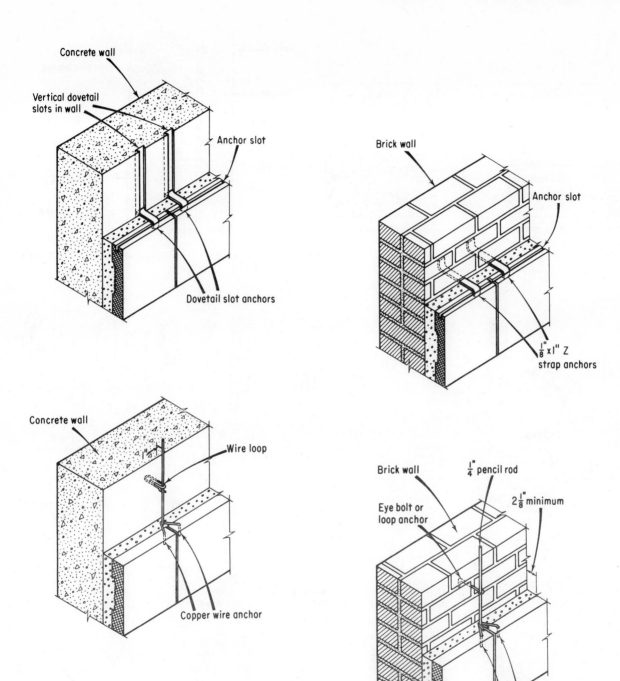

Fig. 14-29. Anchor type architectural terra-cotta

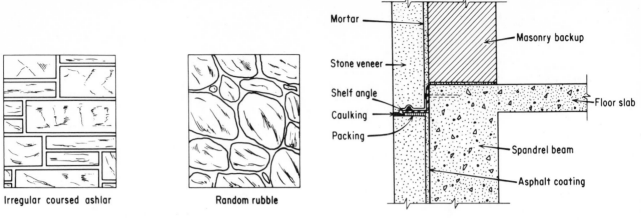

Fig. 14-30. Stone veneer patterns

Fig. 14-32. Stone veneer supported on shelf angle

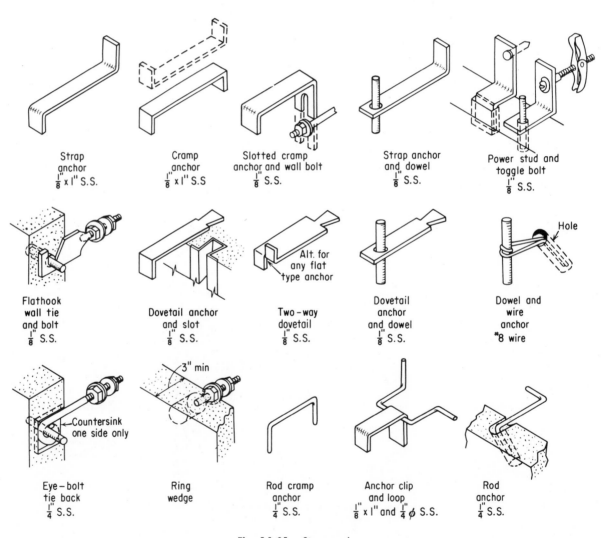

Fig. 14-31. Stone anchors

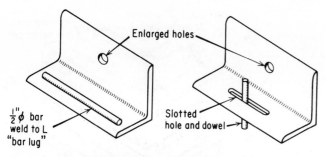

Fig. 14-33. Shelf angle supports

$\frac{1}{2}$" ϕ bar weld to L "bar lug"

Enlarged holes

Slotted hole and dowel

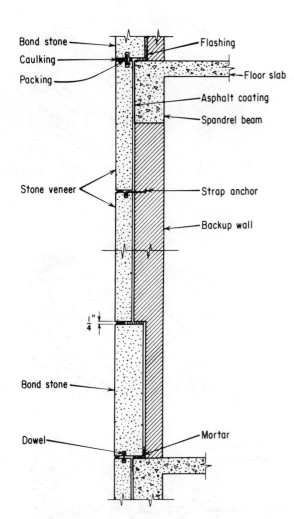

Fig. 14-34. Stone veneer supported on bond stones

Bond stone
Caulking
Packing
Flashing
Floor slab
Asphalt coating
Spandrel beam
Stone veneer
Strap anchor
Backup wall
Bond stone
Dowel
Mortar
$\frac{1}{4}$"

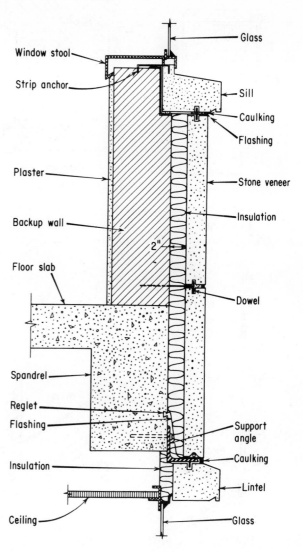

Fig. 14-35. Stone veneer cavity wall

Glass
Window stool
Strip anchor
Sill
Caulking
Flashing
Plaster
Stone veneer
Backup wall
Insulation
2"
Floor slab
Dowel
Spandrel
Reglet
Flashing
Support angle
Caulking
Insulation
Lintel
Ceiling
Glass

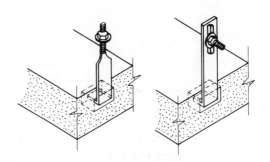

Fig. 14-36. Stone soffit strap hangers

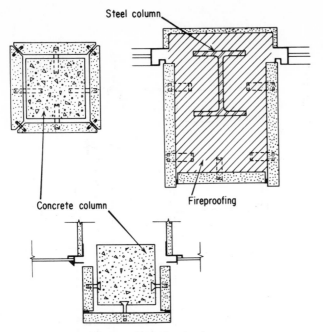

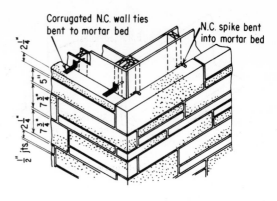

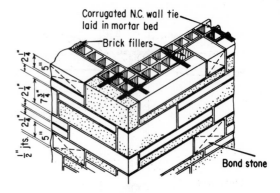

Fig. 14-37. Stone faced columns

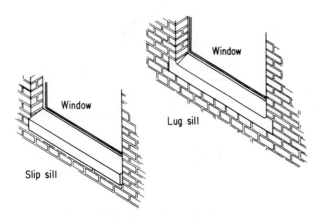

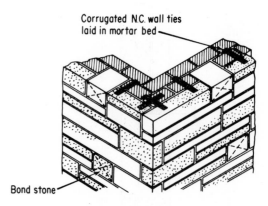

Fig. 14-38. Stone window sills

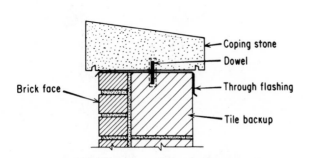

Fig. 14-39. Stone coping on parapet

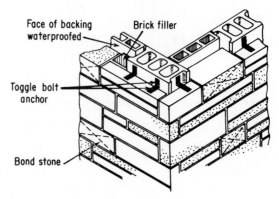

Fig. 14-40. Anchoring stone to various wall backings

When stones are under 24 in. in width, they require only one anchor per stone.

An alternative method of applying stone veneer, shown in Fig. 14-35, is particularly applicable if insulation is used in the wall.

Stone is also used to face soffits and columns or to trim brick and tile walls. Trim stones include sills, lintels, quoins, belts, and copings. Stone soffits are hung from the frame by strap hangers which fit into slots in the edges of the soffit slabs (Fig. 14-36). Several of the methods used to face columns with stone are illustrated in Fig. 14-37.

Belts and copings are secured by strap anchors or dowels, while sills, lintels, and quoins are built into and supported by the masonry surrounding them. Figure 14-39 shows one method of anchoring coping stones to a parapet wall.

Stone ashlar is anchored to solid back-up walls with noncorroding corrugated wall ties, and with bond stones where the back-up material will allow it. If stone course lines do not coincide with those of the back-up material, *toggle* bolts are used to secure the wall ties to the block or tile (Fig. 14-40).

Mortar used for setting stone or for pointing joints should be made with a nonstaining cement. Pointing consists of raking out joints to a depth of ¾ in. and filling them with pointing mortar, packed into place and rubbed smooth to the indicated level. Joints should be wet before the pointing mortar is applied. Pointing mortar is omitted if joints are to be caulked.

Wire brushes and acids should not be used to clean stones. As soon as possible after the mortar has set, they should be cleaned with water, soap powder, and fiber brushes. Approved machine-cleaning processes may also be used.

REVIEW QUESTIONS

1. (a) What are three ways of providing vertical support to concrete block bearing walls? (b) What is meant by a control joint in a block wall? (c) What is the purpose of a control joint? (d) How is horizontal joint reinforcement usually provided in a block wall? (e) Why must a control joint be caulked on the exterior face of the wall?

2. Define the following items of brick wall terminology: pattern bond, mortar bond, and structural bond.

3. (a) What is a *reinforced* brick wall? (b) What is a *brick cavity* wall?

4. (a) What are two distinctive features of a brick veneer wall? (b) What are two methods of anchoring brick veneer to the back-up wall?

5. How is masonry supported over an opening in a brick wall?

6. Differentiate between *external* and *internal* flashing.

7. What two types of structural clay tile are not intended for load-bearing purposes?

8. Differentiate the fireproofing tile used on columns from that used to fireproof girders or beams.

9. (a) Differentiate between structural clay tile and architectural terra cotta; (b) How does the adhesive type of terra cotta differ from anchor-type terra cotta? (c) What is meant by a pencil rod?

10. How are *ashlar* and *rubble* patterns obtained with stone veneer?

11. What are *bond stones* and what is their purpose?

12. Give two reasons for using a belt course in a masonry wall.

15

CURTAIN WALL
CONSTRUCTION

The development of steel or concrete structural frames for multistory buildings has led to the adoption of nonbearing exterior walls known as *curtain walls*. Their primary functions are to protect the interior of the building from the elements and to enhance its appearance.

Curtain walls are not new. They appeared in the nineteenth century, when non-load-bearing walls of clay masonry were first used in tall buildings. Masonry is still used as a curtain wall material, but large units of lighter, colorful, easily installed panelized materials are favored today. These materials must be durable, serviceable, and reasonably priced.

There are a number of advantages resulting from the use of curtain walls in large buildings: (1) There is a reduction in dead load. Since the curtain wall supports only its own weight, wall thickness may be reduced, thus allowing a reduction in the size of beams, girders, columns, and foundations; (2) erection time is shortened because of the relatively large size of many curtain wall components; (3) better insulation is often possible because of the incorporation of insulating materials in the curtain wall panels; (4) more floor space becomes available because walls require less space.

MASONRY CURTAIN WALLS

Masonry curtain walls may be composed of unit masonry (brick, tile, block, etc.), of stone panels, of precast concrete panels, or of a combination of these.

Unit Masonry

There are two methods of incorporating unit masonry into a building as a curtain wall. One is to build the units into the wall openings formed by

Fig. 15-1. Typical curtain wall

Fig. 15-2. Exterior bearing walls

Fig. 15-3. Combination of bearing and curtain walls

Fig. 15-4. Brick walls independent of columns. (Courtesy G. S. Adamson & Assoc.)

columns and beams so that the frame may provide both vertical and lateral support. The other is to erect the exterior walls independently of any vertical support. The walls carry their own dead load to the foundation (Fig. 15-5), but the structural frame provides the wall with lateral support and carries all other vertical loads. This system allows considerable flexibility between walls and frame. Lateral support is provided by flexible anchors called *looped rods* (Fig. 15-6).

Curtain walls supported entirely by the building frame may be laid and bonded to the spandrel beams

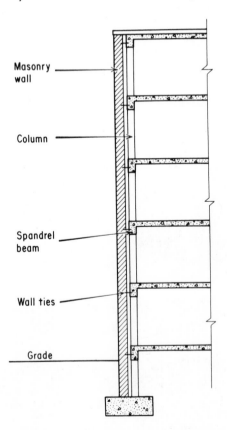

Masonry wall

Column

Spandrel beam

Wall ties

Grade

Fig. 15-5. Curtain wall carried on foundation

with mortar or may be keyed to the beams as in Fig. 15-7. Notice that lateral support is provided here by flat metal ties cast into the column and laid in the mortar joints of the masonry. Also note that the concrete structural frame has been left exposed, as part of the overall design. The faces of a steel structural frame may likewise be left exposed. Figure 15-8 shows a two-wythe brick curtain wall erected in a steel frame so as to leave the column flanges exposed. In Fig. 15-9, a brick cavity wall is used as a curtain wall while leaving the steel frame exposed. Notice the *channels* used to receive the brick, and the *cover plates* used to hold the channels. Figure 15-10 illustrates the same type of construction at a beam.

The structural frame is usually concealed by a masonry curtain wall. In Fig. 15-11, a two-wythe brick curtain wall conceals the exterior of the steel frame. The inner flange is sheathed in furring tile. In this type of construction, the face wythe is carried over the spandrel beams on lintel angles riveted or welded to them. Figure 14-21 illustrates various ways of carrying brick over the face of a beam. A structural frame may be concealed by a cavity curtain wall, as illustrated in Fig. 15-12.

Figure 15-13 illustrates another type of masonry curtain wall, in which a structural tile back-up wall is faced with architectural terra cotta. In this case, the structural frame is steel and fireproofed with concrete. Concrete blocks (standard, lightweight, or cellular concrete) are also widely used as back-up material for a masonry curtain wall.

Standard and lightweight concrete blocks are often themselves used as curtain wall material, particularly with a structural concrete frame. Smooth faced, textured, or sculptured blocks are available for this purpose. Blocks may be laid in running or stack bond, tied to the columns with metal ties (as in Fig. 15-14). Insulation is provided by filling the cells of the blocks with loose fill, such as expanded vermiculite. It is advisable to use either silicone or a *breathing* type

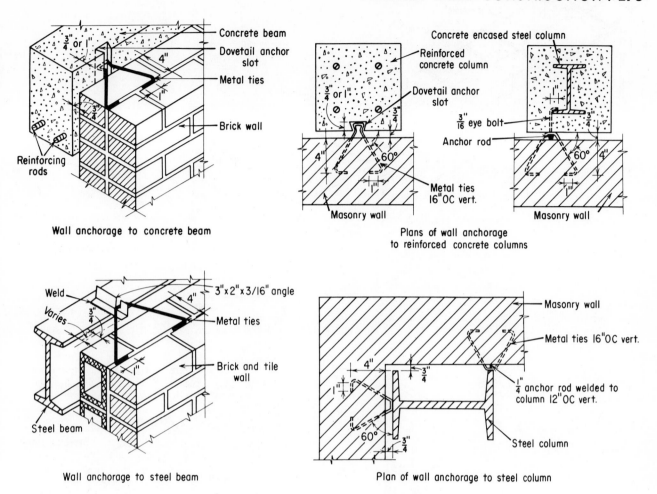

Wall anchorage to concrete beam

Plans of wall anchorage
to reinforced concrete columns

Wall anchorage to steel beam

Plan of wall anchorage to steel column

Fig. 15-6. Lateral supports to beams and columns

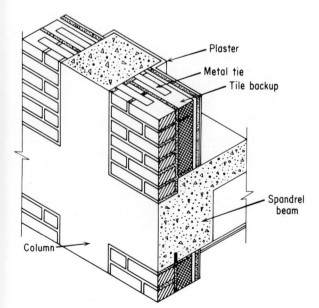

Fig. 15-7. Curtain wall keyed to spandrel beam

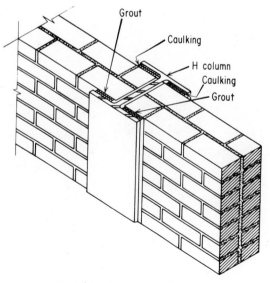

Fig. 15-8. Exposed steel column

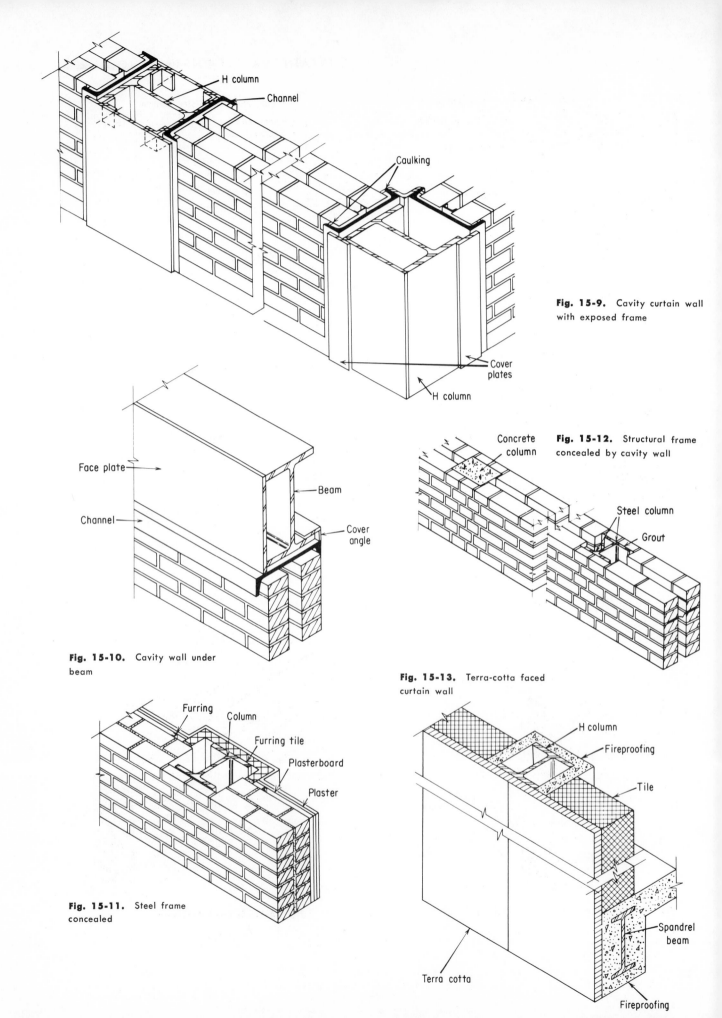

Fig. 15-9. Cavity curtain wall with exposed frame

H column

Channel

Caulking

Cover plates

H column

Fig. 15-10. Cavity wall under beam

Face plate

Channel

Beam

Cover angle

Fig. 15-11. Steel frame concealed

Furring

Column

Furring tile

Plasterboard

Plaster

Fig. 15-12. Structural frame concealed by cavity wall

Concrete column

Steel column

Grout

Fig. 15-13. Terra-cotta faced curtain wall

H column

Fireproofing

Tile

Spandrel beam

Terra cotta

Fireproofing

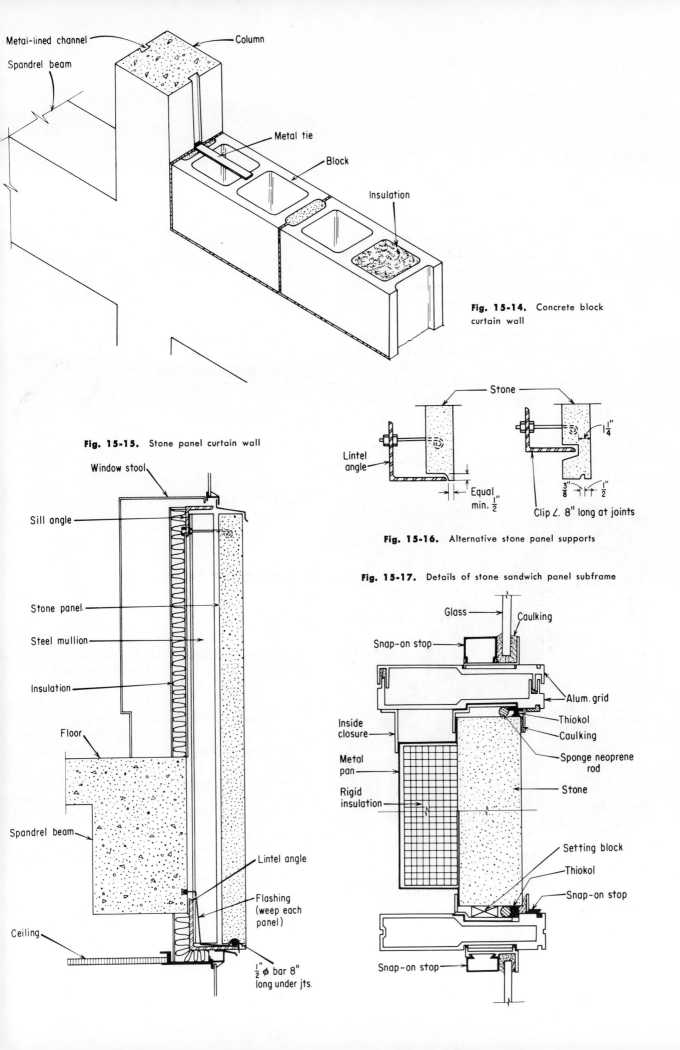

Metal-lined channel

Spandrel beam

Column

Metal tie

Block

Insulation

Fig. 15-14. Concrete block curtain wall

Fig. 15-15. Stone panel curtain wall

Window stool

Sill angle

Stone panel

Steel mullion

Insulation

Floor

Spandrel beam

Ceiling

Lintel angle

Flashing (weep each panel)

$\frac{1}{2}$" ⌀ bar 8" long under jts.

Stone

Lintel angle

Equal min. $\frac{1}{2}$"

$1\frac{1}{4}$"

$\frac{3}{8}$" $\frac{1}{2}$"

Clip ∠ 8" long at joints

Fig. 15-16. Alternative stone panel supports

Fig. 15-17. Details of stone sandwich panel subframe

Glass

Caulking

Snap-on stop

Inside closure

Metal pan

Rigid insulation

Alum. grid

Thiokol

Caulking

Sponge neoprene rod

Stone

Setting block

Thiokol

Snap-on stop

Snap-on stop

of paint waterproofing on the exterior surface. *A vapor barrier* type paint should be used on the interior.

Stone Panels

Several types of stone panels are available to be used as curtain walls. One is a 3 or 4 in. thickness of stone dimensioned to fit the particular job. One method of attaching this type of panel is illustrated in Fig. 15-15. In this case, the panels are held in position at the bottom by rods ½ in. in diameter and about 8 in. long, welded to the lintel angle at joints in the stone. Two alternative methods of support are shown in Fig. 15-16.

Another commonly used type of stone panel is a *sandwich* panel, consisting of a stone face, a layer of rigid insulation, and a sheet metal or hardboard back—all cemented together. This type of panel is relatively light and is often supported by a metal subframe or *grid* which is in turn connected to the structural frame (Fig. 15-17). A great variety of metal grids are available for use with stone or other types of curtain wall panels. Figure 15-17 shows a typical aluminum grid being used with stone sandwich panels.

Fig. 15-19. Panels anchored to frame. (Courtesy Portland Cement Ass'n.)

Precast Concrete Panels

Two types of precast concrete units are used in curtain wall construction. One is a panel which is cast, cured, and finished in a precasting plant, and is then brought to the job for erection in much the same way that stone or terra cotta panels would be used. Such precast panels are custom-made to the required size and surface texture. Figure 15-18 shows typical precast concrete panels being applied over a structural steel frame, while Fig. 15-19 illustrates how those panels are anchored to the frame. Other anchoring systems exist, one of which is shown in Fig. 15-20, where steel pins project through the framing angles into holes cast into the top and bottom edges of the panels. Joints should be bed-caulked with oakum and finished with a waterproof plastic caulking.

Another type of precast concrete unit involves what is known as *tilt-up* construction. Panels are really sections of the wall as high as the building (usually one or two stories) containing wall openings. Forms for the panels are built on the job site, the necessary reinforcing is placed, and the concrete is poured (Fig.

Fig. 15-18. Erecting precast concrete panels. (Courtesy Portland Cement Ass'n.)

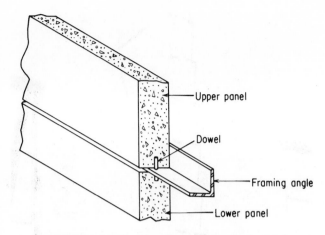

Fig. 15-20. Dowel anchor for precast concrete panel

Upper panel

Dowel

Framing angle

Lower panel

Fig. 15-22. Forms for tilt-up panels. (Courtesy Portland Cement Ass'n.)

Fig. 15-21. Precast concrete panel wall. (Courtesy Portland Cement Ass'n.)

Fig. 15-23. Pouring tilt-up panels. (Courtesy Portland Cement Ass'n.)

Fig. 15-24. Finishing tilt-up panel. (Courtesy Portland Cement Ass'n.)

15-23). Finishing produces the specified surface and the concrete is properly cured. When the slabs have gained sufficient strength, they are lifted or tilted into position (Fig. 15-26). They are held in place by dowels projecting from the foundation or by welding together plates which have been cast into the bottom edge of the slab and the top of the foundation. In this type of construction, columns are usually poured *after* the panels are in place. Panels are properly spaced (Fig. 15-27), and reinforcing bars project from their edges to be cast into the columns. After plumb-

Fig. 15-25. Openings formed in tilt-up panel. (Courtesy Portland Cement Ass'n.)

ing and bracing the panels, simple wood forms are built around the openings, and the columns are poured. Columns may be either the same width as the opening or may be wide enough for the edges of the slabs to be cast into them.

Fig. 15-27. Space for column between panels. (Courtesy Portland Cement Ass'n.)

Fig. 15-26. Hoisting tilt-up panel into place. (Courtesy Portland Cement Ass'n.)

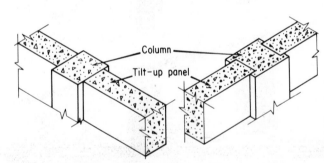

Fig. 15-28. Columns cast between panels

GLASS BLOCK CURTAIN WALL

Glass blocks of various thicknesses are commonly used in curtain wall construction. The thicker blocks are generally incorporated into a masonry wall or a concrete frame, while the thin ones (2 in.) are mounted in an aluminum grid subframe. Figure 15-29 illustrates four methods of inserting glass blocks into a masonry wall. A very important point to remember is that a glass block panel must *float* in the opening—there must be no pressure from the wall or frame bearing on the blocks. This is usually accomplished

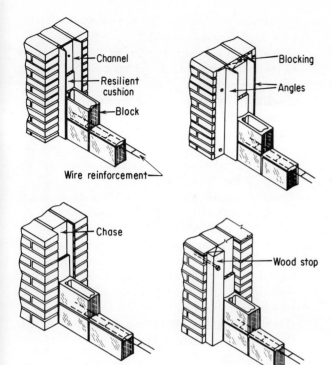

Fig. 15-29. Glass block in masonry wall

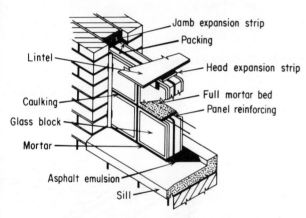

Fig. 15-30. Glass block panel details

undersides of lintels with asphalt emulsion. Be sure that the side strips extend from head to sill and that the head strip is as long as the panel.

3. When the emulsion on the still is dry, place a *full* mortar bed for the first course of glass blocks.

4. Set the first course of blocks using full mortar joints. Do not use steel tools to tap the blocks into position.

5. Lay a bed of mortar half the normal thickness over the first course.

6. Press the panel reinforcing into this mortar from one end of the panel to the other. Laps of 6 in.

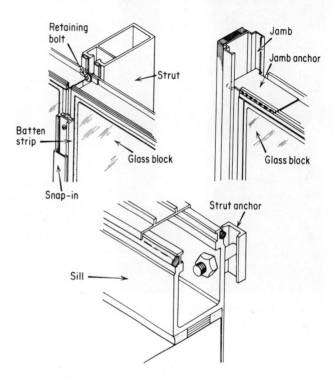

Fig. 15-31. Details of aluminum grid for glass block

by providing a cushion of resilient material (such as fiberglass or foamed plastic insulation) between the block panel and the opening.

Glass blocks are laid in mortar and carefully pointed. The maximum area allowed per panel varies from one code to another, but will usually be about 144 sq ft, 20 ft high, or 25 ft long. The following procedure is recommended for laying glass block panels (see Fig. 15-30):

1. The sill area to be covered by mortar should first be coated with asphalt emulsion.

2. Attach the expansion strips to the jambs and the

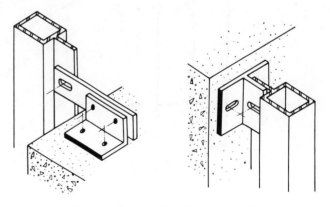

Fig. 15-32. Struts anchored to concrete frame

Fig. 15-33. Steel sandwich panels being installed. (Courtesy Hunter-Douglas Ltd.)

are required at joints. Do not allow reinforcing to bridge expansion joints.

7. Cover the panel reinforcing with the second half of the mortar bed and trowel smooth. Set another course of blocks.

8. Place a full mortar bed for joints which do not require panel reinforcing.

9. Strike the joints smooth or rake out those requiring caulking before the mortar has set. Joints should be raked out to a depth equal to the width of the joint.

10. Remove surplus mortar from block faces before it sets completely, but final cleaning should not take place until after the mortar has set.

11. After the mortar has fully set, pack the spaces between the panel and the sides of the jamb and head construction with oakum or other specified packing. Leave enough space in front of the packing for caulking.

12. Caulk all joints indicated on the drawings with the specified caulking compound.

Figure 15-31 shows details of a typical grid arrangement used with thin glass blocks. The struts may be fastened to the structural frame by any of the methods described on subsequent pages.

LIGHTWEIGHT CURTAIN WALL

In addition to those previously mentioned, curtain wall panels are available in a wide variety of materials, including glass, plastic, steel, porcelain enamel, asbestos-

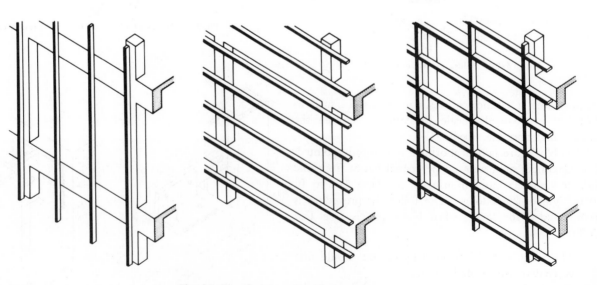

Fig. 15-34. Curtain wall subframe systems

cement, stainless or galvanized steel, aluminum, copper, bronze, and Galbestos. They are made in single skin form and in open or closed sandwich panels in a wide range of dimensions. These panels are comparatively lightweight, and are often supported on a subframe made of vertical or horizontal bars, or a grid (Fig. 15-34). Some types (such as the one shown in Fig. 15-33) require no subframe and are attached to the regular framework, as illustrated in Fig. 15-35. There are many methods for attaching the subframe to the structural frame, four of which are shown in Fig. 15-36. Figures 15-37 and 15-38 illustrate typical applica-

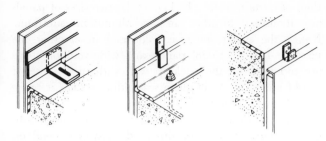

Fig. 15-35. Curtain wall panels clipped to structural frame

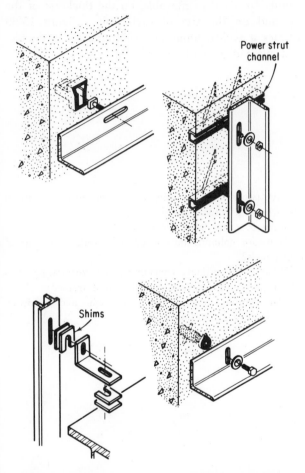

Fig. 15-36. Methods of attaching subframe to concrete or steel structural frame

Fig. 15-37. Curtain wall with subframe

Fig. 15-38. Curtain wall clipped to block back-up

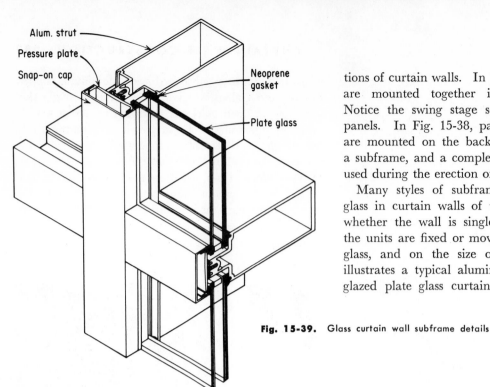

Alum. strut
Pressure plate
Snap-on cap
Neoprene gasket
Plate glass

tions of curtain walls. In Fig. 15-37, two sizes of panels are mounted together in an aluminum subframe. Notice the swing stage scaffold used in erecting the panels. In Fig. 15-38, panels and wide mullion strips are mounted on the back-up wall without the use of a subframe, and a complete scaffolding system is being used during the erection of the panels.

Many styles of subframes may be used to mount glass in curtain walls of this kind. Styles depend on whether the wall is single- or double-glazed, whether the units are fixed or movable, on the thickness of the glass, and on the size of each unit. Figure 15-39 illustrates a typical aluminum subframe for a double-glazed plate glass curtain wall.

Fig. 15-39. Glass curtain wall subframe details

REVIEW QUESTIONS

1. What is meant by a curtain wall?
2. Give four advantages of using curtain walls in large buildings.
3. What is the purpose of a *lintel angle*?
4. How may concrete block curtain walls be insulated?
5. Give two advantages of stone sandwich panels over plain stone facing.

6. Give two reasons for using a subframe to carry curtain walls over a structural frame.
7. What is meant by *tilt-up* construction?
8. How are columns introduced into walls made up of tilt-up panels?
9. What is the primary concern when incorporating glass block curtain wall panels into a structural frame?
10. Differentiate between the single-skin and sandwich types of lightweight curtain wall panels.

BUILDING INSULATION

16

Building insulation is generally considered to be any material which has a particularly low coefficient of thermal conductivity. This is illustrated in Fig. 16-1, where a slab of cellular glass successfully resists the passage of heat. In fact, the term also includes those materials which prevent or reduce the transfer of sound and those which restrict or prevent the migration of moisture and moisture vapor.

THERMAL INSULATION

The ability of a material to resist the passage of heat serves many purposes in building construction. One specific use is the protection of building components against deterioration or failure caused by severe overheating. Materials used for this purpose are generally referred to as *fireproofing*.

Fireproofing Materials

Fireproofing is most commonly used to protect the structural frame of a building, particularly a steel frame (although it may be used for the protection of wood or concrete frames as well). Materials in general use for the protection of a steel frame include regular and lightweight concrete, cellular concrete, gypsum tile, terra cotta tile, plaster made with lightweight aggregates, and sprayed-on asbestos fiber.

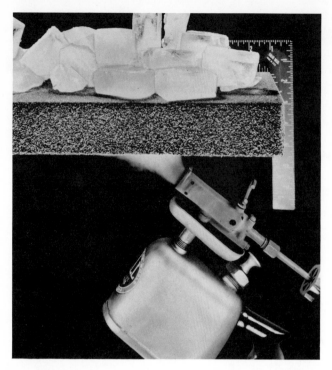

Fig. 16-1. A good thermal insulator. (Courtesy Pittsburgh-Corning Corp.)

Methods of Fireproofing

Fireproofing steel beams and columns with concrete is accomplished by encasing the members in poured-in-place concrete. This involves building a form around the member or using a prefabricated form. When concrete floor slabs are used with a steel frame, fireproofing is usually poured as part of the slab.

Many systems of forming are available, but three common ones are illustrated in Figs. 16-2, 16-3, and 16-4. In Fig. 16-2, the forms are supported from below by posts. Notice that the fireproofing form is built in such a way that the sides may be removed without interfering with slab form supports or beam bottom supports. This is done by using *kickers* near the top edges of the sides and ledger strips along their bottom edges. The form shown in Fig. 16-3 is supported by the steel frame. This is accomplished by hangers which are placed over the beams. The formwork is suspended from the legs of these hangers and is in this particular case held in place by standard wedges. Fixed spreaders eliminate the need for soffit spacers.

The formwork shown in Fig. 16-4 is also hung from the steel frame but heavy duty steel strapping is used in this case to support the form and concrete load. Note that soffit spacers and *blockouts* are used here to hold the form in its proper position.

Columns are fireproofed with concrete by first building or fitting a form around them and then filling it with concrete. It is sometimes advantageous to build the form in two sections—upper and lower. Place and fill the bottom section first, then the top section.

Cellular concrete makes an excellent fireproofing material because of its high insulation value and its light weight. It is used in 2, 3, or 4 in. slabs which may be fabricated to suit any particular situation. Figure 16-5 illustrates a typical application of cellular concrete fireproofing to a steel girder, while Fig. 16-6 shows the same material used to fireproof a column.

In addition to standard rectangular fireproofing tiles, special gypsum and terra cotta tiles are also manufactured for fireproofing beams and girders. Three special shapes are made: *shoe tile, angle tile,* and *soffit*

Fig. 16-2. Fireproofing form supported from below

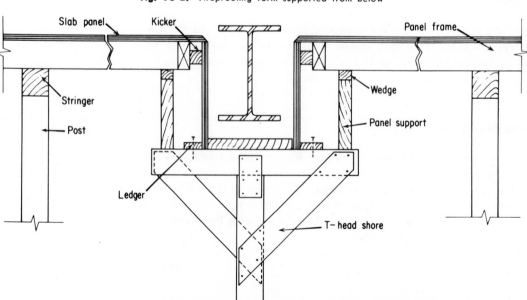

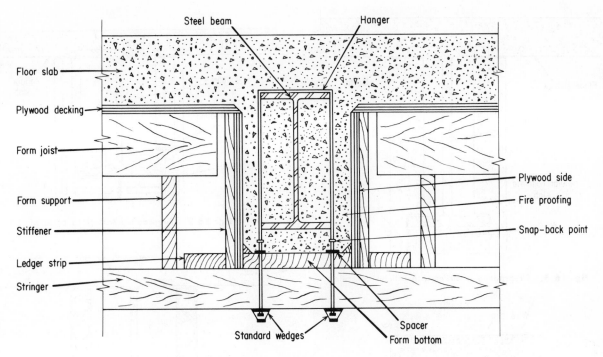

Fig. 16-3. Fireproofing form supported by hangers

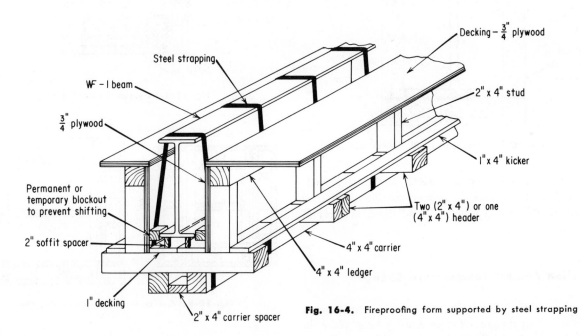

Fig. 16-4. Fireproofing form supported by steel strapping

tile. Figure 16-7 illustrates how shoe tile and standard tile may be used together, while Fig. 16-8 shows the use of angle tile, soffit tile, and fillers. Standard gypsum and terra cotta tiles are used to fireproof columns in much the same manner as that shown for cellular concrete. The space between tile and column may be either left empty or filled with concrete, depending on the degree of protection required

A great deal of fireproofing is done with vermiculite or perlite plaster. Not only do these plasters resist heat transmission, but they are very light and can be applied quite rapidly. The steel members are sheathed in wire mesh or metal lath, stiffened by the addition of light rods if necessary, and the plaster is sprayed over the wire to the required depth.

Asbestos fiber mixed with adhesive may be used the

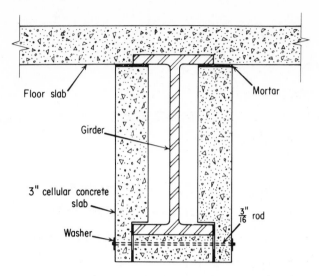

Fig. 16-5. Fireproofing a girder with cellular concrete

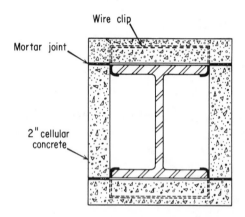

Fig. 16-6. Column fireproofed with cellular concrete

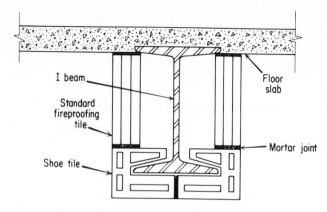

Fig. 16-7. Fireproofing with terra cotta tile

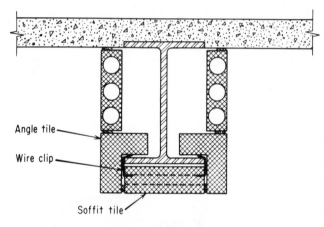

Fig. 16-8. Gypsum fireproofing tile

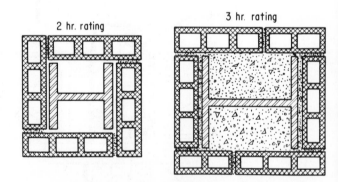

Fig. 16-9. Column fireproofing with clay tile

same way or may be applied directly to the steel member. In the latter case, a primer coat must first be applied to the steel in order to bond the fiber layer to its surface.

Insulation Against Temperature Changes

Another use of insulating materials is to prevent significant temperature changes from taking place in structural members. Such changes would cause movement through thermal expansion. This applies particularly to tall buildings where expansion of long columns could be considerable. Figure 16-10 shows a concrete column being insulated against temperature changes. Cellular glass slabs are held in place by mastic and pins which have been cast into the column. Clips are driven over the ends of the pins projecting through the insulation.

Insulation of Heat Conveyors

An important use of insulation is to prevent heat loss from hot water pipes and hot air ducts. Rigid slabs, mineral wool blankets, and asbestos insulation are all used for this purpose.

Rigid insulation is shaped around pipes (as shown in Fig. 16-11) and is held in place by fabric or asbestos wrapping. Large pipes may be covered by a heavy

Fig. 16-10. Insulating a column against temperature changes. (Courtesy Pittsburgh-Corning Corp.)

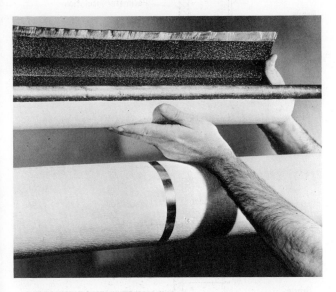

Fig. 16-11. Insulating a pipe with cellular glass. (Courtesy Pittsburgh-Corning Corp.)

layer of plaster made from asbestos fiber mixed with adhesive and water and wrapped in cloth or fireproof paper.

Air ducts may be sheathed in rigid slab insulation, asbestos fiber plaster, rigid boards of corrugated asbestos paper, or mineral wool blankets.

Building Insulation

Heat always seeks lower temperature levels. As a result, whenever there is a difference in temperature between two surfaces of a material, heat will flow to the colder side. This means that when the outside temperature is low, heat from a building will flow to the outside. Conversely, during hot weather, heat tends to flow inward and warm the inside of a building.

Any material will retard the flow of heat to some extent—but in order to effectively control this flow, insulating materials are used in the foundations, floors, walls, ceilings, and roofs of buildings. Heat is transferred by three means: conduction, convection, and radiation; insulation must control all three if it is to be effective. Most insulating materials are effective in controlling heat transfer by conduction and convection, but a special kind of insulation, one with a reflective surface, is necessary to control heat transfer by radiation.

Insulation Application

1. *Perimeter insulation*. Buildings constructed on surface foundations are subject to considerable heat loss around their perimeter. Perimeter insulation controls this loss of heat and keeps floors warm.

Rigid slabs or mineral wool batts are most commonly used for perimeter insulation because of the ease of application. Insulation is usually applied to the inner face of the foundation, but may be applied to the exterior of existing buildings (Fig. 16-12). Walls should be cleaned, dried, primed with asphalt primer, and the insulation should be attached with hot asphalt mastic or with special clips. When applied to the exterior of a foundation, the material should be carried at least 12 in. below grade, or preferably to the frost line. The exposed face of the insulation should be covered with a protective facing such as asbestos-cement board, and metal flashing must be installed above the insulation.

When a concrete slab-on-grade construction is involved, install the perimeter insulation prior to backfilling the foundation trench. The insulation should be carried to the frost line (Fig. 16-13). Notice that the insulation reaches the top of the floor slab. If the area under the floor slab is to be used as a crawl space, several steps are necessary to install perimeter insulation. First, the ground surface must be covered with a moisture barrier which is lapped at least 2 in. up the wall. Wall ventilators which will not allow water to enter the foundation, must be provided. The insulation must cover the entire crawl space walls down to ground level, or preferably to the frost line. If the floor slab

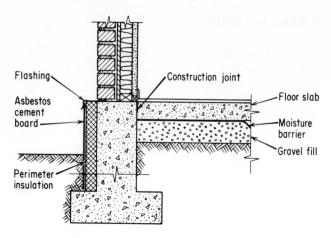

Fig. 16-12. Perimeter insulation outside

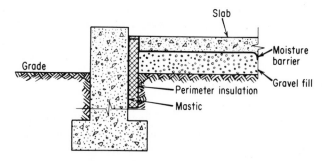

Fig. 16-13. Perimeter insulation with slab on grade

is to contain heating or air conditioning ducts, insulation should be carried along the ground under them (Fig. 16-15).

2. *Foundation wall insulation.* Foundation walls are usually insulated with some type of rigid insulation, including insulating boards and rigid slabs or blocks. The insulating boards include wood and cane fiber boards, straw board, and laminated fiber board. Rigid slab insulations include cellular glass (see Fig. 16-10), foamed plastic rigid insulation, and cellular concrete. Additional insulation may be introduced into concrete block walls by pouring loose fill into the block cores during construction. Vermiculite is commonly used for this purpose.

Rigid slab insulations are applied to the wall surface with hot asphalt, Portland cement mortar, special synthetic adhesives, or wire clips. Walls must be clean and smooth before insulation is applied to insure a good bond. It may be necessary to back-plaster the wall to achieve the necessary finish.

If asphalt is used as the adhesive, the surface must first be coated with asphalt primer and allowed to dry. Adhesive is then applied to the insulation by dipping

the back face and two adjacent edges of each block in hot asphalt. Blocks are applied to the primed surface while the asphalt is still molten. Cellular glass, foamed plastic, and cellular concrete may all be applied by the hot asphalt method.

When synthetic adhesive is specified, the back face and two adjacent edges of each slab are given a trowel coating of adhesive approximately 1/8 in. thick. Sufficient pressure must be applied to the blocks to assure tight joints and good contact with the wall. Both cellular glass and foamed plastic may be applied with synthetic adhesives.

Rigid slab insulation may be applied to block or brick walls by either of the methods described above or may be held in place by wire clips, one end of which has been embedded in a mortar joint (Fig. 16-16). The edge joints should still be sealed first with hot asphalt or some other adhesive.

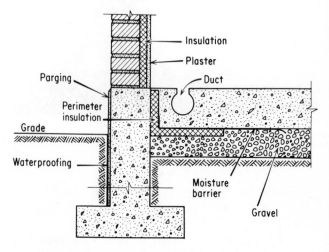

Fig. 16-14. Perimeter insulation in crawl space

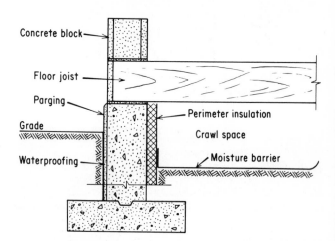

Fig. 16-15. Perimeter insulation with slab ducts

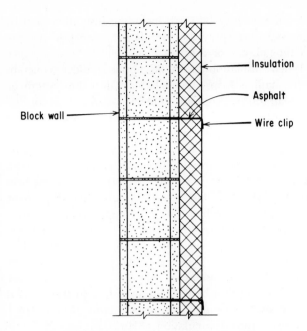

Fig. 16-16. Insulation held by wire clips

Block wall

Insulation

Asphalt

Wire clip

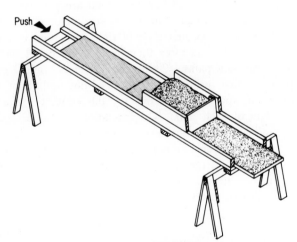

Push

Fig. 16-17. A simple push box

Portland cement mortar is frequently employed in the application of cellular concrete and foamed plastic insulations to masonry walls. When using the latter, mortar is often applied by means of a *push box*—a simple device illustrated in Fig. 16-17. To use the push box, place a slab of insulation in the frame with one end directly below the front end of the box (which may be adjusted to regulate the depth of coating), fill the box with mortar, and push the slab through with another directly behind it. Keep the hopper full for best results.

Rigid boards may be applied to foundation walls in several ways. One method is to strap the wall, as in

Fig. 16-18, and attach the board insulation to the straps with nails. If the foundation wall is poured-in-place, insulation may be attached inside the inner form face. This may be done with nails, or, if the boards are thick, with wires through the form sheathing and insulation. The concrete adheres to the face of the insulation and the insulation remains permanently attached to the wall when the forms are removed. The hot asphalt or the synthetic adhesive method may also be used to secure board insulation to foundation walls.

3. *Curtain wall insulation.* Masonry curtain walls may be insulated by any of the methods applicable to foundation walls. In addition, brick or tile curtain walls are often built as cavity walls, in which case insulation may be installed within the cavity. It may be loose fill, such as vermiculite, perlite, cellulose fiber, or gypsum fiber, or it may be rigid slab insulation thick enough to fill the cavity. Care should be taken that mortar does not protrude from joints so as to restrict the flow of insulation being poured or blown into place. When using slabs, insulation must be installed as construction proceeds, since the metal ties between the inner and outer wythes of the wall should occur at joints in the insulation.

Another insulating technique for masonry walls involves the use of cellular concrete blocks. These are used to build a back-up wall which is faced with a veneer of brick, tile, terra cotta, or stone.

Curtain walls having a stud frame may be insulated with batts placed between the studs, with rigid insula-

Fig. 16-18. Foundation wall strapped for insulation

tion applied over plywood or other sheathing, or by *foamed-in-place* insulation. Insulation is foamed-in-place by placing a specified amount of plastic resin and activating agent in each space to be insulated. The two materials react to form a thermosetting, insulating foam which will fill each space to a predetermined depth. The operation is repeated until each space is completely full.

Prefabricated panels for curtain wall construction are very often manufactured with the insulation built in as the core of a sandwich. Such walls usually require no further insulation. If single skin panels are used, provision must be made for applying the insulation to the back of the panels or to a rigid sheath erected behind them.

Insulation for glass curtain walls is provided by the use of sealed units. In the case of glass blocks or tiles, the two halves of each unit are fused together, enclosing a dry, low-pressure air space. Sheets or plates are hermetically sealed around the edges, in pairs, leaving a space between them.

4. *Ceiling insulation.* Insulation may be applied directly to the underside of floors, or a suspended ceiling system may be employed. In either case, many kinds of insulation may be used, including insulating boards, rigid slabs, or sprayed-on insulation consisting of vermiculite plaster or asbestos fiber.

When insulation is to be applied under concrete floors, nailing strips should be cast into the bottom of the slab on appropriate centers for the type of insulation being used (Fig. 16-19). The surface must be primed and the first layer of insulation is applied at right angles to the nailing strips, using hot asphalt or an approved adhesive on the contact face and edges. This layer is further secured with nails and washers (see Fig. 16-19). The second layer is then applied at right angles to the first, using the appropriate adhesive.

Suspended ceilings are usually supported by hanger rods from the roof, floor frame, or the slab above. They support a system of T bars or metal pans which in turn support the rigid insulation (Fig. 16-20) or the material which will act as a base for sprayed-on insulation. The space above the insulation must be thoroughly ventilated by free or forced circulation of air.

T bars of steel or aluminum are suspended on 18 or 24 in. centers by rod hangers which are placed close enough together to prevent any deflection of the completed ceiling. The first layer of rigid insulation is laid between the T bars after they have been coated with asphalt priming paint. The second layer is applied on top of the first, using a flood coat of hot asphalt or a coating of approved adhesive on the contact surface and edges of each slab. The insulation should be laid in parallel courses, staggering joints between courses and between layers. Finally, the upper surface of the insulation should receive a flood coat of hot asphalt or a $\frac{1}{8}$ in. coating of asphalt emulsion. The hanger rods should also be insulated to a distance of about 18 in.

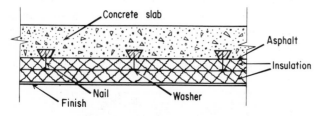

Fig. 16-19. Insulation on solid ceiling

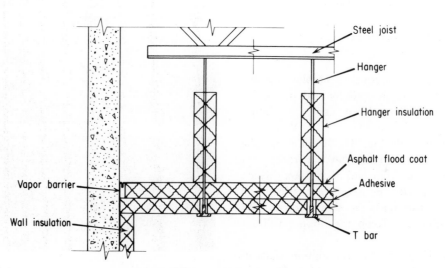

Fig. 16-20. Suspended T-bar ceiling

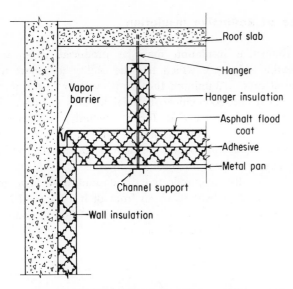

Fig. 16-21. Suspended metal pan ceiling

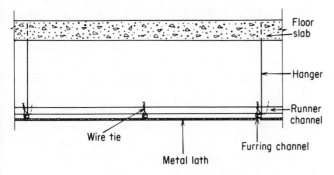

Fig. 16-22. Suspended ceiling frame

from the surface of the insulation (see Fig. 16-20) with at least half the thickness of insulation used on the ceiling.

When sprayed-on insulation is specified, the T bar or metal pan support system may be used to carry some type of rigid board or gypsum lath. Another alternative is to suspend a system of *runner channels* and *furring channels* and to wire metal lath to the underside of this framework. Sprayed-on insulation may be applied to either of these two bases. Figure 16-23 illustrates the application of sprayed-on asbestos insulation on a suspended ceiling.

Framed ceilings may be insulated with batt insulation between the framing members, and any rigid ceiling with accessible space above it may be insulated with loose fill poured or blown into place.

5. *Roof insulation.* Roof decks may be insulated with any type of rigid insulation, including cellular glass, rigid foamed plastic, straw board, fiber boards (usually double- or triple-laminated), and cellular concrete. With concrete, gypsum, precast slab, or steel decks, no undercoating is normally required, but sheathing paper or roofing felt is nailed over a wood deck.

In order to obtain a proper bond between insulation and decking, all surfaces must be dry before and during the application of the insulation. It is applied to the prepared surface by embedding it in hot asphalt, used at the rate of about 25 lb per 100 sq ft. On steel decks, the long dimension of the insulation boards should be parallel to the ridges of the deck, with the edges of the boards resting on the ridges.

Fig. 16-23. Sprayed-on asbestos insulation over suspended ceiling. (Courtesy Columbia Acoustics & Fireproofing Co.)

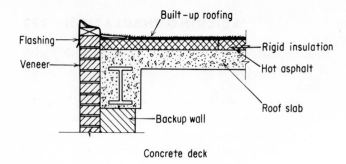

Concrete deck

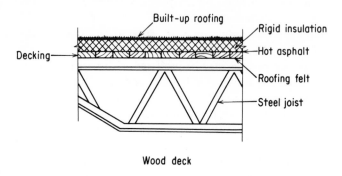

Wood deck

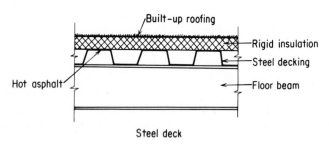

Steel deck

Fig. 16-24. Insulation applications to roof deck

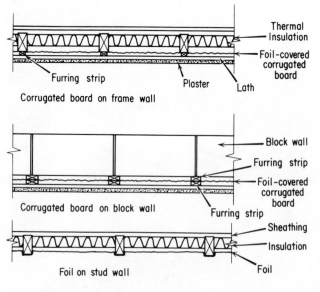

Corrugated board on frame wall

Corrugated board on block wall

Foil on stud wall

Fig. 16-25. Typical applications of reflective insulation

Use of Reflective Insulation

Reflective insulation may be produced from any metallic substance which has the ability to reflect infrared rays. Aluminum foil has proved to be the most practical and economical material for this purpose. It is produced in several forms, including foil-backed gypsum lath, rigid insulation with foil back, foil laminated to kraft paper, corrugated paper with foil on both sides, and plain sheet foil in rolls.

To be effective, reflective insulation must have an air space of at least ¾ in. in front of it. Figure 16-25 illustrates a few typical applications of foil insulation in which the air space is provided.

SOUND INSULATION AND CONTROL

Two types of problems exist in building construction concerning sound and its control. One is the improvement of hearing conditions and reduction of noise in any given room and the other is the transmission of sound from one room to another through walls, floors, and ceilings.

The improvement of hearing conditions and reduction of noise is accomplished by the proper design of inner walls and ceilings, the shape of the room, and a reduction in the amount of sound *reflected* from walls and ceilings (reflected sound causes reverberations or echoes). The ceiling shown in Fig. 16-26 is one example of how part of a room may be designed to affect acoustics.

Sound-Absorbing Materials

The control of reverberations is accomplished by the use of products which have a much greater ability to absorb sound waves than most building materials. These sound-absorbing substances are called *acoustic materials* and can generally be classified in three groups —*acoustic tiles, assembled acoustic units*, and *sprayed-on acoustic material*.

Acoustic tile is intended primarily for ceilings, but may be used on upper wall surfaces as well. When used over a solid surface, such as plaster, plywood, hardboard, etc., the surface must be smooth, even, and clean. Tiles may be secured with nails or adhesive, depending on the type of backing used. In any case, the two center lines of the ceiling should be drawn first and tiling should begin at the intersection of these lines. If adhesive is to be used, some should first be rubbed on the corners

Fig. 16-26. Room with effective sound control. (Courtesy Columbia Acoustics & Fireproofing Co.)

of each tile to act as a prime. A walnut-sized dab of adhesive is then applied to each corner. The tile should be placed close to its final location and forced to slide into place in order to spread the adhesive more completely and insure a good bond with the backing.

Tiles may be nailed to furring strips attached to the undersides of solid decks or framed ceilings (Fig. 16-28). As usual, tiling should begin along a center line snapped across the furring strips.

Acoustic tile may also be installed in a suspended ceiling framework. Some tiles are made with square edges which rest on T bars while others fit over H bars (Fig. 16-29).

Assembled acoustic units consist of sound-absorbing material such as mineral wool or fiberglass insulation fastened to hardboard, asbestos board, or sheet metal facing which has been perforated to allow sound waves to penetrate. These units may be fastened to the wall face on furring strips, suspended in front of the wall or from the ceiling, or incorporated into the wall paneling.

Sprayed-on acoustic materials are widely used for sound control because of the relative ease of application on surfaces of almost any shape (See Fig. 16-26). Vermiculite, perlite, and asbestos fiber mixed with adhesive are all commonly used for this purpose.

Vermiculite plastic is a ready-mixed product requiring only the addition of water. It can be applied over any firm, clean surface such as plaster base coats, masonry, galvanized metal, etc. It is applied in two coats if no more than $\frac{1}{2}$ in. is required or in three coats if a greater thickness is specified. The first coat should be about $\frac{3}{8}$ in. thick, straightened with a darby, and allowed to dry. The second coat is then sprayed on to the desired thickness and texture. The temperature should not be less than 55°F for a week prior to the application of

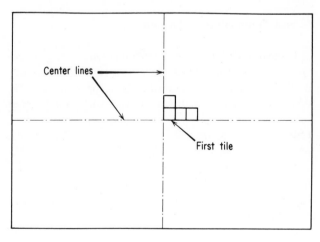

Fig. 16-27. Ceiling layout for tile application

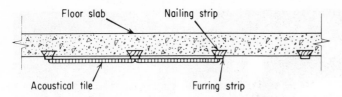

Fig. 16-28. Acoustical ceiling tile on furring strips

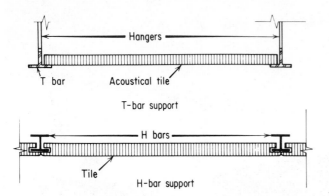

Fig. 16-29. Acoustical tile in suspended ceiling

the plastic, during its application, and for long enough after its application to allow it to set thoroughly. Adequate ventilation must be provided.

Asbestos fiber insulation is a prepared material containing an adhesive mixed with the fiber. It is sprayed on any solid surface or on metal lath backing in several thin coats to a total depth of from ½ to ¾ in. The surface to be coated must first be primed with an adhesive (except in the case of metal lath). Prime only as much area as can be sprayed with fiber while the primer is still tacky. The ceiling in Fig. 16-26 has been sprayed with asbestos acoustic insulation. Notice that additional sound absorption is provided by the carpet and the drapes.

Sound Transmission Control

In nearly all types of construction, sound transmission from room to room takes place as a result of diaphragmatic vibration through walls, floors, or ceilings. The vibrations may be initiated by impact, such as a footstep, or by the action of sound waves striking the surface. One is known as *impact transmission* and the other as *airborne transmission*.

Impact transmission normally takes place through floors and ceilings and there are several ways of reducing it. One is to cover the floor with a resilient material, such as cork tile or a heavy carpet to absorb the impact. Another is to use a suspended ceiling between floors. This is particularly effective if resilient hangers are used.

Good results are also obtained by using a *floating* floor. The floating floor may be a separate 2 in. concrete slab, isolated from the structural slab by a 1 in. foamed plastic or paper-covered fiberglass quilt, it may be a wood floor nailed to sleepers which are supported on flat steel springs (Fig. 16-30), or it may be a wood floor laid on sheets of resilient material such as fiberboard or foamed plastic.

The sound insulating efficiency of a wall or floor is known as its *transmission loss* and is measured in *decibels* (db). It is usually desirable to provide walls and floors with transmission loss ratings of from 35 to 50 db or better, depending on the purposes for which the building is to be used.

A high transmission loss may be achieved by using either a heavy wall or one composed of two or more relatively independent layers. In either case it is essential that the wall be as airtight as possible.

Several types of construction will produce walls with transmission loss ratings of 50 db or better. Among them are:

1. A single masonry wall weighing at least 80 psf (e.g., 8 in. of brick or 7 in. of concrete), including plaster, if any.
2. A masonry cavity wall consisting of two wythes weighing at least 20 psf each, held together with metal ties, and enclosing a 2 in. cavity.
3. A composite wall, consisting of a basic masonry wall weighing at least 22 psf (e.g., 4 in. of hollow clay tile or 3 in. of solid gypsum tile), with a sheath made of ½ in. gypsum lath mounted with

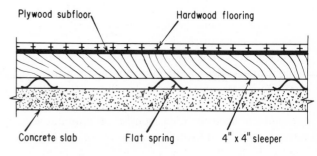

Fig. 16-30. Wood floor on springs

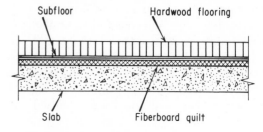

Fig. 16-31. Wood floor on insulation cushion

resilient clips (see Fig. 16-32) and plastered with
¾ in. sanded gypsum plaster.

4. A stud wall consisting of 2″ by 4″ studs with ½ in.
gypsum lath mounted on resilient clips (see Fig.
16-32) on each side and plastered with ½ in.
gypsum plaster. Mineral wool or fiberglass batts
are placed between the studs.

5. A staggered stud wall made of 2″ by 3″ studs set
at 16 in. centers on a common 2″ by 6″ plate;
½ in. gypsum lath is nailed on both sides and
plastered with ½ in. sanded gypsum plaster.
Paper-backed mineral wool or fiberglass batts are
hung between studs on one side only.

Wall construction which will produce transmission
loss ratings of from 45 to 49 db include:

1. A single masonry wall weighing at least 36 psf
(e.g., 4 in. solid gypsum tile or 4 in. brick wall)
including plaster, if any.

2. A composite wall similar to #3 above but with
furring strips to support the gypsum laths.

3. A staggered stud dry wall, consisting of two sets of
2″ by 3″ studs at 16 in. centers on a common
2″ by 4″ plate. Two layers of ⅝ in. gypsum
wallboard are applied to each face, the first nailed
and the second cemented. The joints must be
staggered and both surfaces must be sealed. A
mineral or glass wool blanket is placed between the
boards (Fig. 16-33).

A single masonry wall weighing at least 22 psf including plaster, if any, should have a transmission loss
rating of from 40 to 44 db.

Walls with ratings of from 35 to 40 db include:

1. A 2″ by 3″ or 2″ by 4″ stud wall with ⅜ in.
gypsum lath and ½ in. sanded gypsum plaster on
both sides.

2. A 2″ by 3″ or 2″ by 4″ stud wall with two layers
of ⅜ in. plasterboard on each side, the first one
nailed, the second cemented, with staggered joints.

Floors which will have an airborne transmission loss
rating of 50 db or better include:

1. A 4 in. solid concrete slab or its equivalent, weighing at least 50 psf, plastered directly on the underside and covered with wood flooring on wood
furring strips. However, its impact rating will not
be more than 30 db.

2. A 4 in. concrete slab as above, covered with a 1 in.
quilt of foamed plastic or paper-covered fiberglass
supporting a 2 in. concrete top slab. The impact
rating will again not be more than 30 db.

3. An open web steel joist framework covered by a
paper-backed fiberglass or foamed plastic quilt sup-

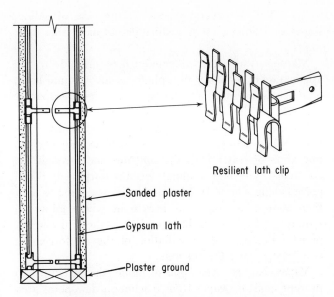

Fig. 16-32. Sound insulation with lath clips

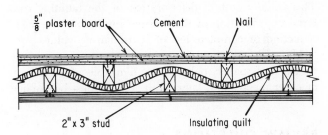

Fig. 16-33. Sound insulation with staggered studs

porting a 2 in. concrete slab. The ceiling consists
of ½ in. gypsum lath mounted on resilient clips
and plastered with ½ in. sanded gypsum plaster.
This floor will not have an impact rating of more
than 30 db.

MOISTURE INSULATION

Moisture may migrate either into or out of a building,
but it is a different type of moisture in each situation.
Moisture entering a building is normally in liquid form,
while that leaving a building does so as water vapor.
Protection against both is available: *moisture barriers*
prevent the passage of water, while *vapor barriers* prevent the passage of water vapor.

Moisture barriers are applied to the outside of a wall
or roof to prevent water from entering the structure.
On a roof, the roofing material is the moisture barrier.
The cladding or exterior finish on a wall is also a moisture barrier, though not perfect in every case. Therefore it is sometimes desirable to apply a moisture barrier
(usually an asphalt-impregnated paper) behind the

finish. This is generally done in the case of siding, shingles, or other materials which do not have watertight joints.

Masonry walls are protected below ground by the application of a coating of asphalt. Above ground level, masonry walls may be given a coating of transparent sealer to prevent the penetration of water.

Concrete slabs on the ground should have a moisture barrier between them and the earth to prevent the migration of water from the soil into and through the concrete. The best material for this purpose is 6 mil polyethylene film. It is available in wide sheets, but there should be a lap of at least 6 in. where joints are required. Care must be taken that the film is not punctured during the installation of the reinforcement or while pouring the concrete.

Vapor barriers are applied inside the structure to prevent moisture vapor from reaching a dew point area *within the wall* where it could condense and collect. This could result in deterioration of the building material or saturation of the thermal insulation, causing a reduction or complete loss of its insulating value.

Materials commonly used as vapor barriers include waxed kraft paper, polyethylene film, foils of aluminum or other metals, and latex paint. They must be applied on the warm side of the insulation and must be one unbroken surface over the entire area.

Vapor barriers produced in strips, such as waxed paper and aluminum foil, should be applied vertically over stud walls or furring strips with their edges lapped on the studs so that they may later be sealed by interior finish. The ends of these strips should extend 6 in. under the ceiling finish and under the flooring. If it is necessary to cut the vapor barrier at openings such as electrical outlets, etc., care should be taken not to make the hole larger than is absolutely necessary.

Polyethylene film is usually available in sheets wide enough to reach from floor to ceiling, and this type of barrier is desirable if there is no practical method of sealing the joints in narrower strips.

Latex paint usually serves a dual purpose—it is decorative and it is a vapor barrier.

Whether or not a vapor barrier should be applied to a ceiling depends on the type of construction. If the space above the ceiling is sealed and cold, a vapor barrier should be used, but if it is ventilated, a vapor barrier is not needed since moisture vapor can escape through the ceiling and then be carried to the outside by cross ventilation.

REVIEW QUESTIONS

1. (a) Define insulation in general terms. (b) What is thermal insulation?

2. Give an advantage and a disadvantage in the use of concrete as fireproofing for a steel floor frame.

3. Why is cellular concrete a good fireproofing material? (Two reasons.)

4. What is the specific purpose of *shoe tile* in fireproofing?

5. The space between fireproofing tile and columns being fireproofed may either be filled with concrete or left empty. Which provides the better fire rating?

6. Give two advantages to the use of vermiculite or perlite plaster for fireproofing.

7. Why must the following be insulated: (a) Long columns; (b) hot air ducts.

8. Describe an *ideal* thermal insulator.

9. Describe three important steps that must be taken when applying perimeter insulation to the exterior of a foundation wall.

10. What is a thermal bridge?

11. What particular steps must be taken to insure the effectiveness of reflective insulation?

12. What are the two basic problems of acoustic insulation?

13. Briefly describe an assembled unit to be used for acoustic insulation.

14. List three methods of reducing impact transmission through floors.

15. (a) Differentiate between a *moisture barrier* and a *vapor barrier;* (b) on which side of an exterior wall should the vapor barrier be placed?

DOORS, WINDOWS, AND STAIRS

17

DOORS

Doors vary widely in material and style, depending on the type of building and location of the door. They may be wood, glass, metal, or combinations of these. They may swing on hinges or pivots, slide on rollers or glides, fold up accordion-style, or roll up on overhead hardware.

Hinged doors may be hung in wood, steel, or aluminum frames. Wood frames are usually made with rabbeted jambs, but plain jambs and doorstops (Fig. 17-1) may be used. Steel frames are made in several styles and widths, some of which are shown in Fig. 17-2. Figure 17-3 shows cross sections of typical aluminum frames.

Wood frames for exterior doors are held in place with blindstop, while those for interior doors may be held with nails and wedges or jamb clips (Fig. 17-4). Steel frames are provided with appropriate jamb anchors and a bottom anchor to be fastened to the floor. Figure 17-5 illustrates the installation of steel frames in different walls.

It is common practice for the manufacturer to fit the doors into their frames, so that they are brought to the job site ready for installation. The doors must be removed from their frames and stored until building has progressed to the finishing stage. The frames can be placed in their openings as required. When hinged doors have to be fitted and hung on the job, proceed as follows:

1. Cut the door to length and width. The bottom of the door should be left approximately ¾ in. above the finish floor unless otherwise specified. The long edges are straightened and dressed to a slight taper (see Fig. 17-2), allowing at least 1/16 in. clearance on either side.
2. Mark the position of hinge gains on the jamb and the edge of the

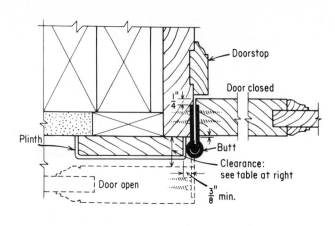

Fig. 17-1. Hinge clearance details

Clearance of stock size butts		
Thickness of door	Size of butt	Maximum clearance
$1\frac{3}{8}''$	$3'' \times 3''$	$\frac{3}{4}''$
	$3\frac{1}{2}'' \times 3\frac{1}{2}''$	$\frac{7}{8}''$
	$4'' \times 4''$	$1\frac{5}{8}''$
$1\frac{3}{4}''$	$4'' \times 4''$	$1''$
	$4\frac{1}{2}'' \times 4\frac{1}{2}''$	$1\frac{3}{8}''$
	$5'' \times 5''$	$2''$
$2''$	$4\frac{1}{2}'' \times 4\frac{1}{2}''$	$1\frac{1}{4}''$
	$5'' \times 5''$	$1\frac{3}{4}''$
	$6'' \times 6''$	$2\frac{3}{4}''$
$2\frac{1}{4}''$	$5'' \times 5''$	$1\frac{1}{4}''$
	$6'' \times 6''$	$2\frac{1}{4}''$
	$6'' \times 7''$	$3\frac{1}{4}''$
	$6'' \times 8''$	$4\frac{1}{4}''$

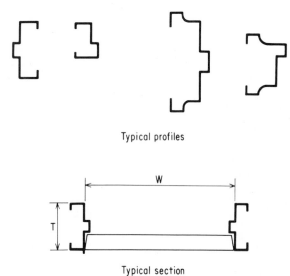

Typical profiles

Typical section

Fig. 17-2. Steel door jambs

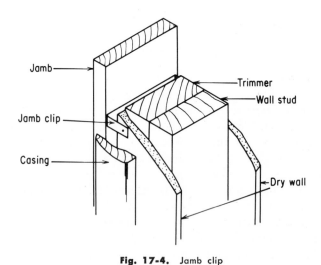

Fig. 17-4. Jamb clip

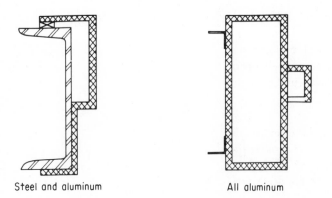

Steel and aluminum

All aluminum

Fig. 17-3. Aluminum door jamb

door. Steel frames will already have hinge recesses in them and it will only be necessary to mark the position of the corresponding hinge gains on the door.

3. Cut out gains in the jamb and the edge of the door. The door gain should be approximately $\frac{1}{32}$ in. narrower than the corresponding one in the jamb (See Fig. 17-1). The depth of the gain is the thickness of the hinge leaf, while its width depends on the amount of clearance required when the door is open (see table in Fig. 17-1).

4. Remove the hinge pins and fasten the leaves in place. Set the door in its frame, replace the pins, and test the swing of the door.

5. Install the lockset. The details of this operation

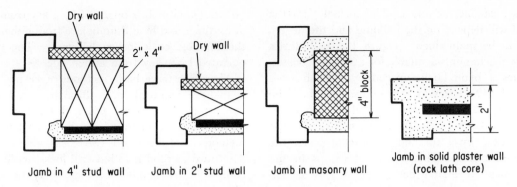

Fig. 17-5. Steel jamb in various walls

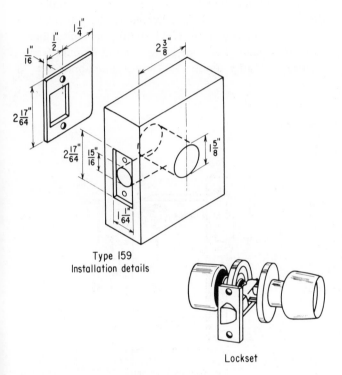

Type 159
Installation details

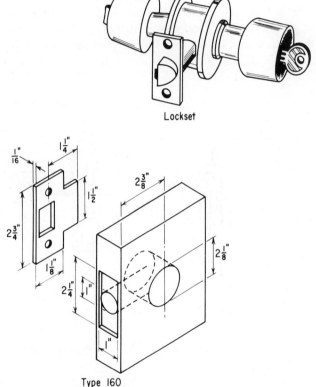

Fig. 17-6. Tubular lockset

Type 160
Installation details

vary, depending on the kind of lockset specified—cylindrical, tubular, or mortise—and the particular type of each. Figures 17-6, 17-7, and 17-8 outline boring and mortising dimensions for particular types and kinds of locksets. (This information must be obtained for every particular type and kind used.)

6. Mount the strike in the jamb. In the case of steel frames, the strike recess is pressed in and the lock must be mounted to correspond.

Various items of hardware may be specified for any particular door. Figure 17-9 shows a number of these and indicates their proper location.

There is a wide range of locking and unlocking

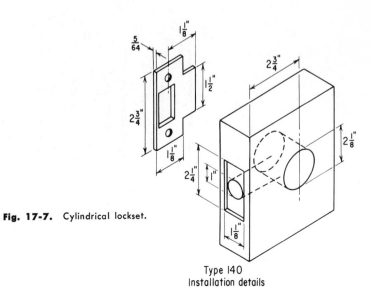

Fig. 17-7. Cylindrical lockset.

Type 140
Installation details

mechanisms available for any kind of lockset, and the one selected will depend on the building and the degree of security to be maintained. Figure 17-10 illustrates a few of the mechanisms available for a mortise lockset. (1) indicates a plain latch, opened by a knob from either side. In (2), a key locks the outside knob. The outside knob in (3) is always rigid, and the latch bolt is operated by a key. In (4), the latch bolt is operated from the outside by a thumbpiece—except when the thumbpiece is locked. This is done by stops in the edge of the lock. The latch bolt is operated by a knob from the inside at all times and by a key from the outside at all times. The latch bolt in (5) is operated by a thumbpiece from the outside, except when the thumbpiece is locked by the stops. It is operated by a knob from the inside and by a key from the outside at all times. The dead bolt is operated by a key from the outside and by the thumbpiece from the inside. In

(6), the latch bolt is operated by a key from the outside at all times and by a thumbpiece from either side, unless the thumbpiece is locked by stops. The dead bolt is operated by a key from either side.

There are three basic methods of keying locks. One is to have identical locks throughout a building or a floor—for convenience. Using this system, any number of locks can be operated by the same key. A second method is to have no two locks alike—for security. The third method is to have all locks master-keyed—for control. Any number of locks may be operated by different keys, and all are operated by a single master key.

The hardware for glass swinging doors is installed in the shop, and the door is delivered to the job ready to be set in place. Figure 17-11 shows the typical hardware on a plate glass door hung in an aluminum frame.

Steel swinging doors are hung and operated in

Fig. 17-8. Mortise lockset

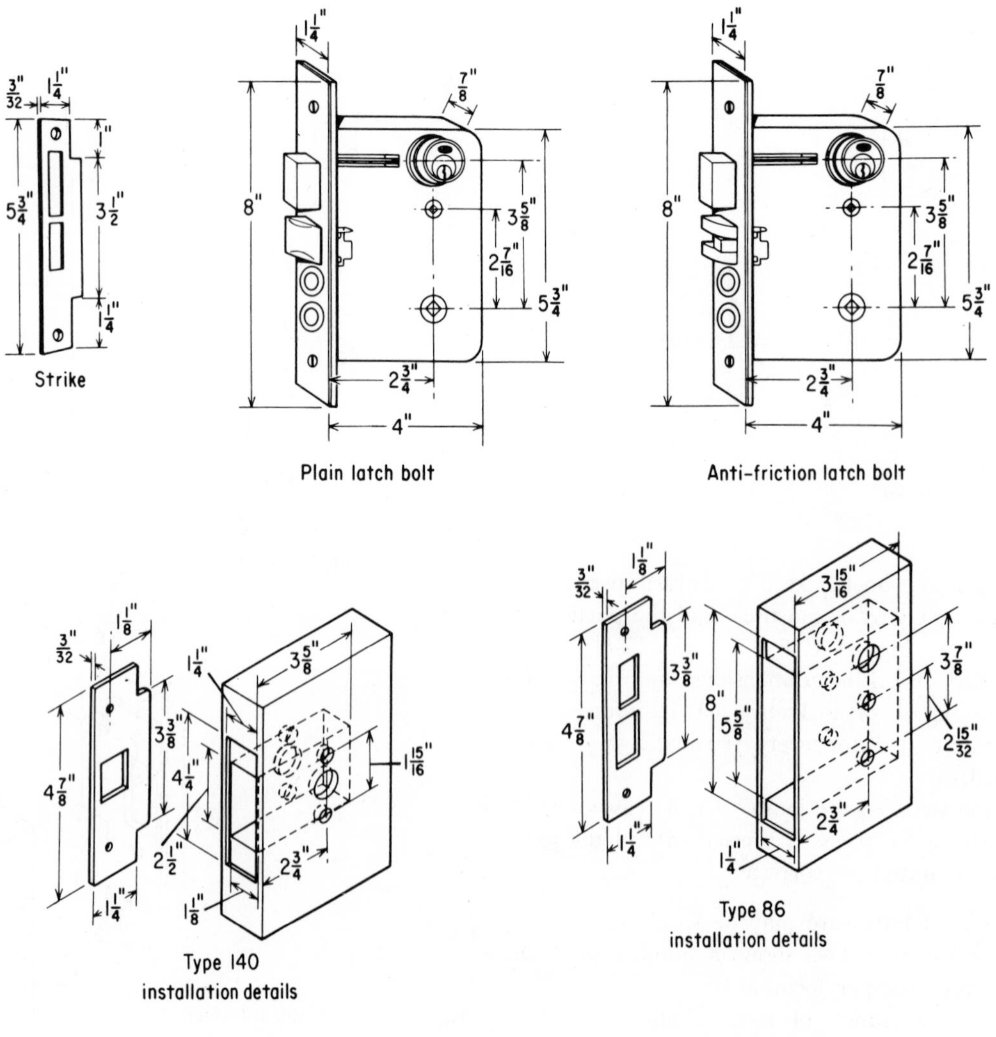

Strike

Plain latch bolt

Anti-friction latch bolt

Type 140
installation details

Type 86
installation details

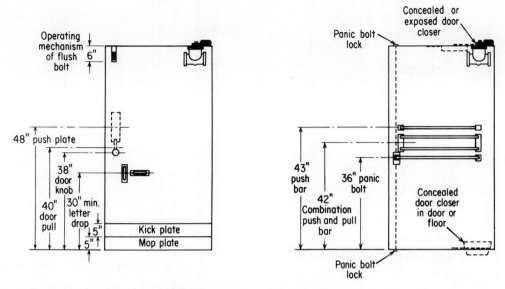

Fig. 17-9. Location of door hardware

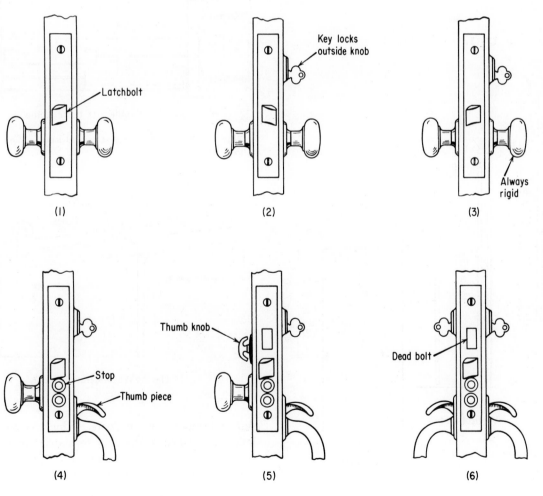

Fig. 17-10. Locking systems

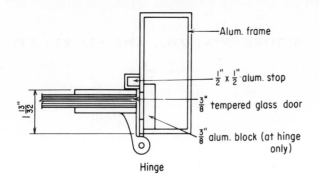

Hinge

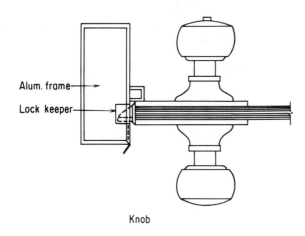

Knob

Fig. 17-11. Hardware on glass door

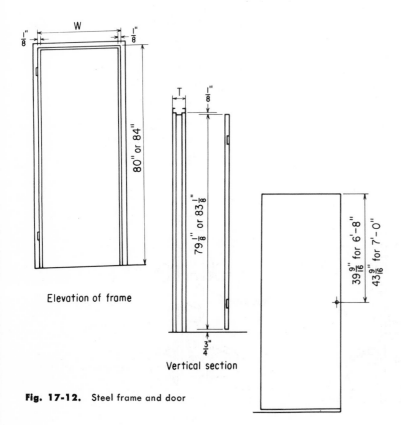

Elevation of frame

Vertical section

Elevation of door

Fig. 17-12. Steel frame and door

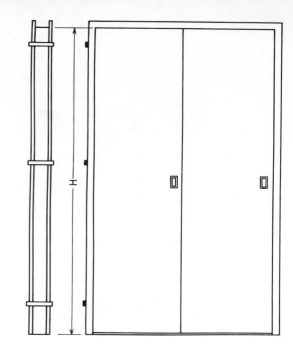

Fig. 17-13. Elevation of sliding doors

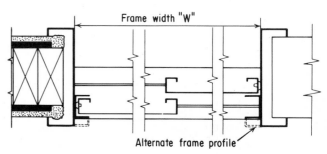

Fig. 17-14. Cross section of typical metal sliding doors in steel frame

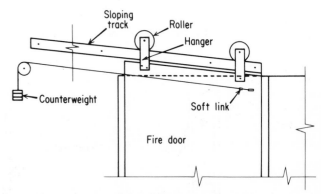

Fig. 17-15. Metal fire door

similar fashion to wood doors. Hinge recesses and lock holes are formed in the door to match hinge and strike recesses in the frame. Figure 17-12 gives some basic details of steel door and frame sizes.

Sliding doors, wood or metal, operate on either top or bottom rollers or glides. They may slide past one

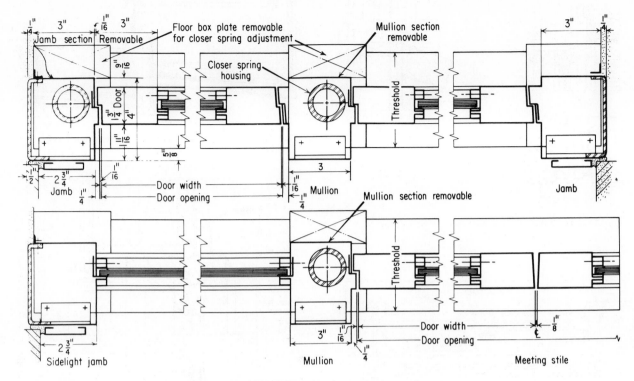

Fig. 17-16. Installation details on metal and glass doors

another in an opening (in which case a double track is required) or each may slide back into the wall on its own track. Figure 17-14 shows a horizontal cross section of metal sliding doors in a metal frame. Glass sliding doors run in aluminum guide channels, top and bottom, and usually have nylon glides at the bottom.

One common use of metal or metal-clad doors is as fire doors—to prevent fire from spreading from one part of a building to another. This type of door is mounted on a track sloping toward the closed position, and is counterbalanced by a weight suspended on a cable. The suspension system contains a link which will melt at a relatively low temperature, releasing the counterweight, and causing the door to shut automatically.

Combination metal and glass doors usually consist of aluminum stiles and rails with a plate glass panel. Jambs for such doors are often also made of aluminum. Figure 17-16 outlines manufacturing details for two styles of combination aluminum and glass doors. One consists of a pair of swinging doors with center mullion and the other of a pair without mullion, but with a sidelight.

WINDOWS

Window styles for large buildings range from the conventional single glazed wood sash (Fig. 17-17) to large areas of glass curtain wall, consisting of plate glass set in an aluminum subframe (see Fig. 15-39). Many of the windows shown in Fig. 17-23 are made with the type of sash shown in Figure 17-17. Two of the more common ones are the double-hung window (Fig. 17-18) and the window with horizontal sliding sash (Fig. 17-19).

Fig. 17-17. Conventional wood sash

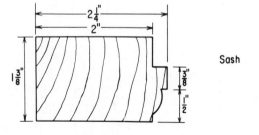

Sash

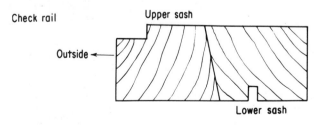

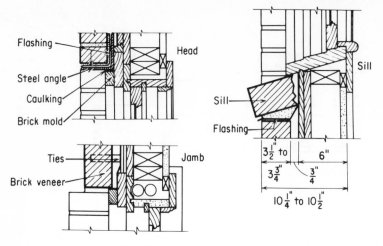

Flashing

Head

Steel angle

Caulking

Brick mold

Ties

Jamb

Brick veneer

Sill

Flashing

$3\frac{1}{2}''$ to

$3\frac{3}{4}''$

$6''$

$\frac{3}{4}''$

$10\frac{1}{4}''$ to $10\frac{1}{2}''$

Fig. 17-18. Double-hung wood sash in brick veneer wall

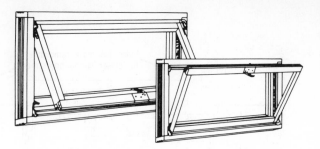

Fig. 17-20. Single light sash and frame, preassembled unit

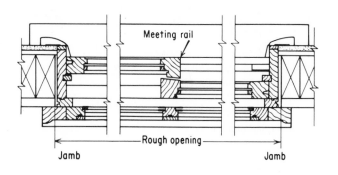

Meeting rail

Rough opening

Jamb   Jamb

Mullion   Mullion

Fig. 17-19. Installation details, horizontal sliding wood sash

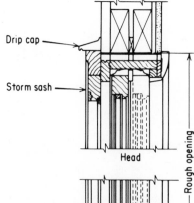

Drip cap

Storm sash

Head

Rough opening

Sill

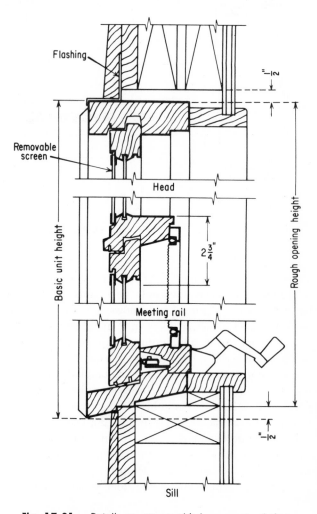

Flashing

Removable screen

Head

Basic unit height

$2\frac{3}{4}''$

Meeting rail

Rough opening height

$\frac{1}{2}''$

$\frac{1}{2}''$

Sill

Fig. 17-21. Details on preassembled casement window. (Courtesy Andersen Corp.)

Fig. 17-22. Installing a preassembled window unit

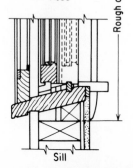

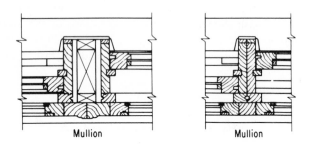

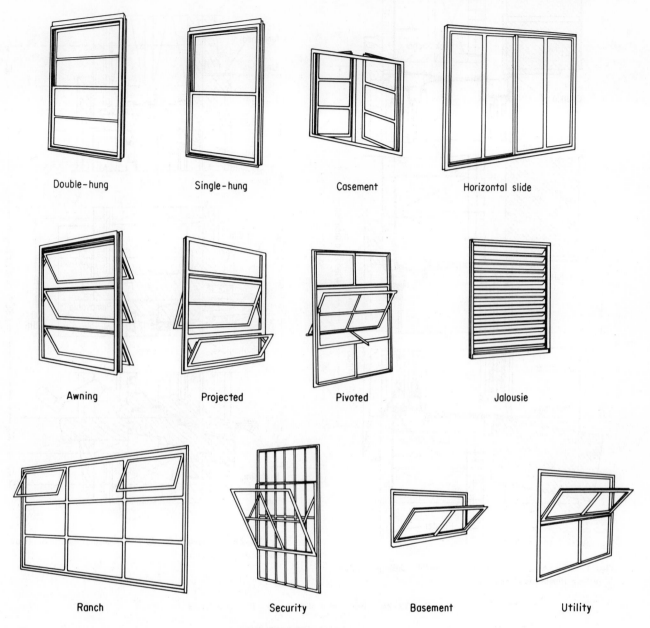

Double-hung   Single-hung   Casement   Horizontal slide

Awning   Projected   Pivoted   Jalousie

Ranch   Security   Basement   Utility

Fig. 17-23. Steel frame window types

Several manufacturers of wood sash windows include the frame, subsill, exterior casings, and removable screen as parts of a complete preassembled unit, containing the required number of lights. Figure 17-20 illustrates one of the easiest types to install, a single light unit consisting of sash and frame with the necessary hardware. Manufacturers' details show the approximate size of the opening required for any given window (Fig. 17-21), and the frame is fastened in place according to instructions. Flashing and sealing gaskets may also be supplied by the manufacturer if they are required. The sash are then simply slipped into place and no fitting is necessary. Most of the

styles shown in Fig. 17-23 are available in windows of this kind. The type shown consists of a fixed sash over an awning sash.

Windows with a steel or aluminum sash are in common use (Fig. 17-23). In some cases these windows are set in a wood frame, while in others the unit is set directly into the opening (Fig. 17-24).

Another type of window consists of a double-grooved frame (Fig. 17-25) containing two sheets of glass which overlap one another at the center of the frame and slide horizontally past one another.

A great many windows are made with insulating glass. This consists of two sheets of glass sealed with

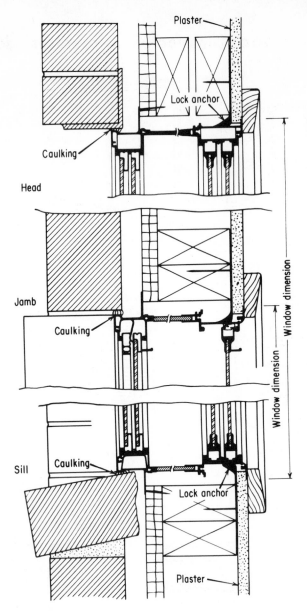

Plaster

Lock anchor

Caulking

Head

Jamb

Caulking

Window dimension

Window dimension

Sill

Caulking

Lock anchor

Plaster

Fig. 17-24. Aluminum frame horizontal sliding window. (Courtesy Humphrey Products)

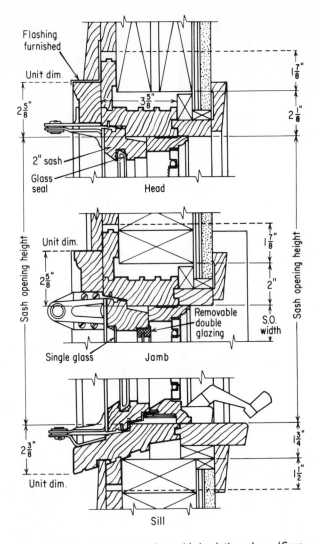

Flashing furnished

Unit dim.

$2\frac{5}{8}''$

$1\frac{7}{8}''$

$3\frac{5}{8}''$

$2\frac{1}{8}''$

2" sash

Glass seal

Head

Sash opening height

Unit dim.

$2\frac{5}{8}''$

$1\frac{7}{8}''$

2"

Removable double glazing

Single glass

Jamb

S.O. width

Sash opening height

$2\frac{3}{8}''$

$1\frac{3}{4}''$

$1\frac{1}{2}''$

Unit dim.

Sill

Fig. 17-26. Casement window with insulating glass. (Courtesy Andersen Corp.)

Fig. 17-25. Horizontal sliding glass in wood frame

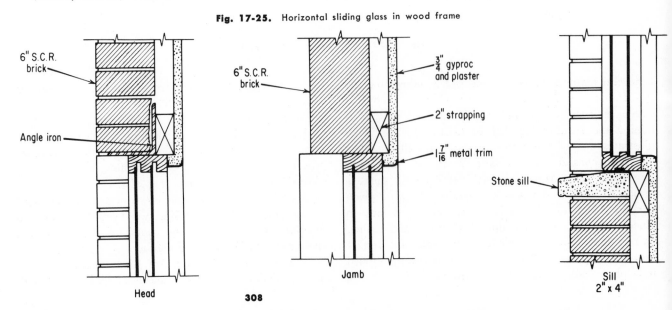

6" S.C.R. brick

Angle iron

Head

6" S.C.R. brick

$\frac{3}{4}''$ gyproc and plaster

2" strapping

$1\frac{7}{16}''$ metal trim

Jamb

Stone sill

Sill
2" x 4"

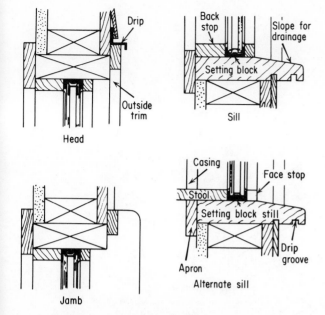

Fig. 17-27. Details on sealed unit in wood frame

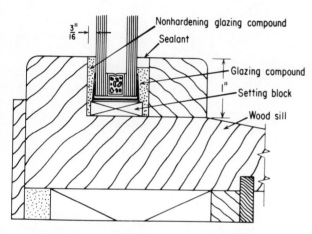

Fig. 17-28. Caulking sealed unit in wood frame

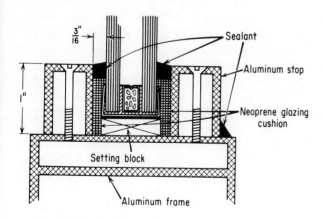

Fig. 17-29. Caulking sealed unit in aluminum frame

an air space between them. Sealing is done by an all-glass seal (Fig. 17-26), by a lead separator fused to both sheets, or by a steel channel around the edges of the unit (Fig. 17-28). Glass-sealed units are most frequently used in conjunction with a wood or metal sash, while the other two, usually made in larger sizes, are commonly set directly into a wood or metal frame. Figure 17-27 shows the details of a wood frame designed to hold a sealed unit, fixed window. The frame should by $\frac{1}{2}$ in. larger than the dimensions of the glass unit to be set. Figure 17-28 illustrates the use of setting blocks under the bottom edge of the glass and the proper glazing procedure when using a wood frame. A neoprene glazing cushion is used instead of glazing compound when working with aluminum frames.

STAIRS

Stairs of one kind or another are a necessary requirement in any building of more than one floor. Plans sometimes call for prefabricated stairs, and temporary stairs are then required until the permanent ones have been installed. These will usually be made of wood. In other cases, stairs will be "roughed in" as construction progresses from floor to floor and are later finished as part of the interior finishing schedule.

Stairs may be of wood, concrete, stone, or steel, but the same general principles apply to their planning and design. These are:

1. The stairwell opening must be long enough to allow ample headroom under the opening header. The usual minimum is 6 ft 4 in.
2. The stair must be at a slope that makes climbing as easy as possible. The angle of the line of flight should be from 25° to 35°.
3. The height of risers must be kept within reasonable limits. In many public buildings the maximum rise is 6 in., and in most cases risers should not be allowed to exceed 7 in.
4. The tread must be wide enough to provide safe footing (10 in. is the minimum width that should be considered).
5. All risers must be exactly the same height.
6. Long, straight flights of stairs without a break should be avoided. Most codes provide a maximum allowable length of stair without a landing.
7. Stairs should be at least 36 in. wide.
8. Nonslip treads should always be provided.
9. Handrails must be provided at the proper height (36 to 42 in.).
10. Stairs with treads of varying width from one end to the other (*winders*) should be avoided whenever possible.

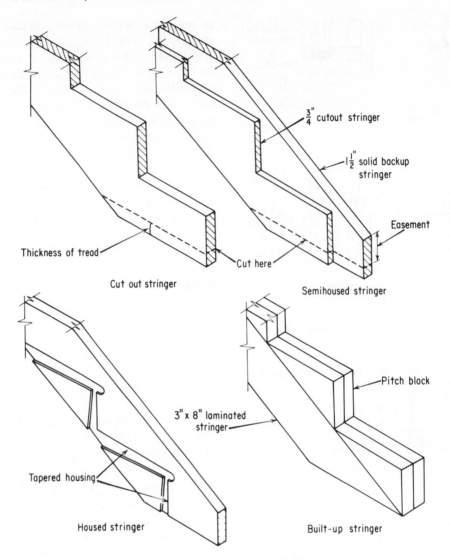

Fig. 17-30. Wooden stair stringers

Wood stairs may be made with an *open* or *cut-out* stringer, a *semi-housed* stringer, a *housed* stringer, or a *built-up* stringer (Fig. 17-30).

The exact riser height is determined by measuring the vertical distance from one finished floor to another and dividing that distance by the desired riser height. The result, to the next whole number above or below that figure, will provide two alternative numbers of risers which may be used. Those two numbers divided into the total rise will provide a choice in the exact height of riser to be used. The width of treads is determined by the total run available for the stairs (keeping in mind that there will normally be one less tread than riser in the complete flight) and by the requirement for headroom (if any).

It must be remembered that with all types of wood stairs except those with housed stringers, the height of the bottom riser must be reduced by an amount equal to that of the thickness of tread being used (See Fig. 17-30). If stairs are resting on a subfloor, the thickness of the finished floor must be added to the height of the bottom riser.

Stringers for housed stairs may be laid out from either the back edge or the front, and edges must be straight and parallel. The top and bottom ends of housed and semi-housed stringers can be extended to provide the *easement* required (see Fig. 17-30).

Steel stairs may be made in several ways. One simple method is to use two structural channels, back to back, as in Fig. 17-31, and weld or bolt steel treads between them. Notice the nonslip tread employed in this stair and the handrails provided on both sides.

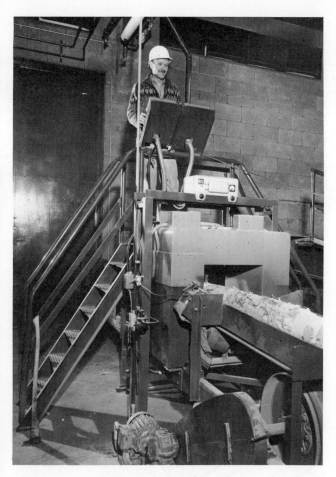

Fig. 17-31. A simple steel stair

Fig. 17-32. Built-up steel stair

Another method of building a steel stair is illustrated in Fig. 17-32. Two or more structural steel members (depending on the width of the stair) are used as stringers. They may be channels, I beams, or heavy plates. Tread brackets are welded to the top edge or to the inside face of the stringers, and steel treads or *subtreads* are then welded to the brackets. In the stair shown in Fig. 17-32, the subtreads are hollow steel pans which will later be filled with concrete, terrazzo, or magnesite.

A somewhat similar type of stair is made by bolting pressed steel risers and treads to steel stringers (Fig. 17-33). The tread mold may receive a stone slab or may be a pan to be filled with poured-in-place tread material.

A spiral steel stair is made by welding nonslip treads or subtreads in rising succession around a central axis such as a steel pipe. This is one type of stair in which the tread is wider at one end than the other, and every effort should be made to build them as wide as possible in the normal line of travel.

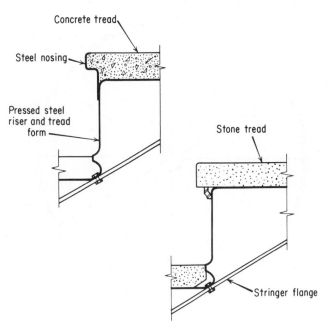

Fig. 17-33. Stone or concrete treads on steel stair

Reinforced concrete stairs may be precast or poured-in-place. Precast units must be tied into the structure, which may be done by casting the topping slab around the lower end, as in Fig. 17-35. Anchor plates cast into the end of the stair may be welded to a matching plate in the lower floor. The top end of the stair usually rests on a beam ledge (Fig. 17-35).

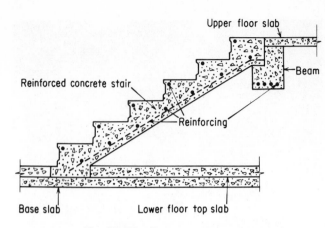

Fig. 17-35. Precast concrete stair

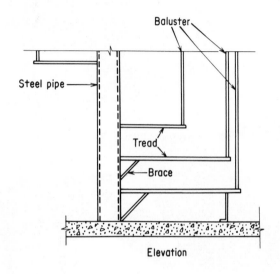

Elevation

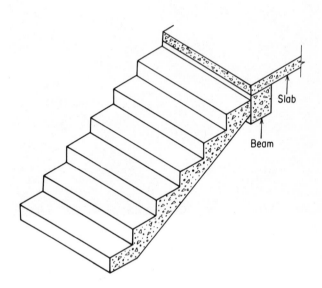

Fig. 17-36. Open flight concrete stair

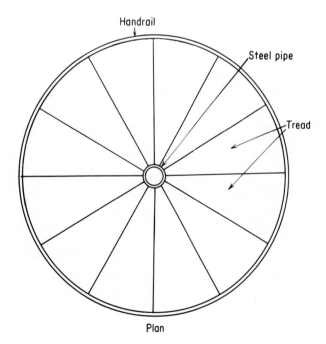

Plan

Fig. 17-34. Steel spiral stair

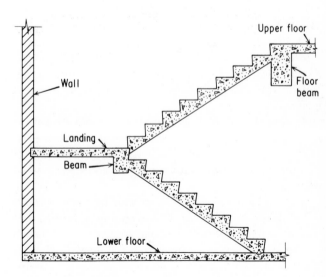

Fig. 17-37. Monolithically poured stair

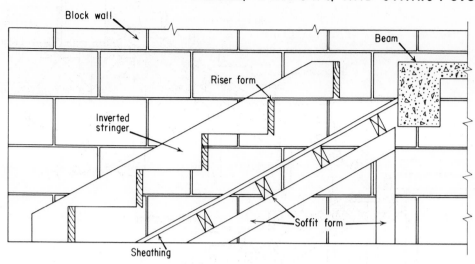

Fig. 17-38. Form for closed stair

The method used to form a poured-in-place stair will depend on the type of stair to be constructed. A *closed* string or flight (between enclosing walls) will require forms that are different from those used for an *open* flight (Fig. 17-36). If the stair is poured monolithically with the landing and upper floor (Fig. 17-37), the method must again be different from that used to form a stair cast between two existing floors.

A stair to be cast between existing walls requires a soffit form (Fig. 17-38) and riser forms held in place by inverted stringers. The stringers must be supported independently of the soffit form, and this may be done by wedging across the stair, from one stringer to the other.

An open flight stair also requires the soffit form, but in this case the stringers rest on the framework which supports the soffit form. The bottom edge of the riser forms should be beveled so that the surface of the treads may be troweled back to their junction with the next riser. A wide stair may require extra support at the center of the risers to prevent them from bowing under the pressure of the concrete. A 2″ by 6″ cut out as a stringer and inverted may be placed against the face of the risers and braced at the bottom to provide that support.

Figure 17-40 illustrates one method of forming a stair being poured monolithically with floor or landing (as is shown in Fig. 17-37).

Circular poured-in-place concrete stairs present special forming problems. In the first place, the stringers must be flexible enough to be bent. Secondly, although the total rise of both inside and outside stringers is the same, the total run of each varies because of the difference in radius of the circles circumscribing the inside and outside edges of the stair. Finally, the soffit must be made in sections of relatively thin material if it is to

fit the warped surface of the underside of the stair. To lay out and build the forms for a circular concrete stair, proceed as follows:

1. Draw circles representing the inside and outside circumferences of the stair to scale (Fig. 17-41).
2. Measure the total rise and also determine the number and height of risers required. This will be the same for both inside and outside stringers.
3. Determine the number of treads and calculate the width of each on the outside circumference. This is the tread run for the outside stringer.

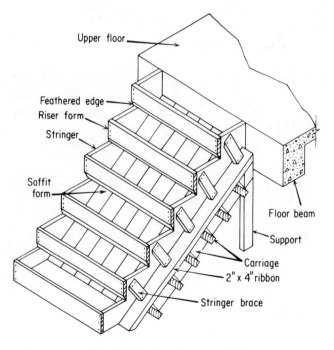

Fig. 17-39. Form for open stair

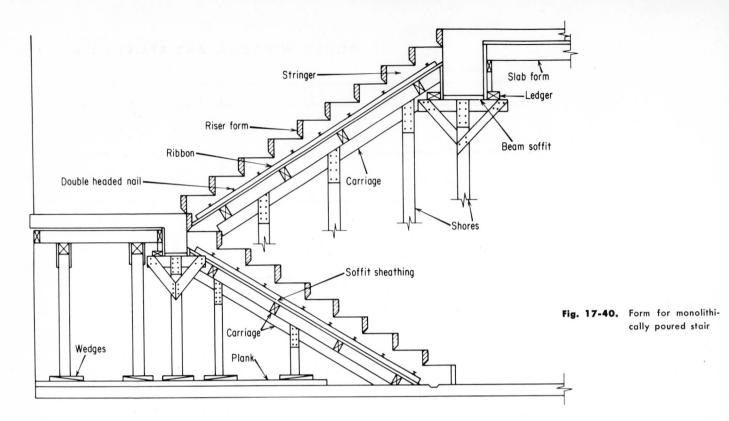

Fig. 17-40. Form for monolithically poured stair

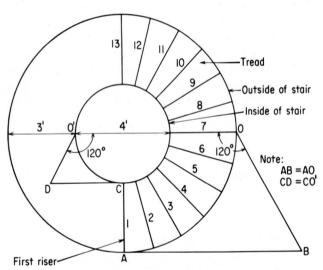

Fig. 17-41. Plan view of half-circle stair

4. Step off these tread widths around the outside circle and join each point to the center of the circles. The distance between points at which the inside circle is cut represents the tread width at the inside of the stair, and is the tread run for the inside stringer.

5. Calculate the total run for both stringers and lay both out against a common total rise (Fig. 17-42).

6. Make the vertical distance from the junction of the rise and the run to the bottom edge of the stringer (distance *x*, Fig. 17-42) the same for both stringers.

7. Build inside and outside circular walls to carry the stair form. Make the necessary allowance for the thickness of the stringer material, as in Fig. 17-43.

8. Bend the stringers around the face of the walls and fasten them in place.

9. Make a template for one section of soffit. Lay out a full-size plan view of one tread and draw in the center line (Fig. 17-44). On either side of this center line, lay out half the length of distance *a* at one end and half the length of distance *b* at the other, at right angles to the center line. Join the ends of these lines. The figure *LMNO* represents the approximate shape of the soffit section.

10. Cut this template out of thin material and shape its ends until the piece fits snugly against the form walls under the stringers. Cut as many soffit sections of this shape as there are treads in the stair.

11. Nail the soffit sections to the bottom edge of the stringers, nailing a ribbon under them for support.

12. Nail riser forms with tapered bottom edges to the stringer risers, and nail blocking in front of each to provide further support.

13. Place the necessary shoring under the center of the soffit to keep the soffit sections in line.

14. Place the specified reinforcement in the stair form.

Stone stairs are usually a combination of either stone and steel or stone and reinforced concrete. In the stone and steel combination, steel stringers and subtreads are capped with stone treads (See Fig. 17-33). In the second case, the stair is formed of concrete, and stone slabs provide the finished surface.

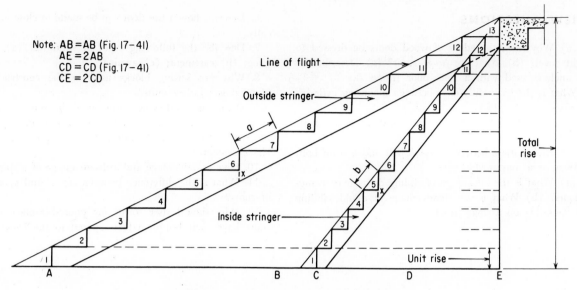

Note: AB=AB (Fig. 17-41)
AE = 2AB
CD = CD (Fig. 17-41)
CE = 2CD

Fig. 17-42. Layout of stringers for half-circle stair

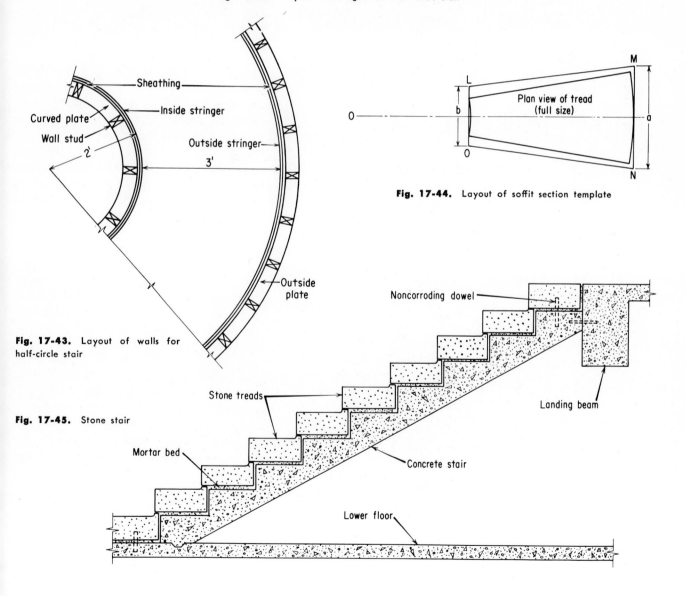

Fig. 17-43. Layout of walls for half-circle stair

Fig. 17-44. Layout of soffit section template

Fig. 17-45. Stone stair

REVIEW QUESTIONS

1. (a) Why must the edges of wood doors be dressed to a slight bevel? (b) What are *hinge gains*? (c) Describe the jamb anchors used with a steel door frame.

2. What is the basic difference between mounting *cylindrical* locks or *mortise* locks.

3. Where is the *strike* of a lockset located? What is its purpose?

4. (a) Differentiate between a *latch* bolt and a *dead* bolt. (b) What is a master key?

5. (a) What is the advantage of sliding doors over swinging doors? (b) What is the disadvantage of double sliding doors operating on a single track?

6. Describe how a fire door can be made to close automatically.

7. Describe the following types of windows: (a) double-hung; (b) casement; (c) awning.

8. Why are setting blocks used in the construction of plate glass window units?

9. Define the following terms used in stair design and construction: (a) line of flight; (b) headroom; (c) tread run; (d) total rise; (e) baluster; (f) newel post; (g) winder; (h) easement.

10. Give an advantage and a disadvantage of a spiral stair.

11. What is the difference between *closed* and *open* flights of stairs?

12. Why should riser forms for poured-in-place concrete stairs have their bottom edges tapered to the back face?

INTERIOR FINISHING

18

The application of interior finish is usually the final phase in the construction of a building. There are a number of reasons for this—one, of course, is that the base for finishing materials must be ready before the finish itself can be applied. Finishing materials are often relatively delicate or easily damaged, and could not withstand the rough use to which they might be subjected during earlier phases of construction. Finishing materials are also often affected by major changes in temperature and humidity—factors which can only be stabilized after the building is enclosed or near completion.

Finishing operations include the application of the final interior facing (plaster, wood paneling, wall tile, hardboard, gypsum board, plastic laminates, terra cotta, stone, steel), laying of finish floors, and the installation of trim around doors, windows, base, etc.

PLASTERING

Plaster is well known and widely used for finishing walls and ceilings in many types of buildings. Either Portland cement or gypsum plaster may be used, depending on the composition of the wall and the conditions to which the surface will be subjected. Portland cement plaster may be applied to concrete, masonry, and metal lath bases, and is used where walls, ceilings, and partitions are subject to rough use or extreme moisture conditions. Gypsum plaster bonds well to gypsum lath, metal lath, fiberboard lath, and gypsum or clay tile. Plaster is usually applied in three coats: the first, or *scratch* coat; the second, or *brown* coat; and the finish coat.

Portland Cement Plaster

Portland cement base plaster is made by mixing 1 part of normal Portland or masonry cement with 3 to 4 parts of plaster sand. Sand grading should be as follows:

Passing #4   sieve: 100%
Passing #8   sieve: 80% to 98%
Passing #16 sieve: 60% to 90%
Passing #30 sieve: 35% to 70%
Passing #50 sieve: 10% to 30%
Passing #100 sieve: not more than 10%

Larger proportions of aggregate to cement may be used when the aggregate is well graded, with a good proportion of coarse particles. When normal Portland cement is used, a plasticity agent may be used to increase the workability of the mortar.

The scratch coat should be approximately $\frac{3}{8}$ in. thick. It should be *dashed* on concrete walls unless the surface is sufficiently rough to insure an adequate bond for a troweled coat. The scratch coat must be troweled on clean, dry masonry walls. Before plastering begins, they should be evenly dampened to control suction. Hair or fiber (at the rate of about 1 lb per bag of cement) should be used in a scratch coat applied to metal lath. The scratch coat must be cross-hatched before it hardens to provide a mechanical bond for the brown coat. It should be kept damp for at least two days immediately following its application, and should then be allowed to dry thoroughly.

The surface of the scratch coat should be dampened evenly before beginning the application of the brown coat, which is about $\frac{3}{8}$ in. thick, brought to a true, even surface, and then either roughened with a wood float or cross-hatched lightly. The brown coat should be damp-cured for at least two days and then allowed to dry.

Finish coats may require a slightly finer aggregate, but excessive fineness should be avoided. Color may be added in the form of mineral pigments, at the rate of not more than 6% of the cement, by weight. The usual finish on interior Portland cement plaster is a sand float or low-relief texture finish, but plaster may be troweled smooth, if specified. Moist curing should take place for at least 7 days. During plastering operations, the temperature should be maintained at or above 50°F.

Gypsum Plaster

Several types of gypsum plaster are manufactured, each for a specific use. They include *hardwall* plaster, for scratch and brown coats; *cement bond* plaster, for base plaster (to be applied to a concrete surface); and *finish* plasters, for the finish coat over a gypsum plaster base.

Either sand or vermiculite may be used as aggregate with gypsum hardwall plaster for scratch and brown coats. Use two parts of dry sand by weight to one part of plaster for the scratch coat over gypsum lath, wood lath, or metal lath. For the scratch coat over gypsum tile, brick, or clay tile, use three parts of sand by weight to one part of plaster. The same general specifications apply for sand used in gypsum plaster as for that used in cement plaster.

The scratch coat is approximately $\frac{3}{8}$ in. thick and is cross-hatched to receive the brown coat. Curing is carried out in the same manner as for cement plaster.

For the brown coat, use three parts of dry sand by weight to one part of plaster. This coat is also approximately $\frac{3}{8}$ in. thick, floated, and broomed to a straight, even surface, ready for the finish coat.

If vermiculite aggregate is specified, use 1 cu ft of aggregate to 1 sack of hardwall plaster over gypsum lath. If the plaster is to be applied over masonry, $1\frac{1}{2}$ cu ft of aggregate may be used per sack of hardwall. For the brown coat, use approximately $1\frac{1}{2}$ cu ft of vermiculite per sack of plaster.

Cement bond plaster requires only the addition of water. It is applied in two coats to a total thickness of approximately $\frac{3}{8}$ in. on ceilings and $\frac{5}{8}$ in. on walls. Before it has set, the surface must be broomed to receive the finish coat.

Several types of gypsum plaster are available for the finish coat. One is the widely used gypsum finish plaster. It is mixed with lime putty to make the putty coat. Lime putty is produced either by slaking quick lime or by soaking hydrated lime for about 12 hr. The two ingredients are mixed in the following ratios: 1 part finish plaster to two parts dry hydrated lime by weight or 1 part plaster to 3 parts lime putty by volume. Water is added to the mixture to attain the desired degree of plasticity.

This putty finish is applied in two coats over a fairly dry brown coat base. A thin first coat should be ground into the base thoroughly and a second coat should then be used to fill in the imperfections. The surface is troweled to a smooth finish, sprinkling water on with a brush to provide workability.

A sand float finish is produced by using screened (hairs or fibers have been removed) hardwall plaster and sand in the proportion of one part plaster to not more than two parts of sand by weight. The maximum size of sand particles will determine the coarseness of the finish. This plaster is applied in two coats to a

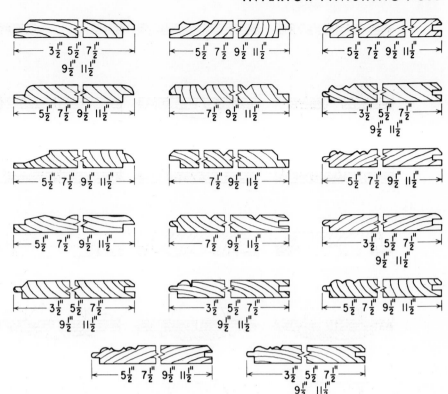

Fig. 18-1. Softwood paneling patterns

total thickness of not more than ⅛ in. over a set but not fully cured hardwall base coat. After leveling, the surface is floated with a carpet or cork float to produce the desired texture.

A prepared finish plaster is available which requires only the addition of water. It is mixed at the rate of approximately 2 parts plaster to 1 part water by volume. The plaster should be allowed to soak for at least 30 min. before it is used. Application and finishing are essentially the same as for a lime putty coat. This plaster does not produce as white a surface as lime putty, but since it contains no lime, it may be decorated as soon as it is dry.

Plaster of Paris and Keene's cement are two other types of gypsum finish plaster with special applications. Plaster of Paris is used where a very rapid set is required, and Keene's cement is used where sanitary conditions or high humidity necessitate a hard, impervious surface.

Vermiculite Finish Plaster

A finish plaster in which vermiculite is used as the aggregate is made by mixing vermiculite and screened hardwall at the rate of 100 lb of gypsum to 1 cu ft of vermiculite finish aggregate. The plaster is first mixed with water and the aggregate is added to the putty.

More water may be added to make the plaster workable. This finish may be applied over any gypsum base plaster to a depth of ⅛ in. The procedure for applying, leveling, and troweling is the same as that used for other finish plasters.

WOOD PANELING

Boards and plywood are both used for interior wall and ceiling finishes. Boards are dressed in a variety of patterns (Fig. 18-1), while finishing plywood is produced with an etched, embossed, or plain surface.

Boards are usually applied vertically and are supported by two rows of girts evenly spaced between top and bottom plates and nailed between the studs or furring strips. Boards may be blind-nailed or nailed at grooves in the surface.

Both hardwood and softwood plywoods are used for finishing. Sheets are normally applied with the long edge vertical, over studs or furring strips not over 16 in. o.c. They are held in place with nails, nails and glue, or by *wood-welding*. The last method involves the use of high frequency glue and a wood-welding machine which sets the glue rapidly. Great care must be taken not to scorch or burn the surface when using this type of equipment.

There are many methods for providing joints

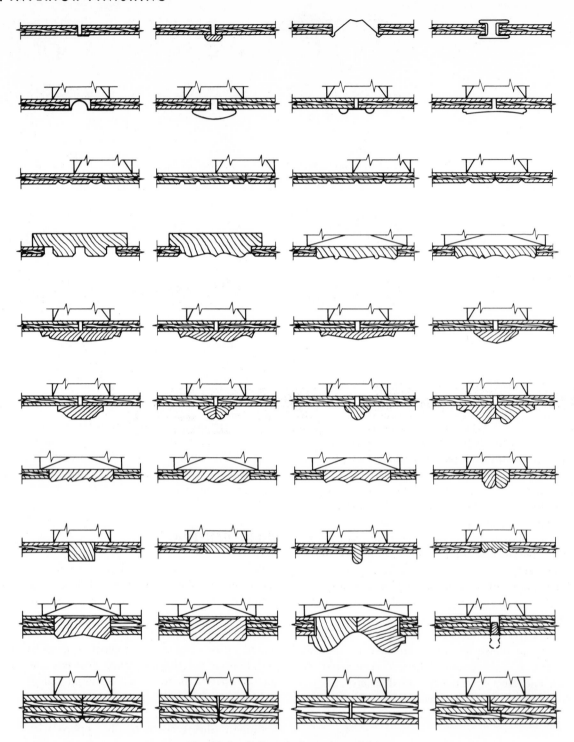

Fig. 18-2. Softwood plywood panel joints

between softwood plywood sheets, some of which are illustrated in Fig. 18-2. When hardwood plywood is used, sheets may be selected to allow grain matching or patterning. In this case, a simple butt joint with its edges slightly beveled to the back is usually best.

Panel effects are produced by the use of a number of hardwood moldings (Fig. 18-3). These moldings are: (1) casing; (2) stool; (3) stop; (4) chair rail; (5) base; (6) and (7) quarter round; (8) corner molding; (9) crown mold; (10) shoulder molding; (11) batten strip; (12) batten insert; (13) cove; and (14) door jamb.

WALL TILE

Several kinds of wall tile are produced in various sizes for interior finishing—including ceramic, glass, steel, copper, and plastic tile. Accessories—such as base, cap, triangles, and corners—are available for most of them. Figure 18-4 illustrates the shapes available in plastic tile. Figure 18-5 shows ceramic wall tile shapes and typical lay-up patterns.

Wall tile may be applied with adhesives to most hard, smooth surfaces such as concrete, hardboard, plywood, gypsum board, or plaster. Ceramic tile may also be set in mortar.

Tile laying should begin at established level and vertical lines on the wall. If tile is to cover the entire wall from floor to ceiling, a level line should be drawn at a convenient height from the floor, measured to accommodate the base and a specified number of tiles. If the tiled surface is to be a *dado,* draw the top line of the tile and a plumb line down the center of the wall. Tile laying should begin at the intersection of these lines. All materials should be at room temperature, 60° to 70°F. Apply the adhesive to the wall with a notched trowel, using a wavy motion. The coating should be of sufficient thickness so that when tile is pressed against it, the ridges of cement will flatten and contact at least 60% of the back surface of the tile. Do not force the edges of tiles tightly against one another; grouting compound, made for that purpose, is applied to the joints by tube or by narrow spatula after the tiles are in place. Joints are then wiped out to the desired depth.

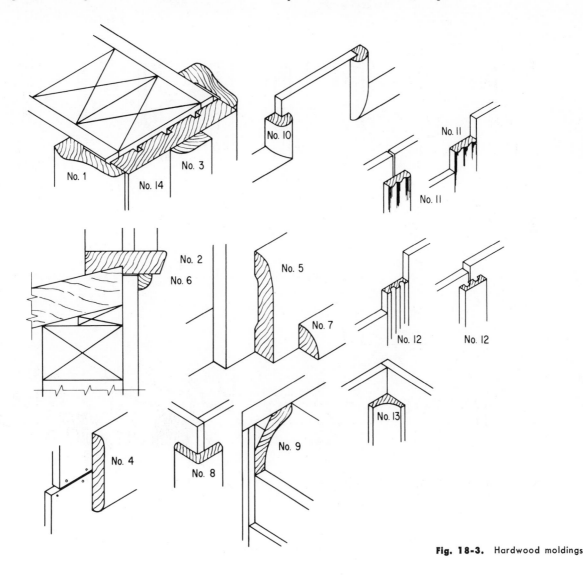

Fig. 18-3. Hardwood moldings

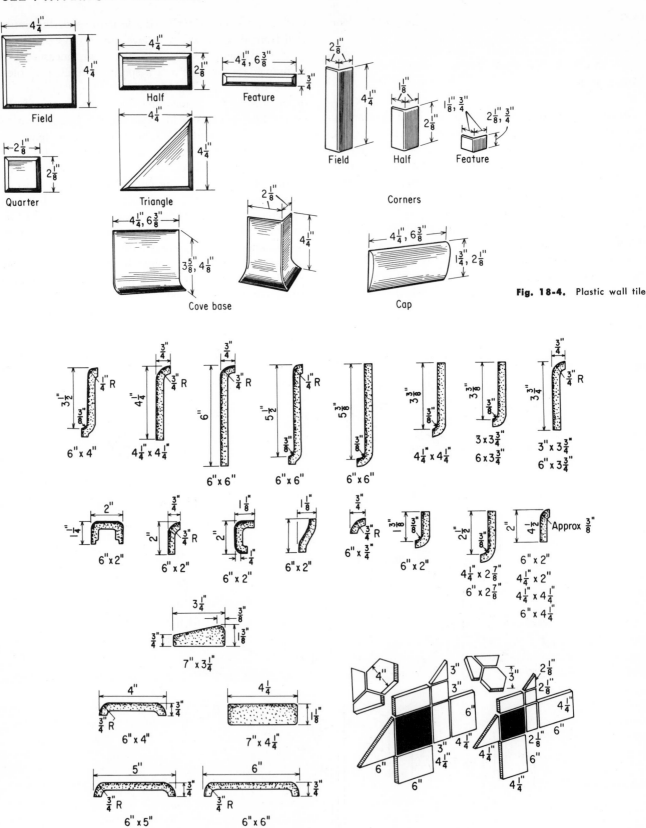

Fig. 18-4. Plastic wall tile

Fig. 18-5. Ceramic wall tile

HARDBOARD

Hardboard with various face designs—such as embossed leather or wood grain, striated, grooved, plastic-coated, either plain or cut into squares like tile—is used for interior finish.

Panels should be *conditioned* before being applied to the walls by allowing each to stand separately on its long edge for at least 24 hr. Do not try to install hardboard panels in abnormally damp areas.

Hardboard may be attached to the wall with nails, with batten strips, or with adhesives. If nails are used, drill a shallow hole at nail locations with a drill slightly smaller than the shank of the nail. Nails should be spaced about 8 in. apart at intermediate supports and 4 in. apart around the edges. A solid backing must be provided when the board is to be applied with adhesive. Spread adhesive over the entire back surface with a saw-toothed applicator and brace the panels in place until the adhesive sets.

GYPSUM BOARD

Gypsum board is often used instead of plaster as interior finish for walls and ceilings. This is known as *drywall* construction. It may be a single application of $\frac{1}{2}$ or $\frac{5}{8}$ in. or a double thickness of $\frac{3}{8}$ in. board. The single layer is secured with special nails or by gluing to studs or furring strips. When a double thickness is used, the inner layer is nailed vertically and the outer layer is cemented to it horizontally with a gypsum cement. The outer layer is held in place with double-headed nails which are removed once the cement has set. Nail holes are filled with gypsum joint filler at the same time as the joints are taped and filled. The joints are sized after sanding, and the surface is ready to be painted.

Gypsum board is produced with printed wood grain patterns and with a plastic-fabric-coated surface. The former is applied with nails whose heads have the same color as the pattern, while the fabric-surfaced board is usually held by aluminum battens, producing a paneled effect. The battens are placed at studs, held in place by screws to the stud, and are capped with a plastic batten strip (Fig. 18-6).

PLASTIC LAMINATES

Plastic laminates in thicknesses ranging from $\frac{1}{16}$ to $1\frac{1}{2}$ in. are used in various ways for interior finishing. The thin sheets, $\frac{1}{16}$ in., $\frac{1}{10}$ in., $\frac{1}{8}$ in., etc., are used

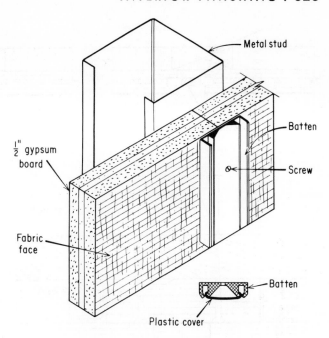

Fig. 18-6. Gypsum board over metal studs

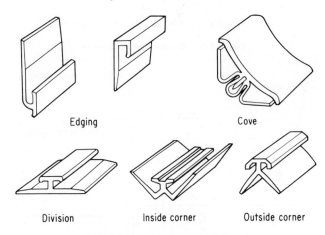

Fig. 18-7. Aluminum panel moldings

by themselves or laminated to plywood backing to line interior walls. Thin sheets are applied directly by the use of contact adhesives. Edges may be butted together, but aluminum edge moldings are generally used (Fig. 18-7). These moldings may be used with other types of wall paneling as well as plastic laminates.

The application of a thin plastic laminate sheet to plywood backing is usually done in a factory or shop. The plastic laminate may be applied to a flat sheet of plywood or may be *postformed* over a curved surface. Faced plywood sheets or strips are used as paneling, base, or ceiling cove. Figure 18-8 illustrates two methods which may be used to attach panels to walls for a flush joint fit. Paneled effects can be produced

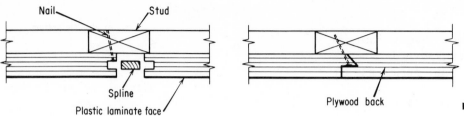

Nail — Stud

Spline

Plastic laminate face

Plywood back

Fig. 18-8. Flush joint panel assemblies

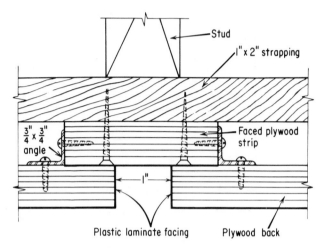

Stud

1" x 2" strapping

$\frac{3}{4}$" x $\frac{3}{4}$" angle

Faced plywood strip

1"

Plastic laminate facing

Plywood back

Fig. 18-9. Divided panel assembly

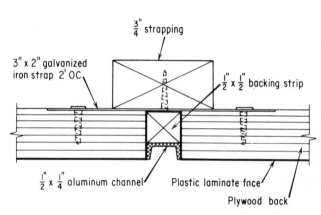

$\frac{3}{4}$" strapping

3" x 2" galvanized iron strap 2' OC

$\frac{1}{2}$" x $\frac{1}{2}$" backing strip

$\frac{1}{2}$" x $\frac{1}{4}$" aluminum channel

Plastic laminate face

Plywood back

Fig. 18-11. Paneling with aluminum channels

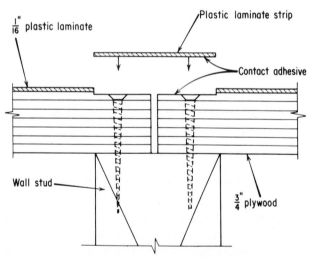

$\frac{1}{16}$" plastic laminate

Plastic laminate strip

Contact adhesive

Wall stud

$\frac{3}{4}$" plywood

Fig. 18-10. Recessed panel joint

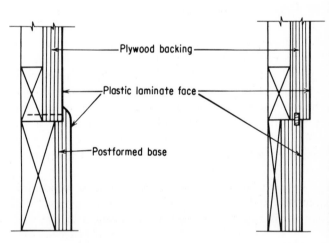

Plywood backing

Plastic laminate face

Postformed base

Plastic laminate face

Fig. 18-12. Base or ceiling cove assembly

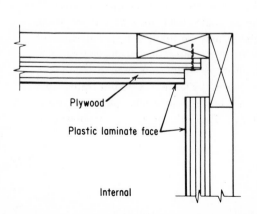

Plywood

Plastic laminate face

Internal

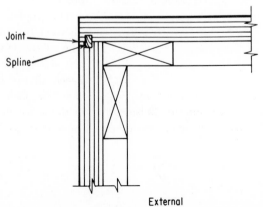

Joint

Spline

External

Fig. 18-13. Panel assembly at corners

in several ways. A method to be used if the panel is accessible from the back is shown in Fig. 18-9. In Fig. 18-10, a finish strip of thin plastic laminate is applied to the recessed joint with contact adhesive. Figure 18-11 illustrates still another method using an aluminum channel to finish the joint.

Base or ceiling cove may be applied as shown in Fig. 18-12, while Fig. 18-13 illustrates a method of jointing at internal and external corners.

Thick plastic laminates are used for partitions, sliding doors, baseboards, window sills, table tops, etc., and are manufactured to specifications.

TERRA COTTA FINISHES

Ceramic wall tile is one of the terra cotta products available for interior wall finishing. Others include common and face brick, facing tile, and ceramic mosaic.

Facing with Brick

Interior walls may be faced with standard 4 in. wide brick or with thin brick veneer units. Standard brick may be either common or face brick, depending on use and appearance. For example, common brick with protruding mortar joints is often used for interiors if a rustic effect is desired.

The procedure for applying face brick to interiors is similar to that used for exterior facing brick, except that stack bond is more commonly employed. The brick may be bonded to the back-up wall with metal ties or by a mortar coat between back-up and face brick. Particular attention should be paid to the mortar joints.

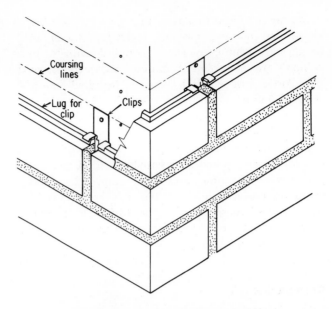

Fig. 18-15. Brick veneer secured by clips

Sand should be fine enough to pass a #16 sieve. Where nonstaining mortar is specified, ammonium or calcium stearate is added at the rate of 3% of the weight of cement used.

Thin brick veneer facing consists of units 8″ by 2½″ or 11½″ by 2½″, both approximately ¾ in. thick (Fig. 18-14). The units may be fastened to the wall with nails (two per unit) or with metal clips, as in Fig. 18-15. A solid wood backing at least ⅜ in. thick is required. Mortar is applied to the joints with a tuck pointer's trowel or a caulking gun after the veneer is in place.

Facing Tile

Facing tiles are available in thicknesses of from 2 to 8 in. and may be laid with either horizontal or vertical cells. Tile laid with horizontal cells should have divided bed and head joints. Enough mortar should be used so that the excess will ooze from the joints as the unit is pressed into place. Excess mortar is then struck off and the joints are tooled to a flush or concave surface.

When facing tile is laid with vertical cells, the mortar bed should not carry through the wall on the connecting webs and end shells except at corners and at ends. The cells should not be filled with mortar, but should instead be left open to allow drainage of any moisture penetrating from the surface. Weep holes should be provided at the bottom of the wall to allow moisture to escape.

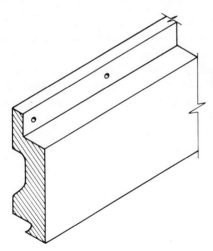

Fig. 18-14. Thin brick veneer

Mortar for tile is similar to that used for face brick. If pointing mortar is specified, regular mortar is raked back, and pointing mortar is applied with a tuck pointer's trowel. Pointing mortar should consist of 1 part Portland cement and ⅛ part of hydrated lime to 2 parts of fine sand (50 mesh or finer). Ammonium or calcium stearate is added at the rate of 2% of the weight of cement used.

Brick and tile surfaces should be cleaned with burlap as work progresses and later scrubbed with a stiff brush and water when the walls are completed. Mortar stains on unglazed brick or tile may be removed by using a wash consisting of 1 part hydrochloric acid to 9 parts of water by volume. Do not use this solution on glazed brick or tile.

Ceramic Mosaic

Ceramic mosaic are small, flat tile units which have been assembled into sheets in the plant and held by cement on a polyethylene coated backing material or by a paper sheet over the tile faces. Back-mounted units are applied to the wall with tile cement, while face-mounted ones are usually applied by pressing the sheets of tile into a wall coating of mortar. When the mortar has set, the paper mounting is scrubbed from the face of the tile.

Joints are grouted with either fine mortar or prepared grouting compound once the tiles are in place.

STONE FACING

Stone used for interiors is normally applied as a veneer over walls and around columns. Cut stones in thicknesses of from 1 to 4 in. and of various face dimensions are employed. The procedure for laying

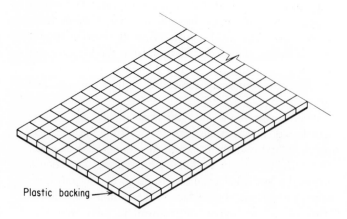

Fig. 18-16. Ceramic mosaic

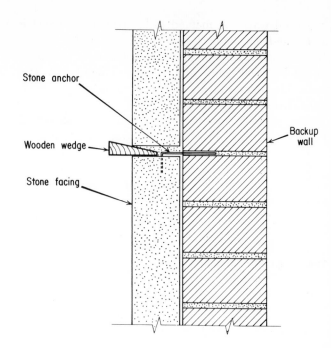

Fig. 18-17. Stone panel wedged in place

stone in interior work is essentially the same as that used for stone exteriors. Small stone units are laid in mortar beds and anchored to the wall with corrugated metal ties (see Fig. 14-40). Larger slabs may be secured by any of the stone anchors illustrated in Fig. 14-31. Because of the stones' weight, two wedges are placed under the bottom edge of each stone in a course and are allowed to remain there until the mortar bed hardens. The wedges are then removed and the holes are filled with mortar.

STEEL FACING

Interior facing material of sheet steel is available in several forms. Steel wall tile has already been mentioned. A somewhat similar product is made to fit over standard concrete blocks (Fig. 18-18). Joints between blocks must be raked out to allow the facing unit to fit around the edges. Adhesive is applied to the back of the panel and it is then pressed into place over the face of the block.

Large steel panels are used as room dividers and partitions, as in Fig. 18-19. Steel supporting members and channels used to anchor panels to ceiling or floor are also available. Notice also the steel cover plates for window mullions in Fig. 18-19.

Still another steel unit for interior use is a steel-faced suspended ceiling panel. The one shown in Fig. 18-20 consists of a perforated steel sheet to which is

Fig. 18-18. Steel facing units for concrete block. (Courtesy Steel Co. of Canada)

Fig. 18-19. Steel partition panels. (Courtesy Steel Co. of Canada)

Fig. 18-20. Steel faced ceiling panels. (Courtesy Steel Co. of Canada)

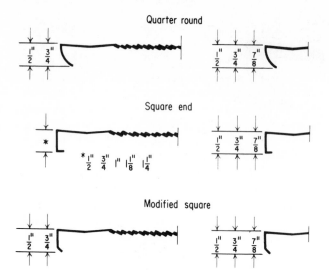

Quarter round

Square end

Modified square

Fig. 18-21. Metal edge moldings

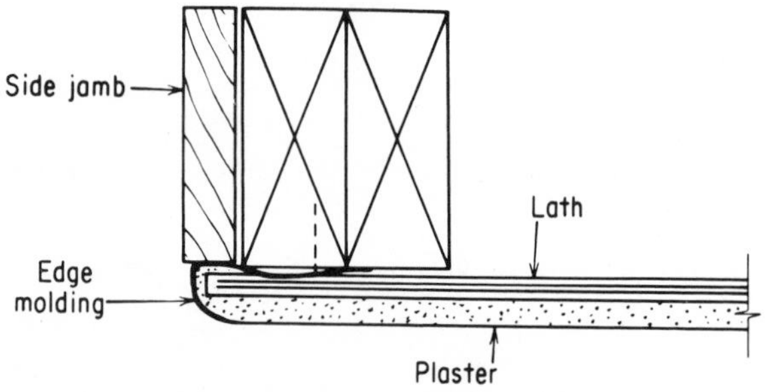

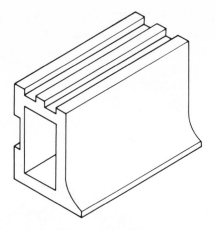

Fig. 18-25. Cove base tile

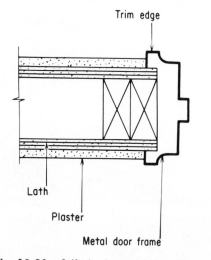

Side jamb

Edge molding

Lath

Plaster

Fig. 18-22. Edge molding under lath

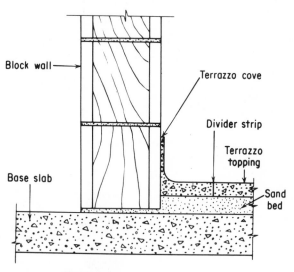

Block wall

Terrazzo cove

Divider strip

Terrazzo topping

Base slab

Sand bed

Fig. 18-26. Terrazzo cove base

attached a rigid acoustical board backing. The units are simply supported by the T bars of the suspended ceiling frame.

FLOOR LAYING

See Chapter 11.

INSTALLATION OF TRIM

The method of trimming around door and window openings, at wall and floor junctions, at wall junctions, etc., depends on the wall finish, the type of window and door jambs, the type of floor, and personal preference.

Trim edge

Lath

Plaster

Metal door frame

Fig. 18-23. Self-trimming metal door frame

Fig. 18-24. Bullnosed jamb block

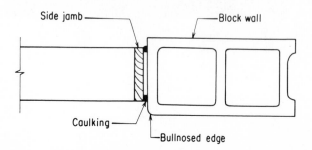

Side jamb

Block wall

Caulking

Bullnosed edge

Windows and doors in wooden frames may be trimmed with conventional wood casing, with stool and apron at the bottom of windows. Here the trim fits over the wall finish and covers all but about ¼ in. of the jambs. When the inside finish is plaster, metal edge molding (Fig. 18-21) may be used. It is fastened to the wall frame either over or under the lath, with its edge set back slightly from the inner edge of the jamb.

With a drywall finish, a similar type of trim may be used. It consists of a thin metal angle covered with paper on the outside. One leg of the angle fits into a kerf in the edge of the jamb and the other fits over the edge of the wallboard. The paper cover is cemented to the wall with joint filler.

Metal door and window frames require no trim because the edges of the frame act in that capacity.

The need for trim around openings in block and glazed tile walls is eliminated by the use of bullnosed jamb units. The projecting, rounded edges of block or tile provide the only trim.

At wall and floor junctions, the type of trim-base used will depend on the composition of walls and floors. With wood floors and wood-framed walls, a wood base is common. Rubber cove base is used with most types of resilient flooring. Glazed tile and block walls include cove units which provide the base trim.

Terrazzo cove base is commonly used in conjunction with a terrazzo floor to form the base trim. The base is really an extension of the floor, and special grinding and polishing tools are needed to finish it properly.

REVIEW QUESTIONS

1. Under what conditions is Portland cement plaster preferred to gypsum plaster?

2. Why should masonry walls be dampened before applying the scratch coat?

3. (a) What purpose does hair or fiber serve in a scratch coat? What is meant by cross-hatching a scratch coat?

4. (a) What is the maximum amount of pigment which may be used to color Portland cement finish plaster? (b) What is the moist curing period for a finish coat? (c) What is the minimum temperature to be maintained during the curing period?

5. Why may more sand or lightweight aggregate be used in mixing the brown coat than in the scratch coat?

6. Differentiate between *regular gypsum* finish plaster and *prepared* finish plaster.

7. Describe a sand float plaster finish.

8. What special use is made of Keene's cement as a plaster material?

9. What is meant by *wood welding*?

10. What is the reason for beveling the meeting edges of two sheets of plywood that are to be butt-jointed?

11. Why should wall tile be started from established horizontal and vertical lines?

12. What is meant by *conditioning* hardboard panels prior to application?

13. (a) Define ceramic mosaic; (b) how is this type of finish applied? (c) How are joints between tiles of this type filled?

14. What is the purpose of trim in interior finishing.

19

COLD WEATHER
CONSTRUCTION

Experiments in cold weather construction have been carried out by contractors and subcontractors for many years, and much valuable experience has been gained. This experience, together with new techniques and materials which have recently appeared on the market, has led to a marked change in the attitude of owners, builders, architects, and engineers toward cold weather construction.

Most industrial building projects are not interrupted during the winter months, though it has been considered desirable to have the building "closed in" before the advent of cold weather. But "closing in" meant completing exterior walls and roofs, a long job in the case of large buildings. So it has become common practice to enclose a structural frame with large tarpaulins or polyethylene film, as shown in Fig. 19-1. Polyethylene has the added advantage of letting light into the enclosed space.

Within the enclosure, the use of equipment such as gas-heated steel pipe (Fig. 19-2) or automatic oil furnaces permits temperatures which allow most types of construction work to continue throughout the winter.

In multistory construction, too large to be completely covered, enclosures may be used one floor at a time. This takes the form of a hanging scaffold enclosed in tarpaulin or plastic film which protects masons and masonry while closure walls are being built (Fig. 19-4). When heat is required, oil- or coke-burning salamanders like the one shown in Fig. 19-5 or other types of heaters are used on the scaffold.

In recent years it is becoming more and more common for major projects to be initiated during the winter. In most regions except the northern states, the Prairie Provinces, and northwestern Ontario, frost penetration under

Fig. 19-1. Polyethylene film enclosure. (Courtesy Portland Cement Ass'n.)

Fig. 19-2. Steel pipe heater. (Courtesy Portland Cement Ass'n.)

snow cover seldom exceeds one foot. This presents no problem for modern excavating machinery and, in fact, sometimes facilitates excavation by providing firmer footing for equipment and trucks.

When it is known in advance that excavating is to be done in soil having considerable frost penetration, the depth of frost can be kept to a minimum by leaving the snow undisturbed over the area or by covering the site with a thick layer of straw before the first snowfall. As soon as an excavation has been completed, steps must be taken to prevent frost from getting into the ground. Straw may again be used, or a shelter such as that shown in Fig. 19-6 may be provided for even better protection.

Protection for concrete during pouring and curing operations is essential whenever below-freezing temperatures are to be expected. Concrete should be warm when poured and should remain at a reasonable temperature until it has gained sufficient strength to prevent frost damage. Concrete which has developed a strength of 500 psi is usually considered past the danger stage, although it cannot withstand repeated cycles of freezing and thawing. To attain a minimum of 500 psi, the American Concrete Institute recommends that the temperature be maintained at 70°F for three days, or 50°F for five days.

In cold weather, it is sometimes necessary to heat the water and aggregate in order to produce concrete which will have a placing temperature of between 50° and 70°F. Water is the most practical component to heat, since more heat units can be stored in water than in other materials. However, water should not be heated above 175°F. because of the danger of causing a *flash* set. If the bulk of the aggregate has a temperature appreciably below 45°F, it must also be heated. Aggregate is usually heated by either steam coils or by the injection of live steam.

A formula has been devised to calculate the temperatures to which water—and aggregate, if necessary—must be heated to produce concrete of a given temperature. It is:

$$X = \frac{Wt + .22\,W'\,t'}{W + .22\,W'}$$

where $X =$ desired concrete temperature
$W =$ weight of water
$W' =$ weight of cement and aggregate
$t \;=$ temperature of water
$t' =$ temperature of solids

Remember that the moisture in the aggregate will have the same temperature as the aggregate. Remember also that if it is necessary to calculate a temperature to which aggregate must be heated, it is assumed that the added water will also have been heated to a given temperature.

Large exposed areas, such as floor slabs, should be protected on both sides. It is difficult to supply heat to the upper surface of the slab if it is not enclosed, but it should be covered with insulation, as illustrated

Fig. 19-3. Oil burning heater. (Courtesy Portland Cement Ass'n.)

Fig. 19-4. An enclosed hanging scaffold. (Courtesy Portland Cement Ass'n.)

Fig. 19-5. Coke-burning salamander. (Courtesy Portland Cement Ass'n.)

Fig. 19-6. Tarpaulin-enclosed foundations. (Courtesy Portland Cement Ass'n.)

Fig. 19-7. Surface of slab insulated against heat loss. (Courtesy Portland Cement Ass'n.)

in Fig. 19-7. Heat can be supplied to the underside of the slab by heaters, as in Fig. 19-8.

Enclosures such as that shown in Fig. 19-9 may be used while erecting concrete or masonry walls. As building progresses, protection may be removed from one location and reused in another.

It may at times be very difficult to supply heat to isolated structures during their curing period. An alternative to doing so is to build insulated forms (Fig. 19-11) and to use concrete with the maximum allowable placing temperature. The insulation will allow the concrete to retain its heat and to cure properly despite low temperatures.

The precautions necessary to pour concrete in cold weather also apply to masonry work. Unless protection is provided, the bond between mortar and masonry may be very poor, and water will penetrate the joints quite readily. Adequate protection should be provided for at least 48 hr.

Warm mortar is the first requirement. Sand may be kept warm by piling it around a large pipe (such as that shown in Fig. 19-12) to which heat is applied by a fire or a gas jet. A simple method of heating water for mortar is illustrated in Fig. 19-13. A steel drum containing a coil of pipe is placed over a fire. One end of the pipe is connected to a water line, and warm water is drawn from the other end as required. But warm mortar is not enough—masonry units should

Fig. 19-8. Supplying heat to underside of slab. (Courtesy Portland Cement Ass'n.)

Fig. 19-9. Wall enclosures for winter construction. (Courtesy Portland Cement Ass'n.)

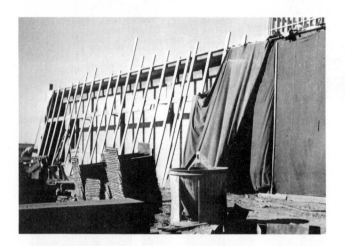

Fig. 19-10. Removing part of protective enclosure. (Courtesy Portland Cement Ass'n.)

Fig. 19-11. Insulated forms. (Courtesy Portland Cement Ass'n.)

Fig. 19-12. Keeping mortar sand warm. (Courtesy Portland Cement Ass'n.)

Fig. 19-13. Heating water for mortar. (Courtesy Portland Cement Ass'n.)

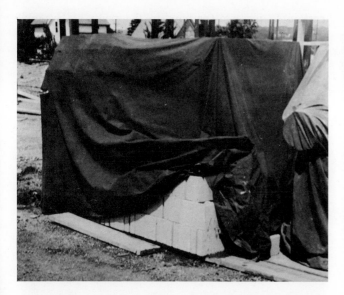

Fig. 19-14. Heating blocks just prior to use. (Courtesy Portland Cement Ass'n.)

Fig. 19-16. Oil burning forced-air heater. (Courtesy Portland Cement Ass'n.)

Fig. 19-15. Laying block behind a protecting tarpaulin. (Courtesy Portland Cement Ass'n.)

also be warm to prevent the sudden cooling of warm mortar as it comes in contact with cold masonry. It is often difficult to store quantities of bricks or blocks in heated enclosures, and one alternative is to heat smaller quantity of units just before they are to be used. This may be done by covering a small pile of bricks or blocks with a heavy tarpaulin (Fig. 19-14). With warm mortar and warm masonry, work can go on within a shelter and full bond strength can be developed. For best results, heat should be maintained for as long as possible. Figure 19-16 shows another type of portable oil

heater which forces hot air into an enclosed space for as long as necessary.

There are two particular precautions which should be taken when using heaters in enclosed spaces. Heaters in spaces containing freshly poured concrete should be adequately vented. Failure to do so may result in an accumulation of carbon monoxide gas which presents a hazard to health and acts as a retarder to the setting of concrete. Another precaution concerns the use of oil burning heaters in rooms which have received their base plaster coat. An oily film may be deposited upon the plaster surface and may very seriously affect the adhesion of the finish plaster coat.

Shelters used in winter construction can be divided into two general groups. The first is the self-supporting type. One example of this is a shelter made from light laminated arches covered with plastic film, now in fairly common use. Another is an air-supported unit made from plastic-coated fabric and often large enough to cover an area the size of a football field. The second type of shelter uses the existing frame of the building for support and encompasses all the shelters discussed earlier in this chapter.

Cost is a prime factor in deciding whether or not to build in the winter. It is generally conceded that the average increase in costs for winter construction will vary from 5% to 10%. This includes the cost of providing tarpaulins, heaters, insulation, fuel, and snow removal. Indirect savings may result from higher productivity, uninterrupted schedules, and greater control of temperatures on the job—thus offsetting direct costs.

It now appears likely that as further study is given to the problem, and as people become more accustomed to a year-round building schedule, winter construction is certain to increase, perhaps to the point of becoming equal in volume to that done in the summer months.

REVIEW QUESTIONS

1. How are large building projects *closed in* in modern cold-weather construction practice?

2. How may frost be prevented from penetrating deeply into soil which is to be excavated during cold weather?

3. (a) What minimum strength must concrete attain to be considered relatively free from frost damage? (b) How is this minimum strength attained in cold weather?

4. (a) How may concrete requiring a placing temperature of 70°F be produced in cold weather? (b) What are the maximum and minimum temperatures involved?

5. Describe briefly how to obtain a good mortar bond with masonry units during cold weather.

6. Give reasons for developing cold weather construction techniques.

INDEX